Montagu Stephen Williams

Round London, down East and up West

Montagu Stephen Williams
Round London, down East and up West
ISBN/EAN: 9783743384101
Manufactured in Europe, USA, Canada, Australia, Japa
Cover: Foto ©Andreas Hilbeck / pixelio.de

Manufactured and distributed by brebook publishing software (www.brebook.com)

Montagu Stephen Williams

Round London, down East and up West

ROUND LONDON

DOWN EAST AND UP WEST

MONTAGU WILLIAMS, Q.C.,

AUTHOR OF "LEAVES OF A LIFE" AND "LATER LEAVES"

London
MACMILLAN & CO.
AND NEW YORK
1894

First Edition printed December, 1892 (*8vo*).
Reprinted December, 1892, *January and February*, 1893.
Second Edition printed July, 1893 (*Crown 8vo*). *Reprinted,* 1894.

PREFACE

IT was the intention of the author of this book to add to it, by way of preface, a few lines of assurance to its readers that every story and every incident contained in it is based upon actual fact, and that only so much disguise has been anywhere assumed as was absolutely necessitated by the exigencies of publication. Unhappily, the severe illness against which Montagu Williams has been struggling with so much courage and fortitude for so long a time prostrated him immediately after the last sketch was written, and he was consequently unable to do anything with regard to the little preface.

Under these circumstances I may perhaps be permitted, as one of Montagu Williams's earliest friends—he and I were boys together in the same pupil-room at Eton forty-two years ago—and as the editor of "Household Words," in which magazine these sketches originally appeared, to convey to his readers the assurance which, if it had been possible for him to do so, he would have laid before them on his own behalf.

Those who have followed the unsavoury histories of the Society scandals of the last few years will readily recognise in the "Up West" division of these sketches many stories with which they are already familiar, and will appreciate the graphic force and the dramatic effect with which they are told; but I venture to think that the "Down East" experiences which Montagu Williams gained during his term of office as a magistrate at Worship Street and at the Thames Police Court will have even greater interest for the general reader. For Montagu Williams was not only content to do his duty as a police magistrate, and to do it admirably too, but devoted himself heart and soul and with all the masterful energy which characterised him to the acquirement of a perfect knowledge of the neighbourhoods and of the people among whom his work lay; to the keenest and most humane study of the wants, the difficulties, the temptations, the daily lives, in a word, of the struggling poor about him; to the earnest consideration of how best to help them in their need, and to make them look upon him, not only as the dispenser of justice, stern and severe as he knew how to be on occasion, but as a friend, always ready to listen patiently to the sad stories which so often came before him, to give wise and sympathetic counsel, and to dispense the charitable funds entrusted to him with the thoughtful care and the kindly words which give such alms a double value.

How well Montagu Williams succeeded in what was to him a real labour of love was amply proved by the lamentations of the poor people—"my poor people," he used to call them—who had learned to know, to trust, and to love him, when, much against his will and only in consequence of the urgent requirements of his medical advisers, he was transferred to the Marylebone Police Court. Even his own modest accounts of what he did tell the same story, and it is easy to see that proud, and justly proud, as Montagu Williams was of his brilliant career at the bar, he was prouder still in his later years of the title, "the poor man's magistrate," which he so well and worthily earned "Down East" in London.

CHARLES DICKENS.

December 1st, 1892.

CONTENTS

Part I.—DOWN EAST

CHAPTER I

EAST END SHOWS

Houses to let—Messrs. Stuckey & Co.—East End hats—Failure of the drapery business—Change after change—At last a penny show—An informal set-to—Weight-lifting—A sickening sight—A favourite spot with pickpockets—Objects exhibited—Poor hospital patients—Summonses taken out—Wholesale correction—Its good effect 3

CHAPTER II

MATCH GIRLS

East End match manufactories—Great improvement since 1880—Wages before the strike—Bryant and May's—Bell's—The Salvation Army—Phosphorus poisoning, termed "phossy jaw"—Wages since the strike—Matchbox-makers—Their sufferings—"Twopence three-farthings a gross, because they are big ones"—Match girls—Their fashions—Early marriages—Their sympathy in time of trouble—Clifden House Institute—Why not a dozen such? 12

CHAPTER III

SCLATER STREET BIRDS

"Thank God for Sunday"—Fisher, of Eton—Summer Sunday morning in Hyde Park—Commercial Street, Shoreditch—Sclater Street—Remarks overheard—Singing matches—Love in humble life!—"Julks"—Winning a "gate"—Sunday morning marketing—Michael Angelo Taylor's Act 20

CONTENTS

CHAPTER IV
MY DEPÔT

Poverty in the East End not exaggerated—Preparing for winter—My letter to *The Times* and *The Daily News*—Generous response thereto—My depôt opened—Bed-clothing the most pressing want—Messrs. Jeremiah Rotherham and Company, High Street, Shoreditch—I interview the partners—Their liberal spirit—I have the articles stamped—No grey blankets—A valuable stock—How we distributed our collection of clothing—A few noteworthy cases—Mr. Massey and his wife 29

CHAPTER V
GRIDDLERS, OR STREET SINGERS

Common lodging-houses in Deptford—I visit one of them—Their occupants—"What is a griddler?"—His haunts—"The Wandering Boy"—Episode in the north of London—Musical répertoire—Police regulation 38

CHAPTER VI
THE LONDON HOSPITAL

Its position—Its staff—The nurses—Admission—The district served—Wards for Jews—Scenes therein—Strength required by nurses—Out-patients—Daily routine in the wards—Dietary—Hospital experiences of a friend of mine—Terrible sights—Humorous incident 47

CHAPTER VII
MEDLAND HALL

Opened by the London Congregational Union—The proprietors summoned for permitting overcrowding—I propose an arrangement—It is accepted—A conference—Resolutions—Speakers' experiences of casual wards—Various classes of casuals—A "stiff," or hawker's license—Why Medland Hall was founded—Encouraging results 56

CHAPTER VIII
CLERKENWELL GREEN

"Hicks's Hall"—Celebrated names—My first appearance—Sir William Bodkin—The granting of licenses—The Argyll Rooms—Cremorne Gardens—A ludicrous incident—Wretched accommodation—The poor juryman!—How service was once evaded—The "Slaughter House"—Lockyer—Mrs. Howe—Changes in the Sessions 64

CONTENTS

CHAPTER IX

RATCLIFF HIGHWAY

Its situation—Its condition twenty-five years ago—Poor Jack in the hands of the Philistines—A modern Babel—The Thames Tunnel—"The Forty Thieves"—"Paddy's Goose"—I visit the neighbourhood—An opium den—"Amok! Amok!"—We conceal ourselves—Scene in the street—Its cause—Strange manner of taking an oath—Watney Street—Thames Police Court—An interesting case—Its termination—A revengeful design frustrated by accident—A curious batch of summonses—Ratcliff Highway improved—Its causes—Further improvement required . . . **74**

CHAPTER X

SUNDAY AT THE EAST END

Open spaces wanted—Cricket reminiscences—Cricket in Bethnal Green—Bat, ball, and stumps—A remarkable suit—Cricket technicalities—The game is suddenly stopped—Half-penny rides in Shoreditch—An extraordinary public-house—Brick Lane—Revolting scenes—Long list of night charges on Monday morning—Sunday closing—Parallel between England and Scotland—East End clubs **84**

CHAPTER XI

BURGLARIOUS BILL

Two kinds of burglars—Argument against the abolition of capital punishment—Occasional burglars—A remarkable specimen—The professional burglar—The Cornhill burglary—Thomas Caseley—Great booty—"Beautiful instruments"—Arrests—Conversation on the way to the station—Female prisoners acquitted—Sentence—Action against the safe-makers—Evidence of Caseley—Which is the easiest safe—"Lawful" and "unlawful" tools—The Alderman, the citizen, and the citizen's friend—How the signals were given—Receivers—My suspicions aroused—The effect—Capital verses in *Punch* **93**

CHAPTER XII

FROM THE EAST END TO RAMSGATE

Modern Jews—The Isle of Thanet—"L'homme propose"—Ten in a compartment, besides a perambulator—The coster and his bride—A happy family—Why they brought the cat and bird—They "take a bite," while I smoke—A skin-dresser—"Look at the fields, Lill!"—Why they chose Ramsgate—Ramsgate sands—The two seasons—Dr. Robson Roose's opinion—Attractions of Ramsgate—The lodging-houses—Old habitués thereof—The Bath-chair men—"Doctor Ramsgate" **102**

Part II.—UP WEST

CHAPTER I
CLIMBING THE LADDER

Exit aristocracy, enter plutocracy—Old estates in new hands—A gambling establishment a hundred years ago—Mordecai Morris—His earliest recollections—His marriage—His death in harness—His will—A worthy successor—Keenness in pursuit of riches—Change of name by deed-poll—Herbert Maurice, Esq.—Cannot look the gentleman—His son not a success at Eton—Peculiar in his dress 115

CHAPTER II
CLIMBING THE LADDER—*continued*

Mr. Maurice changes sides—His reason therefor—Mrs. Maurice and her dear friends—The house in Belgrave Square—The guests—Broadstone Hall, in Northamptonshire—The shooting there—The elder daughter "knows her value"—The noble pensioner . 121

CHAPTER III
DESCENDING THE LADDER

Lord Bythesea at Eton—The Earl of Woking—Bythesea comes of age—Is taken to the Queen's Bench Prison—We visit him there—Racquet courts—"Tap is open!"—No distinctions of rank—Slowman's sponging-house—The last Earl of Woking—The proposed marriage—It takes place—Its sequel—Death of my old friend 127

CHAPTER IV
MODERN STOCKBROKERS—TOPSY-TURVYDOM

Changes in stockbroking—The aristocratic "runner"—His way of conducting business—Stock Exchange gambling amongst women—Its cause—A typical case—The conversation at modern dinner-parties—An old friend—Strawberry Hill—The Grange—My life at Bushey—The new system 137

CHAPTER V
HUCKSTERING HYMEN

Where are marriages made?—Some typical announcements—Their history—Ralph Dobbs—Goes to America—Marries—Retires from business—But dies suddenly—His will—His widow and daughter come to London—The "American heiress" the centre of attraction—She meets the Marquis of Merrivale—Accepts him—Remonstrances unavailing—A clear understanding—The wedding—Separate existences 146

CHAPTER VI

HUCKSTERING HYMEN—*continued*

A wedding at St. Peter's, Eaton Square—Silas Davis—The Earl of Thanet—Lord L'Estrange—A love match—Ruin—The match at an end—Coercion—The marriage arranged—Where was it made?—The Limelight Theatre—The "Johnnies"—Intellectual effusions—Miss Scarborough—A great hit—Fifty pounds a week—She draws the line—Viscount Millington—Engaged—Parents stop supplies—Marriage takes place—Parents still obdurate—"Lady Millington" returns to the stage—Society touts—Huckstering 154

CHAPTER VII

THE PROMOTER

The company promoter—The gullible British public—Leopold Stiff—His office—I visit him there—He is "so busy"—A remarkable sight—An invitation to dinner—Mixed company—Excellent entertainment—The Gull Gold Mine, Limited—Wound up—Stiff arrested—Committed for trial—The Old Bailey—A great crowd—The trial—Sentence—From the West End to Millbank . 163

CHAPTER VIII

THINGS THEATRICAL

The old Adelphi—The Lyceum—Why is extravaganza dead?—Dramatic authors—Henry Byron—Frank Burnand—The Princess's—Mr. and Mrs. Kean—Alfred Wigan—The Haymarket—Benjamin Webster—John Baldwin Buckstone—Compton—Edward Sothern—"First nights"—The opera—Operatic singers—Theatrical managers—Is there room for all the theatres?—Theatrical expenditure—Theatres *versus* music-halls—Suggested alterations 172

CHAPTER IX

COVENT GARDEN

The flower hawkers—Counter attractions to bed—Short history of "Convent Garden"—Distinguished residents—Reminiscences—Murder of Martha Ray—Hackman hanged—Ceaseless stream of traffic—Din of voices—Scene in the market—The man in blue—Flower sellers—Plant sellers—A hard case—I am able to assist . 181

CHAPTER X

FLOSS AND FLOSS

The office in Lincoln's Inn—The partners—Their home-life—Unfortunate clients—The confidential clerk—His methodical habits—Time brings changes—Appearances deceptive—The old circus proprietor—An amazing discovery—A desperate expedient—Ugly rumours—A terrible blow—Left alone—The alternative—The choice—Flight—The arrest 189

CHAPTER XI

THE ROAD TO RUIN

List betting—Its temptations—Centres for betting—Monotony of the evening papers—Betting in the West End—Racing clubs—Betting on the increase—The "commission agent"—What is his crime?—An old client—A plunger—Police raid on a West End club—Playing baccarat declared illegal—Decision upheld on appeal—The son of an Indian officer—Becomes popular in society—Does not know poker—Nor loo—My remark thereon—Justified by the result—A similar case in Paris—Prompt detection . 193

CHAPTER XII

MONEY LENT

The money-lender—His style of living—His victims—The regular course of events—"The —— Bank of Deposit"—Its rules and manner of conducting its business—An illegal act connived at—A case in point—The jury stops the case—Discounting tailors—Experiences of a comrade—Leviathan money-lenders—A good-natured act 209

CHAPTER XIII

TALENT IN TATTERS

The sandwich man—Charges of costume—His remuneration—Keen competition—A true story—Sudden disappearance—Reappearance as a successful author—Terrible news at the zenith of success—I visit my dying friend—His history—Writes for the stage—"Returned with thanks"—Goes on the stage—Not unsuccessful—Marries—Out of employment—Has typhoid fever—From bad to worse—Desperate poverty—The doctor orders fresh air and wine!—He becomes a sandwich man—His wife dies—The end 220

CHAPTER XIV

THE LONDON SEASON

The last day of the season—Its beginning—Ladies at the races—The Fourth of June at Eton—Eton in my young days—The procession of boats—Reminiscences of Ascot—The Master of the Buckhounds—Amusing scene at Ascot Races—A contemptible manœuvre—A funny story of this year's race meeting—His lordship outwitted—Falling off in political entertainments—How marriages are "knocked up"—The Row on a Sunday morning—Coaching Club meets—The July Meeting at Newmarket—Goodwood—Exclusiveness of Cowes society—The river forty years ago—A complete change for the worse—All is vanity . 2.8

Part I

DOWN EAST

ROUND LONDON

CHAPTER I

EAST END SHOWS

Houses to let—Messrs. Stuckey and Co.—East End hats—Failure of the drapery business—Change after change—At last a penny show—An informal set-to—Weight-lifting—A sickening sight—A favourite spot with pickpockets—Objects exhibited—Poor hospital patients—Summonses taken out—Wholesale correction—Its good effect.

DOES misfortune attach to premises with the same diabolical persistency that it sometimes shows in its attachment to individuals? Does ill-luck haunt the portals of a house just as it often dogs the footsteps of a man? These are matters, I confess, that have exercised my mind for a considerable time. I was extremely doubtful at first, but experience and observation have taught me that the correct answer to those questions is an affirmative one.

In my wanderings about the East End, I have often noted premises that seem to be in a chronic state of insolvency. The announcement "To Let" appears in the windows, at short intervals, with absolute regularity. I will give an example —a shop in the Whitechapel Road, almost immediately opposite the London Hospital.

How my attention was, in the first place, called to these premises I really cannot say. If my memory serves me, when the shop originally attracted my notice it had just passed through a sort of resurrectional process. The outside was redolent of fresh paint; the inside had a comfortable and well to-do appearance. Large posters on the clean windows announced that the shop would be reopened, at an early date, as a first-class draper's; and the public was informed that the new proprietors, Messrs. Stuckey and Co., who had had great experience in the trade, were prepared to offer, on the lowest possible terms, the magnificent stock of a leading West End firm which had gone into liquidation.

On the morning of the first of May—and a particularly bright morning it was—the premises were duly opened. Several sandwich men, who paraded to and fro on the pavement, advertised the fact, and three small boys, stationed outside the door, delivered to the passers-by handbills announcing the great benefits that would accrue to them if only they would enter the establishment of Messrs. Stuckey and Co. The windows were most tastefully dressed. In the right-hand one were silks, dresses, shawls, and the like, the price of each being stated on a ticket, which set forth the number of shillings very prominently, with a smaller figure for the pence, and a still smaller one for the farthings. In the other window was exhibited a most remarkable collection of hats—with regard to which I have a word to say.

No one who is a stranger to the East End of London can have any idea of the kind of female headgear in vogue in that locality. The material is cotton velvet, the colour, gaudy, and the size, enormous; and let me parenthetically observe that, no matter how shabby or dirty be the rest of the clothing of the ladies to be seen in every street, court, and alley in the neighbourhood of Commercial Road, Whitechapel, and Shoreditch, if they have any covering at all to their heads, it is certain to be one of the hats to which I refer. In a case that came before me some time ago it transpired that these head ornaments are, in many instances, let out on hire, at so much per week or month; and I have frequently had testimony borne to the fact that the East End girls will part with everything they possess in the world—will sell themselves, body and soul—to become the proud possessors of the articles in question. The size and colour of the feathers are points on which there is keen rivalry among the denizens of court and alley. Day by day, at the Thames and Worship Street Police Courts, the women of the locality are brought before the sitting magistrate, on charges of drunkenness, assault, and so forth; and though their dresses may be torn and bloodstained, and their faces scratched and otherwise disfigured, there, sure enough, is the accustomed hat, cocked jauntily on one side, and having apparently escaped all injury. Whether these Amazons are careful to bare their heads before coming to close quarters, I am unable to say.

But to return to the shop in the Whitechapel Road.

The drapery business, as I have shown, was duly opened, apparently under the most brilliant auspices, and with every outward promise of success; but when I passed the premises some six weeks afterwards, I found that a doleful change had come over the scene. The green iron shutters were up; bills announced that the place was once more to be let; and already the paint was begrimed with soot and dirt. The whole building, indeed, had a neglected and forbidding appearance.

I was at the time about to leave London for my vacation, and on my return, two months later, I had occasion to revisit this locality. The premises had opened once more, this time as a furniture warehouse. The inside of the shop had been entirely removed, together with the windows, and a considerable stock was in view, both on the ground floor inside and on the pavement without. But it was all to no purpose. In a very short time there was the same climax—bankruptcy. So things went on month after month. Sometimes the shop was a greengrocer's, sometimes a milk-shop, and once a pawnbroker's. But even the lucrative trade of a pawnbroker would not do. Subsequently the shop came under my notice judicially as an undertaker's.

The undertaker seemed to do a little business at first, and one day, when I was passing the shop, I saw him looking quite cheerful as he surveyed a large oak coffin that was being carried out. But the reign of prosperity was brief. There had been a good deal of scarlet fever about, and trade had been brisk. As time went on, the mutes standing at the door became more and more seedy-looking, and the same may be said of the proprietor himself, who, by-the-bye, was a half-hourly visitor to the gin-palace round the corner, and emitted an aroma very like that of a cask which has lately contained a few gallons of old rum.

The end very soon came, and even the velvet trappings found their way to the nearest pawnbroker's. I had the curiosity subsequently to enquire what had become of the undertaker himself, and learnt that he had indulged in a moonlight flitting—a proceeding on the part of the proprietor of these ill fated premises which surprised no one.

In the beginning of the winter I found myself once **more**

in the neighbourhood, and I was naturally very curious to ascertain whether any one had had the audacious courage to succeed the absconding undertaker. Judge of my surprise when, on nearing the London Hospital, and casting my eyes across the way, I saw that the upper part of the house was covered with a huge sheet of canvas, on which were depicted, in glowing colours, a Fat Lady, who appeared to be double as broad as she was high, and whose arms resembled sacks of flour; a Black Dwarf, whose hat was level with the ponderous female's knees; an armadillo, some snakes, and a few other attractions. At the entrance stood a woman, dressed in brilliant attire, and playing a barrel-organ. Beside her was a man with a set of Pandean pipes, who invited the public—which was represented by a crowd reaching well into the roadway—to enter at the moderate charge of a penny per head.

It was quite obvious what had happened. The undertaker had for his successor an East End showman. This was ringing the changes with a vengeance. Mutes had given way to masqueraders; tights and spangles had taken the place of crape; and, as it subsequently appeared, the solemn realities of death had been succeeded by a coarse burlesque of murder.

I paid my penny and entered.

In the body of the room was a waxwork exhibition, and some of its features were revolting in the extreme. The first of the Whitechapel murders were fresh in the memory of the public, and the proprietor of the exhibition was turning the circumstance to some commercial account. There lay a horrible presentment in wax of Matilda Turner, the first victim, as well as one of Mary Ann Nichols, whose body was found in Buck's Row. The heads were represented as being nearly severed from the bodies, and in each case there were shown, in red paint, three terrible gashes reaching from the abdomen to the ribs.

One of the attractions of the place was a couple of athletes, who, at the end of their contortions and feats of strength, put on boxing-gloves and announced their readiness to have a round with any one—a challenge that was conveyed to the outer world, through a speaking-trumpet, by the gentleman whose chin rested on the tips of the Pandean pipes. Nor were these individuals the only exponents of the art of self-defence. Among the company was a lady boxer and weight-lifter, who announced that she was the strongest woman on earth, and offered to fight any male creature of less than ten stone. This "female Samson," who did not appear to be more than sixteen years of age, wore fleshings, to which circumstance, no doubt, must be attributed much of the interest which, while standing outside the building in company with the barrel-organist, she excited among the passers-by.

After the curious and prurient had been allowed sufficient time to examine the waxworks, this young woman came inside to go through her part of the programme, and was introduced to the audience as Miss Juanita. Behind the small platform on which she took her stand, a roll of canvas was suddenly let down, and on it were depicted coloured representations of her feats of strength. In one picture she was shown swinging, with the greatest ease, heavy Indian clubs; in another, supporting on her chest six fifty-six-pound weights; and in a third, lifting by her hair four hundredweight. In the centre of the canvas she was represented holding in her teeth a table on which was perched a fat Jew of about twelve stone; and underneath was written " The Lifting of Bacchus."

The audience consisted of some hundred persons. Just as Miss Juanita was about to commence her performance, there was a sudden movement in the crowd behind me, and, on turning round, I witnessed an informal set-to between two of the ladies of the Whitechapel Road. They had been imbibing very freely, and it was clear that the pugilistic air of the place had proved infectious.

The combatants having been summarily ejected, Miss Juanita went through her part of the programme. Her hair, which was very abundant, was let down her back and plaited, a rope was tied to the coils, and an article closely resembling a meat-hook was attached to the rope. Two weights were then produced, and submitted to the close scrutiny of the spectators. One was represented to be ninety pounds, and the other fifty pounds. Miss Juanita bent backwards, attached the rings of the weights to the hook, and then, slowly returning to an upright position, raised the great pieces of metal about a foot from the ground. It was a sickening sight. So great was the strain that, when the performance was over, every nerve in the poor creature's body seemed to be quivering. She drank something from an old cracked mug, and, after a short interval, put on the boxing-gloves for a spar with one of the athletes. The lady came off victorious, and was hailed with shouts of approval by the spectators.

Pugilism obviously was high in favour with the management, for the audience was privileged to see yet another personal encounter. "Daniel the Dutchman" took the field against the "Welshman," and worked the spectators up to a high pitch of enthusiasm by the masterly way in which he dealt with his antagonist. The victorious Daniel received a most flattering ovation; and with that the entertainment came to an end.

On returning home I determined to make enquiries concerning this place. I learnt, among other things, that there were four or five establishments of a similar character in the immediate neighbourhood, and that the existence of such places constituted an old grievance among the more respectable portion of the community. I was told that in every case the proprietors were literally coining money, and I could easily believe it.

It was not long before I had personally visited and closely inspected all these premises, and anything more degrading and debasing than the performances that went on there I never saw. Nor was the evil confined within doors. I was informed by the police that the pavement outside these places was a favourite spot with the Whitechapel pickpocket for the exercise of his calling. Watch robberies, it appeared, were of almost hourly occurrence there; and my informants stated that in many cases there was a working agreement between the thieves and the proprietor of the show, the latter receiving within the articles that had been stolen without.

I have no space to describe these establishments in detail. Besides fat women, dwarfs, "living skeletons," and giants, they contained a number of monstrosities, including "a man with no neck," and a creature which purported to be a five-legged pig. One attraction, which was alleged to have been brought to this country by Buffalo Bill, was described as "half gorilla and half human being," and was certainly a most disgusting-looking object. The Whitechapel murders were favourite subjects for representation; and while several showmen merely dabbled in these crimes, so to speak, one enterprising member of the fraternity dealt exhaustively with the whole series by means of illuminated coloured views, which his patrons inspected through peep-holes Jack Sheppard, Charles Peace, and a host of other similar celebrities lived again on the canvas screens, and there repeated, before an audience of awe-stricken and admiring East End youths, some f the more daring acts of their graceless lives. Outside one show stood a coloured man scowling over a representation of the murder of Maria Martin in the Red Barn.

To those who had the misfortune to live near these places, the noise they occasioned must have been a great curse. Organs were played, drums were beaten, bells were rung, and it was in stentorian tones that the public was invited to enter. It occurred to me, when pondering over what I had seen, that such a state of affairs could not be allowed to continue. One thing, I must confess, caused me much surprise. Why had no steps been taken at the initiative of the suffering neighbours, to put down the nuisance? Take the case of the London Hospital, for instance. The patients must have undergone agonies from the constant din, and I marvelled why the authorities of the institution had not ended it by proceeding against the proprietors of the show. What more easy than to prosecute them for causing an obstruction of the public thoroughfare?

As I have shown, the premises opposite the London Hospital had had a very chequered existence, and, as if to confirm their reputation for ill-luck, the "penny gaff" established there was the first to be informed against by the police. The authorities, however, lost little time in dealing with the others; and quite a crop of the cases came before me within a very short period. In applying for summonses against the proprietors, the police placed me in possession of further details respecting these places. The principal time for the performances, it appeared, was from eight in the evening until half past eleven, though in the case of some fat women and performing Zulus the entertainment was open during the day as well. Subsequently an inspector stated what he saw on the occasion of a visit he paid to one of the shows for the purpose of serving a summons on the proprietor. He said he witnessed an exhibition of female boxers, and a woman "mit nodings on" swimming in a tank—features of the programme that were announced as "novelty attractions." Outside the show, he said, a man was standing on some steps, shouting to the public to enter, and calling attention to the nature of the entertainment by striking a canvas with a stick. Another man was standing by who alternately played an organ and beat a drum.

It appeared from the evidence that it was impossible to find the actual owners of the premises, who, it would seem, kept in the background so as to avoid the service of process.

The authorities of the London Hospital and a number of tradesmen of the locality testified to the nature and extent of the nuisance, and proved that it had been in existence for years. One witness stated that he had visited the show at the corner of Thomas Street, and had found that the proprietor was doing a roaring trade. He stated that while the crowd stood gazing at the blood-stained pictures that blocked up the pavement, the pickpockets were making the best of their opportunities. This gentleman, speaking from an intimate knowledge of the locality, declared that no idea could be formed of the extent to which young men and women were morally corrupted by witnessing the exhibitions that were on view at those places. He said it was terrible to hear the jesting remarks that fell from the lips of young girls concerning the murders and other horrors that were illustrated inside and outside the shows.

Counsel appeared for the defence, and urged that the defendants were merely the hired servants of the proprietors, and, consequently, not the responsible parties. One of the defendants stated that he did not even know the address of his employer; all he knew concerning him was that his name was John. As a matter of course, this would not do for me. I saw at once that the only way to put a stop to the nuisance was to deal with it with a strong hand. I fined the defendants forty shillings for each performance, and as that meant, in the aggregate, a good deal of money, they left the court in the prison van.

Subsequently other summonses were applied for by the police and granted by me.

In one case, the defendant, Thomas Baker, of the Whitechapel Road, said that his employer was a man named Alfred Eaton, and that he resided in Warner Street, Euston.

"What is Mr. Eaton by trade?" I enquired.

"A novelty dealer," was the reply.

Upon my observing that I had heard of many trades in my life, but never before of the one referred to, my informant said:

"He is an importer of things the public has never seen. He travels all over the world in search of them."

I could not help remarking that he evidently travelled so much, and in such distant climes, that it was impossible for the law to get hold of him; and, as before, I fined the defendant forty shillings for every performance that had been proved. The money not being forthcoming, he also went to gaol.

This wholesale correction had the desired effect, and the proprietors of other establishments of a similar character, finding the law too strong for them, shut up shop and decamped; and these horrible dens, at any rate so far as the Whitechapel Road is concerned, have become things of the past.

This amount of good has been effected — it has been definitely established that private houses cannot be put to this vile use; and the proprietors of these exhibitions have been driven from the public thoroughfares, and compelled to take refuge on plots of ground and other places where the law cannot reach them. It is indeed a matter for surprise that, in a civilised and an enlightened country, possessing so extensive a system of local government, it should have been possible for such a state of things to have continued so long; and one cannot help deploring the pernicious influences which these places must have exercised in the past over the poor and ignorant.

CHAPTER II

MATCH GIRLS

East End match manufactories—Great improvement since 1880—Wages before the strike—Bryant and May's—Bell s—The Salvation Army—Phosphorus poisoning, termed "phossy jaw" — Wages since the strike — Matchbox-makers — Their sufferings — "Twopence three-farthings a gross, because they are big ones"—Match girls—Their fashions—Early marriages—Their sympathy in time of trouble—Clifden House Institute—Why not a dozen such?

It is very difficult to make those who have always lived in a cheerful and comfortable home—and who have never had the opportunity or inclination to contrast their own happiness with the misery of the poorer classes—understand how an empty cupboard, starving children, and a sick wife can make life so hideous as to be almost intolerable; how night can be robbed of the blessing of sleep through the whole family being huddled together in one miserable little room; and how damp walls and a leaky roof can make the best-tempered person uncomfortable, peevish, and finally ill.

In these papers on life in the East End I shall place before the reader truthful pictures of some of the places I have visited, and some of the industries I have investigated, in that quarter of London.

There are six or seven match manufactories in the East End, and they give employment to some thousands of women and girls. Until within a few years ago this industry was associated with a system of slavery of the very worst description; but I am happy to say that since the great strike at Bryant and May's in 1880, matters have considerably improved.

This firm, or, rather, company, is the largest of the kind in London, and, in the busy seasons, employs about twelve hundred hands. In 1877 the business paid a dividend at the rate of twenty-five per cent., and at that time the hours of work were from six a.m. to six p.m. in the summer, and from eight a.m. to six p.m. in the winter, an hour being allowed for dinner and half an hour for breakfast. The earnings of the great majority of the girls were from four shillings to eight shillings a week. Strict discipline was maintained, and penalties were inflicted for the slightest breach of the regulations. If, for instance, a girl arrived at the factory five minutes behind time, she was frequently shut out for half a day; and for any little act of untidiness, such as omitting to clear away the litter from under the bench, a fine was imposed.

The business is now much more humanely managed, and the labour of the workers has been considerably lightened by the introduction of improved machinery.

Next to Bryant and May's comes Bell's, where some five hundred girls and women are engaged; and the Salvation Army have a match manufactory which gives employment to about sixty persons. On visiting these establishments, you will find that the women are very contented and cheerful. They work with great rapidity—which is but natural, for they are paid by results. Men are employed in mixing the materials into which the matches are dipped; the girls prepare the wood and make the boxes.

Speaking generally, the factory hands are a healthy class. One woman who was interviewed had worked continuously in the same establishment for twenty years, and she was as robust as could be wished. Nevertheless, it is a mistake to suppose that phosphorus poisoning is a thing of the past. There is still a terrible amount of the disease, which is termed "phossy jaw." The first sign of the disorder is toothache, accompanied by swollen cheeks. As soon as these symptoms appear the sufferer has several teeth removed, in order, if possible, to save the entire jaw.

The factories are fairly well ventilated, and I am bound to say that, to all appearances, the comfort of the girls and women is studied by their employers. I speak, of course, only of those factories which I myself inspected; whether or no there is equal consideration shown in other establishments of the same class I cannot say.

I have already described what wages were paid before the strike, and I will now explain what wages have been paid since that event. The younger girls, that is to say, the novices fresh from school, are allowed, while they are learning their trade, four shillings and sixpence a week standing wages; though I understand that in some of the smaller firms they receive no remuneration at all. The ordinary hands now make from seven to ten shillings a week, which is a great advance on former figures.

I understand that the Salvation Army have a slightly higher scale of payment than the purely business firms, but it must be remembered that they make only one kind of matches, the "safety"; and I was informed by the manager of one of the other establishments that, if his firm had the same demand for those matches as the Salvation Army, they could pay the same rate of wages.

It should be understood that box-making is a very important branch of the industry, and is largely carried on by the girls and their parents in their own homes. During the few years that I was at Worship Street and Thames Police Courts, many cases of matchbox-makers in distress came before me, and I was consequently enabled to obtain exact information with reference to their earnings. The payment is at the rate of twopence farthing, twopence halfpenny, and twopence three-farthings per gross, the workers finding not only their own paste, but also the twine used for tying up the bundles of boxes.

Matchbox-makers are to be found in nearly every house—and, indeed, in nearly every room—in all the courts and alleys in the immediate vicinity of Pereira Street. The materials are generally supplied by middle men, or "sweaters," whose existence as connecting links between employer and employed it is very hard to justify. The children of the matchbox-makers are set to work with knife and paste the moment they return from the Board-School. They have no play, and—Heaven help them!—very little time for rest. At early dawn the "skillets," as the bundles of wood are called, are brought out, and the whole family is soon at work.

In order to illustrate the sufferings of these poor creatures, I will give a few particulars of cases which came before me at Worship Street.

A thin, pale woman with sunken eyes applied, in a trembling voice, for some slight assistance from my poor-box. I caused enquiries to be made at the address she gave, and a piteous state of things was at once brought to light. The applicant and her daughter, who were alone in the world, had in the past earned a precarious livelihood by making match-boxes; but the young girl had fallen into a decline, and was then on her death-bed, and the poor mother, prostrated by anxiety, privation, and ill-health, had found herself quite unable to toil on single-handed.

In another case a man was summoned by the School Board for not sending his boy to school. In this case also I caused enquiries to be made. The man, it appeared, was a dock labourer, but could only get an occasional day's work; there were four children, two of whom were under three years of age; and a rental of six and sixpence a week had to be paid for the one room. When the missionary called there, the father was away trying to obtain work, and the mother had gone out to beg or borrow a loaf of bread. One of the children was away at school, the other three were at home crying with hunger. There was no food in the cupboard, and, though it was bitterly cold, no fire in the grate. The children were very poorly clothed, and one of the boys had nothing on his shivering body save an old vest. The most deplorable object of all, however, was his brother, an imbecile, who was partly paralysed and unable to walk. The poor crippled, half-witted lad was endeavouring to help his sister in the manufacture of some large match-boxes. In answer to the missionary, the girl explained: "We are paid twopence three-farthings a gross for these, because they are big ones." We subsequently learnt that one person, by working very hard, could make seven gross of this size in a day. That would bring in one and sixpence farthing, after deducting a penny for twine and paste. Before my emissary left both parents returned home, the errand of each having proved a futile one.

I gave the family such assistance from the poor-box as was in my power, taking care that the money was spent upon food, coal, and a blanket or two. As the man had broken the law by not sending his child to school, and as he had been previously convicted by another magistrate for the same offence, I could not tax the poor-box to pay the fine I was compelled to impose. Suffice it to say the money was forthcoming, and I presume justice was satisfied.

With regard to the match girls who, to use a vulgar expression, are on their own hook—that is to say, who have detached themselves from their families, if they have any—I am bound to confess they are not the very best of girls. But what can be expected, seeing the way in which they are compelled to live? I am sorry to say that there is a considerable amount of drunkenness among them, though they are not often brought up on that charge before the magistrates presiding at the East End Courts. On looking over the statistics of my cases at Worship Street, I find that there were only about half-a-dozen charges of the kind over a period of several months.

I only remember one occasion on which match girls were brought before me on a charge of theft. Two sisters, while very much the worse for liquor, had stolen three glass tumblers from the Paragon Music Hall. They were very young, and as it was their first offence, I was able to take a lenient view of the case and discharge them.

Every now and then one of these girls is charged with disorderly conduct, and I am bound to admit that their ideas of law and order are very lax; but how can you wonder at this when you think of the conditions under which they live? Think of their squalid and wretched homes, without air, without the most ordinary arrangements for preserving decency, and often without a ray of sunlight even in the midst of glorious summer.

Taking the class as a whole, I think the good preponderate over the bad. Most of them have an exuberancy of spirits truly astonishing. You can do nothing with them by hard words or angry looks, but a great deal by kindness. As to their drunkenness, that is mainly attributable to the fact that the male hands take them into the public-houses and "treat" them.

Match girls come out very strong on a Saturday night, when any number of them may be found at the Paragon Music Hall, in the Mile End Road; the Foresters' Music Hall, in Cambridge Road; and the Sebright, at Hackney. The Eagle, in the City Road, used to be a favourite resort of these girls, and in bygone summers dancing on the crystal platform was their nightly amusement. They continue to be very fond of dancing, but they are even more attached to singing. They seem to know by heart the words of all the popular music hall songs of the day, and their homeward journey on Bank holidays from Hampstead Heath and Chingford, though musical, is decidedly noisy.

The police are as a rule extremely good to the match girls, and a constable will rarely interfere with them unless positively compelled to do so. It must be admitted, however, that to have half-a-dozen of these girls marching down the Bow Road singing at the top of their voices the chorus of "Ta-ra-ra-Boom-de-ay," or "Knocked 'em in the Old Kent Road"—these are at the present moment their favourites—is a little irritating to quiet-loving citizens.

Dress is a very important consideration with these young women. They have fashions of their own; they delight in a quantity of colour; and they can no more live without their large hats and huge feathers than 'Arry can live without his bell-bottom trousers. They all sport high-heeled boots, and consider a fringe an absolute essential. As a class they are not attractive in looks; still, there are some very pretty faces among the feather-headed, brown-fringed factory girls of the East End.

So much for their out-door existence. Their home life is not so bright, and the cause for this is not far to seek. They can sing a good song, or dance a break-down with any one; but can they wash clothes, or cook a dinner? Alas! neither the one nor the other.

They are eager to marry, and do so very young. Many a match girl of sixteen marries a dock labourer or factory hand who is no older. Their happiness is of short duration. Very often one of these poor creatures, a month or two after marriage, has applied to me for protection against her husband; and frequently, when I have heard the case, I could not help admitting that the latter had a good deal to complain of. He has very likely worked hard, and never failed to take his earnings home to his "missis," as he calls her; and yet, night after night, he has returned to a dirty and neglected fireside, and found no dinner and no wife awaiting him. However, the marriages of the match girls do sometimes turn out well, and I think that such a result is somewhat surprising. With so many temptations around them, with so much vice in their midst, and with so many troubles in their lives, it is really astonishing to see the great affection these young people entertain towards one another.

There is a good deal of downright sympathy among the match girls. Quite lately one of the hands in a match factory had a succession of domestic troubles—sickness and other visitations—and her fellows collected between them as much as thirteen pounds, which, freely, and with the brightest of faces, they handed over to their sister in distress.

I am informed by the missionaries, who are far better

acquainted with the inner lives of these girls than I am, that there is not nearly the amount of immorality among them that one would imagine. They will, I am assured, in this respect, compare very favourably with other classes. Their language certainly is sometimes very bad, but I am sure they do not think from one moment to the other what they are saying. It is scarcely surprising that they should repeat the oaths and vile language they hear almost every day of their lives in public-houses, music halls, and dancing rooms, not to mention the so called East End "clubs," which I propose to describe in a later chapter.

In order to counteract the bad influences in the lives of the match girls, there has been formed a Factory Labourers' Union, having its head-quarters at Clifden House Institute, which was founded a few years ago by Lady Clifden. Miss Rawson is the secretary and Miss Nash the superintendent.

The Institute, which is composed of three cottages knocked into one, is a very unassuming-looking building, situated immediately opposite Bryant and May's factory at Bow. There is a very large, comfortable apartment, containing chairs, tables, and other furniture, which serves as the girls' sitting-room, and as many as like can avail themselves of it every evening. At the rear of the premises is a commodious dining-room capable of seating about one hundred and fifty girls. Good hot dinners, consisting of meat and two kinds of vegetables, are supplied at the extremely small charge of threepence per head. Last year as many as twenty-five thousand of these dinners were served to the girls. The number of teas supplied during the same period was nine thousand. On Saturdays, not only are these two meals provided, but every one who chooses can have a breakfast.

Before the Institute was established there was much more drunkenness among the girls than has since been the case, and this is not extraordinary, for in former days many of them were in the habit of bringing their food from home and consuming it in the public-house — an arrangement that naturally led to a good deal of intoxication, attributable not so much to the quantity of beer consumed, as to the filthy maddening stuff put into it after it had left the brewer's dray. In those days, moreover, there was a good deal of fighting among the young women, but this happily is now almost unknown.

Of course it is impossible to sleep any number of these

girls in such small premises, but some ten or twelve can be taken in for the night. Even this limited accommodation proves of great usefulness, for it often happens that these poor creatures are temporarily without any home of their own.

Last year there were some six thousand attendances at the singing, sewing, drawing, and reading classes held at the Institute. One very excellent arrangement is deserving of mention. The girls are allowed to make clothes among themselves, and afterwards buy them at a very cheap rate. As many as six hundred and fifty-two garments were made and disposed of in this way during the last twelve months. There is a savings bank in connection with the Institute, and at the present time the names of two hundred depositors are on its books. Not the least useful feature of this institution is the medical aid which it places at the disposal of the girls. There is, moreover, an excellent library, Sunday services, Bible classes, and what are known as "pleasant evenings."

A girl is able to participate in all the privileges of the Institute by paying the modest sum of two shillings per month; and who shall say that, at all events in some cases, the poor do not try to help themselves?

The establishment of Clifden House has done enormous good, and the condition of the match girls to-day is in sharp contrast with their condition a few years ago, when, if English slavery could be said to exist anywhere, it certainly existed in this industry. The wages of the poor creatures have to a certain extent improved, and they lead cleaner and, therefore, happier lives; but there still remains much to be done to ameliorate their condition.

How is it that there is only one Clifden House? Why are there not a dozen?

CHAPTER III

SCLATER STREET BIRDS

"Thank God for Sunday"—Fisher, of Eton—Summer Sunday morning in Hyde Park—Commercial Street, Shoreditch—Sclater Street—Remarks overheard—Singing matches—Love in humble life!—"Julks"—Winning a "gate"—Sunday morning marketing—Michael Angelo Taylor's Act.

I AM very fond of bed, and always have been. How delightful it is to enter one's sleeping apartment on a Saturday night, after a long week of hard work, and to catch sight of the brass or iron resting-place, with the sheets and b'ankets neatly folded back! Often on such occasions I have exclaimed: "Thank God there is such a thing as bed, and, to-morrow, that glorious institution called Sunday!"

One particular Saturday night is especially imprinted on my memory. After returning from the club, where I had dined, I had sat smoking alone for several hours in my sitting-room. My thoughts had been running at large on the subject of birds, to which, from my earliest youth, I have always been much attached. Seldom have I been without some winged pet or another.

While at Eton I was a constant visitor to Fisher's shop, in the High Street, where one could purchase almost every sort of animal, from an armadillo to a dormouse. Now that I am older, the parrot-house at the Zoo, and the cages of those cruel divers who annihilate so rapidly the dace and minnows, possess for me a strong fascination.

But it was not of divers, vultures, eagles, macaws, or other varieties from abroad to be met with at the before-mentioned establishment that I had been musing; my thoughts had been occupied with our birds—our little English birds—and

I had been mentally comparing their condition when in captivity with their habits when at liberty.

The explanation of this train of thought is a very simple one. I had often heard of the East End bird-fanciers, and, as most of their business is transacted on a Sunday morning, I had resolved to set off, immediately after breakfast on the following day, to visit their haunts, namely, Sclater Street, Shoreditch, and the neighbouring courts and alleys.

It will be observed that I was not going to spend my Sunday in the most orthodox way. I never have been orthodox, and I am afraid I never shall be.

The date of which I am writing was in the eighties, at the beginning of the leafy month of June. The weather was very sultry, and though I did not retire to rest until the small hours, I got very little sleep. At about eight o'clock in the morning I was wandering with my dog in Hyde Park, which is a stone's throw from my door.

The morning was a glorious one. This was an ideal summer Sunday, and the church bells seemed to say, as they chimed, "Thank God for life! thank God for life! thank God for life!" There was scarcely a foot passenger to be seen in Park Lane, and no vehicles save an omnibus or two, almost passengerless, journeying from Victoria to Kilburn, Edgware, or some other remote suburb. Within the Park all was solitude, the gravel walks and green sward being alike deserted. It was a good season for vegetation, and the beds and borders were bright with blossoms and full of fragrance. Those croakers who say you cannot grow flowers in towns can never have seen Hyde Park in June. Who could desire better geraniums, fuchsias, marguerites, and calceolarias than are to be found there?

Sitting down on one of the Park seats, I could not help comparing the beautiful scene around me with the hideous, squalid locality I was shortly to visit. There were no songbirds about, though there were many self-asserting, impudent, well-to-do West End sparrows.

I took my dog home, and set forth on my journey. On looking at my watch I found that I had plenty of time to spare. The hours I wished to spend in Shoreditch were from half-past ten to one. Hailing a hansom, I drove to Baker Street Station, and took a ticket to Aldgate. On my arrival there, I strolled leisurely up Commercial Street by Spitalfields Market, crossing the streets that intersect the main thoroughfare

Here on this Sunday morning every kind of marketing, huckstering, and bargaining was going briskly on. The pavement was crowded, and the roadway almost impassable. I saw an endless array of costers' barrows, loaded with meat, fish, vegetables, and other articles of food. Jews and Jewesses, in charge of truck-loads of old clothes, boots, hats, and other wearing apparel, swore themselves hoarse in praise of their wares. The din was awful, and the stench sickening.

I stopped, leant on my stick, and pondered. How different to the peaceful and beautiful scene I had quitted a few short hours before! There was no sunshine, there were no birds, and there were no church bells. Pulling myself together, I walked on briskly towards Shoreditch.

Sclater Street was soon reached, and at once I felt that the interest of the place had been in no way overstated. Here was to be seen the East End bird-fancier in all his glory, surrounded by his pets and his pals. This little street in Shoreditch forms the common meeting-ground for buyer and seller, chopper and changer, and I can safely say that nowhere in London is there to be seen so interesting a concourse of people. They are all absorbed in birds and bird-life. If you stand at one end of the narrow street and cast your eyes towards the other extremity, the scene presented is one long line of commotion and bustle. You hear remarks such as these: "Don't desert the old firm, guvnor;" "Come, now, that's a deal;" and "Wet the bargain, Bill."

One side of the crowded thoroughfare is entirely taken up with shops, in the windows of which are to be seen all manner of wicker and fancy cages—from the largest "breeder" to the tiniest "carrying cage"—and birds of every description dear to the fancy—linnets, mules, canaries, chaffinches, bullfinches, starlings, and "furriners." The cages are ranged in rows all round the wall.

Each vendor is busy shouting out invitations to the crowd to come and buy or "do a deal," which, in most cases, means a "swop," with a bit thrown in on one side or the other just to balance the bargain. The wares are not confined to the inside and outside of the shops. In the gutter and roadway are crates and boxes tenanted by fowls, pigeons, guinea-pigs, and hedgehogs.

An incessant chatter goes on. Jews and Gentiles squabble and bandy words over the respective merits of their possessions. Nearly every one in the crowd has something under his arm, tied up in a handkerchief—his own dinner, some dainty provender for his dickies, or what not. While Jack is showing to his intimates and admirers the linnet he has matched to sing against Tom Cooper's at the Well and Fountain, Jim is vehemently, and in no very choice language, exclaiming against his bird for losing his last match "by a note."

There are all sorts and conditions of men here—the rough, the coster, the Seven Dials fancier, and the "bricky" from Edgware or Tottenham, with his Sunday shaved chin and his best bright moleskins. The last-named is very busy arranging a trial with a greengrocer from the Hornsey Road. Hard by stands a well-dressed mechanic who is enquiring for a cock linnet of a docker, whose reply is that he is looking for a "chop."

Time runs on, and so dense does the crowd become that one can scarcely elbow one's way through it.

Jack D—— is a well-known dealer, and as I went up to his shop I discovered him leaning against the doorway, with a straw in his mouth and his arms crossed. He stood about five feet ten, was tough and lissom, wore cords and gaiters, appeared happy and well-to-do, and had, fastened somewhat tightly about his windpipe, a red handkerchief. And what a handkerchief! What colour, and what a pattern!

Jack's next-door neighbour suddenly appeared upon the scene in his shirt-sleeves and with a pipe in his mouth. The new-comer enquired laconically:

"'Ow's trade?"

"Oh, very rough," was the reply; "no people about. Always the same at this part of the year, and things don't improve as time goes on."

The two neighbours wagged their heads and exchanged a few friendly grunts. Jack resumed:

"They haven't got any mopusses, Jim; that's what's the matter. They're all stone broke."

"Got any monkeys?" asked Jim inconsequentially.

"No; the monkeys is sold out. Have plenty of 'em in next week—more than I want."

"Any novelties?"

"Well, a couple of piebald squirrels. 'Ad a third, but he's gone to Manchester. Got a good price for 'im."

Looking up at a row of cages over Jim's door, the speaker continued:

"That's a nice canary on the off side. What's the figure for him?"

"Oh, 'im?" pointing backwards with his thumb. "Six bob, and dirt cheap. He's a real genuine Yorkshire, and no mistake. Got some first-class Germans cheap, and blow me if they ain't swine to sing."

"You'll do a stroke or two this morning yet, Jim."

"No; there ain't what you may call any competition, Jack. Maybe we'll 'ave a rush for 'arf an hour or so presently, but then trade 'll clean take its hook and ewaperate again."

Leaving these two worthies to further deliberation and discussion, I pushed onwards, and the next minute came into collision with a girl of about ten, with long, fair hair and a dirty face, and having a dainty little shawl neatly twined round her slim body.

"Scrapers, sir, scrapers?" she cried in my ear.

I told her I didn't want any scrapers. Of course I didn't, for I hadn't the remotest idea what they were.

The public-houses were closed, but there was a temperance bar open. Men kept passing in and out, and several stood gossiping in the doorway. I overheard an interesting conversation there.

"Good morning, Boxer."

"Good morning, old Raspberry Nose."

"What do you want for that collie of yourn?"

"Oh, I'll make it a gift to you—that is, next door to it."

"None of your hanky panky with me. You just tell me what you want for him, and if he's cheap and it's on the square, the dawg's mine."

"Well, he cost me thirty bob, and there's tuppence a week for his grub for ten weeks. Let me see," after a pause, "seeing it's you, you shall have him for half a quid."

"All right," said the other with a complacent smile; "but I must see my customer first, you know."

"Raspberry Nose" took his departure, and Boxer remained lolling against the door of the shop, quite unconcerned. He was a knowing-looking card, for all his sang-froid, and he wore an ugly leer on his newly-shaven face.

I walked on, and the next thing that arrested my attention was an article that hung on the wall outside a shop. It looked like a cross between a doll's house and a bird-cage. In the centre was a linnet standing on a perch, to which he was attached by a tiny chain fastened to his leg. On the right-hand side, separated from the bird by a door, was a string suspending a water glass, and working on little pulleys. The linnet had to exercise a good deal of ingenuity in order to slake his thirst. He had to hop forward, push open the door, pull up the string with his bill, and, when the water vessel came within reach, steady it with his claws while he drank.

Further on I came to a very large establishment where hundreds of cages and birds were exhibited for sale. I was informed that the proprietor, one Brown, designed all his cages himself, and certainly he was to be complimented on his handiwork. As I was passing by, Mr. Brown said:

"Can I do anything for you to-day?"

"No."

"All right," he answered, with a grin; "better luck next time."

Strange to say, three of the largest bird-dealers in "the Row" are teetotalers, and have been so for many years. They bear excellent characters, and are liberal and fair in all their dealings with the other fanciers. Naturally they are not very polished in their manner or choice in their language. They could not sign their names if you paid them fifty pounds, yet when they receive a telegram in Spanish or French—a not infrequent occurrence—they can usually interpret its meaning. When the words completely fog them, they get their message translated at the free school in Bell Lane.

Upon the day of my visit the trafficking continued until one o'clock, and then the crowd rapidly melted away. This is the usual hour for the market to close.

Where do all the fanciers go to? it may be asked. To no locality in particular; they come from all parts of the metropolis.

During the week a considerable portion of the fancier's time is spent in listening to the birds that are matched to warble against one another. The places of venue for these contests are various coffee-shops and public-houses. Very often a large concourse of people will assemble to listen to the competitions.

A word or two about these singing matches may be of interest. A long course of preparatory training is essential. To induce a young bird to sing, he is brought into the presence of a tried songster, the cages being placed side by side. In the case of some beershops in Shoreditch, Westminster, and Seven Dials, the bar-parlour is used so frequently for matches that it wears all the appearance of a bird-dealer's shop, being crowded with cages and other paraphernalia of the fancier.

But I shall have more to say in reference to these contests further on. In the meantime I will describe a further incident that occurred on the occasion of my visit to Sclater Street.

I was about to take my departure from the neighbourhood when I perceived a number of persons entering a public-house which had just thrown open its doors. I could not resist the temptation to follow them. There were a number of people in the bar. They were not bird-fanciers, but loafers who had either been playing pitch and toss and banco on the waste ground adjoining the railway, or otherwise whiling away their time until the welcome hour when the "public" could legally open its doors. The language I heard was fearful.

Among the crowd stood a young girl of about sixteen years of age. Her face was terrible to behold. Both eyes were blackened, and her cheeks resembled swollen pulp.

"Why, Poll," said one of her pals, "how the —— did you get in that state? What cheer, lass? Why, who did that for you? Have a drink, my gal," and he handed her a pint pot half full of porter.

The girl, after taking a pretty long pull at the pewter, replied carelessly:

"Why, my young man, of course. He couldn't have done much more if he'd been my 'usband, could he?"

"I shouldn't call 'im much of a young man," rejoined her companion.

"Ah, well," she said, "if you loves 'em, Jim, you know, you can take anything from 'em."

And this, thought I, is love in humble life!

At the other end of the bar stood several coarse, bloated, blear-eyed women who had apparently not yet quite recovered from their Saturday night's debauch. One of them turned to a man who stood close by, and said:

"Pay for a pot for me, Jack, for I'm stony broke."

I turned my eyes towards the gentleman addressed, and saw that he was a slim specimen of the London prig. He was eating a hot sausage which had just been served him from a hissing utensil standing on the counter.

"You be ——," he replied; "I'm nothing more than blooming bankrupt myself. Go and tout young Bill there," pointing to a man who stood hard by. "He has got the pieces to-day. He and Darky did a bust* last night, and he is flush of coin."

She crossed over to Bill, but I did not wait to see the result. I thought I had heard quite enough.

But to return to the birds.

The fancier's love for his pets is truly astonishing. He will sit for hours in his favourite "public" listening to their trills and encouraging them to further effort. Birds are trained not only by the example of other birds but by the whistle of the fancier himself. Some birds can warble as many as seven or eight "julks," as each change of trill is called. At a singing match the victory goes to that bird which, in a given time, trills the greater number of "julks." The cages containing the little competitors are hung on the wall, and needless to say no other birds are permitted to remain in the room while the "race" is going on. It sometimes happens that one of the competitors will refuse to utter a note. It is against the rules, and a most serious offence, to coax a bird to sing. Absolute silence, indeed, has to be maintained by all present.

The way in which the scores are kept is most interesting. As a bird calls off with a trill, he is scored "1" on the table with a piece of chalk, and a fresh mark is put down for each change of trill. When five chalks stand to the credit of a bird he is said to have won a "gate." The origin of this term is at once apparent, for the fifth mark is made to run transversely across the preceding four—thus: ℍ.

A match will sometimes fail owing to one of the competitors being out of sorts, or because they have been matched together before and know one another, in which case it is no uncommon thing for the little creatures to sulk and remain dumb.

The language which the fanciers use to denote the different "julks" sounds very strange to unfamiliar ears. Such expressions as these are used: "Tollick-tollick," "tug-whizzy," and "tollick, tollick ikki qua." So far as orthography is concerned, I have rendered these words about as correctly as is possible; but where it becomes a matter of pronunciation, I can assure my readers that only a genuine bird-fancier can properly interpret the language of his pets.

In the neighbourhood to which I am referring hundreds of costers with their barrows are to be seen every Sunday morning. If they are an evil, I am convinced they are a

* A slang expression signifying a burglary.

necessary one. It is practically impossible for a great many of the East End poor to do all their marketing on a Saturday night. Many a toiler does not leave the workshop of the sweater until after the shops have closed, and of course the wages are not paid until the last stitch has been put in. Again, those who do their work at home are frequently unable to deliver it until the last thing at night. Then it must not be forgotten that the barrow-men, having no rent or taxes to pay, can sell their meat, fish, vegetables, and other commodities at a lower price than the shopkeepers. Moreover, the costers, with their wives and families, form no small portion of the community, and if their occupation were gone, they would go to still further flood the already overflooded labour market.

I am aware that, according to the strict letter of the law, this trading is illegal. It was made so by an Act (known as Michael Angelo Taylor's Act) passed in the reign of George the Third. The sixth section empowers the local authorities and their street keepers, utterly irrespective of the police, to summarily, and, if necessary, forcibly remove the barrows and their contents after notice has been given; to confiscate the latter and impound the former; and to take police-court proceedings against the offenders.

Shortly after my visit to Sclater Street, proceedings were taken before me against a number of barrow-men who traded in that locality; but I am happy to say that an amicable arrangement was come to. I paid a special visit to the locality—on the 9th of March, 1889—to ascertain how far it was correct to say that these costermongers caused an obstruction. I found them quiet and orderly, and it seemed to me that there was very little ground for complaint.

When the cases came on for hearing, I ordered each defendant to pay the cost of his summons—two shillings—and I informed those who appeared for the prosecution, of the results of the personal inspection I had made in the locality. The Vestry and the street inspector behaved with great forbearance. They suffered the law to fall practically into abeyance, and up to last March not more than a dozen more summonses had been taken out.

Thus the East End poor are still able to purchase their necessaries cheaply, and the East End coster is still permitted to ply his trade, and maintain his wife and ofttimes numerous family.

CHAPTER IV

MY DEPÔT

Poverty in the East End not exaggerated—Preparing for winter—My letter to *The Times* and *The Daily News*—Generous response thereto—My depôt opened—Bed-clothing the most pressing want—Messrs. Jeremiah Rotherham and Company, High Street, Shoreditch—I interview the partners—Their liberal spirit—I have the articles stamped—No grey blankets—A valuable stock—How we distributed our collection of clothing—A few noteworthy cases—Mr. Massey and his wife.

SOME weeks ago, while scanning a well-known morning paper, I came across a remarkable statement in the columns that are devoted day by day to metropolitan fashionable and other intelligence. The precise words I do not remember, but they were to the effect that the poverty and misery in the East End had been very much exaggerated.

Were I acquainted with the writer of the paragraph, I would invite him to accompany me on a stroll through Bethnal Green, Shoreditch, and some adjoining localities, and I do not for one moment doubt that, without my bringing any pressure to bear, he would hasten to publish a correction of his former assertion.

When I left Worship Street Police Court in the autumn of last year, a number of grateful creatures tendered me their thanks for what, after all, were the very small services I had been able to render them, and with their thanks they mingled expressions of regret at my approaching departure. I told them that, although circumstances over which I had no control caused me to migrate to another court, I had become so interested in their welfare, and in the institutions of their neighbourhood, that, so far as my health would permit, I should continue to do all in my power on behalf of both. I had not forgotten, I added, and never should forget, the terrible sufferings they underwent every winter.

As we had scarcely any summer in 1891, it is a little difficult to say when the winter began. However, my preparations for its advent were made some time in advance. Long before I decided to leave the East End, a plan to meet the distress had been maturing in my mind, and my removal to Marylebone in no way prevented my putting it into execution. I proposed to open a depôt of my own for the relief of distress in the Thames and Worship Street districts. I discussed the matter at some length with Mr. Massey, the leading missionary at the latter court, and we came to a complete understanding as to what should be done.

On November 21st I sent the following letter to *The Times* and *The Daily News*:

"A PLEA FOR THE EAST END.

"SIR,—Winter troubles are now coming thickly upon us, and from what I can learn of my late district at the East End of London, the trials and miseries of the last two years are not likely to be mitigated. I no longer preside as one of the magistrates over the neighbourhood, but I think I have hit upon an expedient by which, with the help of the public, I may still be of some use to the suffering poor with whom I have officially parted. Last year I found I was enabled to do much good by distributing, throughout the severely cold months, blankets and warm clothing. I have therefore taken some premises in the immediate neighbourhood as a sort of clothes depôt; and I invite all those who are in a position to do so to send me blankets and old clothing, especially warm undergarments for women and children, together with shawls and cloaks. The London Police Court Mission have kindly given me the aid of the missionaries of the Thames and Worship Street police courts, who will be of the greatest use to me in my venture. I need hardly add that I have the hearty assistance and co-operation of my brother magistrates who preside over the courts to which I have alluded. Parcels should be addressed to John Massey, police court missionary, 7, Coombs Street, Haverstock Street, City Road.

"Your obedient servant,
"MONTAGU WILLIAMS

"9 Aldford Street, Park Lane,
"Nov. 21st, 1891."

MY DEPÔT

As will be seen, I only asked for blankets and clothes, but, besides those articles, I received, from private friends and others, various sums of money to assist in purchasing a stock for my depôt. Among other interesting letters, I received the following:

"DEAR SIR,
"I have been a parsimonious man all my life, and so I have no old clothes to give you. I myself wear out everything that I have, and perhaps this is the reason that I am able to send you the enclosed cheque to buy blankets for the poor creatures whose cause you are espousing."

My appeal met with a generous response, and my depôt was opened in the first week of November. We did not close it till the 24th of March in the present year.

I have always thought, and recent experiences have confirmed the belief, that, in endeavouring to ameliorate the condition of the poor in the East End, the first want one should supply is warmth. Nobody who is not intimately acquainted with that quarter of London can form any idea of the misery that young and old, sick and healthy, endure, during the winter months, through their lack of adequate bedclothing.

In starting the depôt, therefore, my first thought was blankets; and for several weeks I really think I had blankets on the brain. Not being a family man, I know very little about these articles, their price, relative qualities, and so on; but a kind-hearted creature, a tradesman living not a hundred miles from my late court, was the means of relieving me from much embarrassment under this head. When sending me a most liberal cheque, he wrote: "I quite agree with you as to the necessity for blankets, and if you want to know where to buy them, I should recommend you to go to Rotherham's, High Street, Shoreditch. Of course, they will know you; but if you like to present my card, you will, I am sure, find yourself most liberally treated."

After I had finished my day's work I took a hansom and journeyed to High Street, Shoreditch. Proceeding down that thoroughfare, after passing the railway station, the cabman drew up outside a modest-looking draper's shop. At first I thought there must be some mistake. Could these be the premises of Messrs. Jeremiah Rotherham and Company, who,

I knew, employed on their establishment nearly five hundred persons? On alighting from the cab my doubts were set at rest, for I perceived that the shop was only a small section of the premises, the frontage of which extended down the High Street for about one hundred and eighty feet.

I entered the establishment, and five minutes later was shown into the counting-house, and introduced to Mr. Robert Dummett and Mr. Frederick Snowden, who were almost immediately joined by their fellow-partners, Mr. William Ellis and Mr. George Gotelee. After briefly telling them the object of my visit, I said:

"I hope to be able to spend a considerable sum of money with you, in the purchase not only of blankets but also of flannel and knitted petticoats for women and children, and as I am only a trustee for money entrusted to me for charitable purposes, I hope you will meet me on reasonable terms. Of course, I cannot ask you to supply me with goods at cost price, but I do beg and entreat you, considering the cause for which I am endeavouring to enlist your sympathy, to let me have the goods at the smallest margin of profit."

I am bound to say that they met me in the most liberal spirit, and I there and then gave them a very large order.

In revolving in my mind the details of my project, I had not lost sight of the temptations, associated with drink and the pawnbroker's shop, which beset the poor creatures I was desirous of assisting. In this direction a very great difficulty presented itself; but I had at last hit upon a plan which seemed to promise a satisfactory solution.

"We have," I said, "agreed upon the price of the goods, and I want you now to tell me what it will cost to have such articles stamped in the centre, so that to cut out the piece bearing the impression would be to destroy the value of the entire blanket or petticoat."

"I don't quite understand," one of the partners replied.

"What I mean is this," said I; "I intend them all to be stamped in the centre with the words in blue, 'Montagu Williams' Relief Fund.' I propose to let this fact be known to the police in my late districts, and to cause them to keep it in mind on the occasion of their periodic visits to all the pawn-shops. The result, I think, will be that the articles of clothing we distribute will not be turned into drink."

It was at once decided that the blankets and petticoats should all be stamped in the manner I had suggested.

MY DEPÔT

Perhaps I ought to mention that the blankets I ordered were not grey ones.

"Of course, sir," said the shopman, as he spread out before me a large white blanket with a blue border, "we have a great number of grey ones in stock at a much lower price."

"Thank you," I replied emphatically, "but I have no intention of purchasing them."

As I knew perfectly well, the poor do not like grey blankets. "Not like them, indeed!" I fancy I hear some one exclaim. "Not like them! Then they don't deserve any at all. Let them go without." But this is not my view. Human nature is human nature.

There are few more interesting places of business than a large wholesale and retail draper's. At Messrs. Rotherham's you see one department stacked with carpets; another, with merinoes and dress goods; a third, with rich and beautiful silks; a fourth—resembling a gigantic and well-stocked conservatory—with artificial flowers, the pick of the Paris and London markets; a fifth, with thousands of rolls of ribbon, representing every colour known to the dyer; a sixth, with great heaps of straw hats, and so on. As one looks around, it is impossible to help wondering what must be the value of the entire stock. Mr. Dummett was good enough to throw some light on this point.

"Sometimes," he said, "we have a greater quantity of the more costly goods than at others, but at the present time the value of the stock is something not far short of two hundred thousand pounds. Our insurance is distributed among all the English companies, and some American and Continental ones."

Messrs. Rotherham and Company devote one entire house to the making and storing of boxes in which to despatch their goods. To the right of this house are the stables, which are models of what stables should be, being roomy, light, and scrupulously clean. Let into the wall, at the back of each stall, is a plate bearing the name of its occupant—"Jess," "Spot," "Vic," "Dolly," "Punch," and so forth.

Would that the human beings living hard by were as comfortably housed as those horses! The back of Messrs. Rotherham and Company's premises overlooks the infamous Boundary Street area, which I am thankful to say the London County Council has scheduled for demolition. At one extremity of the firm's establishment, the High Street is connected

D

with Boundary Street by Hare Court, which in days gone by enjoyed the unenviable notoriety of being the scene of numberless robberies.

But to get back to my depôt.

Among those who assisted me in my scheme were, as I have already said, many of my personal friends; and I herewith tender them my warmest thanks. But how can I find words to express my gratitude to my other supporters, many of whom were perfect strangers to me? I hope some of them will read these pages, as they will thereby learn the results of our collaborative efforts. Let me add that little, if any, good could have been effected without the co-operation of Mr. Massey.

I find that we were able to help, within the period I have indicated, over four hundred families, representing considerably over that number of adults and as many as sixteen hundred children. We have assisted fifty families in one day. Besides over a thousand blankets, we distributed about four thousand articles of clothing — coats, vests, trousers, boots, shoes, stockings, hats, caps, shirts, overcoats, undervests, and mufflers for men and boys; shawls, dresses, and every other conceivable article of warmth for women and girls; and an enormous quantity of baby-linen. The balance of the money—and it was not a large one—we expended on coal.

One woman was so delighted when some blankets were given her that she exclaimed, with a face never to be forgotten:

"Oh, sir, I've not had a blanket in my house for twenty years."

It was pleasant, though very pathetic, to see the delight with which many poor creatures huddled round the fires our coals had provided. In a number of instances, to our certain knowledge the grate had been empty during several preceding weeks, and even months. And yet, forsooth, some one writes, amid the fashionable intelligence of a morning paper, that the winter sufferings of the East End poor have been greatly exaggerated!

I cannot, of course, give an account of all the cases that were relieved by us; but I propose to briefly deal with a few that struck me at the time as being worthy of notice.

One bitterly cold Sunday night a visit was paid to Mrs. F., who lived—or rather endeavoured to live—in Hoxton. The family consisted of the father, mother, and five children. They had a single room, for which they paid five shillings and ninepence a week. On the occasion of the missionary's visit they were all huddled about a small fire, made with some wood which had been given them by neighbours who were almost as poor as themselves. The only food in the room was a small piece of fried fish. Mr. F., a tailor, who had been out of work for months, was busily engaged in trying to make a pair of trousers out of an old piece of cloth he happened to have by him. He was going to try to sell them next day, he said, to help pay the rent.

Here are my entries of another case visited on the same evening: "Mrs. G., —— Street, Hoxton; husband, wife, and six children. Husband had been a printer; out of work for months; eyesight failing him. Wife near her confinement. All the children without boots and clothes. No firing."

Next door to Mrs. G. lived a man, his wife, and their five children. A few days before they were visited the woman had been confined. They owned neither bedstead nor bed; but a neighbour had lent the poor mother a mattress and a sheet. The children were all on the point of starvation. We lost no time in sending them coals, blankets, baby-linen, and other necessaries.

Here are some further notes that were made at the time:

"Mrs. S., No. — in the same street. Four children. The woman has been a widow for two years. They live in one small room, paying two shillings and ninepence rent. She makes hair-brushes, for which she is paid one shilling and ninepence per dozen. Has lived on six shillings a week for two years. Her wedding ring sold to pay rent and buy food. Next-door neighbour equally badly off. Makes paper bags at fourpence halfpenny per thousand."

Several cases came before us that illustrated the misery often brought about by strikes. Here are the details of two of them:

"At —— Street, Cambridge Heath, husband, wife, and seven children huddled together in small back room (rent two shillings and sixpence per week). Husband out of work owing to dispute in the boot trade. Absolutely and literally starving. Children on an old mattress; no bed-covering. One child very ill, suffering from pneumonia."

"Family in —— Buildings, Shoreditch. Husband out for the same reason. Wife goes into the streets to sell oranges. Her face terribly thin and pinched. No fire. Two children; no food to-day. The woman has no under-garments, not even a chemise. Covered by an old bodice and skirt. No boots. Children also nearly naked."

The next case in point of date was rather a peculiar one. I dare say some of my readers will think that the persons concerned were not entitled to much consideration; but have we not been taught that, as we are ourselves to be judged, we should not judge others too harshly?

At Worship Street a man named S. was charged with stealing a coat, and was remanded for enquiries. It transpired that he was in receipt of a small sum (army reserve pay), and that this was his first offence. There was a girl in question, and he said he would marry her if he got out of his present trouble. The cause of his fall, he said, had been drink, and upon his promising to give it up, my excellent brother magistrate remanded the case for four weeks to see if he would keep his word. The stolen property, it should be mentioned, had been returned.

The man did not abuse the kindness shown him. He married the girl, my missionary seeing the banns put up and being present at the ceremony. We gave them some clothing, and set them up with a small sum of money; and I am happy to be able to add that the pair are now living prosperous, respectable, and happy lives.

The distress in Bethnal Green was terrible in the extreme. We did what we could, but of course our means were limited. Here are some of the cases:

"Mrs. M., husband and three children. Husband a labourer. Rent, four shillings and sixpence per week. Wife and one child ill. Average income for months past, eight shillings a week. No bed; no bed-covering."

"Mrs. P., a widow; three children. Just buried a fourth. One room; rent, two shillings. Paper bag-maker; fivepence per thousand. One old blanket to cover them all."

"Mrs. C., widow; three children. Matchbox-maker; twopence farthing per gross. One child ill; mother in very weak state. No bed or covering. Desperate state of poverty."

The case of Mrs. B., of Mile End, was a very sad one. There were three children, and the husband was out of work. A pitiful sight met our eyes when we called at the room. One child was in the last stages of consumption, and another lay *in extremis* with spinal disease. The poor woman was nearly worn to a skeleton from watching and tending her dying boys.

MY DEPÔT

On calling at the room a second time, I had touching evidence of the sympathy the poor feel for one another. The woman had gone to try and get an hour's sleep at the room of a neighbour, who, though very ill herself, was now taking charge of the children.

Here are the particulars of another case:

"Mrs. G., her husband (who was out of work), and their six children, lived at the top of a house in a little room which contained neither chairs nor table. In a corner of the room, on a straw mattress, lay the woman, dangerously ill. The children—white little creatures, almost naked—were crouched around her. There was no food in the cupboard. A doctor, it appeared, had called in that morning out of pity. We at once procured further medical aid, and supplied the family with food, coals, blankets, and warm clothing.

There was almost as bad a case in the same house.

Mrs. D., who was near her confinement, lived in a room with her one child and her husband, who had been out of work for over a month. The rent was three shillings and sixpence a week. That same morning a neighbour (very poor and ill herself) had given them threepence, which the woman had laid out as follows: Coal, three-halfpence; bread, halfpenny; tea, halfpenny; dripping, halfpenny.

We kept a diary at the depôt in which we recorded, for future reference, full details of all the cases relieved; and from this source I have drawn the foregoing particulars, which conclusively prove, I think, what a terrible amount of destitution exists, and what good service can be done, in the direction of meeting it, by private enterprise.

It will, I am sure, be a great satisfaction to my coadjutors to learn that their assistance has been the means of driving misery and death from the home of many a starving family in, as I believe, the poorest district in the world.

The services of the Worship Street missionary and his good wife were invaluable to me, and I hope, with their assistance, with a renewal of public liberality, and with the experience I have gained, to be able to help my poor East End friends, in their winter troubles, on a far more extensive scale in the future.

CHAPTER V

GRIDDLERS, OR STREET SINGERS

Common lodging-houses in Deptford—I visit one of them—Their occupants—" What is a griddler?"—His haunts—"The Wandering Boy"—Episode in the north of London—Musical répertoire—Police regulation.

My first real introduction to a common lodging-house occurred shortly after I took my magisterial seat at Greenwich. The establishment in question was in Mill Lane, Deptford.

I was, at the time, already tolerably well acquainted with the predatory habits of the poor and criminal (though do not let me be understood as bracketing the two together, for to do so would be grossly unjust), but I was completely ignorant of the sort of life that was led in "kips" or "doss-houses." I had, it is true, visited such places before, but my observation had never proceeded further than a superficial glance, accompanied, it may be, with a shrug of the shoulders.

The courts and alleys of Deptford abound with rotten houses and tumble-down tenements that are the abodes of thieves and unfortunates. It is hardly necessary to enter these places in order to understand their true character; what you see from the outside tells its own tale of poverty, vice, misery, and crime.

Here and there, written in legible characters on the outside of a building, are the words, "Registered lodging-house." As I have elsewhere remarked of these establishments, there is no adequate supervision over them, nor, let me frankly admit, do I see how matters can be mended without fresh legislation in the direction of further restraint. At present the authorities have absolutely no power over the owner of a common lodging-house. The business is sufficiently profitable to enable him to laugh at the law. For conducting his house improperly, he should, in my opinion, be liable to a fine of, say, one hundred pounds. I do not doubt that the enforcement of such a penalty would have a very salutary effect.

You get a tolerably good clue to the character of these dens even from an external scrutiny. At the windows you see some hideous human heads, male and female, with blotched, bloated, and bestial faces, matted and tangled hair, and hungry, desperate eyes.

Some lodging-houses are for one sex only, and others for both men and women.

On entering one of these establishments for the first time, even if you have never been astonished before, I can guarantee that you will experience the sensation.

The visit I am about to describe was paid one foggy morning in February, on a day when I was off duty. The place was warmed by coke stoves, which are to be met with in every lodging-house. From the bent and broken gas brackets a sickly light was shed on a number of wan, pinched faces and emaciated forms that were but scantily clothed in rags.

The gathering included many disciples of Bung, as was proved by red and pimply noses, beery breath, and sour skins. Obviously the East End brewers and publicans are thoroughly appreciated by the "dossers."

A sergeant of police accompanied me, and what struck me as extremely ludicrous was the way in which the poor wretches watched him. There was an unmistakeable look on their faces—a look that assumed a speaking form, and was interrogative—"What do you want me for?" And then, as the officer passed, it was equally amusing to note the look of delight—the gleam of sunshine. "I'm still free! It isn't me after all;" these were the words you could read in their grateful eyes.

I don't believe any of them knew me at all; but I was regarded with the closest suspicion. They were civil, almost servile, to the sergeant; but there was a curious, puzzled look at me, accompanied by an enquiring glance from one to the other—a glance to which, so far as I could see, there was no response.

I was at the time unused to these places, and I confess that, though it was in the daytime, I should not have felt very comfortable had I been by myself.

"Now, what are these fellows?" said I to the sergeant, when we had returned into the street.

He replied:

"Tramps of both sexes—mat-sellers, griddlers, hawkers of lace, makers of fire-screens and fly-papers, brush-makers, street flower sellers, and so on."

"What on earth are griddlers?" said I.

"Well, sir," he replied, "if you've had enough of this place, I'll tell you all you want to know while we are walking on to another."

But I had not had enough of that place. I don't know what possessed me, but I was seized with a strange desire to go back to the lodging-house. We did so, and proceeded to inspect several rooms that we had omitted to enter previously. These rooms were in total darkness, save for a ray or two of light shed from the coke stove.

"Now then, light up here," shouted the sergeant, and the "deputy" lost no time in obeying the injunction.

Among the poor wretches huddled together in these rooms were several shabby-genteel men in dreadfully old black clothes. There were also a few little children.

The conversation carried on between the sergeant and the deputy was very amusing.

"Where's Billy Goff?" asked the officer.

"Left here on Saturday, sergeant."

"Where's he gone?"

"Well, I think if you were to look for him at Notting Hill you wouldn't be far wrong."

"Where's Mog Sullivan?"

"Not up yet. She's in that room," pointing to a door along the passage.

"Rout her out, then! Time she was up! It's eleven o'clock!" and Mog's slumbers were disturbed without more ado.

I watched the dinner being cooked with considerable interest. The favourite article appeared to be what they termed "'addicks." The sergeant informed me that the principal meal in the common lodging-house is supper, of which all the inmates partake. He added that chops and steaks often figure at this meal, and that many a toothsome morsel is yielded by the "scran bag" of the professional beggar. That individual, it appears, distributes his dainties for a consideration among his comrades of the night.

On our regaining the street, and proceeding on our journey, I again enquired what was a "griddler."

"A griddler?" said the sergeant. "Don't you know that, sir? Why, he's a chaunter—one of them as gets a living by singing in the streets. They never have any fixed home. They go about all day and sleep together in gangs—that's my experience. The doss-house ain't got no better customer than the griddler."

It must always have struck the ordinary observer as difficult to understand—it certainly has so struck me, and I consider myself an ordinary observer—how any man or woman (a child, of course, has no option) can adopt street singing as a regular business. There are so many adverse circumstances to be taken into account—for example, the variations in our climate; the physical exhaustion and mental depression resulting from singing in the open air for any considerable time; and the degradation of such a vocation.

Chaunting has become an actual profession, and it is followed in London alone by hundreds, not to say thousands, of individuals. Of course in some instances street singing is adopted as a temporary expedient, to tide a man over a slack period; but with such unfortunate persons I have nothing to do in this article. The real "griddlers" are men who have never worked laboriously in their lives. They form a large section of the vast army of human parasites who suck away the substance of the industrious.

Why these people are called "griddlers," again I say I do not know. I have made every enquiry on the point, but have hitherto failed to learn the origin of the expression. A great many "griddlers" come from Birmingham, and the word seems to have a Brummagem ring about it.

Addressing my companion, I said:

"I suppose these people have sunk about as low as they possibly can?"

"No, sir," he replied, "that is wrong. The ordinary working man," he proceeded, "never sticks to it long. There is such a dreadful sense of shame about it that few really honest men can bear it. I may tell you, sir, that it is very easy for any one experienced in the ways of the griddler to tell a new hand. It's as easy, sir, as to tell a ha'penny from a penny. Any one not used to the game drops the thing as soon as he or she has got enough coppers to get food and a bed. With the regular hand, however, it isn't so much board and lodging that they think about as drink, and they often sing on and on until they've got enough money to get drunk on. Added to chaunting, the griddler often goes in for patter. The other day I came across a strong, able-bodied chap, a loafer every inch of him, and his hands as white as a woman's, and he pitched a fine yarn, I can tell you;" and the sergeant indulged in a chuckle over the reminiscence. "The fellow," continued the officer, "stopped in front of a lot of people and said: 'My dear friends, it is no doubt very degrading for a strong young man like me to be standing singing in the street, but it's only the want of food for my dear wife and children which compels me to do so. Not long ago, when I was earning good money, it was my greatest pleasure to sit at home of an evening with my wife and children, and the thought of this compels me to do what I am doing for them.' Then he went on with his psalm, and several coppers were thrown to him by some old ladies, who carried on about him being a 'poor dear man,' and I don't know what all."

"And you knew as a fact, I suppose, that the fellow was an old stager?"

"Lor' bless you, sir, I've seen that same man on the streets, off and on, for six or eight years past. That sort of patter I was just speaking of is the thing to get the posh, they'll tell you. By the way, the griddlers don't often appear at the police court, as you must have noticed, sir."

Yes; on thinking it over I decided that the sergeant was right. I can remember only a very few cases of street singers being brought before me.

The lodging-house is the common meeting-place of the "griddlers." There they sit after the "labours" of the day, smoking any amount of tobacco, drinking pot after pot of beer, and debating as to what neighbourhoods are, and what neighbourhoods are not, "good for money."

Spitalfields, Whitechapel, Holloway, the Borough, Westminster, and Notting Hill are the haunts of these gentry, who, however, occasionally vary their movements by a run out to the suburbs.

By the virtue, or rather vice, of his calling, the "griddler" is no respecter of weather. The full glare of an August sun, the fogs of November, the snows of January—it is all one to him. In the winter people do not often ask him why he does not get work; but the question is frequently put in the summer. He has his answer pat—"I've just come up from the country, please, sir, and I've been travelling all day looking for work. I haven't had the luck to find any yet, and so I'm just trying to get a few coppers to buy food, for I haven't touched a bit of anything all day, if you'll believe me, sir."

As a rule the "griddler" journeys alone, but occasionally he picks up a female companion, and the two walk and sing in company.

The sergeant told me that at one time it was the daily custom of two old stagers to proceed to Highgate Ponds, kick the white dust all over themselves, and then sing their way back to the East End, looking for all the world as if they had just come off the road.

A man who was once a "griddler" relates the following experience. He was singing "The Wandering Boy" in a very disconsolate condition one day, when a butcher's wife, calling to him, said:

"Are you 'the wandering boy'?"

"Yes, ma'am," was the answer.

"Well," she returned, "it's time 'the wandering boy' was in bed."

"Yes, ma'am," moaned the "griddler"; "but 'the wandering boy' hasn't got the price of a bed;" and thereupon the good woman gave him a substantial sum of money.

It is not an uncommon thing for a trio to sing the streets, and in such cases the "swag" is shared equally, that is, if the collector can be trusted to "brass up" all the earnings.

I gained a good deal of information about these people from the missionary of one of the courts; and he told me a story about three of these gentry who were chaunting in a fairly respectable road in the north of London. They presented a rather ludicrous appearance. One was very tall and remarkably thin, while his companions were short and thickset. As trade was dull that day, they were very depressed, and so much out of heart that their joint mutterings were only just audible to the passers-by.

While they were favouring the public with "I will Guide Thee with Mine Eye," a lady appeared at the door of one of the villas and spoke to them. She said:

"You men sing so nicely that I want you to come and stand on the pavement here and go on with that hymn. There's an invalid lady upstairs, and she wants soothing. When you've finished you shall come into the house, and I'll give you something to eat and some money."

At this the "griddlers'" spirits rose, for they were hungry and thirsty. They came forward eagerly, stationed themselves immediately in front of the house, and went on with their dirge. They continued singing for about a quarter of an hour, and then, thinking they had imparted sufficient comfort to the poor invalid, they knocked at the door.

The lady who had previously spoken to them answered the summons, and bade them follow her downstairs.

The three vocalists, with their caps in their hands, and a happy, greedy look in their eyes, were making their way to the basement, when there suddenly emerged from the back parlour a stern, powerfully built man, who carried a large whip.

"Get out of this, and look sharp about it," he exclaimed, standing in their path, and pointing to the open door with his whip.

They protested, remonstrated, and swore; he repeated his injunction, got very angry, and threatened to thrash them. They refused to budge, and there appeared to be every prospect of an animated quarter of an hour; but at length, perceiving that bullying would not do, the man with the whip condescended to explain.

"There's no invalid in the house," said he, "and the lady who spoke to you is suffering from a fit of D.T.s. I'm in here to look after her while her husband is away at business. If you want to know anything more you had better call when he is at home, though I shouldn't advise you to."

The wandering singers grasped the situation, turned on their heels, and, as soon as they had reached the pavement outside, burst into noisy laughter. The next minute a voice called to them from the house, and, on looking round, they perceived that the lady had again come to the door. She beckoned them, and one of the three, with some trepidation, retraced his steps.

"There," she said, handing him a great pyramid of fresh-cut bread and butter, "demolish this, and, when you've done so, just you come back and polish off my old man. Give him a good hiding, and I'll pay you for it."

The trio polished off the bread and butter, but, as my informant added, they took a little time to think about the rest of their instructions.

The "griddler," where he is refused money, does not hesitate to substitute a request for clothes or underlinen, for all is grist that comes to his mill. He will resort to any artifice to obtain his ends.

One of the fraternity, who had been a compositor, prided himself on being the gentleman of the profession. He was always very clean and respectable-looking, and, being rather a handsome fellow, he succeeded in making a very fair living. He had a great weakness for wearing white shirts, perfectly got up and scrupulously clean.

It is very amusing to hear a discussion among members of the brotherhood as to the relative drawing powers of the various items in their musical répertoire. "There is a Home Eternal," "Brightly Gleams," "Onward, Christian Soldiers," "Shun Evil Companions," and the perennial "Wandering Boy" all have their measured value, and where one fails another is tried.

Saturday night sometimes brings in five or six shillings, and Sunday morning in the slums often yields a couple from seven to fifteen shillings. It must not, however, be supposed that money can be coined at this rate all the week. Monday generally finishes the "griddler's" earning week, and he does not try again until the following Friday evening, save and except for an occasional turn to get the "price of a pot."

Two or three years ago street singers came out in such amazing force that a stringent police regulation was issued regarding them. The force were directed to call upon every person found singing in the street to desist, and if he refused to do so, they were empowered to arrest him on a charge of begging. Very seldom were "griddlers" interfered with by the police anterior to this. It must be remembered that in many instances they went about in large numbers singing "We've got no work to do," and it would, of course, have been rather a ticklish thing even for three or four constables to tackle these gangs.

I remember once seeing a number of these gentry carrying about a labourer's shovel, on which were chalked the words "Rusty through idleness." Notting Hill used to be invaded by a large gang of Lancashire men, very strong and strapping fellows, who went about with a piano organ. After spending an extremely profitable year in the metropolis, they betook themselves to pastures new.

At some period of his life the "griddler" has, in all probability, worked at some trade. A love of idleness and the want of self-respect have caused him to take up with gutter singing. If he has children he apprentices them to the business and thereby permanently doubles and trebles our vagrant population, for in only a very few instances, unfortunately, have the young people sufficient strength of character to raise themselves to a nobler calling.

CHAPTER VI

THE LONDON HOSPITAL

Its position—Its staff—The nurses—Admission—The district served—Wards for Jews—Scenes therein—Strength required by nurses—Out-patients—Daily routine in the wards—Dietary—Hospital experiences of a friend of mine—Terrible sights—Humorous incident.

HAVING resolved to include among my sketches some description of a leading metropolitan hospital, I was not long in deciding to which one I should direct my attention. I chose the London Hospital, and I will give my reasons—I always like to do so—for my selection.

There is a greater variety of people admitted into this hospital than into any other in London. Moreover, its district contains my old Courts of Thames and Worship Street. The magistrates presiding there hear of no other hospital, and from time to time they have occasion to visit it to take a dying deposition.

I would preface my remarks by saying that I do not believe there is another institution of the kind conducted so admirably in the whole of England—not to say the whole of the civilised world.

The hospital consists of a large building facing the Whitechapel Road, from which it is divided by a courtyard, which serves as a carriage way. The main entrance leads into the receiving-room, which, if I am not much mistaken, was opened as recently as last June. One side of the building runs down Turner Street, and the other down East Mount Street, while the rear looks out into Oxford Street and Philpott Street.

The institution was founded in 1740, and greatly enlarged in 1859. The Alexandra wing was added in 1866, and the Grocers' Company's wing was opened by the Queen in 1876.

His Royal Highness the Duke of Cambridge is the president, and the establishment is conducted by a house committee, of which Mr. Edward Murray Ind is the present chairman. A quarterly court of governors is held on the first Wednesdays in March, June, September, and December. There is a matron; and there are nearly thirty sisters, and over two hundred nurses. Some ten physicians, and an equal number of surgeons, are aided by a large staff of junior surgeons and dressers.

Four separate rooms constitute a ward, and each room contains either fifty-two or fifty-six beds. On an emergency seven hundred and seventy-six beds can be made up. As a rule between six and seven hundred are occupied. On each floor there are some thirteen or fifteen nurses and one sister.

There is an entire building, practically detached, set apart for the use of the nurses. It contains a large dining-hall for all, and each nurse has a separate bedroom, with her name and a number written on the door. The nurses are allowed two hours' leisure every day, and they have one day's rest every month. They all have to serve two years as probationers, and if, at the end of that period, they decide to remain on, and the authorities are willing, they are permitted to take a month's vacation before resuming their duties. From that time forward they have three weeks' holiday every year. These rules, I believe, are similar to those in force in other large hospitals.

The *modus operandi* of the admission of patients is very simple. In the receiving-room a porter is stationed night and day, and when patients are brought in by the police or others, he promptly admits them, and hands them over to the nurses. To the right and left are two rooms, one for the reception of women, and the other for the reception of men. Here the patients are examined by the nurses, with a view to seeing whether the cases are medical or surgical, and whether they are of a pressing nature. The nurses of course afterwards report to the surgeons and physicians.

That the hospital is by far the most important in the metropolis is proved by the extent and character of the district it serves. This district comprises Bethnal Green, Spitalfields, Whitechapel, Shadwell, Mile End, Commercial Road, Commercial Street, Limehouse, and all the surrounding neighbourhoods, including the Docks. A heterogeneous mass of humanity, representing nearly every nationality on earth, is brought together within its walls.

Communications between the doctors and nurses on the one hand, and the patients on the other, have very largely to be conducted by signs and symbols, and having regard to the sufferings of many of the patients, it is marvellous that they succeed so well in making themselves understood.

A great many foreign Jews enter the hospital, and this is not to be wondered at considering the number living in this part of London.

Two of the wards are specially endowed by the Rothschild family for the use of Jews. They are in every way distinct from the rest of the establishment, and have their own kitchens and cooks. In these wards the Jewish Sabbath is kept, the Passover is celebrated with the greatest solemnity, and all the fasts and feasts of this ancient race are duly observed.

To judge by the accounts given me, the occupants of these wards are not for the most part very courageous. They frequently make a considerable uproar when asked to uncover and show their wounds, the noise of their bellowing being, I am assured, in inverse proportion to the severity of their injuries. They are always very loth to leave the hospital, and many of them would, I am sure, like to remain there to the end of their days.

These Hebrew patients are, as a rule, very well-conducted people. Though the race to which they belong is notoriously slow to part with money, it invariably happens that, when anybody is dying in these wards, some one is found to defray the cost of a "watcher." This individual remains by the bedside until death takes place, and performs the necessary offices afterwards. Christian nurses are not permitted to touch the body; everything is left to the "watcher."

Another peculiarity of this most peculiar people is that they will not eat from a plate that has been previously used by Christians. What is more, it is insisted that no plate from which a Jew has eaten shall leave the ward until it has been washed. The strangest part of the business is that the nurses themselves are Christians. The patients would not on any account permit one of their own race to give them their draughts and otherwise minister to them.

The inmates of these wards are allowed to receive visitors on Tuesday and Friday from four till five, and on Saturday (their Sabbath) from three to five. The friends of those who are on the dangerous list, however, have a right of entry at all hours.

As they speak nothing but "Yiddish," they find it very difficult to make themselves understood, but by hook or by crook they manage to express the grateful feelings they almost invariably entertain towards their nurses. Sometimes very singular scenes result from the patients' ignorance of the language that is being spoken around them.

Once there was a little boy in one of these wards suffering from a serious complaint, and suddenly he died. A fatal termination to the illness had not been anticipated, and it happened that neither a "watcher" nor any of the family were present when the end came. The mother was sent for, and promptly arrived. She would not believe that her little one was dead, and proceeded to blow into his mouth. While she was thus engaged, the father put in an appearance and called upon his wife to desist. She took no heed, whereupon he endeavoured to force her from the bedside, and there ensued a most unseemly scuffle between them. A nurse tried to quell the disturbance, but this only led to further friction, and matters were beginning to assume a very serious aspect when the "watcher" fortunately arrived, and succeeded in throwing oil on the troubled waters.

When a Hebrew who is known in the neighbourhood dies in the hospital, all his or her friends and relatives — men, women, and children—flock into the institution and congregate and wail around the bed, with the result that the medical and nursing staff are greatly inconvenienced and hindered in their work.

On Saturday nights and Bank holidays there are so many applicants for admission into all parts of the hospital that the resources of the institution are taxed to the utmost.

If any one has any doubts as to the brutalities practised on women by men, let him visit the London Hospital on a Saturday night. Very terrible sights will meet his eye. Sometimes as many as twelve or fourteen women may be seen seated in the receiving-room, waiting for their bruised and bleeding faces and bodies to be attended to. In nine cases out of ten the injuries have been inflicted by brutal and perhaps drunken husbands. The nurses tell me, however, that any remarks they may make reflecting on the aggressors are received with great indignation by the wretched sufferers. They positively will not hear a single word against the cowardly ruffians.

"Sometimes," said a nurse to me, "when I have told a woman that her husband is a brute, she has drawn herself up and replied: 'You mind your own business, miss. We find the rates and taxes, and the likes of you are paid out of 'em to wait on us.'"

One day a German woman, who could not have been more than twenty years of age, was introduced into the general ward to be treated for a broken jaw. On the following day several friends came to see her, and among them her reputed husband, who had inflicted the injury. As soon as she saw him she burst into tears, and begged the nurse to allow her to return home with him at once. Upon being told that her removal from the hospital would be attended with danger, she reluctantly consented to remain there for the time being; but she left two days afterwards. As she was taking her departure, the nurse warned her that the slightest additional violence on her husband's part must be fatal, whereupon she exclaimed impatiently:

"Ah, ma'am, you don't know anything about it. You see, I love him with all my heart."

And at this time the jaw had not even been set.

The nurses as a body possess great amiability, patience, and gentleness; but it is often useful if to these qualities is added that of muscular strength. It sometimes happens, indeed, that the nurses have to combine the functions of ministering angels with those of police constables, as the following experience of one of them will show.

"One day," she said, "a woman who had been very much maltreated by her husband was brought into the hospital. She was too tipsy for the doctors to examine her, and so she was sent up to the general ward, where she refused to undress, and began to scream and utter the most fiendish noises. I and another nurse tried to take her in hand, but it was of no use. She wrenched off my apron, and tore my dress terribly. It was, in fact, impossible to do anything with her, and so, after we had, with a lot of trouble, removed her skirt and bodice, we let her go to sleep. Two hours afterwards, when we awoke her, it took three of us to remove her things. She was a foreign Jewess—a Pole, I think."

Every afternoon some five or six hundred out-patients are treated at the London Hospital. When they arrive, if the inspector is satisfied, they are passed through at once; if he is not satisfied, enquiries are made. On passing the barrier, they are presented with numbered books for the prescriptions, and they then proceed to interview the physician or surgeon.

There are separate departments for the different classes of disease, one entire ward being devoted to ophthalmic cases. The out-patients, most of whom attend between the hours of nine a.m. and six thirty p.m., are for the most part wretchedly poor.

The daily routine in each ward may be briefly described. The majority of the patients are called by the night nurse at a quarter to six in the morning. Those who are able to wash themselves do so; the nurse washes the others. Between six and half-past breakfast is served. Everything is then made ready for the day nurse, who enters the ward punctually at seven. The beds are then made, and the floors swept. The probationary nurse does the dusting, while the regular nurse cleans the tables, etc. At nine the patients have bread and milk, and after that the day nurse makes ready for the doctors. They usually appear a little after ten, and remain with the patients till about twelve.

Then comes the patients' dinner, which—save of course in special cases—consists of meat from the joint, vegetables, and pudding, the different quantities of each being carefully weighed out by the nurse. After dinner the ward is kept very quiet, unless a visiting physician or surgeon comes in. If one makes his appearance he is accompanied by a whole army of students. The beds are all visited in turn, and he lectures on those cases that are worthy of remark. Sometimes his harangue will occupy twenty minutes or half an hour. One would imagine that the patients themselves would find this very galling and obnoxious. The very reverse, however, is the case. There is a great deal of jealousy on the subject, and if A's case is lectured on and B's is not, B passes the rest of the day in the highest possible dudgeon.

Tea is served at four, and when this has been cleared away, the day nurse makes the beds for the second time, does the evening dressing, and tidies up the ward for the night. At seven the saucepans are put on for the soup and beef-tea, and soon afterwards supper is served. At eight the lights are turned down, and a cup of milk is placed by the bedside of every patient. Between eight and ten the doctors come round again, and at twenty minutes past nine the day nurse is relieved by the night nurse.

Before concluding this paper, I think I may appropriately describe the experience of a friend of mine.

On leaving my court one morning I repaired to one of my

clubs, as is my custom, for luncheon. On enquiring for a friend who usually sat at the same table as myself, I was informed that he had met with an accident and was in —— Hospital.

Though very anxious to learn the nature of his injuries, I had no leisure to make any enquiries that day. Subsequently I learnt that my friend, while outside Ludgate Hill Station, slipped on a piece of orange peel and fell to the ground, fracturing his thigh. He was picked up, put into a four-wheeler, and taken to ——, where he arrived at about one o'clock in the afternoon. He was placed in the —— ward, where some eleven other patients were being treated.

As soon as I learnt what had taken place, I was all anxiety to go and see my friend, and on the day following that on which I had first heard the news, I took a cab from Worship Street for the purpose of doing so. I had no order of admission, and knew nothing about the visiting regulations.

In the gateway stood a good-looking old pensioner, and as I was hurrying past him, he exclaimed :

"Hullo! where are you going?"

"Well," I replied, stopping short and confronting him, "I'm not quite sure. Perhaps you can assist me. I understand that there's a friend of mine in the hospital, and I'm going to see him. Mr. ——, fractured thigh. Perhaps you can direct me."

"Oh," said he good-naturedly, "we don't do things in that sort of way here. I know the case; but you haven't come at the right time; besides, he's seen one visitor already to-day."

"Well," I replied, "that's awkward, though I don't see any just cause or impediment why he shouldn't see another."

"No," he replied with composure; "only that it's agin the rules."

"Is the principal in, or any one I can refer to?"

"Well, you see, it's just about dinner-time."

This was true enough, for I had driven round immediately after adjourning the court for luncheon. The gate-keeper's remark served to remind me that I had no time to spare, so I observed:

"Come, come, you can make a difference with me. Don't you know me? I'm your magistrate."

"Lor bless me!" he exclaimed; "why, it's Mr. Montagu! Oh, sir, of course you can go in when you like. Go through that door, sir."

I entered, and two minutes later was standing by the bedside of my friend. He was very cheery, and, as he explained, wonderfully comfortable considering the circumstances. He spoke with enthusiasm and gratitude of the way in which he was being treated.

I visited him several times, and was greatly impressed by the quiet and order that prevailed in the hospital, and by the excellence of the arrangements generally.

Pleasant as it was to see my friend from time to time, I was anything but happy while in the hospital. Terrible sights necessarily meet the eye there. For example, in the bed next that of my friend lay a little boy who was deaf and dumb, and, as if these afflictions were not sufficient in themselves, he was suffering and dying from a contraction of the limbs. One day I saw the nurse dressing him for bed-sores, and never before in my life had I set eyes on so pitiable an object. As I was taking leave of my friend on this occasion, I said:

"You will be out, the doctor tells me, in a fortnight. Forgive me if I don't come again. I can't bear these terrible sights."

When the fortnight had elapsed, and he was once more out and about, we talked over his hospital experiences.

"A night or two after I was taken in," he said, "a man was admitted who had fallen off the flies at the Britannia Theatre. What with this poor fellow on one side of me and the little dumb boy on the other, the experience was one I am never likely to forget. The Britannia man died next day, and the lad was suffering still when I came out. But," added my friend, with a smile, "things, even in a place like that, sometimes have their comic side," and he went on to describe an incident that greatly amused me.

It appeared that, during the last week of his stay in the hospital, two new patients were introduced into the ward, and placed in opposite beds. By a remarkable coincidence both were suffering from the same malady—*delirium tremens*. They were of different social status, they came from different districts, and they were—as was most conclusively established—utter strangers to one another.

When admitted—the one at nine o'clock in the evening, and the other at half-past ten—they were not then drunk, but recovering from the effects of drink. Each fell sound asleep immediately he was put to bed.

The night passed, and the morning found them somewhat

restless. All that day they took very little food, and, of course, no stimulants. Night again came on, the candles were put out, the patients for the most part fell asleep, and quiet and stillness reigned—for a little while.

Suddenly a bed creaked, and the next moment a terrible oath was uttered in a guttural whisper. One of the men was sitting up in bed; my friend could just descry him in the semi-darkness.

"Now," said the man, leaning forward and speaking in the direction of his fellow-sufferer, "we ain't going to stand this sort of thing any longer. We'll make our escape from this —— place, and I'll tell yer 'ow we'll do it."

My friend turned his head, and, behold! the other man was sitting up in bed. He, too, muttered a fearful oath. Then he said:

"Right you are. The Home Secretary is the boy for us. We'll make these minions tremble. Not one single drop all day!"

The two spectral forms in night-shirts proceeded with one accord to scramble out of bed.

My friend had a stick beside him, and with it he drummed on the floor as hard as he could. The nurse ran in from the adjoining ward, assistance was procured, and the two delinquents were removed and placed in separate parts of the building.

CHAPTER VII

MEDLAND HALL

Opened by the London Congregational Union—The proprietors summoned for permitting overcrowding—I propose an arrangement—It is accepted—A conference—Resolutions—Speakers' experiences of casual wards—Various classes of casuals—A "stiff," or hawker's license—Why Medland Hall was founded—Encouraging results.

THERE are many charitable institutions in London about which the general public know little or nothing, and among the number may be reckoned Medland Hall. Opened at the beginning of last year by Mr. Sydney Halifax, situated near the Stepney railway station, and owned by the London Congregational Union, Medland Hall is to all intents and purposes a casual ward for men run on an improved method.

On the first night of its existence the Hall had twenty inmates, and on the day the census was taken the number was six hundred and eighty-three, including four hundred under fifty years of age. Thousands of persons have benefited by the institution since its establishment.

The shelter opens its doors at eleven o'clock at night, and the inmates are allowed to remain there until six in the morning. It sometimes happens that a man will leave before that time, in which case there will always be several poor outcasts anxious to take his place. One or two hours' rest and shelter are very welcome to those who have passed the night wandering about the streets or crouching in a doorway. During the winter nights a number of men are usually to be seen waiting outside the building on the chance of being admitted.

Last September Medland Hall came before my notice

officially at the Thames Police Court. The proprietors of the place were summoned by the Limehouse Board of Works, under the Nuisances Removal Act, for permitting overcrowding, and thereby endangering the health of the inmates. The sanitary inspector, at whose instance the proceedings were taken, stated that, when he visited the premises, which consisted of four floors, they contained three hundred and eighty-four persons, whereas they were only capable of properly accommodating two hundred. After explaining that he had found the house similarly overcrowded on other occasions, he said that the inmates had nothing to lie on but the bare boards, and that, in his opinion, such a condition of things was not conducive to health.

Mr. Gates, the superintendent of the Hall, next gave evidence. He explained that the premises the Union then occupied were of a temporary character, the original building having been destroyed by fire, and a new one being in course of erection. He went on to say that their lease would expire on the twenty-fourth of October, and that they would then be able to move into their new quarters.

It occurred to me that if I made a peremptory order for the closing of the premises, I should be depriving hundreds of poor fellows of a shelter. I therefore proposed that an arrangement should be come to between the authorities and the London Congregational Union, suggesting that the former might withdraw from the prosecution on the latter undertaking to limit the number of inmates to two hundred. This proposition was accepted and acted upon.

On Tuesday, the fifth of April in the present year, a conference was held at Medland Hall, respecting the condition of casual wards in the metropolis. Mr. Sydney Halifax presided, and was supported by Mr. Gates, Mr. Stapley (of the London County Council), and other gentlemen. There were also present over four hundred men, most of whom had been inmates of casual wards.

The resolutions proposed and passed were:

" 1. That the casual ward accommodation of the metropolis should be largely increased, so that neither men nor women need be turned upon the streets because the wards are full.

" 2. That casuals be admitted to the wards up till midnight on any night, and that they be at liberty to leave at five o'clock in the morning.

"3. That no task should be required of those casuals who only need shelter and medical attendance, but that when they need food, whether supper or breakfast, or both, the labour performed should be in proportion to the meals consumed.

"4. That the dietary be improved, and the scope of the tasks so arranged as to give to casuals the opportunity of doing that class of work for which they are best adapted, and that the plank bed be prohibited.

"5. That the property qualification for election to Boards of Guardians be abolished, and the method of electing them be so reformed as to admit of working men taking a direct part in the administration of the casual wards.

"6. That no limits be placed upon the number of visits by men or women to the casual wards, provided that they are destitute at the time of application."

Several casuals were called upon to state their views, and the speeches they made were so amusing and interesting that I propose to give some quotations from them.

Mr. E. ascended to the platform, and addressed the conference as follows:

"Mr. Chairman, ladies and gentlemen—my comrades—I shall never forget my first experience of casual wards. I am speaking of about fifteen years' experience. I didn't know what sort of a thing the inside of a casual ward was; but I had been fifteen nights in the streets, and I had got to that pitch that I thought I would go to the casual ward, and I went to the best I could find—Shoreditch. A tall gent about six feet high came to the door and looked down on me. 'What do you want?' says he. 'I want a night's lodging, if you please,' says I. 'Oh, come in, young gentleman,' says he. 'We are here for that purpose; come in. I'll give you yer supper in a minute.' In I went, and down I sat, quite comfortable like. Presently I heard a voice through a little wicket window say: 'Come here. What's yer name?' I told 'im. 'What are you?' says he. I told 'im. 'What's yer age?' says he. 'Well,' thinks I to myself, 'you'll know enough presently.' Howsoever, I told 'im, and then he looks me up and down, and says: 'You ain't partic'lar strong, are you? I shall talk to you in the morning.' 'Well,' says I to myself, 'that cove's all right.' Next morning they gave me my breakfast, and the same cove opens the door, and says, with a grin: 'D'yer see those stones?' Should think I did see 'em—great lumps of granite. 'Well,' says he, 'you've got to break 'em before you go out of here.' Thinks I to myself, 'if they wait till I break 'em they'll have to wait a long time.' There were two hammers lying there, and I took the biggest and struck at the stones. The hammer flew up to the ceiling and I didn't know where I was. I did no good with those stones. The cove came back in about an hour, and said: 'Can't you do no better than that?' My hands were all bleeding, and I says: 'No; I can't do 'em.' Then he brings me four or five pieces of oakum, and I started to pick 'em. When I had got through about five ounces he comes back, and says: 'Why, you're no good at anything. I've a good mind to run you in.' 'What for?' says I. ''Cause you ain't done your task,' says he, and he goes on to say as how there's an old chap in the next cell what had done his little lot by four o'clock. 'Don't you come here again,' says he to me. I've 'eard say that a Cabinet Minister in the 'Ouse of Commons said there wasn't any poverty in London, and that it was greatly exaggerated, and that the casual wards weren't 'alf full. Well, now the very same night I went to four casual wards and I couldn't get in 'cause they said as how they was all full. Something has been said about Mile End. Well, I've been there, and the bloke has come to the door, and said: 'How many of yer?' 'Ten,' says we. 'Well,' says he, 'I can only take in five. The others must go away.' And would you believe it, when I got inside I found there was eight cells empty! If any gent calls what's a-looking after 'em, they go and fill up all the cells pretty quick. That's 'ow they work it, and I think it's about time some one did look into it. Well, I think I'll leave this now in better hands. This is my maiden speech."

Mr. E. was loudly applauded, and was complimented upon his speech by the chairman.

A Mr. B. next addressed the meeting. He said:

" This is the first time I have ever occupied this platform; perhaps it will not be the last. I think it an honour to stand up here. I wish to relate to you in a few simple words my experience. One of my experiences was in 1889, when I entered Whitechapel ward. I was perished with cold. They gave me a small portion of bread and some skilly. I was told to wash my face in water which resembled broth, and I wiped my face on a towel that would disgrace a rag-shop. Then I was told to go to bed, and after wrapping myself in a blanket you could see to read a newspaper through, I got to sleep. In the morning I had four pounds of oakum to pick in an ill-lighted and ill-ventilated room. I tried to pick it, but got nervous because I thought I should get run in. At five o'clock they took my oakum away from me and booked the quantity. They then gave me a pint of skilly resembling bill-stickers' paste, and a small portion of bread. I was put back with others, as I thought, to go to bed, but the fates had ordained that I was not to go to bed, but to prison. After waiting for some time the casual master came in with a list of seven names, and I was among them. We had to stand out in a line, and after we were all assembled, three policemen took us into custody and we were marched round to the police station, taken before the magistrate and sentenced, three of us to fourteen days and the others to eighteen days. I was better treated in prison, and had better food, and was altogether much more comfortable than when I was in the casual ward. I fought shy of casual wards after that, and went on into the country and got a little work. But it soon failed, and then I had to go back to casual wards. The next experience I had was in 1890, when I went into Rotherhithe. I dare say you know what sort of a shop that is. I was received more like Bill Sikes and his dawg than anything else. They gave me ten hundredweight of stones to break. I knew no more of breaking stones than the whale did of the inside of St. Paul. I had a poisoned ankle when I went in, and I was afraid of hitting it. After knocking the stones about till five o'clock in the afternoon, the master looks in and he says: 'Young gentleman, I don't wish to hurry you, but if you haven't done I shall have to charge you.' I didn't finish my task, and I was taken to the Greenwich Police Court next day and received fourteen days. Why should we have our hands bleeding because we haven't got fourpence? Why should we have our hearts bleeding because we are set to tasks which no convicted criminal has to perform? I ask you who are assembled here to-night, *bonâ fide* working men, some of you fellows like me—I ask all of you to do your best. If you never spoke before in your lives, open your mouths and let these gentlemen know what we have to suffer at the hands of the casual masters. I say to these ladies and gentlemen, if they do their best to help us, and to alleviate our sufferings in our daily march through this life, I am sure they will not only have the plaudits of thousands like me, but the approbation of the Divine Mediator and Friend who is always willing and who is always quick to reward those who give even a cup of cold water in His name."

Another casual gave an account of his experiences. His story was similar to that of the others. He was ordered to break ten hundredweight of stones—a task, he declared, that no novice could perform if he were offered a thousand pounds as his reward—and because, by the end of the day, he had only got through about half the quantity, he was taken into court and sentenced to fourteen days' imprisonment.

A magistrate sees a good many frequenters of casual wards. For the most part they are brought before him charged with neglecting their allotted tasks. In some cases they are poor, miserable-looking creatures, weak physically and without any moral backbone. Another class are the sturdy, impudent beggars, who, I verily believe, abstain from work on principle. Again, it sometimes happens that the delinquent is an apparently honest man, who, having lost his means of livelihood, through no fault of his own, has been forced to resort to the casual ward.

It is, of course, impossible to generalise with regard to this class of prisoners. Each case must be judged on its own merits. Obviously, if a man is quite capable of performing his work, but wilfully abstains from doing so, he must be sent to prison. On the other hand, if he is unable, either through physical weakness or want of knowledge, to accomplish his task, it would be grossly unjust to punish him; but there is always a doctor in attendance, I believe, and he certifies whether or no the person is able-bodied.

The question of the capacity of the casuals to do the particular kind of work that is set before them is one that apparently needs to be looked into.

"They gave me a lot of oakum to pick," said a casual in describing his experiences, "and as I had never done such a job before, and didn't know how to do it, of course I hadn't finished in time. Now, I'm a basket-maker, and what would be the good to put a man to make a lot of baskets when he had never done work of that kind before? And where's the difference, I should like to know!"

Among the tramps, who constitute a large proportion of the inmates of casual wards, are many men who have been navvies. They also include a number of soldiers—some of whom are pensioners—and a sprinkling of broken-down professional men. Oddly enough, you seldom or never find an old sailor in the ragged army of tramps.

The crafty, indolent individual who begs his way from door to door, and from street to street, has several ways of evading the law. His principal expedient is to procure a hawker's license, which is known among the brotherhood as a "stiff." It is the easiest thing imaginable to do this. All a man has to do is to go to the police station, pay five shillings, give his name, and ask for a hawker's "brief."

The license confers upon the holder legal authority to call at any house, provided he has something to sell. Two or three pencils, one or two sticks, half-a-dozen boot-laces — these, or any other equally trifling goods, are sufficient for the purpose. Under cover of this pretence, for it is no better, begging is carried on all over the country. When confronted by a constable, all the delinquent has to do is to produce his license and declare that he is merely pursuing the legal calling of a hawker—an explanation he not infrequently conveys in language that is none of the choicest.

I cannot forbear to describe a police inspector's experience of one of these individuals.

The officer found the fellow, to all intents and purposes, begging, though he carried, ostensibly for sale, a packet of cards on which scriptural texts were inscribed.

"Do you know," said the former, "that you want a license to do this sort of thing?"

"No, I don't want a license," was the reply.

"But you do," retorted the inspector, "and if I catch you at this game again, I shall have you locked up."

"You will, will you? Well, we'll see about that;" and the mendicant bade him farewell in terms both flippant and filthy.

Later in the day the police inspector met the same man, as he was skulking out of the gateway of a gentleman's mansion.

"Hullo, there!" said the officer, "now, you know I've warned you that you want a license for this business."

The fellow retorted:

"I suppose you know best, but I know better. I don't want a license—because I've got one;" and as he spoke he drew his "brief" from his pocket and laughed in the officer's face. "Take me to the station, my friend," he continued, "and see what your superior will say"—an invitation, it is needless to say, that was not accepted.

It sometimes happens that men of this stamp will enter the casual ward with money successfully concealed about their persons. A tall fellow of twenty, who, though as strong as a horse, had never done a proper day's work in his life, was heard to boast that he once went into a casual ward with fourteen shillings in his pocket, did his task without perspiring, and left the establishment next day as rich as he entered it.

What with pots of four ale, plenty of fresh air, and the constant meeting with old friends, the tramp's life, though it has its intervals of imprisonment, is a tolerably merry one. The philosophy of the thing appears to be that it is easier to idle, and eat and drink, than to work hard and only do the same.

It would seem that nothing can be done to put down our vagrant population, which increases year by year, the children inheriting the lazy and roving proclivities of their parents.

Medland Hall was founded, in the first place, because it was felt that the casual wards are not able to accommodate all who desire to enter them, and, in the second place, because there was a desire to try the experiment of letting out the inmates sufficiently early in the morning to admit of their obtaining work. A man has to stay in the casual ward the greater part of the day, breaking stones, picking oakum, or doing some other work as a set-off against his food and night's lodging; and as, when he is set at liberty, it is much too late to find a job anywhere, he is unable to get the money to pay for a bed. Unless, therefore, he has the luck to secure the loan of a few pence, he is driven back at night to the casual ward, with the same consequences as before, and in the end, it may very likely be, he is sucked down into the vortex of chronic pauperism. How easy to sink! How difficult to rise again!

As I say, Medland Hall, in which I take a very great interest, was established on lines intended to enable its inmates to regain an independent footing in the world. The experiment, I am delighted to think, has been attended with very encouraging results. Undoubtedly our Local Government Board and Boards of Guardians can learn some very useful lessons from Medland Hall.

CHAPTER VIII

CLERKENWELL GREEN

"Hicks's Hall"—Celebrated names—My first appearance—Sir William Bodkin—The granting of licenses—The Argyll Rooms—Cremorne Gardens — A ludicrous incident —Wretched accommodation —The poor juryman! — How service was once evaded—The "Slaughter House"—Lockyer—Mrs. Howe—Changes in the Sessions.

OLD names cling to old places, or else, why Clerkenwell Green? There is nothing verdant about the spot so designated. It is a small open space surrounded by dingy-looking houses, and situated in one of the most crowded districts in London.

Clerkenwell itself is peopled by small tradesmen. Several nationalities are represented there, including Germans and French, who for the most part are engaged in the manufacture of watches, clocks, and jewellery.

Between Clerkenwell and Holborn is to be found a very large Italian colony, consisting of organ-grinders, image-sellers, ice-cream vendors, and the like.

The principal building of the neighbourhood stands on Clerkenwell Green itself, and is known as the Middlesex Sessions House. It was originally called "Hicks's Hall," though who Hicks was I really do not know, nor is it my intention to pause to enquire. It may be that Hicks erected the building; possibly he merely lived in it; or did the name originate by reason of so commanding a structure evoking the exclamation, "Bravo Hicks!"? Again I say I do not know.

When I was called to the Bar, there were, besides the Central Criminal Court, two buildings used for sessional purposes — the Middlesex Sessions House, on Clerkenwell Green, and the Surrey Sessions House, at Newington. A barrister was not allowed to practise at both Courts. If he were a member of the Home Circuit, he could choose between the two; if not, the Court on the north of the Thames was the only one open to him. As an inevitable consequence, the Bar of the latter tribunal was always an exceedingly large one.

Many celebrated men have commenced their career at Clerkenwell, notably the late Lord Chancellor, Serjeants Ballantine and Parry, Mr. Poland, Q.C., and Serjeant Sleigh. On special occasions, too, the walls have echoed the eloquence of Lord Chief Justice Holker, Sir Henry James, Sir Charles Russell, and other men of like eminence.

It was at Clerkenwell that I made my first appearance as a criminal advocate, and here it was that I laboured, day in and day out, during a long series of years. The sessions were nearly always held twice a month, and they usually lasted from Monday till Friday.

There were two Courts at Clerkenwell—one presided over by the Assistant-Judge to the bench of magistrates, and the other by the Deputy Assistant-Judge, with whom sat the justices themselves. The Assistant-Judge was appointed by the Home Office, and received a salary of fifteen hundred pounds a year. He enjoyed the privilege of appointing his deputy, who was remunerated at the rate of five guineas per diem while the Sessions lasted. The Assistant-Judge also presided in the Court of Quarter Sessions for hearing appeals from the decisions of the magistrates in the Courts below; but the justices who sat with him had equal voting power with himself.

When I joined the Sessions, a new and very excellent Judge had just been appointed. This was Mr. (afterwards Sir William) Bodkin. His deputy was Mr. Payne, part editor of Carrington and Payne's Reports.

The two Judges had nothing to do with granting either public-house or music and dancing licenses. This was left to the justices themselves. Within the last few years the power of granting music and dancing licenses has been vested in the London County Council. I scarcely feel justified in criticising a method of which I have had no direct personal experience, but I may say with reference to the old system—and I had a large licensing practice—that I regarded it as very far from satisfactory. It has always struck me that, in default of a system of local option, the best persons in the London district

F

to have the power of granting or refusing licenses would be the stipendiary magistrates. Each one knows his own district and its requirements, and—what is of still greater importance —he is familiar with the character of all the licensed premises it contains, having them brought constantly under his notice. If the present number of licenses is to be reduced—and the interests of the community certainly demand that it should be —surely the best way to effect the reduction would be by cancelling those attached to disreputable houses. If a confirmation committee were found to be desirable, one could be composed of, say, ten of the metropolitan magistrates presided over by the chief. The amount of extra work that would thus be thrown upon them would not be very considerable.

In times gone by, some of the greatest field days at Clerkenwell were those upon which the applications for music and dancing licenses were heard. I am speaking of the time when the Argyll Rooms and Cremorne were in existence.

For many years the license for the Argyll Rooms was granted on the application of counsel as a matter of course. The inspector of police was asked the usual question by the chairman: "Any complaints, inspector?" His invariable reply was: "No, sir." The chairman then put the question to his brother magistrates: "Those in favour of renewing the license hold up the right hand. On the contrary." There were few, if any, votes in opposition, and the application was duly granted.

But a change suddenly came over the spirit of these proceedings. Whether the public became better, or the places became worse, or both, I do not know; but one thing is certain, year by year the license of the Argyll Rooms met with determined opposition, and year by year Mr. Bignell, the proprietor, was represented by the most eminent counsel that wealth could procure. There was usually a magisterial "whip," and the bench was crowded. The attendance of justices was sometimes, indeed, so large that several of them had to be relegated to the jury-box.

Of course each justice had a vote, and the result was therefore always in doubt until the hands were counted. The license of the Argyll Rooms was ultimately refused, I believe, in consequence of a kind of riot that occurred one night in Windmill Street, just as the Casino was closing.

For years the license of Cremorne Gardens was held by Mr.

Simpson, who was also the proprietor of Simpson's Restaurant in the Strand. Subsequently Cremorne passed into the hands of Mr. E. T. Smith, the lessee of Drury Lane, a most popular and genial man, who had, I should think, seen more of life, with its ups and downs, than any other individual then living. He was a great favourite with every one, not excluding the Middlesex magistrates, who always granted his license without a murmur. In the course of time this admirable caterer for the entertainment of the public died, and Cremorne Gardens passed into new hands.

I think I was one of the counsel who appeared on behalf of the applicant on the occasion when the license was refused. Sir John Holker (the Attorney-General) led. The opposition, which was instituted by Canon Cromwell and petitioners in the district, was represented by the late Mr. Bottomley Firth, afterwards Deputy Chairman of the London County Council.

On the same day a rather ludicrous incident arose out of the application for the renewal of the license of a well-known music hall in the West End. The applicant appeared before the bench in the usual way, and the license was about to be granted without any opposition being raised when up jumped Major ———, a magistrate, who had an unfortunate habit of objecting to everything and everybody on the very smallest provocation.

The Major said he desired to put some questions to the applicant, who straightway went first white and then red, and began to tremble visibly.

"Now, sir," said the Major, "attend to me. Is it true that on one occasion, some few weeks back, two private soldiers of the Guards were refused admission to your hall because they were in uniform?"

"No, sir," replied the wretched man, "not because they were in uniform, but because we thought they were a little in— a little in———"

"In what?" retorted the Major angrily; "a little in what, sir?"

"Well, sir," faltered the applicant, "not quite the better for drink."

"You thought, did you!" shouted the Major, growing purple in the face with rage. "You ventured—you actually ventured——! I move that this license be refused."

There was an awkward pause, during which the miserable

applicant murmured something about meaning no harm. Almost going down on his knees, he proceeded to stammer out this unfortunate observation:

"I assure you, Major—believe me, Major—I should be the last to cast a slur upon any member of the British army. I'm the son of an officer myself."

This was too much for the Major.

"You, sir!" he shouted, almost jumping out of his seat with indignation. "You! I call upon the chairman to put the question to the vote."

The applicant had a narrow escape, for though the bench was extremely full, the license was granted only by a majority of two. I don't suppose the applicant ever alluded to his military connections in public again.

In the Clerkenwell Sessions House, as in most criminal courts, there is very poor accommodation for the public. I always felt exceedingly sorry for the witnesses. Day after day they had to be in attendance, and until their services were actually required they had to kill time as best they could by loitering about outside the building or lolling in the neighbouring public-house. When at last their case came on they had to stand outside the door of the Court—huddled together with pickpockets, housebreakers, and other depraved characters who come under the general head of "prisoners' friends"—waiting until their names were called out.

Considering what discomforts and hardships had to be endured at the Sessions House, I often marvelled that any persons could be found to come forward as witnesses and prosecutors.

Then, too, how hard is the lot of that long-suffering individual, the British juryman. I have always had the greatest pity and admiration for him, probably for the same reason as that given by Jo in "Bleak House": "'E was wery good to me, 'e was."

There is, I believe, no Court in the world where the juryman has suffered more than at the Clerkenwell Sessions House. He, too, while in waiting, has no place of rest and shelter. He had, and no doubt still has, to attend from ten in the morning till five in the afternoon every day during the Sessions. It is true that, while in waiting, the juryman can sit in Court, that is, if he is able to find a vacant seat; but it is not a very great privilege to be permitted to spend many hours in a vitiated atmosphere, with, very likely, some specimens of untubbed humanity as next-door neighbours.

One hears of a proposal to pay Members of Parliament, but surely jurymen should be first considered. A Member of Parliament has many privileges. He may like to write "M.P." after his name; he may enjoy belonging to "the best club in the world"; he may even not be averse to seeing his name in the papers; and have there not been known politicians who were not wholly displeased to hear the sound of their own voices? A Member of Parliament has, I admit, anxious and laborious duties to perform, but no one would deny that there is a credit as well as a debit side to the account. What, however, of the poor juryman? Where are his privileges? To be fined by the Judge if he arrives in Court a minute late; to be censured if, worn out by the verbosity of counsel, he allows his eye to rest upon the newspaper he has surreptitiously abstracted from his pocket; and to have withering glances shot at him if he ventures to return a verdict not quite in accordance with the views of the bench—these are his rewards.

While upon the subject of jurymen, I cannot resist describing a whimsical incident that occurred many years ago. It was a Monday morning, in the middle of July, and I remember, as I journeyed to Clerkenwell, remarking how lovely was the weather. The Judge was a little late, the grand jury was being charged, and we—that is, the Bar—had either robed or were robing, and stood chatting together in our room. While we were thus engaged my clerk ushered in the well-known form of a celebrated journalist, who was an old friend of mine. He was very smart, in his snow-white waistcoat, and looked like a visitor at a garden-party.

Shaking hands with him, I exclaimed:

"What on earth brings you here?"

"I'm on the jury," he replied; "that is to say, I've been summoned. For goodness' sake get me off. I never was so busy in my life, and from what they tell me I should be kept here for a week or a fortnight. You go down and say a word for me to the Clerk of the Peace before they begin calling over the names."

I need hardly say that I did so at once, but returned in a few minutes only to report a failure in my mission. The clerk had informed me that he dared not erase the name without the permission of Sir William Bodkin, who, on being appealed to, had turned a deaf ear to our prayer.

On hearing of the result of my efforts, a blank expression came over my friend's face. It did not, however, remain there long; and the next minute a smile lit up the features of this most genial of men. It was clear that he had bethought him of an expedient, and I awaited the developement of events with interest.

The usher came and announced that the grand jury were charged, whereupon we all proceeded into Court. On entering that chamber, my friend, without waiting for his name to be called, made straight for the jury-box, as if only too anxious to discharge the onerous duties his country had imposed upon him. I observed that he took the seat usually allotted to the foreman of the twelve gentlemen who are called upon "to true verdict give," etc.

The other eleven in due course entered the box. Whether they recognised the eminent journalist or not, or whether the attraction of the white waistcoat and genial face proved irresistible, I cannot say; but while preliminaries, such as taking the pleas, were engaging the attention of the Court, my friend in the box became the centre around which all his fellow-jurymen gathered, like flies about a jam-pot. He appeared to be in excellent form, and as he chatted his hearers all wore smiling and delighted faces. It was a very happy family.

In due course the jury were called upon to elect one of their number as foreman, and when my friend rose, apparently with a view to quitting his seat, I was not surprised to see him at once thrust back by his comrades, who appeared to be quite unanimous in their desire to appoint him their spokesman. After a very pretty show of hesitation, he consented to act, and was duly sworn as foreman.

The first case was called on. It was, if I remember aright, a very simple one of robbery from the person. The evidence, which seemed pretty clear, was given, the prisoner grew more and more dejected, the Judge summed up in a manner not too favourable to that individual, and the jury were directed to consider their verdict.

The white waistcoat turned round, there was a whispered colloquy, during which my friend seemed to be shaking his head a good deal, and finally the white waistcoat faced about again.

The officer of the Court put the usual question: "How say you, do you find the prisoner at the bar guilty or not guilty?"

With the blandest of smiles, the foreman replied: "Not guilty."

The prisoner gave a start, and the Judge looked down as though considerably surprised.

Another prisoner was given in charge of the jury, the trial was gone through, and the result was the same.

When the second verdict was returned, the Judge turned very red, and, addressing the foreman, said:

"Perhaps, gentlemen, in the next case I had better read the whole of the evidence over to you."

The sarcasm, I need hardly say, had not the slightest effect.

A third case was tried, and again, though the evidence seemed at least open to another interpretation, the prisoner was pronounced to be "not guilty."

This was too much for the Judge.

"Rumbelow," he said, addressing the usher, "call a fresh jury." Then, turning to the occupants of the box, his lordship added, in a voice not quite under control: "Gentlemen, your attendance will not be required any more during the Session."

I shall never forget the face of the foreman as he stepped from the box. As he passed me, on his way to the door, I fancied I detected the faintest contraction about his left eye.

There were usually from a hundred to a hundred and thirty prisoners tried every fortnight at Clerkenwell. The cases were of all kinds, from prosecutions of sharpers for indulging in the three-card trick, to those raising the question of the legality of baccarat as played at a West End club. Occasionally trials of considerable public interest took place there.

Criminals had a wholesome dread of the Sessions House, and the magistrates in the Courts below were constantly asked to send cases to the Central Criminal Court rather than to Clerkenwell. In criminal circles the Sessions House was known as the "Slaughter House," and certain it is that very few malefactors escaped who came before Sir William Bodkin, who had a most successful way of handling a jury.

Lockyer, the Sessions officer, was a very remarkable man.

He had been more or less connected with criminals all his life, and knew the history of half the prisoners brought into Court. As the reader is probably aware, unless the accused himself opens up the question of his character, that issue cannot be raised until the verdict has been returned.

It was very amusing to watch the countenance of a prisoner who had been found guilty, when Lockyer entered the witness-box, book in hand, to give an account of the culprit's life. He performed the task in the most business-like way, totting up the convictions with as great a rapidity as the waiter reckons up a customer's score in a City restaurant. His statement was usually something like this:

"Known him all my life, my lord, ever since he was sent away as a lad to the Reformatory. Twenty-five convictions and two tickets in thirty-seven years."

Then there was Mrs. Howe, the female prison officer, who had an extensive knowledge of malefactors of her own sex. She had been, I should say, not a bad-looking woman in her youth; but she always seemed to press the more heavily upon a culprit if that unfortunate creature were of a comely appearance.

I remember on one occasion unsuccessfully defending a well-known female omnibus thief, with reference to whom Mrs. Howe, after reading a long list of previous convictions, said, addressing me rather than the Judge:

"She's as bad in prison, sir, as she is out."

Not quite seeing how this could be, I ventured to ask the witness what she meant.

"Why, sir," was the reply, "she corrupts everybody she comes across."

It immediately struck me that, under certain circumstances, ignorance is bliss; and I asked no further questions.

With the creation of the London County Council, considerable changes were brought about in reference to the metropolitan criminal courts. The Surrey Sessions and the Middlesex Sessions have, in name, ceased to exist. The two areas have been thrown into one, and their Sessions are known as those of the County of London. They are presided over by one Judge, Sir Peter Edlin, who now has to do the work of both sides of the river; and when one considers the additional duties that this involves, and the number of assessment appeals he has to hear, it is obvious that his must be a very laborious life.

It was at one time suggested that the whole of the criminal work of the metropolis should be transferred to the Old Bailey, that additional Judges should be appointed, and that the Courts there should sit continuously. It would, in my opinion, have been of advantage to the public had this arrangement been adopted.

CHAPTER IX

RATCLIFF HIGHWAY

Its situation—Its condition twenty-five years ago—Poor Jack in the hands of the Philistines—A modern Babel—The Thames Tunnel—"The Forty Thieves"—"Paddy's Goose"—I visit the neighbourhood—An opium den—"Amok! Amok!"—We conceal ourselves—Scene in the street—Its cause—Strange manner of taking an oath—Watney Street—Thames Police Court—An interesting case—Its termination—A revengeful design frustrated by accident—A curious batch of summonses—Ratcliff Highway improved—Its causes—Further improvement required.

THE condition of Ratcliff Highway some five-and-twenty or thirty years ago was a terrible disgrace to London. Matters have vastly improved since that time, though even now the thoroughfare is very far indeed from being a model one.

Ratcliff Highway, running parallel with the river, extends from Little Tower Hill to Shadwell, and is in close proximity with the London, the Wapping, the Regent's Canal, and other docks, which at the period I have alluded to were continuously crowded with shipping. In those days the Highway was the scene of riots, debaucheries, robberies, and all conceivable deeds of darkness. Such, indeed, was the character of the place that it would have been madness for any respectable woman, or, for the matter of that, for any well-dressed man, to proceed thither alone. The police themselves seldom ventured there save in twos and threes, and brutal assaults upon them were of frequent occurrence.

The inhabitants of Ratcliff Highway lived upon the sailors. There were a great many lodging-houses there; still more clothiers and outfitters; and any number of public-houses and beershops, nearly every one of which had a dancing saloon at the back of the bar. Jack came ashore with his pockets full of money, but they quickly emptied. He was ready enough to spend his pay, but there were other persons still more ready to despoil him of it. In those days there were no Government officials to board the vessels and arrange for the safe despatch of Jack's money, and Jack himself, to his home. No sooner did a vessel reach her moorings than she was swarming with boarding-house touts, crimps, outfitters, runners, and other rapacious beasts of prey. Poor Jack was soon in the hands of the Philistines.

From the public-houses in Ratcliff Highway there constantly issued the sound of loud laughter, mingled with shouting and fearful imprecations. Far into the night the women and the drunken sailors danced and sang to the accompaniment of screeching fiddles. For the most part the women wore white dresses and white shoes. If the sailors were not entirely fleeced inside the saloons, the process was completed by bullies and fighting men when they staggered out into the street. The poor fellows were frequently drugged, and sometimes half murdered.

Sailors of every nationality were to be met in this thoroughfare, including a great many Portuguese, Spaniards, Italians, Greeks, Norwegians, and Scandinavians. The Highway was indeed a veritable modern Babel. Among the disreputable characters to be met there were men dressed as sailors who sold parrots and parrakeets, many of which could blaspheme almost as naturally as their owners.

The Thames Tunnel was open in its original form at the time of which I am writing. As my readers are aware, it is now used by a railway. Previously, besides a roadway, there was on one side a pavement set apart for the use of pedestrians. The charge for admission was a penny for each person. One of the features of the place was a bazaar, where a variety of goods were exposed for sale. Several times during the year a regular fair was held in the tunnel, among its attractions being swings and donkey-riding. Those fairs certainly ranked among the curious sights of old London.

The immediate neighbourhood of Ratcliff Highway was as bad as the thoroughfare itself. In Albert Street half the houses were of the vilest description, and very much the same may be said of Albert Square, Victoria Street, Chancery Lane, and Baroda Place. These places were frequented by a band of robbers, who openly called themselves " The Forty Thieves,' and who plied their nefarious calling by day as well as by night. Sometimes these ruffians went the length of attacking and robbing pedestrians in Devonshire Street and Commercial Road.

One of the vilest houses in the Highway was the "White Swan," better known as "Paddy's Goose"; oddly enough, its site is now occupied by the Wesleyan Methodist Home Mission Hall. This excellent institution has done much to purify the neighbourhood.

My last visit to Ratcliff Highway, which was paid early in the seventies, very nearly resulted in serious consequences to myself. The adventure is worth describing, as it throws some light on the horrors of the district.

If any one in those days desired to visit Ratcliff Highway and its environments, it was usual, and indeed necessary, to get permission from the authorities at Scotland Yard for either a lodging-house inspector or a police officer to act as an escort.

One day I and some friends, after dining at the "Ship and Turtle," proceeded to the Leman Street police station, where, as had been arranged, we picked up two officers who were to act as our East End guides. From Leman Street we proceeded at once to Bluegate Fields and Ratcliff Highway.

Going the round of the drinking and dancing houses, we witnessed some curious sights. The women, thieves, and other bad characters appeared to be on the best of terms with our companions, who were repeatedly offered drink, and once or twice invited to join in a dance. Of my friends and myself no notice whatever was taken.

During the evening we went to the Chinese quarter, where are to be found the opium dens, into one of which we penetrated. Ascending a ladder, we entered a loft where about a dozen men were sitting or reclining on wooden benches, smoking opium. Our guides shook hands with the man who "bossed" the premises, and whose manner was the pink of politeness. His language, of course, none of us understood. Motioning us to seat ourselves in this most rudely constructed and uncomfortable of divans, he proceeded to offer each of us the calumet of peace.

The officers had told us what to do. We were to accept the pipes, take one or two whiffs, and then put them down again. That, we were assured, would suffice to satisfy the laws of hospitality.

When the man offered me a pipe, I made certain signs to indicate that I should prefer a cigarette. Being extremely intelligent, he understood my meaning in a moment, and at once folded a little opium in paper and handed it to me. I proceeded very gingerly to smoke it, not without grave misgivings; but, I am happy to add, no unpleasant consequences resulted. The cigarette had a very soothing effect, but it neither drugged me nor made me ill.

After tipping the courteous Chinaman we took our leave, and wended our way back to the Highway, where we proposed to wait a short time preparatory to visiting the "Bridge of Sighs," and the night refuge in its immediate vicinity. It must have been very nearly one in the morning.

Now it was that the serious occurrence to which I have alluded took place.

We had just emerged from a narrow passage, and had proceeded a few yards down the main thoroughfare, when our attention was suddenly arrested by the shrieking and shouting of a number of persons evidently running helter-skelter in our direction. The next minute above the din we heard the cry "Amok! amok!" at which the police officers were evidently very much alarmed.

"This way, gentlemen, and be quick, for God's sake!" they exclaimed, as they unceremoniously hurried us through the nearest doorway. When I looked around me I found we were in one of those East End shows which I have described in a former paper. Having fastened the door, the two officers consulted together in an undertone. We heard the sound of fleeing footsteps outside, mingled with human screams, groans, and oaths. My friends and I stood stock still and listened. The sounds gradually passed away in the distance. In a little while one of the officers opened the door and slipped out. The other remained behind, and in answer to our enquiries said he was afraid it was an ugly business, and that his comrade had gone out to see how the land lay, and to render any assistance in his power. Pending the other's return, he peremptorily forbade us to stir from where we were.

In a little while the other officer came back and said it would now be safe for us to quit the premises. On our emerging into the street an extraordinary sight met our eyes. There were pools and trails of blood on the pavement and in the roadway; here and there was the prostrate form of a human being surrounded by men and women half distraught with grief and fear; a couple of four-wheeled cabs had just arrived crowded with policemen, and, in the distance, men carrying stretchers were to be seen rapidly approaching.

We soon learnt what had occurred. A number of Chinamen had been drinking with some women in a public-house, and just as the premises were about to close, a dispute had taken place. The foreigners alleged that they had been robbed; this was indignantly denied by the women; some Englishmen came forward and had their say in the matter, and, in the end, a serious disturbance took place. Finding that the affair was becoming one of blows as well as words, the Chinamen ranged themselves in a body, drew their knives from their pockets, and, shouting "Amok! amok!" fought their way into the road and rushed upon all whom they met, stabbing and cutting men, women, and children indiscriminately. The knives of these people are peculiarly adapted for ripping flesh, and thus the wounds inflicted were for the most part of a very serious nature.

A body of police arrived upon the scene, and the murderous ruffians were all arrested and removed to Leman Street. It only remained to convey the wounded to the London Hospital, and this was done with commendable despatch.

Subsequently I had the satisfaction of seeing the culprits tried and convicted. For the defence there were several Chinese witnesses, each of whom, on being sworn, went through the extraordinary process of taking up a plate and breaking it—a fate which, if I am not much mistaken, in some instances overtook the oath itself.

As I have said, Ratcliff Highway has greatly improved in recent years. The same cannot, however, be said of its immediate neighbourhood. Certain streets in Shadwell could never have been in a worse condition than they are at present.

While acting as one of the magistrates of the Worship Street district it was a part of my duty to sit on certain days at the Thames Police Court. I found that the most convenient way to reach it from the West End was to go by the underground railway from Baker Street to Shadwell and proceed thence on foot. The distance from the railway station to the Court is an inconsiderable one, but the shortest route is through Watney Street, which is the most disgraceful thoroughfare I was ever doomed to traverse.

On either side of the way are poor, squalid shops. Throughout the day the road and the pavement are crowded with barrows laden with fish, vegetables, and other articles of food, cheap second-hand furniture, old iron, rabbit skins, and many articles besides. So great is the throng of dirty and ragged human beings that it is very difficult to make one's way through the street. There is a good deal of unceremonious shoving in the crowd, but to remonstrate thereat would be to run a very good chance of being sent rolling in the gutter. A few policemen pick their way through the street, but I think they would be slow to incur the displeasure of such an evil-looking crowd.

The stench in Watney Street is sickening. It arises for the most part from the greasy mash formed underfoot by the miscellaneous refuse from the barrows.

Needless to say, this pandemonium contains a number of thriving public-houses. The women who infest the place are of a lower order than those to be met with in the Ratcliff Highway of to-day. When you gaze on their brutal and vicious faces, soddened with drink, you have a difficulty in believing that such beings are fellow human creatures.

While I was discharging temporary duty at the Thames Police Court, several interesting cases from Ratcliff Highway came before me. One was that of a sailor who was charged with stealing a watch. The prosecutrix, who it was evident from her brogue hailed from the Emerald Isle, entered the box and told her story. She said that she kept a lodging-house for sailors, and that the prisoner always stayed there when he was on shore. The good woman proceeded to expatiate upon her own virtues, which, as I had a tolerably extensive knowledge of the class to which she belonged, made me follow her narrative with some suspicion.

"I have been," she declared with emotion, "more than a mother to the boy" (the "boy" being, I should say, over thirty, and standing six feet high). "When he got with bad people and lost all his money some time ago, I took him in, sir, just the same, and gave him clothes and food, and, as if that wasn't enough, I got him a kit when he went to sea again, because he hadn't a farthing in the world to buy one."

While she said this, the alleged culprit, standing bolt upright in the dock, simply smiled.

Stopping the prosecutrix, I begged her to come at once to the subject matter of her complaint.

"Well, sir," she continued, "I had two watches, which I

kept in a drawer in the kitchen. They were safe enough there yesterday, because I saw them, and I went out shopping, sir, leaving the prisoner in the kitchen, and when I came back he was gone and so was one of the watches. I went and told the police, sir, and they've found the watch in a pawnshop, and the assistant what serves there has seen this man, and he is sure it was him as pawned the watch."

Witnesses were called who bore out the prosecutrix's story, and the prisoner declined to put any questions to them. Thus the case against him seemed tolerably clear, and I was about to have the depositions read over, preparatory to committing him for trial, when, not feeling quite satisfied, I said to him:

"You will have an opportunity presently of saying what you like in your defence; but before the witnesses leave the Court, are you sure you would not care to put any questions to them?"

"Quite sure," he replied; "but if you wouldn't mind, sir, I should like to put a question to you."

"Well," said I, "it's a little irregular, but if it will do you any good, I have no objection."

"Thank you," he returned. "What I want to ask you, sir, is this. Can a man be guilty of stealing his own property?"

"Certainly not," I replied. "But what on earth do you mean?"

"Well, sir," said he, "it's just this way. I did take the watch, and I did pawn it, but I had a perfect right to do so, for it is my property. It was given to me by my uncle nine years ago. Before I went my last voyage I gave it to the old woman to keep, and when I returned I asked her for it, but she always put me off with excuses. Yesterday I found out where it was, and after she went out I took it, and thought it would be far safer if I pawned it."

I called the woman back into the box, and asked her what she had to say to the man's explanation. Without changing colour or moving a muscle of her face, she gave an emphatic denial to his statement, which she characterised as a pack of lies from beginning to end.

This did not by any means satisfy me, and, turning to the prisoner, I asked him if he knew the number of his watch.

"Yes, sir," he replied. "Seventeen hundred and ninety-four. My uncle, whose name was ——, bought the watch at Sir John Bennett's two days before Christmas Day in the year 18—."

This detailed statement, I confess, was rather more than I had expected. It made my course of action very simple. Ordering the case to be put back, I despatched an officer to Sir John Bennett's to make enquiries, and, if necessary, request Sir John to send any assistant who might possibly be able to throw light upon the case.

Later in the day the sailor was put back into the dock. An assistant from the watchmaker's entered the box and explained to me that it was the custom at their establishment to enter in a book the name of every purchaser of a watch, together with its number. This book he had brought with him and produced. There, sure enough, under the date in question, was the name of the prisoner's uncle, bracketed with the number "1794."

I told the prosecutrix what was my opinion of her, and at once discharged the prisoner.

For a specimen of villainy and perjury this was bad enough; but the matter did not rest here.

My usual days for sitting at this Court were Monday and Tuesday, but it so happened that, in the following week, I chose the Thursday instead of the Tuesday.

Among the night charges there appeared, to my great surprise, my friend the sailor. Referring to my register, which lay before me, I found that he was charged with stealing a razor from a barber's shop. The barber himself was the first witness. He deposed that the prisoner came to his establishment for a shave, and that soon afterwards a razor was missing from a shelf. It appeared that while he was shaving the sailor, he was called away to another part of the shop to serve a customer, and that, according to his statement, the theft occurred while his back was turned.

I asked the witness whether he had any other evidence to call.

"Yes," he replied, "a woman is here who was looking through the window and who saw the prisoner take the razor from the shelf and hand it to another man."

Hereupon with the greatest effrontery in the world, the lodging-house keeper who had prosecuted in the other case stepped into the box. A few questions sufficed to smash her testimony to pieces, and the sailor was once more discharged. This vile woman had either tricked the barber, or by some means had induced him to enter into the plot, and I doubt not that she craftily arranged for the case to come into Court on a day when I was not likely to be sitting. Happily an accidental circumstance was the means of frustrating her revengeful design.

A batch of summonses of rather a curious character came before me one morning. For years a number of women had, in Ratcliff Highway and the vicinity, kept shops which were ostensibly for the sale of ginger-beer, cigars, and matches, but which were in reality for the sale, without a license and during prohibited hours, of spirits and malt liquors.

The evil grew to such an extent that representations were at length made to the authorities, who decided to take strong measures to put an end to it. It was arranged that two police officers, dressed as sailors, should go the round of the cigar and ginger-beer shops to obtain incriminating evidence against the women who were carrying on this lawless traffic.

Two detectives from the West End were selected for the purpose, as it was felt that there was a likelihood of local members of the force being recognised.

The ruse answered admirably, and a number of convictions were secured. It was curious to watch the faces of the female defendants while the officers were giving their evidence. One old woman shook with fury as the detective recalled the incidents of his visit—how she had said, "Yours ain't much like the hands of a sailor"; how he had replied, "No, of course not, because I'm a purser's clerk"; and how the two had laughed over the ease with which the accused were being hoodwinked. I never, before or since, heard such venomous abuse as that which poured from the lips of this old woman. There cannot be much doubt that if the two detectives had shown their faces in Ratcliff Highway within a year of that date, they would have been somewhat roughly handled.

After the great strikes the maritime prosperity of London began to wane, and one result was that the character of Ratcliff Highway somewhat improved. Other circumstances have assisted to purify that region. New docks drew the shipping lower down the Thames; the great liners are manned by a better class of men than were the sailing vessels of thirty years ago; and I am not sure that the changes brought about in the shipping world by the construction of the Suez Canal had not something to do with the transformation alluded to.

Much good has no doubt been effected by the appointment of certain Board of Trade officials. A sailor is now shipped in proper form. Articles are no longer signed in some disreputable little public-house, and Jack is no longer sent off on a long voyage with a kit barely adequate for a trip to Ireland.

But though it gives me great satisfaction to record that Ratcliff Highway is better than it was, I confess I could wish to see it better than it is.

CHAPTER X

SUNDAY AT THE EAST END

Open spaces wanted—Cricket reminiscences—Cricket in Bethnal Green—Bat, ball, and stumps—A remarkable suit—Cricket technicalities—The game is suddenly stopped—Half-penny rides in Shoreditch—An extraordinary public-house—Brick Lane—Revolting scenes—Long list of night charges on Monday morning—Sunday closing—Parallel between England and Scotland—East End clubs.

ALTHOUGH several plots of land, and notably some disused burial-places, have of late years been added to the open spaces of the East End of London, that quarter is still lamentably deficient in recreation grounds. Thus, most of the children who live there have to amuse themselves in the crowded, squalid streets, with what results all who read the reports of coroners' inquests are only too well aware.

In other parts of the metropolis ample opportunities are afforded for outdoor pastimes. Throughout the warmer months the youths of North, West, and South London may be seen, in all the glory of flannels, taking their full of cricket, boating, lawn tennis, and a dozen other sports, and thereby developing their muscles, chests, and bones, and physically equipping themselves for life's toils and struggles.

Has it not been said that the battles of Alma, Inkermann, and Balaclava were won in anticipation on the Upper Shooting Fields at Eton? It was my privilege as a boy to see, on these very fields, the bowling of Alfred Mynn, playing against the school team, I think for Kent, the wicket-keeping of Chitty, the batting of the elder Sir Frederick Bathurst, and the prowess of other great athletes. I witnessed Yardley's celebrated hit at Lord's in the Oxford and Cambridge match, and even now I never miss an opportunity of being present at a good game.

What has all this to do, you may ask, with "Sunday at the East End"? Well, these reminiscences will serve to remind the reader how the youths of the more favoured classes occupy themselves; and I will now invite him to accompany me in imagination on a visit I paid one Sunday morning to a tiny piece of waste ground in Bethnal Green.

Look at yon ragged, half-starved little fellow; watch him at his game of cricket amid these squalid surroundings; see how he makes his runs, and handles his bat. Why, that attenuated little form hits out with as much heartiness as if he were playing at Lord's or the Oval. A brick wall forms one boundary of the pitch, and another brick wall the other. If the ground falls short of the regulation number of yards, it is at any rate tolerably level. Three chalk lines on the wall do splendidly for stumps, and this arrangement renders a wicket-keeper and a long-stop wholly unnecessary.

The mind of the East End "nipper" is equal to most emergencies. That bat, you will have observed, is not of the most approved type, but see how well the little fellow drives with it. I fancy its component parts are half a broomstick and a piece of an old butter-tub. Then the ball is worth noting. Some cricket-balls are made of leather, but this one isn't. It is formed of a boy's cloth cap, which has been crushed together and tied round with sundry pieces of string. It hasn't got much bounce, perhaps, but how the batsman makes it fly!

Single-wicket is the form of the game being played. Owing to the limited area of the ground there is no necessity for a wide field. The bowling is of the kind known as under-arm. These circumstances might perhaps be expected to militate against the enjoyment of the players; but not a bit of it—both sides are engaging in the contest with as much enthusiasm as characterises a team from the Antipodes.

Our thin little friend has been run out, and an older lad is now wielding the bat. His costume has some points that are worth noting. The left leg of his trousers is split all the way down, and at odd moments naked flesh is exposed. On one foot is a dilapidated button-boot, while its fellow is of the lace-up order. The latter is three or four sizes too large for the wearer, and sadly in need of repair. The front of the sole has become unstitched from the upper, so that at every step the lad takes the two parts of the boot part and meet like an animal's jaws, showing toes by way of teeth. The youngster wears a coat which is a remarkable illustration of maternal ingenuity, the original material having been almost entirely superseded by patches. At the upper part of one of the arms there is an extensive rent, through which at almost every sweep of the bat there appears the shoulder of the lad, who promptly readjusts the rag by a dexterous hitch. He wears no waistcoat, and, his shirt being deficient in buttons, his chest is partially exposed to public view. As is the case with many East End gamins, his head is bare.

The new batsman is even a more vigorous player than his predecessor. He would make many a four, did not the brick walls arrest the progress of his ball.

Heaven knows where these youngsters learnt the game, but they have learnt it well. Their running comments, often uttered at the top of their voices, prove them to be well versed even in its technicalities.

"Now then," shouts the bowler, "see me take 'is off stump with a shooter."

"Like to see yer," jeers the batsman. "Yer can't give nothing but wides, Jimmy Porter. There y'are!"

Wide or no wide, the ball is struck high into the air. Yells of excitement arise, and a ragamuffin in his shirt-sleeves rushes forward with hands outstretched, amid cries of "'ave it, Bill! 'ave it!"

But the ball slips through his hands, whereat there are howls of "Bloomin' butter-fingers!" followed by derisive laughter from the enemy.

The bowler sends another ball.

"Leg afore! leg afore!" screams one of the field, rushing up to the wicket.

"'Twarn't!" protests the batsman. "My leg was 'ere. You 'old yer row, Charlie Fisher, can't yer."

But the majority decide against him, and the next "man" goes in.

And so the game proceeds, the youngsters being all the while oblivious to the absence of green sward and fresh air. What rare enjoyment it is to one and all! Two of the lads had been sent out in charge of baby sisters, whom they have deposited on a neighbouring doorstep, towards which, while snatching the fearful joy of an innings, they direct an occasional glance, to assure themselves that no harm has befallen the little creatures. Manifestly this is in both cases a contravention of parental authority.

SUNDAY AT THE EAST END

In a little while the game is brought to a sudden termination. A powerful man of threatening mien scrambles over the wall from one of the back-yards, and at once spreads a panic among the urchins, who for the most part, gathering up their coats and the implements of the game, flee precipitately, a few of the bolder spirits, as they disappear round the nearest corner, giving vent to "Yah-boo!" and other derisive exclamations.

One lad lingers on the spot, and the man steps up and soundly cuffs him, remarking as he does so:

"Kicking up such a row" (whack!). "You're the worst of the lot" (whack!), "with yer mother lying in bed so ill, and wanting quiet, and you go a-screaming under her very window" (whack!). "Now git along 'ome pretty quick."

Sorry as I felt for the young cricketers, I could not help admitting that no invalid should be subjected to the annoyance of their clamour.

The moral to be drawn from the incident manifestly was that proper places of recreation should be provided for the youth of the East End.

Let us pass from Bethnal Green to some of the quieter lanes of Shoreditch. Many a poor lad has a halfpenny or a penny put by for Sunday morning, and it will be interesting to see how he spends it. It is hardly conceivable that any one, even a Jew, would set himself to make a business out of the children of the slums; but this has been done.

Look at that brake standing in the road, and laden with about forty children. "To Chingford" is painted on a board fixed to the vehicle's side; but this announcement must not be literally interpreted, but taken rather as a figure of speech. The brake has not been to Chingford, nor is it going there.

There is a licensed driver on the box, and on a step at the back stands a burly son of Jacob.

"Now then," shouts the latter, "this way for a long and lovely drive. Only a ha'penny. Just a-going to start. Come along, Johnny; hurry up."

The last words are addressed to a breathless ragamuffin, from whom, after hoisting him up, he demands and receives a half-penny; for this Hebrew gives no credit.

"This way. 'Ere you are!" shouts the man, on catching sight of two more ragamuffins hurrying towards the brake. "You're just in time, young 'uns. Come along, don't miss the treat."

The new arrivals are hoisted in, and, the brake being now tightly jammed with passengers, the driver cracks his whip and sets the horses in motion.

The vehicle passes through several streets and then comes back to its starting-point, where it discharges its living cargo and promptly secures another. "To Chingford" indeed! However, I must say that the lads are treated with every care and kindness, and they really seem to extract enjoyment out of the little excursion.

Christians are not averse to take a lesson in money-making from Jews. See that jolly-looking coster over there; he is doing the same kind of business, only on a more humble scale, he having a donkey and cart instead of a horse and brake, and his complement of passengers being six instead of over forty.

Further on we find yet another form of the same enterprise. Behold that little donkey-cart that is being drawn by a man, a rough-looking customer, from whose face the perspiration is streaming. He can only take four youths at a time. In consideration of the absence of a quadruped, he carries his passengers a good deal further for the half-penny than do either of his rivals. Poor fellow! he will hardly make a fortune at such a vocation.

These Sunday drives have become quite an institution in the East End. The vehicles remain on the road throughout the day, or until the little ones have spent all their half-pennies.

Leaving the children, we will turn our attention to some of the recreations of the adult portion of the East End population.

I must now introduce the reader to an ordinary, or rather very extraordinary, public-house, situated not a hundred miles from Artillery Lane. You will probably say, What can there be extraordinary about a public-house? Well, I will describe the place.

Some public-houses are palaces, light and glittering, while others are shanties, dark and dirty. In outward appearance the one I am referring to represents a pleasant mean between the two extremes. While there is nothing very attractive, there is nothing very repellent about it. In a word, it is like a hundred and one of these places of entertainment for man and beast that are to be seen in the streets of London.

One thing particularly struck me as I stood looking at this establishment, from the opposite side of the street, after opening hours on a certain Sunday morning. I refer to the number of customers who passed in and out. I wondered wherein lay the peculiar attraction of the place; and in order to probe the mystery I crossed the road and boldly entered.

The bar proved a very remarkable one. It was crowded, but no one was smoking, no one ordered a second glass, and no one was using improper language. All was as quiet and orderly as a Sunday school. And this was in the heart of the East End! I confess I was thunderstruck.

As I stood staring about me, I caught sight of a card, headed "Rules," and printed in bold type, which hung upon the wall. I read as follows:

"(1.) No smoking on the premises is permitted.

"(2.) No loud talking or obscene language is tolerated.

"(3.) No customer is supplied with more than one drink until he or she has been off the premises for half an hour, at the end of which period only one more drink is supplied.

"(4.) No refreshment is served to any one who appears to be under the influence of drink, and if one of a company of friends is in this state, none of them will be served."

At the bottom of the card was a note stating that the foregoing rules would be rigidly enforced, and that the proprietor requested all persons who did not care to conform to them, to take their custom elsewhere.

The mystery was solved, and I took my departure with a deep sense of gratitude to the man or woman who had conceived and created this purified public-house. As I wended my way up the street I could not help thinking what an excellent thing it would be if these rules were adopted in all the other public-houses in London. Why should not "the trade" thus join hands with the teetotallers and endeavour to stamp out drunkenness?

I subsequently learnt that the remarkable establishment I had visited is very widely known and esteemed, and does a very substantial business.

Before, however, I pass from this subject, it is only fair that I should mention a doubt that has entered my mind as to whether, in the present state of the licensing law, the enforcement of such rules as I have mentioned would be strictly legal.

It is now night, and we are in the neighbourhood of Brick Lane.

Let us look at the public-houses hereabouts, and observe what is going on within and without their walls. They are frequented by the depraved, the dissolute, and the drunken. The male habitués are very bad, but the female habituées are even worse. Drunkard after drunkard staggers in at the doorway, and is freely supplied with drink. Outside, the scenes are revolting in the extreme. Men, in a ferocious stage of intoxication, quarrel, fight, and kick, and frenzied women fall upon one another, tearing out hair, scratching, spitting, and even inflicting wounds with their teeth. Verily this is a land flowing with beer and blood.

These public-houses account for the long list of night charges that the magistrate has to deal with on Monday mornings at the Thames and Worship Street Police Courts. Whereas on ordinary mornings the number is about twenty or thirty, on Mondays it is from sixty to eighty. They are all of one description in so far as the offences arise from drink.

While I know there is a good deal to be said for Sunday closing, I cannot help admitting that there is also a good deal to be said against it. To begin with, would it not inflict a great injustice on innocent people? Why should a poor man who conducts himself properly be deprived of his glass of ale or spirits on the Sabbath? Do not forget that it is the only day in the week that he has for rest and such recreation and enjoyment as his means will permit. Suppose he has saved enough money to take his wife and children to Hampton Court or Greenwich, or even no further than that extremely pretty, but little known place, Battersea Park—is he to be denied a glass of ale on the journey, or on arriving at his destination, because of the offences of others?

Again, why should the poor man be placed at a disadvantage as compared with the rich man? The latter has his casks and bottles in his cellar, and no power can prevent him consuming their contents on a Sunday; moreover, in many cases he has his club.

Recent statistics, I believe, show that, for offences committed on Sunday in England and Wales, the proportion of convictions for drunkenness is one in every eighty-four thousand eight hundred and sixty-eight; whereas, for offences committed on Sunday in Scotland—where the public-houses are on that day closed—the proportion is one in every seventy-four thousand nine hundred and seventy-six. From these figures it might be assumed that if we had Sunday closing in England and Wales the number of these convictions would increase at the rate of eleven per cent., but I certainly cannot admit the force of such reasoning.

It must not be forgotten that the number of convictions for drunkenness is not by any means a proper measure of insobriety. If a policeman sees a drunken man conducting himself quietly, or sleeping in a doorway, he passes on and takes no notice. Those who are convicted belong, as a rule, to the disorderly classes, who, the moment the liquor rises to their heads, manifest their natural propensities by obstreperous and riotous conduct. For one drunkard of this order there must be fifty who behave quietly, and always manage to reach their homes, however zigzag may be their journey thither.

Thus the parallel between Scotland on the one hand, and England and Wales on the other, would not hold good unless it could be proved that the proportion of disorderly characters to the rest of the community is the same in both cases.

On the whole, I am not disposed to favour the closing of public-houses on Sundays.. I think, however, that a great deal of good would be done by imposing further limitations on the hours during which they may remain open. It would, for instance, in my opinion, be an excellent thing if they were all shut up during the evening and night, from, say, seven o'clock.

You wish to know what that building is across the way from which, every now and then, a man or woman staggers, quite as drunk as some of the habitués of the public-houses we have just left. It is one of the bogus clubs by which this neighbourhood is infested.

There are, in the East End, hundreds of these "clubs," which are a far greater curse even than the beer and gin shops; and I feel very strongly that, while the former are permitted to exist, little or no good would be done by interfering with the latter. The publican, at any rate, is under the eye of the licensing benches and the Excise authorities; but the proprietor of a bogus club is practically under no supervision.

When in the East End districts, I did all I could to suppress these places, by inflicting upon the owners the heaviest punishment prescribed by law. My efforts, however, were attended with little success. The men paid their fines, or went to prison; but the premises passed into new hands, and in a month or two were reopened on the same lines as before.

In most cases these dens are frequented by both men and women, a great number of whom belong to the Jewish community. They are crammed with people on Saturday nights and Sundays, and then it is that the worst scenes of drunkenness, debauchery, and rioting are enacted.

Wretched women constantly came before me at Worship Street, and, with tears in their eyes, besought me to save their husbands and sons from the temptations and dangers of these places. Alas! the will was not wanting, but I had not the power.

CHAPTER XI

BURGLARIOUS BILL

Two kinds of burglars—Argument against the abolition of capital punishment—Occasional burglars—A remarkable specimen—The professional burglar—The Cornhill burglary—Thomas Caseley—Great booty—"Beautiful instruments"—Arrests—Conversation on the way to the station—Female prisoners acquitted—Sentence—Action against the safe-makers—Evidence of Caseley—Which is the easiest safe—"Lawful" and "unlawful" tools—The Alderman, the citizen, and the citizen's friend—How the signals were given—Receivers—My suspicions aroused—The effect—Capital verses in *Punch*.

THERE are two kinds of burglars—those who dabble in the crime, breaking into houses when their funds are low; and those who make it the serious business of their lives.

When for the first time the professional burglar is "unfortunate"—that is, arrested, tried, and found guilty—he is sentenced to imprisonment, while his subsequent convictions result in terms of penal servitude, which, from being of short duration, increase by progressive stages until they cover a period of many years. This he discounts, but as a rule he will not risk the gallows, and here, I think, is to be found one of the strongest arguments against the abolition of capital punishment. A great many burglars carry firearms, but they rarely use them. Is it not reasonable to suppose that, if the scaffold no longer stared them in the face, they would unhesitatingly use their weapons to avert capture?

Burglars of the occasional kind are usually tramps or town loafers, and for implements they are rarely provided with anything beyond an old knife, a bent chisel, and a box of lucifer matches, appliances which, though insignificant compared with a professional equipment, are remarkably effective in adroit hands. A favourite enterprise of these men is to break into a country chapel, with a view to annexing the contents of the collecting boxes, and, possibly, the Communion plate. They are very prone to explore outhouses, in search of workmen's tools, and other buildings not used as dwellings.

I once had to deal with a case in which a rather remarkab'e specimen of this class was concerned. The man in question had during a long series of years been guilty of a number of petty larcenies, and one day, growing more venturesome, broke into a dwelling-house in a somewhat secluded district on the borders of Edgware. The garden at the back of the house was skirted by a country lane, and as a constable was passing along it at about half-past three one spring morning he observed a light flitting about in the basement. His suspicions being aroused, he sought out his sergeant, who was on fixed point hard by, and informed him of what he had seen. The two then made a careful inspection of the house from the lane at the back.

Feeling sure that something was wrong, the sergeant, leaving the constable in the lane, hurried round to the front of the premises. On inspecting the front door and finding that the bolts had been forced, he turned the handle and entered.

Proceeding down the passage he went into the kitchen, where a singular sight met his view. The fire was alight, and a frying-pan stood on the hob. On the table were the relics of a fried rasher of ham, and other evidences of a meal, including half a bottle of sherry. Lying about the floor were several bundles of goods ready for immediate removal. The air was still heavy with the aroma of the fried ham.

No one being visible, the sergeant proceeded to search the apartment, and it was not long before, on opening a tall cupboard, he discovered a middle-aged man about six feet in height. Stepping forth, the culprit cheerfully remarked:

"I say, guv'nor, if you'd been ten minutes sooner you'd have spoilt my breakfast. There's a drop of sherry left, and you'd better help yourself before we start."

While the officer was describing in the box what had taken place, the prisoner in the dock kept up one continuous roar of laughter.

The professional burglar is a very different sort of person. He is generally a married man, or, at any rate, has a female companion. A woman is very useful in keeping watch, in helping to dispose of the stolen property, and in many other ways. A wife can assist in burglaries with tolerable impunity, for, in the event of being arrested, she has only to urge coercion and produce her marriage certificate to ensure an acquittal.

In April, 1865, I was engaged as counsel in a rather remarkable case, which was known as the Cornhill burglary. There were several persons charged—a man named Brewerton and his wife, a man named Caseley and his wife, and three others.

Thomas Caseley (with whom I propose principally to deal) was described as twenty-three years of age, and his wife as twenty-six. The former defended himself, and I appeared for the latter. Caseley was known to be one of the most expert burglars in the metropolis, and he had already undergone one sentence of penal servitude, which proves that he must have entered upon a criminal career at an early age. He had two nicknames, one being "Counsellor Kelly," and the other "Tom the Madman."

The establishment broken into was that of Mr. Walker, a large jeweller's on Cornhill.

It appeared that on Saturday, the fourth of February, the assistant, after placing the whole of the stock in one of Milner's iron safes, left the premises at half-past seven in the evening. As usual, the gas was left burning in the shop, which was open to inspection by the police and other passers-by through apertures in the shutters. The safe was so placed as to be distinctly seen by any one looking through these apertures, and by an ingenious arrangement of mirrors a person standing in any part of the shop would also be visible from the outside.

When the assistant returned to the premises on Monday morning at half-past eight o'clock, he found that the shop had been entered through a hole in the floor, and that the safe had been opened and ransacked. It appeared that the thieves had forced an entry into the rooms of Mr. Mitchell, a tailor, in the lower part of the building, and had cut their way through the ceiling. The value of Mr. Walker's stock was about six thousand pounds, and nearly the whole of it had been stolen. The booty included four hundred and sixty-five watches and one hundred and sixty gold chains. It was manifest that some considerable time had been occupied in the operations of the culprits. In all probability they had remained on the premises during Saturday night and the greater part of Sunday. The safe had been forced very cleverly, there being no external marks of violence upon it. During the trial the police declared that the tools used must have been "beautiful instruments."

The assistant lost no time in communicating with the police, and Inspector Potter, of the S Division, Inspector Brennan, Thomas Foulger, and Sergeant Moss, of the City Police, who were among the cleverest officers in the London force, were told off to investigate the matter. It appeared that, very soon after the burglary, Caseley opened a meat-pie shop at 142, Whitechapel Road, and there, on Friday, the twenty-fourth of February, Potter, Moss, and Brennan arrested the Brewertons and some of the other culprits. On the premises were discovered several articles of jewellery that were stolen from Mr Walker's shop, together with one hundred pounds in cash, and two receipts for money recently lodged at the London and Westminster Bank, one being for a sum of two hundred and fifty pounds and the other for a sum of one hundred and fifty pounds. The officers next proceeded to the Caseleys' private dwelling, 13, Ely Terrace, Bow Road. One of them knocked at the door, whereupon Mrs. Caseley put her head out of a window and said:

"Who are you?"

"We are police officers," was the reply.

They waited for a minute or two, but as the door was not opened they forced the lock, entered, and rushed upstairs. The two Caseleys were at once taken into custody, after which the house was searched, with the result that the officers discovered a box containing a number of Mr. Walker's watches and chains, gold coin to the amount of one hundred and ninety-six pounds, and a fifty-pound note. The proceeds of other burglaries were also found, together with a life preserver, which had been placed in the bed under the pillow, a collection of skeleton keys, several screwdrivers, a revolver, and some caps and bullets.

On the way to the station a conversation took place between Potter and the male prisoner. Caseley was reported to have said:

"What robberies are you going to buff me for? I can prove where I was at the time of Johnson's robbery and the Strand robbery. I was doing time. But I am right for Walker's."

"Who are the others?" asked Potter.

The prisoner gave two names, adding:

"If you will allow me to give evidence I will tell you all about it."

The officer replied :

"I can make no promises. That will be a matter for after consideration ;" and there the conversation ended.

At the close of the case for the prosecution I urged that there was no evidence against my clients, Mrs. Caseley and Mrs. Brewerton, they being married women and having acted under the control of their husbands; and upon my producing their marriage certificates, the Court held that I was right, and directed a verdict of acquittal to be returned as against them.

Thomas Caseley, in the course of a long address, which was not devoid of ability, stated that since he last came out of prison he had been getting an honest living, and that he had been in no way connected with the burglaries for which he was being prosecuted. He criticised the evidence in detail, and explained that the expression he made use of when arrested was not "I am right for Walker's job," but "My God! what will you say next? What next are you going to buff me for?"

Caseley called witnesses, amongst whom was his father, to prove an alibi, but this part of the case entirely collapsed, and in the end all the male prisoners were found guilty. Brewerton and Caseley were each sentenced to fourteen years' penal servitude.

In consequence of the revelations at this trial, Mr. Walker brought an action against Messrs. Milner to recover the value of the stolen property, on the ground that the safe had been guaranteed to resist the violence of burglars. This action was tried before the Lord Chief Justice and a special jury at the Guildhall, and attracted a great deal of public attention. Caseley himself was called as a witness, and his evidence was very interesting and amusing. He was brought up in custody, and wore the convict garb. In describing how the burglary was committed, he said :

"I went to Cornhill on Saturday the fourth of February. There were four others besides myself. Two of them and myself went into the house. We went into Number 68, at the corner of the archway of Sun Court. It was exactly ten minutes to six in the evening. We went to the floor over Sir Charles Crossley's. We sat down there until twenty minutes to eight, when we received a signal that Mr. Walker's shopman had gone by the 'bus. Sir Charles Crossley's is the floor over Mr. Walker's shop. We opened Sir Charles Crossley's safe, and did nothing else for some hours.

"As far as I can remember," proceeded the witness, putting his hand to his forehead, "we did nothing more till twenty minutes to twelve on Saturday night, when we got into the tailor's, where we stayed the whole of Sunday morning. We then cut a hole in the ceiling and let ourselves into Mr. Walker's shop. This was exactly eight minutes to three on Sunday afternoon; we saw the time by a clock in the shop on the left-hand side of the safe. We cut our way through the ceiling, then through the floor, and then through the oil-cloth that covered the floor. One of the two men came in along with me. We took some tools in with us—crowbars and sundries. We had to go back again, because we got the signal that the policeman was coming round; but very soon we got the signal 'All right' and returned. We then tested the safe to see whether we could open it, despite the disadvantages we were labouring under."

"Now tell me," said the Lord Chief Justice, evidently much interested, "how did you test it?"

"Why, you see," replied the witness, with the patronising air of one who enlightens ignorance, "we did it by striking in a small wedge between the jamb and the door, to see if it were capable of bearing the amount of pressure we were about to put upon it."

"Yes, and what was the result of the test?" enquired his lordship.

"It held the wedge," smilingly replied the witness. "The wedge bit, as we say, and so we knew the safe would give. We were agreeably surprised. The police constantly disturbed us. That constable did his duty. He came round every nine minutes, and when he came, of course, we lost our purchase on the safe. Every time the policeman came round we descended into the tailor's. After the first small wedge was put in I put a small bar in also, to feel the amount of resistance. It relieved the wedge, and we found the door giving. I turned round to my comrade and said: 'See here. It's all right. It will do.' Then I put in a larger bar and prised open the door."

Asked how long he was occupied, from first to last, in opening the door, Caseley replied:

"Well, we went in at five minutes to three, and the whole property was cleared out of the safe, and we were in Sir Charles

Crossley's washing ourselves at a quarter to four. Of course there are three minutes to be deducted out of that in every nine, as it took one minute to get from the safe to the tailor's, one minute to get back to the safe, and one minute to replace the tools. I carried the tools in my breast. We only used two bars; the others were not required. We did not expect to find a Milner's safe; we thought it would be one of the easier ones. You see, my lord," addressing the judge, "T——'s safes are easier than Milner's, and G——'s are easier than T——'s. At twenty minutes to five we were three miles away."

The cross-examination of the witness gave rise to a great deal of laughter. Asked how many safes he had opened, he replied:

"Three of Mr. Milner's. We purchased two to experiment on. They were single door Milners. One resisted for hours before it gave way, and then we had to use an unlawful bar to it."

"An unlawful bar!" interposed the Lord Chief Justice; "what may that be?"

"A bar, my lord," explained the witness, "that would not be used to commit a burglary. The tools we use in a burglary we call lawful tools; we call them unlawful when they are too long or when they make a noise."

"You used the best class of lawful tools at Cornhill, I suppose?" said the counsel.

"When you say lawful," returned Caseley, with a slightly puzzled expression, "do you mean the word as a barrister would use it or as a burglar would use it?"

At this there was a roar of laughter, in which the Lord Chief Justice joined.

"I mean the word in your sense," the counsel explained, when silence was restored.

"Yes," said Caseley, "they were the best kind of tools. I carried them in a violin-case. We had a bar, my lord," he added, again addressing the judge, "which we did not use on this occasion, and which we call the Alderman. It will open any safe, no matter how good it is."

"Is there a Lord Mayor as well as an Alderman?" asked the learned counsel.

"No," was the quiet reply; "but we have a citizen—that's a small one; and a citizen's friend, which is smaller still."

Asked to explain how the signals were given, Caseley said:

"There were two men outside at opposite points, and they let us know that a policeman was coming by walking past. That signal was given to a third man, who was seated upstairs in Sir Charles Crossley's arm-chair, and he passed the word down to us by pulling a string."

"What time," asked the Lord Chief Justice, "would you have taken to open the safe in question if you had been quite sure of not being interrupted?"

"My lord," answered the witness, with great solemnity, "I swear I could have opened it in a quarter of an hour with the instruments I used that night. With the Alderman I could have done it at once."

Whether or no the jury believed the evidence of the witness I cannot say. Possibly they did not, because they returned a verdict for the defendant.

Of course burglars of the stamp of Caseley could not get on without the receivers. I doubt very much, however, whether receiving is carried on in anything like the large way it was when I was called to the Bar. The "fences," who were principally Jews, did an enormous trade in those days; but convictions have thinned their ranks, and the area of their operations has been considerably narrowed through the vigilance of the authorities. In the present day stolen articles of jewellery and watches are usually taken to pieces, the gems of the former and the works of the latter being sent to Antwerp and other places abroad, where they are furnished with new settings and cases.

There are still a few public-houses and beershops in the East End of London which are used as storing places for stolen property. In a case that came before me not very long ago at Worship Street it was alleged that a stolen watch had been sold to a barman across the counter of one of the former establishments. As the case assumed a very suspicious aspect, I gave orders for the landlord of the house to attend upon the remand, and so unsatisfactory were his replies to the questions I put to him that I sent for the police inspector of the division, and directed him to keep an eye on this establishment. This action on my part bore good fruit, for within a year the house was surrounded by a cordon of police, who on entering, arrested several well-known burglars, and discovered a great quantity of stolen property.

The landlord of the public-house was arrested, tried, and sentenced to penal servitude. He afterwards made a statement to the authorities incriminating several other men, whose conviction resulted from his evidence.

Apropos of Caseley's trial, my old friend Shirley Brooks wrote some capital verses in *Punch*. Here are some of them:

Proud policeman marches along,
Is very tall, and looks very strong,
Belted and buttoned, bludgeoned and drilled;
Set him to fight, he'll be victor or killed.
"But, bless his eyes," says burglarious Jim,
"What do I care for his bludgeon or him?"

* * * * *

It's Sunday morning—O jangle, bells,
Calling to church the pious swells.
The parson stands on his Humbox high,
Abusing Jim and his friend, hard by.
"Bless his eyes," says burglarious Jim,
"What do I care for his sermon or him?"

A jolly big hole in his "shopship's" wall,
In goes Jim with his pals and all;
Now for a wrench with the strength of four
At somebody's patent impossible door.
"Bless his eyes," says burglarious Jim,
"What do I care for his patent or him?"

Door or side, or something to smash,
Now for watches, and jewels, and cash;
Now for a wash and a tranquil meal.
Hark! the clink of the iron heel!
"Bless his eyes," says burglarious Jim,
"What care I for his boots or him?"

CHAPTER XII

FROM THE EAST END TO RAMSGATE

Modern Jews—The Isle of Thanet—"L'homme propose"—Ten in a compartment, besides a perambulator—The coster and his bride—A happy family—Why they brought the cat and bird—They "take a bite," while I smoke—A skin-dresser—"Look at the fields, Bill!"—Why they chose Ramsgate—Ramsgate sands—The two seasons—Dr. Robson Roose's opinion—Attractions of Ramsgate—The lodging-houses—Old habitués thereof—The Bath-chair men—"Doctor Ramsgate."

> MANY have told of the monks of old,
> What a jovial race they were;
> And 'tis most true that a merrier crew
> Could not be found elsewhere.

There is no doubt about it. In selecting sites for their monasteries the monks always had an eye for the finest deer pastures, the purest water, and the sweetest air; and those ancient brotherhoods have successors in the Jews of modern times. This remarkable and widespread race have a keen scent for the best of everything, which they are not averse to obtaining at the lowest possible figure; and here are to be found the reasons why a Hebrew paterfamilias, when he leaves London for his annual excursion to the sea, commonly hies him to the sandy shores of the Isle of Thanet.

And a very good selection too. I believe that in Margate and Ramsgate—and in the latter more particularly—are to be found the most healthy and invigorating of our seaside resorts.

These Eastern people commence their outings about the beginning of July, and from that time till the end of August the denizens of Aldgate, Houndsditch, Shoreditch, Hoxton, and East and North-East London generally, are to be found disporting themselves on Margate jetty and Ramsgate sands.

Should you be travelling to Ramsgate or Margate during the two months I have indicated, either by the South Eastern from Charing Cross, or by the Chatham and Dover—the fastest route—from Victoria, you will be extremely fortunate if your first-class compartment is not invaded by those who should, strictly speaking, find accommodation elsewhere. The company is not to blame for this. Its ways and means are not sufficiently elastic to enable it to cope with the enormous crowd of passengers which besieges its booking-offices on a fine July or August afternoon. In this respect I have, from time to time, been a sufferer myself, for I have a house at Ramsgate, whither I annually repair in search of that one blessing of life without which there can be no true happiness —namely, health. If, however, there is temporary inconvenience in having one's carriage filled with third-class passengers, it is an ample recompense to watch the delight that is depicted on their faces at sight, first of the green fields, and afterwards of the sea and sands. It is a transition indeed from the fetid atmosphere of Whitechapel and the stenches of Bethnal Green, to the pure ozone of merry Margate, wafted as it is almost in a direct line from the North Pole.

On one occasion when I travelled down from Charing Cross by a train that was crammed, a friendly guard managed to reserve me a carriage, and, just as we were steaming out of the terminus, remarked:

"You will be all right in here, Mr. Montagu. There will be nobody to disturb you. I think I can guarantee that you will have the carriage to yourself all the way."

"L'homme propose," etc. We did not call at Cannon Street, whence another section of the train started, but we did stop at London Bridge. On the platform were, among others, a man and woman, and five children, with a perambulator and sundry articles of luggage of many forms and sizes. The man ran one way, the woman the other, and the porters hurried hither and thither; but seats could nowhere be found in the train. Husband and wife met in the immediate neighbourhood of my carriage, and cried in accents of despair and excitement:

"There is no room! There is no room anywhere!"

"You must wait for the next train," said the guard; and I shall never forget the look of disappointment this remark conjured up upon the faces of the five children, who ranged from a girl of about fourteen to a great chubby boy of three.

I was extremely ill at the time, but this sight was more than I could stand, so, calling out of the window to the guard, who was about to give the signal for the train to start, I bade him unlock the door of my compartment and bundle the family in. Father, perambulator, mother, parcels, children—in they came pell-mell; the whistle was blown, and we were in motion, as well as commotion.

On looking round I discovered that my invitation had been more widely accepted than I had contemplated. Taking advantage of the state of affairs, a couple of late arrivals in the persons of a coster and a young woman had scrambled into the carriage. Thus we were a party of ten. It was a sultry July afternoon, and the outlook was anything but pleasant. However, things soon settled down.

The father of the family sat opposite to me at one end of the carriage, his wife and children took up positions in the centre, and the uninvited pair occupied the remaining window seats. It transpired during the journey that the coster and the young woman had been married that morning, and were on their way to spend a three days' honeymoon at Ramsgate. Their luggage consisted of a small hand-bag, containing, I presume, a brush and comb, a pair of irons for the lady's handsome fringe, and other articles of the toilet.

"Now then, Ikey," said my opposite neighbour as we steamed through Spa Road, "leave that thar bird alone. He'll get shaking enough without your rolling him about."

Looking round, I perceived, in the centre of the carriage, and on the top of a pile of packages, a small cage in which was a linnet. Hard by, I noticed a rush basket, which also, as was proved by its oscillating movement, contained live-stock of some description or other. My curiosity being aroused, I ventured to ask what the basket contained.

"Oh, 'im?" my *vis-à-vis* remarked, jerking his thumb in the direction of the receptacle in question, "'e's the cat—Joe, as we calls 'im. Rachel, if you've got a knife in your pocket, cut one of the strings and give poor Joe some air, for 'e didn't get much from 'Oxton to London Bridge; or perhaps, sir, if you and this 'ere gentleman and lady"—meaning the coster and his bride—"haven't no objection, Joe might come out for a bit and stretch hisself."

The happy pair at once gave their consent, and I, for my part, did not object to the proposal, though I ventured to suggest that the linnet might.

"Lor' bless yer, sir," said the man, with a smile, "they don't mind one another. We are, thank God, a happy and united family, and the cat knows it's the children's bird, and would no more think o' touching it than of jumping out of this 'ere window. Joe's used to railways, sir. We come this journey every year, there and back, and Joe knows when the time comes, and enjoys it just as much as Becky, my eldest girl, or any of the young 'uns."

Joe had now emerged from captivity, and was alternately playing with the children and rubbing his chin against the bars of the linnet's cage.

Before we reached Chislehurst I had begun to experience quite a friendly feeling towards the family with whom I was thus so closely brought into contact. Turning to the wife, I asked her how it was that, having so large a family to look after, she cared to burden herself on her holiday with the care of the cat and bird. The bright, piercing eyes peculiar to women of the Jewish race lighted up in a moment, and she replied:

"Well, you see, it's this way—we ain't got no choice; though I don't think," she added, appealing to her husband, "we should leave them behind even if we had."

"What the old woman means," said the man, "is this. We lives in two rooms, and when we goes away we locks up those rooms, and here's the bloomin' key," producing the article from his pocket. "Now, if we left the cat and bird behind, what would become of them, especially Joe? A neighbour might take in the bird; but then neighbours ain't always to be depended on where dumb animals are concerned, although I admit they're wery good. We shouldn't see Joe no more. He's that artful I believe he'd travel about and try and find us; but, yer see, Ramsgate's a long way off; besides, he only takes his meals from one of us. By the way, sir, if you've got no objection, we ain't 'ad nothing since an early dinner, and we'd like just to take a bite."

Upon this, one of the many parcels was undone, and some cold fried fish and a bottle of milk produced therefrom. My friend was not behindhand in politeness, and invited every one in the carriage to partake of the meal—an invitation which was accepted by the coster, but declined by his newly-married wife and myself. I've no doubt the fried fish was very toothsome, but it emitted a greasy odour, the presence of which in the carriage led me to remark that, if my companions had no objection to tobacco, I would light a cigar.

"Object!" cried the man, with his mouth full of fish, "why, we live in 'baccy smoke—at least, most of us does. My girl there—Becky," pointing to his eldest offspring, "is a cigar-maker by trade, and works at Mr. Isaacs's manufactory in the Commercial Road. She earns good money, too! Perhaps you know Mr. Isaacs, sir?"

As I had seen "Buy Isaacs's Brand" and "Try our Mixture, Ben Isaacs," placarded all over the East End, I felt myself justified in returning an affirmative nod.

"And you see, sir," the man continued, "I'm a skin-dresser by trade; and as it isn't by any means the sweetest business in the world, I smoke a good deal of 'baccy myself; and so," he added, swallowing his last mouthful of fried fish, "if you don't mind, I'll join you in a pipe." And he suited the action to the word.

"What is a skin-dresser?" I enquired.

My friend looked at me with something like an expression of pity on his face, and replied:

"Well, yer know what fur is, don't yer? Well, fur is the skins of animals; and them skins is sent over here in a raw state just as they're stripped off the little varmints—sables, ermines, and other animals what is worth a lot of money, though they're only little bits of things. Well, you see, those skins have to be dressed and pieced together by the likes of me, and then they are made up into ladies' cloaks and mantles, and sometimes sold for hundreds of pounds."

The speaker paused, apparently in a state of hesitation, then, turning to his wife, he had a short conversation with her in Yiddish, which I do not understand. What had passed between the two, however, was revealed by my friend's next remarks.

Looking wistfully at the coster and his bride, who proved to be very much occupied with each other, and leaning well forward, he said in a low tone of voice:

"You see that thar parcel up there," pointing to a small bundle on the rack. "Well, that's full of skins, and that little lot's worth close on a hundred quid. I've worked with my firm for some years now, and our guv'nor trusts me with a little bit of work to take away on our holiday. People don't know their value, that's one comfort; besides, I'm very careful who I trusts, but the old gal thinks with me that you're all right and on the square, so now you know all about it."

As we were passing through Staplehurst we were aroused from our conversation by a shout from the coster's wife.

"Look at the fields, Bill," she cried, in delight. "I knows all of 'em well. Look at the 'ops; ain't they fine? When I was a little bit of a kid mother used to bring us all the way down from London 'opping. 'Opping, you know, begins in about a month's time, and goes on till about the first week in September. We lived in Buck's Row then, and, lor', what a change it was to come down to these beautiful fields and all the lovely country. We'd scarcely ever seen the sun before!"

At this moment Bill closed her mouth with a kiss which sounded all over the carriage, and made some whispered remarks, which evidently related to what would happen, given certain eventualities, in years to come.

The situation obviously afforded considerable amusement to my companion. But the Jew will out, and he could not resist enquiring what was the scale of remuneration for the employment to which the young woman referred. From the reverie into which he fell when the desired information was supplied to him, it was clear he was thinking whether "'opping" was calculated to suit any of the younger members of his household.

"Why do you choose Ramsgate for your holiday?" enquired I later.

"Well, yer see, the fares are very cheap, and when you come to pay for seven that's rather an important point. Then it's 'ealthy for the kids, and, what's more, we can get all the things Jews require just as well as if we were in the middle of Houndsditch. Now, I wouldn't mind wagering half a dollar you don't know what kosher is? Well, you see, we get our kosher meat killed in our own way by our co-religionists accordin' to the law o' Moses, and we get our kosher poultry also, if the pieces will run to it. Besides that, you know we're great people for fish, and that's pretty cheap there. At one or two shops in King Street you can get as good a bit of cold fried as you can get in the Lane, or anywhere in Whitechapel. You take yer basket, yer know, and the whole bloomin' lot can picnic on the sands. There's plenty of cheap amusements at Ramsgate, too. I used to go to Margate, but Ramsgate takes the cake. Margate's very nice, though.

There's the 'All by the Sea, the theayter, and two or three capital 'alls; but when I and the old woman, and the rest, have finished the day, we don't want no 'alls; we're a jolly sight too ready for bed. Beg pardon, did you say you was for Ramsgate, too? Well, I dare say you know the place as well as I do;" and so the conversation went on until we reached our destination, by which time I had quite forgotten the aroma of the fried fish, not to mention that of the parcel of skins.

My new acquaintanceship was not destined to end at the railway station. As I was walking thence to my house I heard footsteps behind me, and turned to find that the man was hurrying after me.

"You must think us very ungrateful, sir," he said; "I forgot to thank you, but the old woman reminded me. If it hadn't a' been for you, sir, we shouldn't have been here till ten o'clock at night. We thank you, sir, all of us, Joe included."

He put out his hand, and I shook it warmly, saying:

"All right, my good friend. I only wish all the better class, as they are termed, took as good care of their dumb animals as you do," and so we parted.

I think there is no more amusing sight, at the height of the season, than the Ramsgate sands. There you can see thousands of people, mostly Jews and East Enders, enjoying themselves. The fun is all very quiet and harmless, and all participate in it, from the youngest to the eldest. By the way, it is always the man who carries the baby, or wheels the perambulator, in accordance, I presume, with the theory that the woman is the weaker vessel.

Two or three days after my arrival at Ramsgate, on paying my usual morning visit to the sands, I there espied the family with whom I had travelled from London. Becky was seated in a chair, amid an admiring, open-mouthed crowd, intent upon the glib patter of a phrenologist who was feeling the bumps of her pericranium. She was listening in wonder and amazement to what was to happen to her in after life. Close by was young Abe, spade in hand, filling up an enormous hole in the sand which he had previously made, if I am not much mistaken, with the funereal idea of burying his younger brother and sister. Young Ikey was dividing his attention between Ally Sloper, the Hokey Pokey man, and a band of Ethiopian serenaders. The father of the flock was seated hard by, pipe in mouth, buried in the columns of *The Daily Telegraph*, and ever and anon he cast his eyes upon his wife, who sat close at hand, on a red cushion, stitching an undergarment. A basket containing fried fish stood at her feet. I don't think I ever saw a happier group ; but, then, who can be anything but happy on Ramsgate sands ?

The last time I saw my honest skin-dresser was a few days afterwards, on the pier, when, coming up to me, he touched his hat, murmured a few sentences in a tone of apology, and ended with the words "your wuship." I felt that I had been betrayed, and that our new-formed friendship was at an end.

It must not be supposed that the Ramsgate season finishes in August, when the excursions practically cease, and the old picturesque town becomes less crowded. Soon the "better class of people" begin to arrive, and they continue to do so during September, October, and November, in which months visitors to Ramsgate enjoy the blessings of an Italian summer —bright blue sky, no fogs, splendid air, and, up to sunset, a climate almost, if not quite, equal to that of Monte Carlo.

Most eminent medical men speak in high terms of the health-giving properties of the town. My own doctor, Robson Roose, is of opinion that the West Cliff of Ramsgate is unequalled as a recuperative resort. A friend of mine, after taking the waters at Marienbad, under Dr. Ott, was suddenly summoned back to England, and was thus prevented from completing the cure, as is usually done, by visiting the Engadine or other foreign place. Upon my friend explaining the position to the German doctor, the latter observed : " Have you ever been to Ramsgate? Go there, for in my opinion you cannot do better."

The attractions of the place are manifold. There is a splendid harbour ; the finest golf links in the world are situated at Sandwich, some four miles distant ; there is fine sailing, with equally fine fishing, presided over by my excellent friend, Stephen Penny, principal fisherman and owner of the *Arona*, which has won the sailing race at the regatta twenty years in succession. A new road, connecting the East and West Cliffs, now in process of formation, and to be opened in a year's time, will prove a great convenience to residents and visitors, and there is a new park for the people just opened. There can, indeed, be no doubt that a glorious future lies before this popular resort

Among the "better classes" who go to Ramsgate in the autumn are many Jewish tradespeople from various parts of

London. For the most part they patronise the numerous lodging-houses that are a feature of the Isle of Thanet. From Saturday to Monday some of these establishments accommodate from sixty to eighty persons, and about forty sit down to dinner there on other days. The boarder pays either by tariff or by the week. The meals are timed somewhat as follows: breakfast, from eight to ten; luncheon, from one to two; and dinner, from six to eight. At the last-named meal there is usually a president elected for the week, whose word is held to be law.

Old habitués of these boarding-houses have their seats at table reserved for them from season to season. For example, at one of these establishments Mr. Marcus Moses has occupied the seat on the right of the chairman for something like twenty years. He is an old gourmand, and as he is always served first, he has the pick of the dish and his food hot, as he is wont to observe with a chuckle.

After dinner the company adjourn to the drawing-room for music and other recreations. A long-haired German Jew of about twenty-one discourses sweet music on the violin. The Misses Marks render the "Battle of Prague," and other bold pieces, on the piano. Young Mr. Simpson, clerk to Messrs. Tripp, Staggers, and Squib, of the Old Jewry, and a constant visitor to the London music-halls, sings the latest songs of the popular Mr. Chevalier.

Another well-known figure is the old raconteur and bore, who is never tired of telling you how many juries he has served on, always in *causes célèbres*, and never misses an opportunity of dragging in the name of his "very old friend, Montagu Chambers." Then there is the conjurer and funny man, who lets off imaginary fireworks, a feat he accomplishes by retiring into a corner of the room, pretending to send up rockets from his coat-tail pocket, and then, pointing to the ceiling, uttering the "pish-pish!" that is supposed to indicate the descent of the sticks.

The Bath-chair men of Ramsgate, or at any rate some of them, are characters. I was driven to Pegwell Bay the other day by a singular specimen of the class. Suddenly stopping the vehicle on the cliff, he turned to me and said:

"Mr. Montagu, would you mind my asking you a question?"

"Certainly not," I replied; "you may ask me twenty."

Up to that moment I had not observed him at all closely.

I now noticed that he was an extremely melancholy-looking man, and a poor, weak-eyed creature, with scarcely any flesh upon his bones.

"Is it true, sir," he enquired, "that you were once on the stage?"

"Yes," I said, "for a few months of my life."

"So was I, sir," he replied, "for something like fifteen years. Then I was converted to the Lord."

"Really!" said I. "And what theatres did you play at?"

"All over the country," he answered; "with Mr. Cave at the Marylebone, and in nearly every provincial town in the kingdom. I used to play Hamlet, Macbeth, Romeo"—he would have made a far better Apothecary—"and all the legitimate. I was a devoted admirer of Shakespeare, sir. But I did not reach the height of my ambition; I was not as successful as I had anticipated, and I am glad of it now, sir. You see, if I had been, I possibly should not have been converted; and you see, when I was I could not remain in such a sinful life any longer, so it was all for the best."

"I don't know," said I. "What salary did you get as an actor?"

"Well," he replied, "sometimes as much as four pounds a week."

"And how much do you get as a chair-man?"

"Well you can make six shillings a day, but not very often, and then you have to give half to the proprietor of the chair."

"Well," said I, "of course you are the best judge of your own affairs, but one thing is certain—if you failed to draw as an actor, you are making up for lost time now."

But there was not the vestige of a smile on the man's face. He was in far too serious a mood to heed any poor joke of mine.

. Let me, in conclusion, remark that I have no interest, pecuniary or otherwise, in the Isle of Thanet or its neighbourhood. I know, however, from experience that an invalid or convalescent cannot do better, at any season of the year, than take a dose of " Doctor Ramsgate."

Part II

UP WEST

CHAPTER I

CLIMBING THE LADDER

Exit aristocracy, enter plutocracy—Old estates in new hands—A gambling establishment a hundred years ago—Mordecai Morris—His earliest recollections—His marriage—His death in harness—His will—A worthy successor—Keenness in pursuit of riches—Change of name by deed-poll—Herbert Maurice, Esq.—Cannot look the gentleman—His son not a success at Eton—Peculiar in his dress.

Go back some fifty years, and ascertain who then resided in Eaton Square, Belgrave Square, Grosvenor Square, and Park Lane. Compare the names with those of the present residents, and you will be considerably astonished at the change that time has brought about. A few of the old aristocracy remain, but the majority have been eliminated, and their places taken by *nouveaux riches*, Jews, and plutocrats. And this is not true merely of the fashionable quarter of London alluded to. Country seats and estates—especially those situated within an easy distance from the metropolis—have also changed hands in a great many instances. In point of fact, England is rapidly becoming a plutocracy; and the reason for this is not very far to seek.

In a number of cases the aristocracy has become very much poorer. The depression in the value of land has had a good deal to do with this; while the reckless extravagance, gambling, and luxurious habits of men who, at an early age, came into their inheritance, have brought practical ruin on those who succeeded them. During the melting process these individuals have not enjoyed life, and have done but little if any good. The principal persons to be benefited by them have been usurers, bookmakers, stockbrokers, and professional gamblers. Mortgage after mortgage has been executed, entails have been cut off, absolute sales have been effected—and the end of it all has been that ancient estates and old family properties have passed into new hands. Who have become possessed of them? Those who have made fortunes with great rapidity, by speculation or otherwise, in the City or in manufacturing districts, in England or the colonies.

The object of this paper is to sketch one of these fortunate individuals — to describe his general habits, his family surroundings, and the efforts he has put forth to obtain a position in society.

I must, in the first place, go back a generation or two in the family of my subject.

Towards the end of the last century, in one of the principal thoroughfares of the West End, stood a house of somewhat dingy exterior, and of an appearance calculated to arouse the curiosity of any passer-by who happened to be ignorant of what, day by day—or, rather, night by night—was passing within its walls. During the daytime the blinds were drawn down, the doors were closed, and the whole building presented an appearance most funereal. At midnight, and for an hour or two before and after, a great change was apparent. The whole house was full of light and animation; carriages were constantly arriving; and men-servants in gorgeous liveries foregathered at and about the doorway. The house was a gambling establishment, and the visitors were the fashionable young bloods of the period.

Gaming-houses were permitted in those days, and this was *par excellence* the first in all London. Here for years fortunes were won and lost, and the place was responsible for much human misery. Lives had here been rendered intolerable, and ruin of the most rapid and remorseless description had been sown broadcast.

Next door to this pandemonium was a shop displaying the glittering stock of a West End jeweller. As you entered from the street you found yourself in a narrow passage, with the door of the shop on the right and a staircase at the further end leading up to the first floor. On the wall of the staircase, painted in large gilt letters, was the name "Mordecai Morris."

Mordecai was a very remarkable man. For years he had pursued the calling of a money-lender and bill discounter. He had a keen eye to business, as he had shown by pitching upon these particular premises. But he had not been content with merely planting himself next door to the gaming-house. He had entered into an arrangement with the proprietor thereof whereby, for a certain consideration, he was permitted to occupy a seat in one of the corridors of that establishment. The corridor led directly into the room where play was carried on. There he was to be seen transacting business night after night all the year round.

Mordecai, so it was said, was a foreign Jew; but it may be doubted whether he himself had the remotest idea what part of the world he had originally hailed from. As a boy he had received little, if any, education. His earliest recollections were of the lowest part of the East End of London, where, during the week, he did odd jobs for his co-religionists. On Saturday, the Jewish Sabbath, he picked up a few coppers by blacking the boots of the inhabitants of Petticoat Lane and its vicinity, who tarried for the purpose on their way to the synagogue.

The shoe-black rose in the world by leaps and bounds. He married above him, and as a comparatively young man was left a widower with two sons and three daughters. After the death of his wife he resided in a remote street in Bloomsbury. He was an excellent father, and he had been a good husband. He had no friends, and said he did not want any. I should add that he was a strict observer of all the rites and ceremonies of his ancient religion.

Mordecai lived and prospered next door to the gaming-house for a long spell of years. The late hours and the strain of business, however, told upon him at last, and one morning his old clerk entered the office to find him seated at his desk—his head fallen on his chest and a bunch of bank-notes in his right hand—cold and dead.

Upon his will being read, it was found that he had not left all his money to his family, but a good portion of it to various Jewish institutions. To his two sons he had bequeathed fifty thousand pounds apiece, and to each of his daughters a sum sufficient to make them more than comfortable for life. The elder son did not long survive his father; he died in less than a year, leaving all his money to his brother.

The latter inherited his father's business qualities. Already he had employed his capital to good purpose. He had put a considerable portion of it into some colliery property in the north of England, which had turned out a veritable El Dorado. Fortune showered favours on him as years went on, and indeed he used laughingly to say that whenever he went out the sun was sure to shine. He put out his money here, there, and everywhere, and always with the same result—everything he touched turned to gold. So prosperous had his collieries become, and so many thousand hands did they employ, that a town grew up around his property. Yet so keen was he in the pursuit of riches that he frequently travelled all night from the north of England, so as to be early at his broker's in the City on the following morning. In fact, wherever there was money to be made he did not allow himself a moment's rest. In due time he died, leaving behind him, besides four daughters, one son, to whom he bequeathed the bulk of his enormous fortune.

The young man, by deed-poll, obtained Her Majesty's permission henceforth to assume the name of Maurice in lieu of Morris. Thus he was known to the world as Herbert Maurice, Esq., of Maurice Town, Lancashire; of Broadstone Hall, Northamptonshire; and of —, Belgrave Square, London.

Let us pass over a number of years, and make his acquaintance as a man of forty-five, with an income of some eighty thousand pounds per annum.

As a young man he had been a light-hearted, genial, and fairly generous fellow; but the acquisition of his enormous wealth changed all that. He exhibits twice as much chest and shirt-front as any ordinary person, and, in fact, is as puffed out as the toad in the well-known fable. The poor fellow is really too large for anything but elastic clothing. Early in life he married the only daughter of a large manufacturer, who, by reason of his having been several times mayor of his native town, had received at the hands of Her Majesty the honour of knighthood. At his death Sir Jacob left the whole of his property to his daughter.

Mr. Herbert Maurice is short, slightly stout, and has bright red hair. In dress he is showy and fond of colour, and, though his garments are turned out by the very best clothes artist in London, he never seems altogether at his ease in them. Mr. Maurice rides the best cobs and horses, and, during the season, is to be seen every morning in the Park on horseback. Though his get-up in the saddle is of the most sporting description, and similar to that of all the fashionable young men of the day, there is always something *outré* about it—either his yellow riding-boots come up higher, or are of a brighter hue than is usual, or the cords that he wears are of a more shiny material th̲ ̲ ̲hose of other frequenters of the Row. In a word, there the̲ ̲ ̲ something about his dress to cause the casual passer-merely
had enter

by to single him out from among the mounted crowd. He seldom or never walks. His brougham is the smartest in London, and the same may be said of all his carriages. Their number is great, for each member of the family has his or her own private equipage. The Maurices' carriages, which are to be seen day by day driving about the West End, bear, in rather large form, the crest of a palm-leaf underneath the motto "Virtute"—armorial bearings of course adopted since the passing of the Disabilities Act.

Mrs. Maurice is not unlike her husband, save that she is very fine and large. She is fair, with prominent features, and a profusion of hair which originally, I believe, was brown, but which by some process has been changed to an extraordinary kind of chestnut.

There are three children—two girls and one boy. The latter is just of age, while one of his sisters is eighteen and the other sixteen. The son and heir is shorter than his father. He is thinner, but his hair is of even a brighter red. The lad has been to Eton. His father thought it the correct thing to send him there, and so perhaps it was. But Gerald was anything but a success at this school of schools. He was neither a "wet bob" nor a "dry bob"; was no good at cricket; hated the river; never took to fives, football, or hockey; and at the request of his tutor, was removed by his father earlier than had been intended.

On arriving at man's estate Gerald became a member of one or two second-rate clubs. He smokes an enormous number of cigarettes, and passes a great portion of his time at the billiard-table. He is very peculiar in his dress, and has apparently correctly studied a picture gallery containing portraits of old veterans of a hundred or two hundred years ago. He wears collars that reach half-way up his cheek, a black satin stock, a gorgeous pin, a tight-fitting frock coat, and trousers that cling so closely to his thin legs as to suggest difficulties in the way of getting them on, and still greater difficulties in the way of getting them off. He has been brought up to no particular business; his health is not good; he is extremely irritable; and, to those who put up with it, purse-proud to such a degree that I really believe his size is the only thing that protects him from utter annihilation. He is not given to saying very much, but a remark he is very fond of making at the Rockingham Club, of which he is a constant habitué, is:

"Hang it all, I think I ought to know a gentleman when I see one."

The girls, Bessie and Jessie, are buxom and extremely self-assertive. When perched in the magnificent barouche, *vis-à-vis* to their mamma, they seem to say to passers-by: "Now, my friends, be good enough to look at this and say what you think of it."

CHAPTER II

CLIMBING THE LADDER—*continued*

Mr. Maurice changes sides—His reason therefor—Mrs. Maurice and her dear friends—The house in Belgrave Square—The guests—Broadstone Hall, in Northamptonshire—The shooting there—The elder daughter "knows her value"—The noble pensioner.

THE several members of the Maurice family vie with one another in their endeavours to climb the social ladder. They are always in London from February to the end of July—from the opening of Parliament to Goodwood. Though the head of the family is not at present in the House, he is rather given to politics. Oddly enough, for years he gave his support to the Liberal party, to which he was of considerable assistance, monetarily and otherwise; but as soon as the cry of Disruption of the Empire and Separation arose, he turned his back on his former friends, and was one of the first to join the ranks of the Liberal Unionists. The reason for this is not difficult to find, and will be sufficiently indicated if I quote a conversation he had with his wife immediately after the split over the Irish question.

"You see, Rachel, my dear," he said, "it is the very thing for people in our position. Matters stand thus. The Tories cannot keep in a day without us, so Lord Salisbury and the big-wigs of the Conservative party are bound to be civil. Cards for their receptions and for political parties will flow in merrily this year, and if in the autumn or spring the Liberals obtain a majority, we shall next session be even in a better position. We have never actually declared ourselves adverse to the Radical programme, you know. On the contrary, the Dissentient Liberals sit on the same side of the House as the Liberals. We have simply detached ourselves on the question of Ireland, and if the Gladstonians come in they will only be too glad to get us back. They are not too flush of cash, you know, and then, a man of my wealth, and the power of such a fortune as mine—a peerage, my dear, a peerage!"

Mr. Maurice made this speech while surveying himself—a habit to which he was much attached—in the Louis Quatorze glass in his wife's boudoir, in their magnificent mansion in Belgrave Square. The lady is, if possible, more subservient to Duchesses, Countesses, and other titled people, even than her husband. She always talks of them as her dearest and most intimate friends, and frequently refers to them by their Christian names.

"My dear," said she the other day to a poorer friend whom she was in the habit of patronising, "you know the dear Duchess of W——. She is the sweetest" ("sweetest" is a favourite word of hers) "thing that ever breathed. Nothing but kindness and simplicity. And the house, my love! You never could have imagined anything so lovely. The blue room is simply perfect, and then the yellow drawing-room! Such taste! And the china! And the pictures! All the old masters, and the most lovely collection of water-colours ever seen!"

She proceeded to give a pretty accurate description of the staircase, hall, and other parts of the house. I need scarcely say that she had never been a guest there in the whole of her natural, or, rather, unnatural life. Her Grace had, however, been in the habit of occasionally lending her mansion for charitable meetings, concerts, and other gatherings, and Mrs. Maurice had never omitted to take tickets for these functions. While others were listening to the speeches and music, she had been making mental notes of the pictures, furniture, and ornaments around her. She is a constant student of the Peerage and Baronetage, and the "County Families," and, in fact, almost knows those publications by heart. So conversant is she with Debrett and Burke, that if the conversation turns upon any Prince, Duke, or peeress, she immediately chimes in with something like this :

"Yes, of course, she married ——. She is the sister of Lord ——, who married and was divorced from poor ——, who was one of the sweetest and most loveable creatures ever created."

The family, though apparently most united, are not averse to saying unkind things one of the other. It was only the

other day that Mrs. Maurice's sister-in-law, after listening to one of that lady's tirades on birth and rank, observed :
"If I did not know that Rachel was studying one of these books," taking up Debrett, "all day long, I should really think she obtained her information from the linkman."

The house in Belgrave Square is replete with every luxury, and the entertainments given there—dinners, concerts, and receptions—the best in all London. It has been said that, provided your cook be good and your cellar beyond reproach, you have only to go out on the doorstep and ring the dinner-bell, to secure the most acceptable of guests. Be that the case or not, all the best men, and some of the best women, are always willing to accept Mr. and Mrs. Maurice's hospitality.

The two grand occasions of the year are those on which they receive Royalty, and I believe these are the happiest days of their lives. Yet I have often wondered whether the host is really happy in the presence of his distinguished visitors. Is it not a dash of bitter in his cup of sweets to know that he is out of his element, that he is merely tolerated, and that he is often treated with something very like insolence ? Apparently not. He has perhaps become used to his position. If you should ask him if he knows the Duke of ——, he will answer that his Grace is the oldest friend he has, and if you should enquire of him whether he is acquainted with the Earl of ——, his reply will be, "Of course—I have known him all my life." Should you afterwards chance to see him in the company of one of the individuals referred to, you cannot but be hugely amused at the scene. The little man, all blandness and smiles, goes sidling up to the nobleman, who, with a curt "Good evening," or possibly without even a word of greeting, turns quickly on his heels and makes his escape. But this sort of thing has no effect. Off goes the busy bee to try and gather honey from another flower.

What a pity it is that the poor fellow cannot enter into a working agreement with needy members of the aristocracy, whereby he would recompense them for their patronage with hard cash ! A regular scale of fees might be fixed upon, varying, of course, with the rank of the patron. Thus, I take it, one pound would not be an excessive sum for the smile of a Baronet, nor five pounds for the handshake of an Earl, and I am persuaded that the little man would not begrudge a couple of one-hundred-pound notes to be greeted by a Duke, before a roomful of people, in some such terms as these : " Hullo,

Maurice, my dear fellow; I'm delighted to see you." Two hundred pounds, did I say?—why, such bliss would be purchased cheaply for five times that sum.

The season over, Mr. Maurice usually retires to his country seat in Northamptonshire, which certainly is a very magnificent estate. Of course, however, if he reads in the newspapers that Royalty is at Carlsbad, Spa, or Homburg, thither he betakes himself with all speed.

His place in Northamptonshire, Broadstone Hall, was the country seat of one of the oldest families of England. The house itself is of the Elizabethan style of architecture, and is in every way a show place. The central hall is one of the finest in the world. Around it winds a splendid picture gallery, filled with works of the old masters—a few Gainsboroughs and Rembrandts, a Romney or two, and some of older date. Mr. Maurice purchased the house as it stood, pictures and all. The first question the hostess asks you, should you be a visitor at the house, is:

"Have you seen our picture gallery?"

Then she points to different works, and explains:

"That is Lady ——, time of James the First; here is Sir Vincent B——; and this picture," pointing to one hung beside a suit of armour, "is Viscount G——, killed in the Wars of the Crusaders."

I believe it is no exaggeration to say that she has really come to believe that the canvases represent ancestors of her own.

The park, pleasure grounds, and gardens all bear the stamp of antiquity, the last-named being laid out in the Italian style. It is manifest that the fruit-trees on the walls have clung there for generations. At the end of the stabling, which is most extensive, stands an old belfry tower, the architecture of which is of so remote a date as to puzzle antiquaries. In the centre of the stable-yard, surrounded by a plot of grass, is an ancient mulberry-tree, which is supposed to have been planted by Queen Elizabeth herself while honouring the then proprietor of the Hall with a brief visit.

In the stable a separate compartment is set apart for each member of the family. There are Miss Jessie's hunters, Miss Bessie's hunters, the master's hunters, and a number of horses belonging to the son and heir.

There is splendid shooting at Broadstone Hall, the beat

shoots excelling in number any bag made up elsewhere in the county. Several of the nobility are asked down for a day or two's shooting, and if slaughtering hundreds of hand reared pheasants be a pleasure, the guests have a chance of enjoying themselves to their heart's content.

Everything is overdone at Broadstone Hall. The elaborate costumes of the beaters, and the gorgeous velveteen of the keepers, call up a smile to the lips of the old country sportsman. The hot luncheon which is brought out on a large vehicle elaborately constructed for the purpose is far superior to the repast usual on such occasions, and would make the mouth of any disciple of Epicurus water. A year or two ago a member of the Royal Family was induced to attend one of these shooting-parties, and ever since the lady of the mansion has spoken of the rooms where her distinguished guest passed the night as "His Royal Highness's suite."

The young ladies shine a good deal at Broadstone Hall. The elder, having heard that young Lady Dorothy B——, a daughter of one of the old aristocracy of the county, is very smart at handling a team and shooting rabbits, has passed a great deal of her time endeavouring, under the tuition of the head coachman and head keeper, to become a proficient in both those accomplishments. She has, in consequence, obtained a mastery over the gun and the reins, together with a slanginess and swagger not infrequently associated therewith. This young lady has studied Zola, and is up in all the latest French novels of the day. She often drives her father to the railway station, or elsewhere, and afterwards joins the shooting-party at luncheon. She has the greatest possible idea of her accomplishments and appearance, and was overheard the other day to remark, while looking at herself in the glass in the billiard-room :

"I don't mean to go cheap. I know my value, and I don't intend to go under it—ten thousand a year and a title. I know I'm clever, and "—surveying herself from head to foot in the glass—"I can't help seeing that I'm handsome."

The younger girl is extremely fast, and openly declares that she is desirous of getting married as soon as possible, stating as her reason that she knows she will be able to enjoy herself so much more as a married woman.

One of the family party I have, up to the present moment, omitted to refer to. This is Sir Hugh ——. At one corner of the Park stands a large antiquated-looking stone house enclosed in walls and with long windows composed of small panes. This building was, and still is, known as the Dower House, and it is inhabited by the gentleman alluded to.

Soon after the family had taken Broadstone Hall, they were introduced in London to Sir Hugh, who was a ruined man, and had scarcely a five-pound note to call his own. They had asked him down to the Hall, thinking that, as he had known every one in the county, he would not only be able to put them *au fait* at entertaining, but be an excellent card to play at dinner. He accepted the Maurices' invitation, and has remained with them from that day to this. As I have said, he occupies the Dower House, but he lives to all intents and purposes at the Hall.

Oddly enough, it was in the gaming-house described in the early lines of my last chapter that Sir Hugh's grandfather had dissipated all the estates and property that would, in the natural course of events, have passed into the possession of this young man. Both he and his host are ignorant of the fact, but so degenerate is human nature that I doubt very much whether, if the former were aware of it, it would make any difference in his relations to the latter.

I now conclude my sketch of this typical family, but shall ask my readers only to say *au revoir* to some of the characters introduced, as they will probably reappear in a later chapter.

CHAPTER III

DESCENDING THE LADDER

Lord Bythesea at Eton—The Earl of Woking—Bytherea comes of age—Is taken to the Queen's Bench Prison—We visit him there—Racquet courts—"Tap is open!"—No distinctions of rank—Slowman's sponging-house—The last Earl of Woking—The proposed marriage—It takes place—Its sequel—Death of my old friend.

It is a remarkable thing that while there are always hundreds of persons trying to climb the social ladder—as exemplified in the two previous chapters—an equal number may be found doing their level best to descend it. Old and honoured names are dragged into the mire, and families that have been esteemed and venerated from generation to generation are, by the thoughtless, reckless, and sometimes criminal acts of one or more of their members, degraded and disgraced almost beyond all hope of recovery.

I was at Eton with Lord Bythesea, the only son of the Earl of Woking, and, as boys say, we were very "pallish." He was an extremely popular boy; a good all-round fellow in the "eight" and the football wall Oppidan eleven; great at "pop"; and, save and except *inter silvas academi*, a beau-ideal Etonian. Our schooldays over, we both left to take our different places in the world.

The Earl of Woking had been an extravagant sporting man, with a weak wife, this son, and three daughters. He possessed a large stud of race-horses, had once owned the favourite for the Derby, and had won some few classic races. His lordship had hunted a very stiff and expensive county, and indulged in many other extravagant tastes. Before coming into his title he excited a good deal of admiration and astonishment as a debater, and he subsequently attained some distinction in the capacity of M.P. for one of the divisions of Kent. On being translated to the quieter atmosphere of the House of Lords, however, he practically gave up politics, and set himself with increased zest to squander what remained of his fortune.

His lordship was, in his way, very fond of his son Ralph, and had great influence over him. The lad did everything his father wished him to do, and the result was that in due time the entail was cut off, and all that remained of an old and valuable property was handed over to the fashionable usurers of the day.

On coming of age, Ralph Bythesea, who inherited all the tastes and habits of his progenitor, purchased a lot of race-horses, and trained in famous stables at Newmarket. Besides his love for flat-racing, he was an extremely game rider over sticks and at steeple-chasing, being second to none in schooling his horses over timber. At this time he was deeply in debt, and his I.O.Us., bills, and post-obits were flying all over London.

Ralph and I met several times at the theatre and opera. We also dined together at the "Wellington and Blue Posts," in Cork Street, and there talked and laughed over old Eton days.

One morning in July, while I was having breakfast in my rooms in Duke Street, St. James's, I was informed that F——, another old schoolfellow of mine, desired to see me immediately.

"I say, Monty, old fellow," he exclaimed, as he entered the room, "I've awfully bad news for you—that is, if you haven't already heard of it. Poor Ralph Bythesea was arrested ten days ago, and is at present in the Queen's Bench Prison, and from what I can see, there is precious little chance of his getting out of it. I have been round to Jimmy Dickinson, the lawyer in Burlington Street, and sent him down to see what can be done. He seems to think it's a bad business. He holds a lot of his paper himself. I know how fond you are of poor old Ralph, and the least thing we can do, as soon as you've polished off your breakfast and dressed, is to drive to the other side of the water and see for ourselves what's to be done."

The news was indeed startling. Needless to say I required no second invitation. I scrambled into my clothes, and a quarter of an hour later we chartered a hansom, and ordered the driver to take us to the well-known debtors' gaol at Southwark.

The Queen's Bench Prison, which has long since been demolished, was familiarly known as Hudson's Hotel, a gentleman named Hudson having been the governor of that somewhat extensive establishment.

Upon our hansom driving up to the gates of the prison we got out, and I pulled the bell. We were at once admitted into what was called "the receiving-room." I gave our names, and enquired if we could see Lord Bythesea.

"Oh," said one of the officials to another, "Bythesea? Yes; show the gentlemen to three in six."

We were at once conducted into the prison yard. Immediately opposite the apartment we had just quitted stood a building which we subsequently learnt was called the State House. Here Humphrey, Brown, and Cameron, directors of the British Bank, were, at the time of our visit, accommodated with a lodging. Other tenants were a Captain, formerly of the Rifle Brigade, and two brothers—the victims of some Chancery proceedings—who had been there for twenty years.

To the right of the State House was an enormously high wall of considerable length. It was utilised for a series of racquet courts, the boundaries of which were marked out upon the gravel. Players were to be seen all along the line, and at the margin of the courts stood a number of spectators, some of whom were betting while others kept the score. I need hardly say that prominent among the crowd was the object of our visit, arrayed in flannels, and playing as if his life depended on the issue of the game. He espied us at once, and holding up his racquet, shouted:

"Must finish this game, old fellows. Will be with you in ten minutes. Meanwhile have a look round the shop."

We acted upon this advice, and made a thorough inspection of the prison yard.

It was not long before we perceived what had been meant when the officer directed us to "three in six." Facing the racquet wall, and bounded by a broad white pavement, was a row of houses four or five storeys high, and with a number painted over the door of each. On entering one of these buildings we found that each room was similarly distinguished by a number; therefore it was clear that "three in six" meant the third room in the sixth house. These houses were occupied by those debtors who could afford to pay for quasi-luxuries and for a laundress to wait upon them.

At the back of the row of houses was the "poor side" of

K

the prison, and those who were forced to live in this portion of the establishment were in a very wretched condition indeed, and had to get on as well as they could. There were no racquet courts for them.

Another interesting part of the building was the kitchen, which resembled that of a West End club more than anything else. It was presided over by a chef, who, if the inhabitants of the prison were to be believed, was one of considerable distinction. As we were emerging from this apartment we were met by our friend, racquet in hand.

"Deuced good of you fellows to come over here," said he. "Come up to my room, and then I'll give you a true, full, and particular account of my latest sheaf of misfortunes."

"Ralph, old man," said I, "will you never be serious?"

"Quite enough time for that, dear old fellow," he replied; then suddenly stopping, and casting his eyes towards a door on the right, he exclaimed: "By Jove, Tap is open! You know, my future Cicero, we can only get liquor here twice a day, between one and two, and five and six, and we can't go beyond one quart of ale or one pint of wine per diem; but you fellows, you know, being visitors, can have what you like. Doesn't it remind you of Jack Knight's, only that old coon at the beer-engine is not a fair representative of little Emily?" And so he rattled on, as though he hadn't a single care in the world.

Having partaken of sundry draughts of shandygaff, we proceeded to "three in six." It was a funny little room, with a table in the middle, an iron camp bedstead behind the door, a chest of drawers against the window, and three or four Windsor chairs standing here and there. In a few minutes the laundress, an untidy, middle-aged woman, made her appearance with a snow-white table-cloth, and proceeded to set out a plain but substantial luncheon. While she was thus engaged we were all looking out of the window, watching the racquet players.

"See that dapper-looking little fellow in flannels?" said Ralph. "That's ——, the tailor of Cork Street. Overdid himself a little with discounting, not to mention a great partiality for Cremorne and a villa at Barnes. That stout fellow playing with him is the heir to the earldom of W——. No distinctions of rank here, I can tell you!" And he was right, for, just as he was uttering the words, the door was kicked open, and a long, loose-built, red-haired man lumbered into the room with the words:

"Got any mustard and things, Bythesea? Think I'll borrow the lot," sweeping up a number of bottles from the table. "Bring them back in five minutes."

"Who is that extraordinary apparition?" I asked, when the fellow had shut the door behind him.

"Oh, that?" was the answer; "that's Gibson. He's a bookmaker, I believe; at any rate he is one in here, and he'll always lay you odds up to a tenner on any race, money staked of course. He's the very deuce at loo. We play a good deal when the weather puts a stop to racquets. All cards are forbidden, you know, so we have to keep them up the chimney. Look!" he added, putting his hand up the register, and producing a sooty piece of brown paper in which were wrapped two packs of cards and a box of ivory counters. Replacing them he continued: "Now I'll tell you about my arrest. I was coming out of the Travellers and was jumping into my tilbury, when a very common-looking fellow put his hand on my shoulder and exclaimed: 'Very sorry, my lord, but you are my prisoner. *Ca sa* unsatisfied judgement—suit of one Joel.' First of all I felt inclined to knock him down, but, remembering that if it were not the enterprising Joel, it would be somebody else of the same calling, I yielded to fate, hailed a four-wheeler, and was whisked off, in company with the myrmidons of the law, to Slowman's, the sponging-house in Cursitor Street, Chancery Lane. Ah, my dear fellow, you've never seen a sponging-house! Ye gods! what a place! I had an apartment they were pleased to call a bedroom to myself certainly, but if I wanted to breathe the air I had to do so in a cage in the back garden—iron bars all round, and about the size of one of the beast receptacles at the Zoo. For this luxury I had to pay two guineas a day. A bottle of sherry cost a guinea, a bottle of Bass half-a-crown, and food was upon the same sort of economical tariff. Well, you know, this sort of thing wouldn't do, so I sent for the governor and talked matters over. He went to his lawyer, who got what they call a *habeas* for me, whereupon I was brought over here, and here I am. Might have been worse, old fellow, you know."

"Has Jimmy Dickinson been over to see you?" said I.

"Oh, yes," he replied. "He said matters would take a long time to settle, so I chucked him up and sent for little P——, of New Inn. He's as sharp as they make 'em, so the best of the fellows in here say, and he's sure to get things brought to a head in a week or two at most."

As he was speaking a knock came at the door, and the subject of his remarks entered. He was a short, stout, fair man, rather fashionably dressed, and with a quick, off-hand manner. After Bythesea had introduced us, I turned to F―― and observed :

"Time is getting on, and as these gentlemen have business to discuss, had we not better be on the move?"

The little lawyer at once interposed.

"Not the slightest necessity, my dear sir," said he. "I know exactly what his lordship wants—to get out of this hole as quickly as possible. I enquired at the gate and found that the amount of Joel's judgement was three thousand five hundred pounds, and there are detainers lodged in the gaol which total up to something like thirty-three thousand pounds. It can all be arranged for his lordship. With the assistance of the noble Earl, his father, the money can be raised, and his discharge procured. All I require is that the matter shall be left entirely in my hands. I never permit any interference. No, my dear sir," he continued, turning to me, "too many cooks—you know the rest," and holding out his cigar-case, he added: "Let me offer you one of the very finest Cabanas in London."

I did not refuse. Seeing, however, that no business could be seriously transacted if F―― and I remained, we wished our companions good-bye and took our departure.

I visited Bythesea nearly every day, and in about a fortnight's time had the pleasure of calling at the prison, in company with the lively solicitor, and taking him away.

It will now be necessary, from want of space, and for other reasons, to skip over a long period. Suffice it to say that, in the fulness of time, the Earl was gathered to his fathers, and Ralph ruled in his stead. Ruled? Yes; but the kingdom to rule over had practically vanished. My old friend was Earl of Woking with scarcely an acre to his name. Since his release from the Queen's Bench Prison, he had married the youngest daughter of an Irish Viscount, who was almost as impecunious as himself. She was extremely beautiful and very haughty, and, though much attached to her husband, was ill suited to face the troubles of the *res angusta domi*. By their marriage they had one child—the most *distinguée* and beautiful girl I have ever seen.

Lady Ethel Marsden was the apple of her father's eye, and she in turn thought there was no one in the world like the author of her being.

Marsden Manor, and the mansion in Park Lane, had been sold by legal arrangement, and the old family estate had passed into the hands of a millionaire, one Sir Samuel ———. He was a widower, and had an extremely vulgar son. One little corner of the estate was preserved—Swallows Fields, which consisted of a house, farms, and grounds—and this had been the home of the Earl since ruin fell upon the family.

His friends—and their name was legion—did not desert him, and, though his wife never accepted invitations, he himself was often to be seen at Newmarket, Ascot, Doncaster, and other fashionable race meetings, all the families in the neighbourhood being only too pleased to receive him as a guest. Besides Swallows Fields the Earl had a small flat in the neighbourhood of Victoria Street, and here he passed a portion of the London season.

The happiest days of his life, as I often heard him declare, were the six weeks he spent every year at a charming nook by the sea not a hundred miles from Cowes. An old schoolfellow who was at the same tutor's as both of us, and who had succeeded to a vast inheritance, was in the habit of placing this, one of his numerous residences, at his lordship's disposal every year.

It was after one of these autumnal sojourns by the sea that I chanced one day upon my old friend at a club of which we both were members. For some time past I had noticed a change for the better in his appearance. He had a more elastic gait than formerly, and his anxious, careworn expression was becoming a thing of the past.

"My dear old fellow," said he, "I am so glad to have met you! Things at last are taking a brighter turn. You know ———, the man who owns our property now? Not a bad sort of fellow——you needn't tell me you don't like him; I know that. Why, my Ethel found it out in a moment! You know, you and the Countess don't seem to hit it off very well—one's old friends before marriage never do—but I think that Ethel likes you, after her old dad, better than any one in the whole world."

"Better than any one?" queried I, smiling.

"What do you mean?" said he, fidgeting with his watch-chain and key.

"Ethel," I said, "is very beautiful. Has it never occurred to you that there might be somebody else? She sees so very little of people, and the time might come, you know———."

"Now, it is a curious thing," he said, "but that is the very matter I was coming down to the Temple to see you about to-morrow if we hadn't met. As I said to you before, —— is a good fellow, a very good fellow, and I can't disguise from you the fact that he has been of considerable use to me of late. I am making a certain amount of money in the City now, for he has put me on several boards. You see, my name and the influence of his wealth make rather a valuable combination. As you must have guessed, I have been considerably embarrassed of late, and I am bound to say he has been generosity itself. I have only had to express a wish, and it has been gratified at once. And then her ladyship, you know, has rather set her heart on this. You know, my father and I, to put the finest point upon it, did not always consider what was our duty to our successors." Throwing away a cigar, and trying to laugh, he added: "You see, it is I who am becoming serious now. As my lady says, the estates will be in the family, if not in the family name."

"What on earth do you mean?" said I.

"You seem remarkably dense to-night; the thing is easy enough to comprehend. In a word," and here his voice took a snappish tone, "Sir Samuel's boy loves Ethel."

I confess I was so startled that my prudence for a moment entirely forsook me, and I was sorry afterwards for what I said.

"Good God!" was my exclamation, "you can't think of giving your girl to a cub like that—and such a girl! Does she know? Have you told her? Has it never struck you that her heart may not be quite her own? Even if it were not so, a girl of such refinement! She is so loveable a creature, with all your good qualities, and—if you will pardon me for saying so—none of your faults."

He retorted irascibly:

"What do you mean about her heart? Ethel has never kept a thing from me."

"Am I talking to a blind old man?" said I. "At Cowes, when her ladyship was good enough to tolerate my presence for a day or two, if your eyes were shut, mine weren't. Don't you remember when Claude Misterton came to say good-bye before rejoining his ship? Why is it, old friend, that since then day after day, when down there, Ethel's eyes were always fixed upon the sea? And have you seen no change? Where is that merry laugh? Where have those spirits flown? Across the sea, and, if I'm not much mistaken—and you know I am by trade a reader of faces and minds—her life, her thoughts have leapt out there."

"This is absolute ruin," he protested, "worse than anything that has gone before. I have always looked upon Claude Misterton as though he were one of my own family; and, consider for a moment—beyond his lieutenancy in the Navy, he has not a shilling he can call his own. No, no, it would break my lady's heart."

I am bound to say that I am a bad hand at weighing quantities, and as I had never gauged the article referred to, I simply replied:

"Possibly."

"It is too late," said he; "my darling Ethel—I would not give her a moment's pain for the wealth of the world; but what am I to do? I thought her heart was free—and in fact, short of your surmises, I don't know to the contrary now—and on Sir Samuel mentioning his hopes and wishes to me I consulted my wife, who was more than delighted; and—well, hang it all—I've told my neighbours that the thing is as good as settled."

Not being a man of fashionable society's world, I observed:

"You have not consulted the principal party concerned?"

"Ah!" he exclaimed impatiently, "that's just like you; you don't understand these things. At dry law books there's no one better, and at addressing a jury you're splendid—give me a light, old fellow—thanks—but you don't understand women. You have no idea how these things are arranged. Forty thousand a year at the least; my girl—all of us—in the position I destroyed. It will be all right—it will be all right!"

A few months after this conversation, on taking up *The Morning Post*, I read a paragraph headed:

"Marriage in High Life."

It ran as follows:

"A marriage has been arranged, and will shortly take place, between Ponsonby ———, Esq., of Marsden Manor, and Ethel, only daughter of Ralph, Earl of Woking. The marriage is to be celebrated early in July."

In due time I received a card for the ceremonial and reception. I did not go, but I read in the next day's paper a glowing account of the marriage—which took place in the

Chapel Royal, Savoy—and of the departure of the "happy pair." Happy! Knowing what I did, I would rather have surrendered all I possessed in the world than have witnessed the sacrifice of that poor child.

The remainder of this somewhat tragic history may be told within the scope of a few sentences.

Two years after the solemnisation of the marriage, a paragraph appeared in the papers with these head-lines:

"Another Scandal in High Life."
"Elopement of Lady Ethel —— with the Hon. Claude Misterton, Lieut. R.N."

I had an enormous number of business engagements at the time, and for a fortnight after reading this announcement I had hardly a moment to call my own. The first time I had a little leisure I jumped into a hansom and drove to my old friend's flat in the neighbourhood of Victoria Street. Upon asking if he were at home, the answer I received was:

"His lordship died this morning."

"Is her ladyship here?"

"No, sir. His lordship came up to town yesterday, suddenly, and he was quite alone when he died."

And this was the end of my poor old friend. There was no heir, and the title is now extinct.

CHAPTER IV

MODERN STOCKBROKERS — TOPSY-TURVYDOM

Changes in stockbroking—The aristocratic "runner"—His way of conducting business—Stock Exchange gambling amongst women—Its cause—A typical case—The conversation at modern dinner-parties—An old friend—Strawberry Hill—The Grange—My life at Bushey—The new system.

PERHAPS no business in the world has passed through more changes than that which is pursued with so much profit in Capel Court and the neighbourhood.

Within my own recollection, stockbroking has undergone a remarkable metamorphosis. My oldest memories of stocks and shares date back to 1846, the year of the railway mania, when George Hudson reigned as king. The whole of my information was picked up from the conversations that took place upon the domestic hearth, for I am afraid mine were long ears even for a lad of twelve. By-the-bye, one thing is proved by this reminiscence: in whatever other ways matters have changed since then, fortunes were won and lost on the Stock Exchange half a century ago as rapidly as they are won and lost in the present day.

Not only were sales and purchases of stock not conducted in my young days as they are now, but both the firms and their clients were of a totally different calibre. In fact, I think I shall be able to show, before completing this chapter, that there has been an absolute topsy-turvydom in this business. I had almost written "in this profession"; but, had I done so, I should most assuredly have incurred the displeasure of any of the old school under whose notice the expression might have come.

At the time of which I am speaking, the business usually

descended from father to son, and it not infrequently happened that a head clerk was taken in as partner, in reward for many years of faithful service.

In those days, members of the nobility who had money to invest, or, at any rate, a great many of them, were in the habit of visiting the City, and personally arranging with their brokers, not for mere time bargains, but for real and permanent investments.

The stockbrokers of that period enjoyed wisely the good things Dame Fortune had been bounteous enough to shower upon them. Most of them had West End houses, some owned country seats, a few sat in Parliament, and I am bound to say that the great majority of them were charitable and generous to their poorer brethren. Punctuality and regularity were their watchwords, and the eldest member of the firm would always be as methodical in his attendance at the office as the youngest clerk.

The stockbrokers rarely speculated, being content with the commission they received from their private clients, or—in the case of those who had the good fortune to be connected with a joint-stock or other bank—the interest that accrued from lending out money, either from day to day or from account to account. Now the whole aspect of things has changed, as I shall briefly show.

In former days, when any young sprig of the aristocracy occupying a position in the Army, diplomacy, or civil service, came to grief, he generally, as a last resource, tried his hand at the wine trade. This course had its advantages, for the young man was very likely, on account of the amiability of his disposition, or the position and influence of his friends, or both, to make sufficient income to live upon fairly comfortably. In the event, moreover, of pecuniary reverse and failure, there was generally a sufficient residue of champagne or brandy in stock to enable him, with very little trouble and with extraordinary rapidity, to pass into those realms where the weary are at rest.

Of recent years, when it has been necessary for the son of Lord This, or of Sir Harry That, to earn his living, he has shown a marked preference for the Stock Exchange, and, as I think, with very good sense. It may be taken for granted that he has no capital. Having, therefore, nothing to lose, he has everything to gain. The position he attains is that of "runner," as it is termed, to some firm of stockbrokers.

The representative of the Strawberry Leaves or of the Bloody Hand thus obtains a chair in a stockbroker's office, and it is arranged that he shall receive half commission on all business introduced by him. He gets on little by little, and in due time, by taking out a certificate, becomes what is known as an "authorised clerk," and has admission to the sacred precincts of the "House."

This new way of conducting business, which has been rapidly on the increase during the past ten years, has, in my humble opinion, been productive of a very great deal of mischief.

The young "runner," who has perhaps been in the Grenadier or Life Guards, or some other crack position in life, belongs to various clubs and has many friends. He repeats to them, innocently enough, all that has been told him by those with whom he mixes in the City; how these shares are bound to turn out well, how those others are safe to run up next week, and how much money must of necessity be gained by the immediate purchase of De Beers, etc. He relates how, by investing in the last-named securities, a friend of his realised over eight thousand pounds in a fortnight, from account to account.

"Indeed; but how?" is the question asked.

"Oh," is the reply, "the thing is very simple. There is no actual money required. You only have to give an order to sell or buy until the next account day."

Further questions are asked, and answered satisfactorily, and in the end the "runner" receives an order, which he cannot run fast enough to execute.

The moth has singed his wings. The first step has been taken in the very worst kind of gambling of the day. It makes very little difference whether the "runner's" client wins or loses. If successful, he decides to have "another flutter for more;" if unsuccessful, he resolves to try his luck again, and see if he cannot win back his losses. The result is obvious; *facilis descensus Averni.*

The hard part of the case is that the punter has not brought his misfortune upon himself. He has not been enticed by the glowing newspaper advertisements of the outside brokers, and he has not sought out and been caught in the Dædalean webs of those gentry; the temptation has been carried to him by his own friend, whose word he would not dream of doubting. Anxious to share in the good fortune of which he hears so much, and delighted to do an "old pal" a good turn, he plunges headlong into a stream which is composed entirely of whirlpools.

But the mischief does not stop here; this is not the worst outcome of the new way of conducting Stock Exchange business. Women—I mean, of course, society women—are fellow-victims with their brothers and husbands.

The women of to-day have a keen relish for gambling. How many hundreds, nay thousands, have delighted in poker, baccarat, and other games of that description! If you have watched these pastimes, where have you found anxious greed most manifest—in their eyes, or in those of their male companions? I appeal to the experience of any man of the world. Again, what scores of women gamble on the turf, at Epsom, Newmarket, Ascot, and elsewhere! Look in at Sandown or Kempton—places almost invented for "grandes dames" and their pleasures—and you will find the betting pretty equally divided between the sexes.

Among the women of the *beau monde*, Stock Exchange gambling is rapidly becoming as dire a disease as baccarat and horse-racing. Why is this? The explanation is as plain as the nose in your face. It is all owing to the "runner."

As I have already indicated, the individual in question has been nursed in society's lap. He is a good-looking, dashing, agreeable young English gentleman, whose superior, nay, whose equal, is to be found in no other country with which I am acquainted. He has been the pet of all the young débutantes who, season after season, have dropped their first graceful curtsy to her most gracious and Imperial Majesty. These have in time married, and no guest is more welcome at their different houses, come when he may, than this young friend and companion of their girlhood. What is the consequence? Without meaning any harm, when he calls to afternoon tea, or at other visiting times, he brings his tempting trade with him.

Young Lady C—— has heard what a run of luck Mrs. B—— has had in the City during the past few months. She has also heard that that lady's business has been conducted through a certain firm of stockbrokers, and by whom? Why, by "dear old Georgie"—to wit, the "runner." Lady C—— at once determines what to do, and sits down and writes the following letter:

"PARK LANE.
"DEAR GEORGE,
"Just saw you for a moment from my boudoir window this morning riding in the Park. Fancy you becoming so industrious as to be compelled to join the Liver Brigade! I want to speak to you. Most important business. At home on Thursday afternoon after five. Come early. I'm going to make some money, and you must help me.
"Yours truly,
"AGATHA ———."

Thursday afternoon arrives, and her ladyship has not long to wait after the clock has struck the appointed hour. Her visitor is duly announced, and as he shakes hands he cannot help exclaiming:

"Why, ever since we were boy and girl together I've never seen you looking so lovely."

"My dear George," says the hostess, slightly blushing, and pushing him into a chair, "we have no time for bandying compliments. I'm in a most serious dilemna. I want money, and money I must have. Of course I have some, but not nearly enough for the straits I am at present in, and so I thought we'd have a little gamble — only a little one, you know. I hear you have done wonders for Mrs. B———, and that you and your firm are absolute conjurers in your knowledge of good things — that's the proper term, isn't it, George? —and you must reserve one of your straight tips for me."

"What is it to be?" he asks gaily. "Berthas (Brighton A's), or Sarahs (Midlands), or Brummeys (Birminghams)? Why do you shake that business-like head of yours? Not railways?"

"No, not railways. Something foreign, of course."

"Indeed; and so you're not scared by the Baring crisis?" he replies, laughing.

"Oh, no, I'm not so silly. You see, George, I want to win a lot. The fact is I've not paid my bills, I mean my personal bills, for the last three years. Madame F———, of Bond Street, and some other big tradespeople are getting very tiresome, and beginning to bore me to death. I seem never to get a moment's peace. The Earl, I know, is himself rather hard hit—he backed Orme for a large amount—I can't possibly ask him, and so what is to be done?"

The conversation continues, and they eventually decide in what securities the speculation shall take place. Whether successful or not, it is not the business of this article to say. I have merely given an example of the way in which the movers in the fashionable world often enter upon their speculations.

At modern dinner-parties, if the conversation does not turn on racing, it is usually about the Stock Exchange. The young men I have endeavoured to describe are considered most eligible guests. Many a young lady having business transactions is not above arranging with her hostess to be taken down to dinner by one of the individuals in question. Instead of the usual society chat, which, Heaven knows, was usually as dull and stupid as it well could be, everybody discusses past City ventures, and the successes which the future may have in store.

Is this or is this not a most unhappy state of things, and is happiness or misery likely to be the outcome of it?

My personal experiences of members of the Stock Exchange date a great many years back, and are associated in my mind with some very pleasant memories.

Years ago, soon after I was called to the Bar, I was living with my wife and a very young child in Gordon Street, Gordon Square; and while we were located there I made the acquaintance of a man for whom I came to entertain the sincerest regard, and for whose memory I shall always have the deepest respect. He lived a simple life with his family—to whom he was much attached—in a large house in a neighbouring square. He was a stockbroker and the head of his firm, his only partner being his son. They did a thriving business, and were sole brokers to one of the largest and most influential private banks in the City.

My friend's tastes were of the simplest description. He delighted in having one or two intimates to dinner every now and then, and cigars and pictures were his only extravagance. He kept no horses or carriages, either for himself or for his family. Punctually at twenty minutes to ten every week-day morning the same four-wheeled cab would call for him and take him to the City; and he was never known to keep it waiting three minutes. The same vehicle brought him back in the evening. His first wish, after his business was done, was to get back to his family. He never stopped on the road, save at rare intervals when he called at a club to which we both belonged.

In the vacation—and he allowed himself a very short rest—my friend was in the habit of taking a furnished house on or near the banks of the Thames. He was careful to keep within easy hail of the City, for fear his services should be required there at a moment's notice. The houses he took were usually in the neighbourhood of Twickenham, Teddington, Walton, or Shepperton.

I have always, in thinking over my past life—its pleasures and pains, its successes and disappointments, its bitters and its sweets—come to the conclusion that my happiest days were spent at the period to which I am alluding.

Besides the family I have referred to, I had many friends living up the river, and it is not surprising, therefore, that, as soon as I could afford it, I pitched my own summer tabernacle there. Who that knew the neighbourhood at the time of which I am speaking will ever forget it?

In those days Frances, Countess of Waldegrave, afterwards Lady Carlingford, reigned supreme at Strawberry Hill. What a beautiful house, and what lovely surrounding country! What gardens, and what a perfect boat-house in the meadow across the way—not "with roses at the door," but covered all over with clusters of them! Who among the many that enjoyed it will ever forget the hospitality of the Grange, the charming country residence of Mr. and Mrs. Edward Lawson, where every Sunday were gathered together the élite of journalism, literature, and the law, and all that was clever, witty, and bright.

Consider what all this was to one who had spent the whole week grinding away in the filthy atmosphere of the closest of law courts! The reader can imagine what were my feelings when, rushing off to Waterloo just in time to catch the train, I proceeded to our cottage at Bushey, a little dwelling just facing the Teddington gates of the Park, and overlooking those glorious avenues of chestnuts which are so lovely at the end of May, but which, alas, flourish for so short a time.

How glorious it was to hurry into one's flannels, bolt up the village, and get old father Kemp, or his son William, or Joe Baldwin to take one out after the barbel for an hour before dark; or, if too late for this sport, to hasten up to Messenger's, jump into one's boat, scull up to the weir, and either lie to in the expiring rays of the sun, or go on shore nd ask the genial master of Weir Bank for a cooling drink!

But alas! all this has passed away, never to return.

I, too, have wandered far from my theme. I crave pardon, and can only plead as my excuse that memory was a little too mi ch for me.

My pen carried me astray while I was describing the place where the summer vacation was passed by my friend, whom I have instanced as a typical member of the Stock Exchange in those days. It was at Teddington, I think, that he took his last furnished house. He afterwards became more attached to his London home, and contented himself with taking rooms up the river for his boys, to whom he would pay brief visits from time to time. As he once said to me: "My halcyon days are gone."

My friend has now been dead some years. He is to this day spoken of with respect and affection by persons of all grades with whom he came in contact. He died very fairly off, but no millionaire. How could it have been otherwise? As I have said, he never gambled, but was always content with his legitimate commission.

At the time of his decease, the proprietors of the private bank with which his firm had business dealings hinted at a desire to make fresh arrangements with reference to their brokers. They had an interview with the remaining member of the firm, and the matter was discussed. Some of these bankers were related to certain members of the aristocracy who had lately set up in business on the Stock Exchange, and at the interview the former agreed to leave their custom in the old channel on condition that their noble kinsmen were taken into the broking firm as partners. The arrangement was ultimately agreed to, and with the new blood was inaugurated the new system.

In days gone by, there was practically only one person to live on the profits of the firm, and I have shown that his income was not a particularly large one. Now there are several partners, each of whom keeps up a much larger establishment than my deceased friend was able to do. The head of the firm—a somewhat extravagant fellow, but with many of his father's good qualities—spends, I should say, not far short of fifty thousand pounds a year.

I think, then, I have proved that a great deal of the business of the Stock Exchange is very different now to what it was in my young days.

CHAPTER V

HUCKSTERING HYMEN

Where are marriages made?—Some typical announcements—Their history —Ralph Dobbs—Goes to America—Marries—Retires from business—But dies suddenly—His will—His widow and daughter come to London—The "American heiress" the centre of attraction—She meets the Marquis of Merrivale—Accepts him—Remonstrances unavailing—A clear understanding—The wedding—Separate existences.

"MARRIAGES are made in heaven." Are they really? I wonder who can really believe this saying. It is intended to apply, I believe, to men and women of all grades of society even to those poor lads and girls of the labouring classes who enter the bonds of wedlock at the age of seventeen or eighteen, without a penny in the world, with scarcely a rag to their backs, and with a prospect of nothing better than casual employment.

But it is not with the poor and ignorant that I am about to deal. I propose to direct attention to the matrimonial ways and customs of those whose lives are spent amid the glare and tinsel of what is termed London society.

The marriages that will come under my notice are of the kind that are announced in *The Morning Post*, and the fashionable weekly papers. In reference to one of them this paragraph appeared:

"A marriage has been arranged, and will shortly take place, between the Marquis of Merrivale, of The Dene, Milford, and Glenginrock, Inverness-shire, and Madeline, only daughter of the late Ralph Dobbs, Esq., of San Francisco."

Again, to quote from a well-known "weekly":

"One of the smartest weddings of the season, and one of which there has been much talk since its announcement, is fixed to take place at St. Peter's, Eaton Square, on July the thirteenth. We allude to that of Silas Davis, Esq., of Melbourne, Australia, and the Hon. Louisa Verrinder, second daughter of the Earl of Thanet. The wealth of the lucky bridegroom is supposed to be beyond that of any millionaire in this country. The wedding presents already received are truly magnificent. There can be no doubt that the bride will be one of the loveliest débutantes of the year."

Run your eye down the page and you will find the following item :

"We have heard on undoubted authority that Viscount Millirgton is about to marry a celebrated skirt-dancer of the Limelight Theatre, who has, for months past, been drawing all the *jeunesse dorée* of the metropolis to that place of entertainment."

Now, what I propose to do is to see under what circumstances these marriages were contracted, and thereby to give some clue to where they were "made" in the sense in which the word is quoted above.

I will deal with these marriages in the order in which I have mentioned them.

When the great news of the gold finds first reached this country, at a time when the now enormous city of "Frisco" consisted of a few straggling shanties, among the first to set out from these shores, bent on making his fortune or perishing in the attempt, was a young man named Ralph Dobbs.

Ralph did not care to follow in the footsteps of his father, who was a shopkeeper at Eton, being averse to what he regarded as a life of drudgery; so, scraping together what money he could—and it was barely enough to pay his passage out—he set off with a light heart to the American gold-fields.

Like most persons in those days, Ralph Dobbs had only heard of the pleasant side of "digging," and he had not anticipated the sufferings and hardships that lay before him. Being a bold, determined fellow, however, he succeeded in pushing his way. Indeed, almost from the moment of his arrival, things went well with him. He was concerned in several lucky "finds"; he became a partner in some prosperous claims; and in the course of time, as the city grew and the country developed, if a stranger asked, "Who built that street?" or "Who owns that store?" the answer was very likely to be "Ralph Dobbs." It is no exaggeration to say that a large portion of the township belonged to him.

When he left England, Ralph possessed no more education than falls to the lot of the ordinary "Brocas cad." Naturally in his new life he found few or no opportunities for mental culture, and thus it came about that he grew up uncouth in manner and in speech, a rough though honourable man.

Shortly after his arrival in America he married the youngest daughter of a small storekeeper, and they had one child, a girl, Madeline by name. From the moment their wealth began to accumulate, the sole thought of both husband and wife was the future of their offspring. They spared no expense on her education, and even imported foreign masters to assist in her training.

In due time Ralph resolved to retire from business and pass the autumn of his life in his native country, and he was never tired of discussing and forecasting with his wife the impression their daughter would make in Europe.

"The girl will not be far behind in looks," he was wont to say, "and as far as fortune is concerned I'll bet my bottom dollar there ain't one'll come within a hundred mile of her."

It took him some years to realise, capitalise, and arrange for the future disposal of his wealth; but a length everything was satisfactorily settled, and the date was fixed for the migration of the whole family to England.

But *l'homme propose et Dieu dispose.* A week before the vessel sailed a clerk found Ralph Dobbs, in his private room at his head office, seated at the table, his head bent over a map of Europe—cold and dead.

All the necessary business arrangements having been made, it was but natural that, at the end of their period of mourning, mother and daughter carried out the project that had been matured, and came over to settle in England.

There were many exaggerated rumours as to the wealth Ralph Dobbs had left behind him, but the simple fact was that it amounted to between five and six millions sterling. The life interest of two millions he bequeathed to his wife; the residue went *en bloc* to his daughter, together with the reversion of her mother's legacy. In the English Press appeared many paragraphs anent Mrs. and Miss Dobbs and their pile of dollars. I quote the following from a leading London fashionable journal:

"Arrangements have been made for the purchase of No. ―, one of the most commodious mansions in Carlton House

Terrace, by Messrs. Fuller and Company, acting as agents for Maria, widow of the late Ralph Dobbs, Esq., who is shortly expected to arrive from San Francisco. Her wealth and that of her daughter, who accompanies her, is reported to be almost fabulous, and rumours of the young lady's beauty and accomplishments have already reached this country."

In due course report became reality. The mansion in Carlton House Terrace, with its superb appointments, was the talk of the whole fashionable world, the doors of all the salons of the great were thrown open to the new-comers, and the balls and receptions they gave in return—under the fostering care of a Duchess or two, and occasionally graced by the presence of a Royal personage—excelled in magnificence, and the evidence of lavish expenditure, everything of the kind that had before been attempted within the area of London society. At the coaching meets, in the Park, on the river, at Ascot, and at all other gatherings of the smart sets, Madeline Dobbs was the centre of attraction, and one of the foremost objects of speculative talk.

The "American heiress," as she was called, was not only extremely pretty but also very clever, inheriting in no small measure her father's shrewdness.

Madeline had come to England with a purpose, and that purpose was to make an advantageous and a happy marriage. Though she had loved her father very dearly, she had been anything but blind to the roughness and coarseness of his manners; and though devotedly attached to her mother, she entertained a very lively abhorrence of that lady's many American mannerisms and gaucheries. No one felt more keenly than she the shrugs of aristocratic shoulders, and the smiles that were exchanged, at certain phrases and exclamations that fell from time to time from her mother's lips. I do not say that this young girl was endowed with any preternatural sensitiveness; any one in her place would have felt the same. The high education she had received, grafted as it was on a good stock, made her a different kind of being from, and in a sense raised her above, her progenitors.

Balls were given, parties were arranged, and all the toils and snares of scheming mothers with marriageable sons were spread before her. She refused offer after offer.

Living under such conditions and amid such surroundings, of the hollow nature of which she was well aware, the girl's better nature gradually hardened. She entered upon her second London season without having met one single individual, male or female, from among the hundreds with whom she mingled, who appeared to be real and genuine.

Having her eyes open to the shams of society, tortured by the thinly-disguised sneers that were directed to her mother, and haunted with thoughts of the treatment that her father, had he been alive, would have received, a marvellous change came over Madeline. She relinquished all thoughts of marrying for affection; became filled with a desire to attain some commanding position from which she could take her revenge on the world; and, in a word, deliberately resolved to make a deal in the matrimonial market in which she had already seen so much huckstering.

She was introduced to, and sedulously cultivated the acquaintance of, the Marquis of Merrivale, one of the leaders of fashion, and in many respects an Admirable Crichton, being handsome and clever, and having that about him which made him *nulli secundus* in the estimation of the reigning beauties. He had inherited and dissipated a considerable fortune, and at fifty—his age at the time of which I am speaking—he had seen more of the world than most men who have come to the end of life's allotted span.

In the case of the American heiress, he came, he saw, and, to all appearances, he conquered.

I implied just now that Miss Dobbs had failed to make one real friend; but this was not quite true. She undoubtedly had one friend in W., a member of my own profession, and an intimate friend of my own. From him it was (let me add in parenthesis) that I learnt the more private details that I am recording in these pages. W. was a rising man, of good birth, and a favourite in society. He had made the young American's acquaintance soon after her arrival in this country, and, without the slightest intention of competing for the prize that was creating so great a stir in the matrimonial market, he learnt to entertain a very genuine regard for her, and was frankly accepted on the footing of a friend. More particularly was he impressed by her stately and reserved bearing, and her clear insight into the character and motives of those who worshipped at her shrine. I remember his one day remarking to me:

"You see, she's so quiet and collected; so still, so unlike her fellow-countrywomen—indeed, so totally different to anything that has come to us from across the Atlantic before."

The Marquis duly proposed, and was accepted. Naturally the news was not many hours old before it became public property. One of the first to hear it was my friend, than whom no one was better acquainted with Lord Merrivale and his reputation.

The moment W. was able to escape from the Temple, he jumped into a hansom and drove to the house in Carlton House Terrace, where he was always a welcome guest.

On reaching the middle of Pall Mall, my impetuous friend began to wonder what right he had to interfere, and what on earth he should say upon his arrival. The cab drew up outside the house before he had come to any conclusion on these points.

Miss Madeline was at home and alone. On entering, he took her by the hand and said:

"So glad you are in. Am I right in offering you my congratulations?"

"If you mean," she replied, "on my marriage with Lord Merrivale—yes. It takes place next month."

"But," he stammered, "I really—I don't know what excuse I have—but——"

She stopped him at once, gently placing her hand upon his arm.

"None is needed," she said. "You and I have always been good friends, and I know what you were going to say. I appreciate the kindness of your coming here, but you can tell me nothing that I do not know already. My mind is made up; nothing can change it." Then, glancing somewhat hurriedly at the clock, she added: "You see, I am very busy now, and must hurry you away. But, remember, the future Marchioness expects you at her wedding."

And so the interview ended.

There was the usual gush in the society papers about the devotion of the intending bridegroom, about the affection of his fiancée, and about their never being seen apart. Rather more to the point were the paragraphs stating how the estates and magnificent properties, that had been lost to his lordship's old and noble lineage, were to be bought back with the wealth of his bride.

As a matter of fact the interviews between the engaged couple were very few. At one of them, when Lord Merrivale was making some conventional remarks about his affection and future devotion, Madeline brought matters to a climax.

"My lord," said she, "we both are used to the ways of the world, and, if I mistake not, understand them thoroughly. You have been good enough to offer me your hand; it is useless for either of us to talk of heart. It suited my purpose to accept that offer. Why did you make it? Did you want to marry me for my own sake? No. Had I been a girl fresh from the wilds of America with nothing but myself, would you have made that offer? Had I arrived here with my simple-hearted mother and without a fortune, would you, or rather, would your aristocracy, have thrown open your doors to welcome us? Would you have fêted us, and sought after us, while in your heart of hearts you despised us both? No. I will act more generously by you than you have done by us. It is not too late. If you wish to retract your offer, you are at liberty to do so. You refuse? Be it so. But remember, the bargain is —my fortune, your rank. You are an English Marquis, and on our marriage I shall take my position as your wife, as all those who have covertly sneered at their country's guests shall know."

The future bridegroom, who desired nothing more, accepted this position at once.

The wedding took place on the appointed day, and it was the occasion for more gush in the society papers. Glowing paragraphs testified to the beauty of the bride, the enormous fortune that had accrued to the bridegroom, and the extreme felicity of the pair. They passed their honeymoon at Holveston Hall, the seat of the Duke of ——, a brother-in-law of the noble bridegroom. On returning to London they took their places among the leaders of the fashionable world.

Their lives were, and still are, as separate as though they were mere acquaintances. Her ladyship passes a great deal of her time in Paris and other Continental cities. The Marquis frequently stays at his country seat, which has been considerably enlarged, and is now one of the finest places this country can boast. His wife is very seldom seen there. She has often been heard to say that English scenery, though very beautiful, has little charm for her. When his lordship is not at his seat or in London, he is away fishing in Norway, or hunting big game in still more distant climes.

When the gaieties of the season are in full swing, the Marquis and Marchioness are usually for a short time in Carlton House Terrace. The entertainments there are still superb, and the society most exclusive. Occasionally they are to be seen together in their box at the opera. With such exceptions their existence is quite apart, and not one single word of affection has ever passed between them.

Some of my readers may remark: "Can this be true? It is impossible such a state of things can exist!" It is, alas, only too true. Each of the three cases I have selected as illustrating the morale of a large section of modern marriages is founded upon solid fact. Each has its parallel in real life.

Then it may be said: "But all this is something quite new. Such a state of things did not exist in our forefathers' time. The world has changed very much for the worse, and there must be something extremely rotten in the present condition of fashionable society. Can you point to the cause of the evil?"

I may mention that I propose to state my views on this point in the concluding portion of my next chapter. Meanwhile, *revenons à nos mariages*.

CHAPTER VI

HUCKSTERING HYMEN—*continued*

wedding at St. Peter's, Eaton Square—Silas Davis—The Earl of Thanet—Lord L'Estrange—A love match—Ruin—The match at an end—Coercion—The marriage arranged—Where was it made?—The Limelight Theatre—The "Johnnies"—Intellectual effusions—Miss Scarborough—A great hit—Fifty pounds a week—She draws the line—Viscount Millington—Engaged—Parents stop supplies—Marriage takes place—Parents still obdurate—"Lady Millington" returns to the stage—Society touts—Huckstering.

It is a glorious summer morning, the date the thirteenth of July. The roadway in the immediate neighbourhood of St. Peter's, Eaton Square, is thronged with carriages, and the very smartest wedding of the season is about to take place.

The happy bridegroom is Silas Davis, Esq., late of Melbourne, Australia, now of Churtston House, Mayfair; the bride, the Hon. Louisa Verrinder, second daughter of the Earl of Thanet.

Every seat in the church is occupied. The Bishop of ——, who is to perform the ceremony, is attended by the Rector of Acol, the Earl's country seat, as well as several fashionable West End clergymen.

The bridegroom has already put in an appearance, accompanied by his best man, an acquaintance he has made at his club during his short sojourn in this country. There is not a single representative of his own family among the throng of spectators.

Silas Davis is a tall, rather engaging-looking man, with sandy hair already turning to grey. He is sixty years of age and slightly inclined to stoop. Though he struggles hard to appear at ease, it is clear that he is very hot and uncomfortable.

The important moment arrives at last. There is a sound of wheels outside, followed by some little stir in the lobby, and then the bride enters the church leaning on her father's arm. As they pass up the aisle they present a striking appearance.

The Earl in his youth was accounted one of the handsomest men of his day, and even now he is of fine carriage, commanding presence, and pleasing countenance. He wears an old-fashioned blue tailed coat—exquisitely cut, and ornamented with brass buttons—a white, double-breasted waistcoat, and a scarf very full, and quite after the old school. In a word, he is a good specimen of the *grand seigneur*.

The lovely bride, as she walks up the aisle, seems to cling somewhat despairingly to her companion's arm. Only a close observer would detect the slight quivering shudder that passes through her frame as she approaches her mother, the Countess, who occupies a front seat opposite the chancel, and is surrounded by her noble relatives.

The set expression on the young girl's face renders her even more beautiful than usual. She is radiant in gems, which are the finest the bridegroom's wealth could procure. Her lustrous black eyes look out from a face that is deadly pale.

She walks up to the altar with a firm step, and, throughout the service, utters the responses in an audible and unquavering voice.

So far as the ceremony is concerned, it does not take long to make these two persons one. After an adjournment to the vestry for the signing of the register, there comes the departure from the church, followed by the usual breakfast and rice-throwing. Then these two beings, who are as much made to be mated as the lion and the lamb, leave town as man and wife, whom God has joined together and whom no man shall put asunder.

Under what circumstances has this union taken place? Let us see.

The bride's father, the Earl of Thanet, is not rich and never has been. His wife brought him but a small dowry. They are the parents of seven girls and three boys. The eldest daughter has already entered into the bonds of wedlock under circumstances much to her worldly advantage. Her mother discovered a *bon parti*, and arranged matters with her usual diplomacy. Nor did the Countess have any difficulty in that case. Her eldest daughter was as prepared to obey her in the choice of a husband as in the selection of a frock,

In the case of the second daughter things had been very different. The Countess had had a very uphill battle indeed, and had her will been one whit less indomitable than it was she must inevitably have suffered defeat.

Louisa had passed the greater portion of her early youth at their country seat. She was her brothers' favourite sister, and joined in all their sports, being never so happy as when they were home for the holidays.

The Earl's nearest neighbour at Acol was Lord L'Estrange, the head of the firm of Messrs. Lombard and Throgmorton, the great financiers. He had received his peerage in consideration of his wealth and influential position.

For many years it had been quite an understood thing that the Hon. Allan Lombard and the Hon. Louisa Verrinder should, when their ages would permit, become man and wife. As lad and girl they had fallen in love, and the prospective match was one that gave complete satisfaction to both families. Allan, I may add, was a schoolfellow and intimate friend of the Earl's sons.

Time went on, Louisa was presented at Court, and it was arranged that the marriage should take place at the end of the season. Then the unforeseen occurred. The great firm of financiers failed, and Lord L'Estrange and his family were ruined.

Of course, as is usual in such cases—I mean in society, where hearts count for so little—matrimony was held to be out of the question. The Earl's family announced that the match was at an end.

The poor girl appealed to her father and pleaded with her mother, but all to no purpose. The answer she received from the Countess was:

"Allan Lombard is a gentleman and a man of honour. He has released you from the engagement, and has wisely made up his mind to go abroad and seek his fortunes in a foreign land."

This was true enough, but the Countess did not mention the arguments she had employed to make the young man come to this conclusion. She had insisted that he would be doing her daughter the greatest injury if he persisted in his suit. There had been, on his part, a long struggle between love and a sense of duty; and at length the appeals to his honour carried the day, and he had made what he knew to be the greatest sacrifice of his life.

Allan stipulated for one thing—a final interview with the girl he so dearly loved. It took place, and resulted in her assurance, based on the roseate hopes always found under such circumstances, that she would patiently await the time when, as a rich man, he should return to this country to claim her as his wife.

The Countess of Thanet belonged to a set of match-making mothers, and, as I have already indicated, was no novice in the art.

At first her ladyship played a waiting game. She did not force her daughter into society, but allowed her to lead a quiet, humdrum life in the country.

At the opening of the season in the following year, when the family returned to London, the Countess altered her tactics. She insisted upon her daughter going once more into the gay world, stating that the interests of her sisters made it necessary for her to do so. So, night after night, the poor girl was dragged off to parties, balls, and receptions, and night after night, on her return home, she would throw herself on her bed, without removing her finery, and sob herself to sleep; or, inspired by some faint spark of hope, she would seek her mother's boudoir and on her knees beg to be released from so terrible a life. The Countess would reply:

"You know our position. Your sisters have to be considered, and it is absolutely necessary for all of us that you should marry and marry well."

When the unhappy girl appealed to her father, he invariably replied:

"My dear, it is useless your speaking to me. These are your mother's affairs."

It was while things were in this condition that Silas Davis made his appearance in England. His enormous wealth became at once a matter of notoriety, and, in spite of his age, he could have made his selection of a wife from among the noblest and most handsome in the land.

Needless to say, Silas Davis did not escape the eagle eye of the Countess of Thanet. She sedulously pursued him throughout the London season, and, when it came to an end, on reading in *The Morning Post* of his arrival in Homburg, she at once set out for that place in company with her daughter Louisa.

I have no space to dwell upon the wiles that were resorted to, the arguments that were brought to bear, and the near approach to actual force that was used, to bring the poor girl to consent to the marriage. It took place, as I have shown, in St. Peter's, Eaton Square, on a bright July morning.

How is such a union likely to end? Was the marriage made in heaven, or—elsewhere?

These are questions I can leave my readers to answer for themselves.

There is no more popular place of amusement in all London than the Limelight Theatre. It is the favourite haunt of the "Johnnies" and "dear chappies"—those singular specimens of the rising generation of England. They are always to be seen there—in summer and in winter, at evening performances and at morning performances—even though the bill remains unchanged for months at a stretch. The front row of the stalls is almost sacred to them. If you drop in from time to time you will always see the same young gentlemen, in the same seats, with the same smiles on their faces, and wearing the same Malmaison carnations in their buttonholes. They seem to live in those stalls.

I don't know, but I suppose some of these young gentlemen have business to attend to. They certainly don't look like it. If they have, I should be very sorry to trust them with any of mine.

The "Johnnies" are on intimate terms with the principal artists. They like nothing but burlesque, and the chief performers, male and female, are their idols. The prima donna calls them "my boys," and they in return rapturously applaud everything that falls from her lips, and never tire of showering floral offerings at her feet. But this is not surprising, for in nine cases out of ten the prima donna is extremely clever, and quite worthy of the enthusiasm she excites.

What strikes me as most extraordinary is the power of the risible faculties of these gentlemen. No matter what their favourite comedian says or does, be the words or the act never so vapid, they simply roar with laughter, twist and wriggle about like eels, and almost drop out of their stalls in fits. Well, he may be very amusing to them, but what about the general public? The fun, if fun it be, usually has reference to some sporting or fighting club, to which these young gentlemen belong, as does possibly the comedian himself.

The songs, which are often not without merit, send the "chappies" frantic with delight. They never tire of hearing

"How I did it on the sly," "Please don't tell my ma," "Pull your socks up, William," and intellectual effusions of that order.

It is sometimes said that in these democratic days class distinctions have vanished. Certainly the remark is true so far as the music-hall performers and their patrons are concerned. The lion comique is "Johnny's" intimate friend. They go to one another's rooms, they play billiards together, they drink together, and, in fact, they seem unable to live apart.

It happened in the autumn of last year that business at the Limelight Theatre became very slack. The enterprising manager went about with his eyes wide open, anxiously in search of some novelty. One day, happening to enter an East End music-hall, he made a very lucky find in the person of a young, pretty, graceful, agile danseuse, with extraordinary kicking powers and any amount of "go."

Being a friend of the proprietor, the Limelight manager went behind the scenes, and had a conversation with the young lady. It was arranged that she should call and see him on the following morning, and the result of the interview was that the danseuse accepted an engagement at the Limelight.

A new burlesque was announced to appear in a week or two, and a special line on the bill was given to Miss Scarborough, "the celebrated skirt dancer."

The first night arrived. Every seat in the stalls was occupied, and some of the "Johnnies" had to be relegated to the orchestra. From the very first the burlesque took well, but the climax of success came with the appearance of the débutante. Miss Scarborough made a great hit. Not for years had there been such applause at the Limelight. Jaded youths leapt from their seats and clapped their hands with zeal, and it is to be feared that, in the enthusiasm of the moment, some of them creased their collars.

"What a jolly pretty girl!" "Light as a fairy!" "Sweet little hands and feet!" Yes; Miss Scarborough had indeed "caught on."

In a few weeks the young lady demanded fifty pounds a week, and received it. At the East End music-hall two pounds a week had been her maximum salary.

Miss Scarborough did not lose her head; she was no fool. Night after night and day after day she was besieged by a host of young gentlemen who professed themselves her slaves. All this was very different from the time when she had for her lover a young Jew, the son of an East End pawnbroker in rather a small way of business. Miss Scarborough soon became very fastidious, and learnt to discriminate between a dandy who only gave her silver bracelets and one who went the length of a diamond brooch. Her ambition developed with extraordinary rapidity, and it was not long before she resolved to play the matrimonial card.

One young Earl, not remarkable for the lucidity of his intellect, and who was already married, gave her jewels to the value of several thousand pounds. She accepted them, and treated him with some little condescension. She allowed him to give her dinners at Richmond, suppers at the Café Royal, and so on; but there she drew the line.

Miss Scarborough received offer after offer, in some cases from men whose fathers were wealthy and titled. But they were not good enough for my lady. "I shan't be content," she was wont to say to her intimate friends (the other young ladies of the theatre), "until I'm a Countess."

One day young Viscount Millington, after dining at his club, dropped in at the Limelight Theatre with a few friends. He was at once completely captivated by the young dancer.

Certain habitués of the theatre are permitted to go behind the scenes with their friends, and among these privileged few was one of his lordship's companions. The proposition was made that they should all "go round and see her," and it was at once agreed to.

Miss Scarborough and Lord Millington supped together that night, and three weeks afterwards they were engaged to be married.

Viscount Millington is the eldest son and heir of the Earl of Claremont. He had no independent means, but had been in receipt of a most liberal allowance from his father.

When the bomb burst and the engagement was publicly announced, the Earl was furious, and the Countess in despair. They positively refused to have anything more to do with their son, and at once stopped his supplies. This was exceedingly awkward, for Lord Millington had, during the three weeks he had known Miss Scarborough, lavished the whole of his income upon her, and he was now practically penniless. However, the young couple decided that when they were married, and it was too late for any further opposition to be raised, the Earl and Countess would relent and come to their assistance financially. In this expectation, however, they were woefully mistaken. The worthy peer was made of sterner stuff than his son had supposed, and a deaf ear was turned to all overtures for a reconciliation.

What was to be done? Of course the bride had her jewellery, which would have realised sufficient money to keep them afloat for some time; but young ladies of her class are not in the habit of making such sacrifices.

Upon her marriage, Miss Scarborough had severed her connection with the stage; but, as soon as financial matters reached a crisis, she resolved to return to her profession. Nor did she experience the slightest difficulty in doing so. Theatrical managers vied with one another in their efforts to secure the prize. Was she not "My lady," and could she not be announced as "Lady Millington, the future Countess of Claremont"?

She was engaged at one of our principal theatres, and there she is still playing. Her august husband either hangs about the theatre during the performances or awaits his wife's pleasure at the stage door.

Again I ask—where was this marriage made and how is it likely to end? and again I leave the reader to solve the matter for himself.

In my last chapter I stated that I should attempt to give some explanation of the evils illustrated by the three marriages I have described.

One question will be uppermost in the minds of many of my readers. It is this: "How did the lady from San Francisco and the gentleman from Australia gain their entry into London society?" Their welcome, of course, was to be traced to their wealth. "Yes," it may be said, "but how was their actual introduction brought about? On their arrival in this country they knew nobody."

Perhaps my readers have never heard of society touts? These are needy individuals who have elbowed their way into society—in many cases through the possession of what is termed "blue blood"—and who, for a consideration, are ready to assist others to do the same. Most society touts are men, but a good many women pursue the calling.

When the wife of a *nouveau riche* desires to entertain, with a view to gaining a footing in the fashionable world, she sends for one of the fraternity, and places herself entirely in his or her hands. This individual has a book in which are inscribed the

M

names of all the noble and fashionable people who are likely to accept an invitation. It seems, indeed, that there are a number of persons ready to go to any good address, even though the occupier of the establishment be an entire stranger to them. Host and hostess count for nothing; the point is—will the cuisine and the wine be good?

Supposing Mrs. A., the wife of the millionaire, gives an entertainment, the tout not only provides a number of aristocratic guests, but also manages to slip in other Mrs. A's, and their families, thereby serving several clients at one and the same time.

Thus it happens in the case of hundreds of parties given in the West End during the season, that the hostess who stands at the head of the stairs is a complete stranger to every one of the guests she welcomes so cordially. If a lady is the medium through which the guests are invited, it is not an unusual thing for her to stand beside the hostess and assist in doing the honours of the house.

Can one expect a healthy outcome from such a system of imposture?

I do not for one moment mean to suggest that huckstering in the matrimonial market is peculiar to this age. What I do say, however, is that never before has the evil assumed the dimensions to which it has attained in the present day, and never before has it been fostered by means so degraded.

Of course, in the case of the third marriage I have described, one must look elsewhere for the explanation of the evil. The fact is, many young men of the present day take no interest in the social gatherings of their own class. They are consequently driven to the music-halls, and other places of amusement, and are there as often as not caught in the toils of attractive, cunning, and ambitious women.

Perhaps, if there were less hollowness and humbug about society functions, and a freer play for good, honest human nature, young men would not be so prone to seek the society of their social inferiors.

CHAPTER VII

THE PROMOTER

The company promoter—The gullible British public—Leopold Stiff—His office—I visit him there—He is "so busy"—A remarkable sight—An invitation to dinner—Mixed company—Excellent entertainment—The Gull Gold Mine, Limited—Wound up—Stiff arrested—Committed for trial—The Old Bailey—A great crowd—The trial—Sentence—From the West End to Millbank.

THERE is no more remarkable being in the city of London, with its many curious trades and vocations, than the company promoter. He has existed there, and flourished like a green bay-tree, for many years past. Though everybody knows him, either personally or by reputation, there is in all quarters much uncertainty as to his origin and antecedents.

The successful company promoters are enormously wealthy, they have palaces at Kensington or mansions in Grosvenor Square, besides charming places in the country, and they are usually aspirants—and, it may be, not unsuccessful aspirants—for Parliamentary honours. They are, as a rule, Conservatives in politics, and have a large circle of titled acquaintances—impecunious lords, baronets, generals, admirals, and the like. The latter, who are termed "guinea pigs," figure as directors of the companies launched by their City friends.

The promoters drive to their business in well-appointed broughams, drawn by high-stepping horses. They are remarkably particular in their dress, and wear a good deal of jewellery, their massive rings being particularly conspicuous. Altogether their appearance, both in the City and in the West End, is calculated to impress the casual observer.

Quick at figures, cool-headed, and gifted with a retentive memory, the company promoter is an excellent business man. There is a good deal of variety in his work. He transforms all manner of going concerns from private enterprises into share investments for the public. One day it is soap; the next, candles; then an hotel or a theatre, and so on. He also finds capital for, and works—by syndicate, or as a company —mines, valuable and valueless. His ability in placing an undertaking before the public in an alluring form is marvellous. What prophetic visions of wealth for those who are wise enough to subscribe! What dividends await the investor—if he will only walk into the parlour! How eagerly the public rushes to secure shares in the Brobdingnagian Diamond Mine, the South African Auriferous Dust Company, and the Borneo Sea Salt Company!

There is no one so gullible as an ordinary member of the British public. He will invest his last penny in an undertaking of which he knows absolutely nothing, although if he reads his newspaper, he must be perfectly well aware that kindred enterprises have, times without number, been exposed as out-and-out swindles. This starting of bogus companies is very like the confidence trick, the ring dropping, and the painted sparrow.

Of course, the "fat," as it is termed, goes in a great measure to the promoter, and between him and the poor investor there are usually several individuals with their mouths very wide open.

Many a company promoter, when he has amassed considerable riches, retires from business, and, as one of the moneyocracy, gives sumptuous dinners and splendid receptions, and, by these and other means, gradually elbows his way into fashionable society. With some of these individuals, however, things take a very different turn, as the history I am about to relate will show.

At the time when I was reading for the Bar, and eating my dinners at the hospitable board of the Inner Temple, no man was better known as a financier and company promoter than Leopold Stiff. Scarcely a new venture was launched but he manipulated the ropes. He had a finger in every pie.

Mr. Stiff's office, which was not a hundred miles from the Old Jewry, was more like an enormous bank than a private establishment. The bustle and commotion that went on there were astonishing. All day long people passed in and out, upstairs and downstairs, dozens of clerks hurried hither and thither, doors slammed, bells rang, and everywhere were noise and movement.

The premises themselves were built in the most costly style, and were an ornament to the thoroughfare. Several broughams and hansom cabs were usually to be seen waiting in the roadway outside.

On entering the building the visitor passed up a broad marble staircase, and his progress was likely to be impeded by the number of persons ascending and descending. In the throng were noblemen, officers in the Army, clergymen, fashionably-attired ladies, mothers and wives of the middle class, and, in fact, all sorts and conditions of men and women.

At the head of the stairs stood a page in livery, who was available for taking the visitor's card into Mr. Stiff's private office.

On the ground-floor were any number of little rooms, each of which contained a chair, a writing-table, and a sofa or small settee. Anybody who wished to have an interview with Mr. Stiff was shown into one of these apartments, where he had to wait until the great man was able to come to him.

One day I paid him a visit, to enquire as to the value of certain securities. He saw me in one of the rooms I have described, and I must confess that his manner was the perfection of politeness and affability.

He explained that he was so busy he scarcely had time to breathe, but that he would make a note of my enquiry, and get his head clerk to write to me on the subject.

"Good-bye," said he, shaking me by the hand. "You must excuse my running away. I have a board meeting going on in room A., and in my large room there are specimens of the gold ore taken from the great Gull Mine, the prospectus of which you may have seen. People from all parts of the country have come up to see it. I wish you had been older, for I would have put you on the directorate. I've put your friend Colonel S. on. He dined with us at home last night."

As we passed out into the corridor a clerk came up and whispered something to him. The next minute he was shaking hands with an elderly gentleman, who was about to be ushered into the little apartment we were leaving.

"I'll be with you in ten minutes," said Mr. Stiff to the new comer; "can't spare a moment now."

He disappeared down the corridor, and the page shut the old gentleman in.

Before leaving the premises I thought I would pay a visit to the large room, being rather curious to inspect the specimens of the Gull Mine ore. Happening to see one of the liveried servants of the establishment I asked him the way thither, and he very graciously volunteered to be my guide.

A remarkable sight met my eyes as I entered the room. It was crowded with men and women of all classes, including country gentlemen, widows, City merchants, and clergymen. Every one was closely inspecting the ore, which lay on tables placed about the apartment, or scrutinising the charts and maps that hung upon the walls.

Standing in the middle of the throng, chatting very affably with those about him, was Mr. Stiff, whom I was surprised to see, as I had fancied he had left me to return to the boardroom. He was admirably dressed for office purposes, wearing a well-cut black velvet jacket and a double-breasted white waistcoat, across which hung a gold and turquoise watchchain. He had a ruddy complexion and iron-grey hair, and I do not think I ever saw a man more calculated to inspire persons with confidence. He looked a philanthropist every inch of him. For my part, however, I confess that I had no consuming desire to take shares in the Gull Mine.

That evening, as I was about to leave the chambers where I was reading, I received a letter answering the enquiry I had made in the morning, and enclosing an invitation to dinner from Mr. and Mrs. Leopold Stiff. I had never been to their house, and as I had a curiosity to go there, I accepted the invitation.

The house, which was situated in a fashionable quarter of London, was magnificently appointed—in fact, a little too magnificently appointed. As you entered, you were literally mobbed by footmen, who were ablaze with yellow and crimson. The drawing-room was hung with exquisite watercolours, which must have cost any amount of money. It called up a smile to my lips to see the host pointing them out to Lady H., one of the reigning beauties, and discoursing to her on Art.

The company was a little mixed. There were one or two

City magnates and their wives pompously marching about the room, the Marquis and Marchioness of A., Lord H. L., whose name, at that time, figured on many boards of directors, and several others *ejusdem generis*.

The dinner was excellent, the wine beyond reproach, and the flowers among the choicest I have ever seen. After dinner there was a concert. It was arranged by Signor P., who was the conductor of the Italian Opera at the time, and among the performers were several of the leading lights of the musical world. In fact, I am bound to say that, could one have only forgotten how the money which procured the entertainment was acquired, it would have been possible to pass a most enjoyable evening.

Years rolled by, and it came about that dark clouds gathered over the London money market. A disastrous drought crippled the finances of a foreign land, two large English houses were reported to be hopelessly involved, a panic spread through the City, and half-a-dozen bubble companies burst in a single day. Several directors were prosecuted, and our friend Leopold Stiff was in an extremely bad way.

It was rumoured that, though apparently ruined, the well-known promoter, having executed some timely settlements, and having, in days gone by, sent large sums of money out of the country, was still a wealthy man. Whether this was so or not I am unable to say. One thing is certain—if he had escaped ruin, a large percentage of those who had placed money in his concerns were less fortunate.

Of all the companies that had gone to grief, the Gull Gold Mine, Limited, proved to be the greatest swindle. Remarkable as it seems, though some pieces of very rich ore were found on the estate before the company was floated, not another solitary speck was discovered there after the capital had been subscribed.

Unfortunate individuals in all parts of the country had placed their savings—in some cases to the extent of the last shilling they could scrape together—in the Gull Mine, and the consequence was that when calls were made, prior to the winding up, thousands of persons of all grades were involved in absolute ruin.

It was rumoured one day in the City that Leopold Stiff had sought an asylum in a foreign land; but this, strangely enough, proved not to be the case. Within forty-eight hours a vigilant press informed the country that a warrant had been issued for his apprehension, and that, it having been duly executed, he had made his appearance before the Alderman at the Mansion House.

It would have been an odd coincidence had the presiding justice been one of those City magnates who were guests at the sumptuous entertainment I have described as having been given some years before at the company promoter's magnificent West End house. This was, I am happy to say, not so; but —which comes to very much the same thing—one of these very individuals, actuated, it may be, by a not unnatural curiosity, was seated throughout the proceedings on the bench beside the Alderman.

The proceedings, as is usual in this Court, were of a quiet and businesslike nature. Sufficient evidence was tendered to enable the accused to be sent for trial, and the very able counsel who represented him asked but a few questions. Leopold Stiff was committed to take his trial at the next sessions of the Central Criminal Court.

Bail was applied for and tendered to a very considerable amount, but refused, and the prisoner was conveyed to Newgate in the prison van. An application was afterwards made to the Court of Queen's Bench for the removal to that—the highest criminal court in the kingdom—of any indictment that might be found against the prisoner at the Old Bailey. This application, as might have been expected, was at once refused. I may remark in passing, that so far as these applications are concerned, things have very much changed since that time. The late Lord Chief Justice Cockburn had the greatest objection to sanction such removals, and only did so on rare occasions and under very exceptional circumstances; but now, provided the defendant be a man of means, the application is seldom refused.

The day for delivering the gaol of Newgate soon arrived, and the date was fixed for the trial of Mr. Leopold Stiff.

This was, of course, a *cause célèbre*, and the rush of persons seeking to obtain admission to the Court was almost unprecedented. The number of witnesses, too, was unusually large.

Has the reader ever visited the Old Bailey while the sessions are on? Possibly not, and he may therefore like me to give some description of the *locus in quo*.

Turning to the left from Ludgate Hill you find yourself in a narrow, unimportant thoroughfare, with less than its fair share of pavement. The roadway is pretty sure to be choked with vans, either lumbering along with Smithfield or some City warehouse as their destination, or hovering about the railway and steamboat goods depôt.

On the right-hand side is the Court-house. What an interesting medley of human beings you find inside the lobby and on the pavement!—weeping women in black shawls, a couple of well-drilled, compassionate policemen, shabby Jews with anxious faces, Bill Sikes and his young woman, a few detectives, and any number of nondescript males consorting in groups and talking in a whisper.

Of course there are a few public-houses hard by. You always find them in the immediate vicinity of criminal courts. During the sessions these places do a roaring trade. Witnesses, prisoners' friends, prosecutors, and solicitors' clerks mingle together in a heterogeneous mass, all eager for drink, a few for food. The public-house immediately opposite the Court-house is always so full as to be scarcely approachable. I wonder how many alibis have been concocted on those premises, how many prosecutions have been, as they term it, "squared," and how much false swearing planned!

Of course, when executions were public the proprietors of these houses, in addition to their ordinary profits, received large sums of money from persons who came from the West End and elsewhere to witness those terrible spectacles. The culprits were hanged early in the morning, and it was no uncommon thing for parties of men and women to proceed to these public-houses overnight, provided with hampers of food and champagne, with which, by way of killing time until the "show" took place, they kept up the most disgraceful orgies throughout the small hours. I was told by the late Mr. Jonas, who for a great many years was governor of the gaol, that the scenes which used to be enacted on those premises were a disgrace to civilisation. Happily executions are no longer public.

There are two entrances to the Old Bailey, one approached from the public thoroughfare, and the other approached from the court-yard of the prison. You reach the latter by passing up some stone steps which are on the right-hand side as you enter through the broad gateway. This entrance is used by the Judges, Aldermen, Sheriffs, and other officers of the Court, by counsel, and, on occasions such as the one to which I am referring, by the few privileged members of the public who have been furnished with tickets of admission. In order to prevent a crush, wooden barriers are erected at the bottom and top of the stone steps, and they were certainly needed on the day of Mr. Leopold Stiff's trial.

On the occasion in question the roadway outside the Old Bailey was blocked with carriages and hansoms, and from half-past nine to ten o'clock in the morning the pavement and lobby were crowded with people, many of them ladies. The moment the doors of the Court were opened every inch of available space was seized upon, and the Sheriff ordered the outer gates of Newgate to be closed.

It was a pouring wet morning, and on a rainy or foggy day I don't think there is a more depressing place in the world than the Old Court of the Old Bailey. There are two doors leading into the Court from the corridor. One is used by the Judges, the Aldermen and Sheriffs, and the few selected visitors, who either take their seats upon the bench or in a contiguous enclosure that looks like a huge private box. The second entrance from the corridor is used by barristers and their clerks, solicitors, and other persons having business in the Court. The centre of the chamber is occupied with seats for the members of the Bar, and below them is the solicitors' bench. Between the Judge and the jury — both of whom command a fine view of the dock—is the witness-box.

Underneath the jury-box sits the usher, an individual who must enjoy very little sleep in a natural way at night, for while the trials are on he is rarely to be seen with his eyes open. Once or twice during the day, however, he rouses himself by a great effort and, in stentorian tones, shouts "Silence!" and this, generally, at a time when everything is so still that you could almost hear a pin drop.

Over the jury-box are three large windows furnished with reflectors, in front of which hang huge lamps for use in foggy weather.

Just over the dock is one of the most interesting places in the Court. I refer to a little gallery that is principally used by the friends of the prisoners. Most of the celebrated murderers of the century, including Lamson, the Stauntons, the Mannings, and Catherine Wilson—to take a few names at haphazard—were tried in this Court. What scenes those walls have witnessed! What terrible agony have I seen suffered there myself! The cries of despair that have issued from that little gallery from time to time when a verdict has been pronounced, or a sentence passed, will never be forgotten by those who heard them.

At length there are the two knocks, and the Judge, the Lord Mayor, and the Sheriffs, preceded by the mace bearer, enter the crowded Court. The prisoner ascends from below into the dock, steps up to the rail, and is called upon by the Clerk of Arraigns to plead to the indictment. "Not guilty," he replies in a firm voice.

Leopold Stiff has very little changed in appearance. His hair has grown a shade or two greyer, that is all. The same scrupulous care is observable in his dress, and the same smile plays upon his face.

The *dramatis personæ* in this most interesting act in a remarkable drama have a peculiar interest for me. At the back of the Court I catch sight of two ladies who were among the guests at the dinner-party I attended at Mr. and Mrs. Stiff's house several years before, and there, ready to ascend the witness-box, is one of the very clergymen whom I had seen handling the gold ore of the Gull Mine.

Very distinguished counsel appeared for the prisoner, but the result of the trial, which occupied the whole day, was a foregone conclusion. Mr. Leopold Stiff was found guilty, and sentenced to five years' penal servitude.

From a West End mansion to Millbank is truly a curious transition!

CHAPTER VIII

THINGS THEATRICAL

The old Adelphi—The Lyceum—Why is extravaganza dead?—Dramatic authors—Henry Byron—Frank Burnand—The Princess's—Mr. and Mrs. Kean—Alfred Wigan—The Haymarket—Benjamin Webster—John Baldwin Buckstone — Compton — Edward Sothern — " First nights"—The opera — Operatic singers —Theatrical managers — Is there room for all the theatres?—Theatrical expenditure—Theatres *versus* music halls—Suggested alterations.

EVEN before, as a young man, I myself became connected with the stage, theatres had for me a great attraction. When I came home from Eton for the holidays I was a frequent visitor to the pit of the old Adelphi Theatre. There I have seen casts which, with all the talent of the present day, it would be hard indeed to beat.

Webster, Céleste, Alfred Wigan, Leigh Murray, Mr. and Mrs. Keeley, and Miss Woolgar in one piece! What would the public say to a treat like that in the present day, when actors and acting are far more widely popular than they were at the time of which I am writing?

The pit at the old Adelphi was not the most comfortable place in the world, and if you were unfortunate enough to be relegated to a back seat you could only see the performance at the cost of a cricked neck. I used often to pay this penalty, and I did so without complaining.

How my heart quailed at the melodramatic acting of O. Smith as Grampus in " The Wreck Ashore"; how my sides shook with laughter at the delightful comedy of Wright and Paul Bedford in " The Flowers of the Forest "; how breathlessly I sat watching the superb acting of Benjamin Webster in "The Sea of Ice," and "Janet Pride"; and how deep was my juvenile admiration for Miss Woolgar and other beautiful actresses who appeared on those boards !

I sometimes transferred my affections to the Lyceum, which for some time was under the joint management of the Keeleys and a partner. Subsequently the theatre passed into the hands of Madame Vestris and Charles Mathews. At that time it was the home of burlesque and extravaganza. How I have delighted in "The Fair One with the Golden Locks," "The King of the Peacocks," and "The Golden Branch"! How very witty and elegant were the lines of dear old Planché, who was pre-eminent in this field of dramatic authorship!

Why is extravaganza dead? Why has the same fate befallen burlesque—I mean true burlesque, not mere sketches filled in with gag, and pulled through by skirt-dancing and limelight?

Who, among the playgoers of my early days, will ever forget Jem Bland and such pieces as " Valentine and Orson," and "The Forty Thieves"? Among the authors of distinction at that time were William and Robert Brough, Tom Taylor, Albert Smith, and Charlie Kenny, not to forget Charles Dance, who wrote one or two excellent pieces. But Planché stood head and shoulders above them all. Then came the days of Frank Talfourd, whose fame is particularly associated with the Olympic and Haymarket. What a treat it was to see Robson in "Medea" and Shylock, and Compton in "Pluto and Proserpine"!

Subsequently we had the less classical and, if I may use the expression, more emphasized burlesque of that most popular author, my old friend Henry Byron. Originally his pieces were produced at the Strand, which was then under the management of the beautiful Miss Swanborough. The interpreter of his excellent lines was Marie Wilton, that perennial favourite, whose equal, in my humble opinion, we have never seen. I would travel any distance, or get up in the middle of the night, for the privilege of once more seeing her in the "Maid and the Magpie." This period also gave us the burlesque of " Kenilworth," in which Miss Swanborough herself played, looking simply magnificent. It was written, if I remember rightly, by Andrew Halliday, also an author of no mean repute.

Who ever saw the equal of Jemmy Rogers as an impersonator of female characters? I remember laughing over the Widow Twankey until my sides ached. Among his contemporaries one gratefully recalls Johnny Clarke, Martha Oliver, and Charlotte Saunders.

Of course my old and intimate friend Frank Burnand was the last of this school of authors, and his burlesque of " Black-eyed Susan " undoubtedly entitles him to take a foremost place among the famous men I have mentioned. I suppose his multifarious engagements prevent him giving us another piece of the same sort. I confess that I wish he would do so. It is doubtful whether any other living man is capable of writing a really fine burlesque.

In my youth of course I did not neglect the Princess's. Here as elsewhere I patronised the pit, a part of the house which in the days of Charles Kean was made very comfortable. This was as it should be, for is not the pit the financial backbone of the theatre?

I think I saw Mr. and Mrs. Kean in all their Shakespearian revivals. They were the first to mount the plays with splendid scenery and stage accessories, and, as we know, successive managers have vied with one another in this direction until Mr. Henry Irving—who, I think, besides his foremost position as an actor, is the cleverest theatrical man of business of the age—has, in his recent productions, attained a point of scenic excellence which apparently does not admit of being improved upon.

The Keans were backed up by Walter Lacy, John Ryder, Meadows, Carlotta Leclercq, and the incomparable Miss Kate Terry; but otherwise their companies were not, as a rule, very strong ones.

I remember a rather funny story that was told about Ryder. Charles Kean was very particular about the language and conduct of every one engaged about the theatre, from the principal of the company to the call-boy. One day something seriously annoyed Ryder, and, in a fit of temper, he gave loud utterance to a big, big D. The incident came to the knowledge of Kean, who lost not a moment in carpeting the delinquent and pointing out to him the enormity of his offence. Poor Joe Langford, for so many years a favourite at the Garrick Club, on hearing of the occurrence, wrote some very witty lines, entitled : " The man who said ' damn ' in the green-room."

I was a very great admirer of Mr. Kean; but a still greater admirer of Mrs. Kean. The former I think I liked best in the part of Louis the Eleventh, and, after that, as the twins in "The Corsican Brothers." Alfred Wigan was simply perfect as Chateau Renaud. Though it was my privilege to see Fechter in the principal part on this side of the English Channel, I never saw the piece in Paris, where, however, it could not have been better performed than at the Princess's.

Wigan was one of the most accomplished men I ever met. He was a magnificent fencer and a masterly swordsman. He spoke French with the accent of a Parisian, he was tolerably well acquainted with every other modern language, and he was the most delightful and amusing of companions, being an excellent conversationalist and possessing one of the most pleasant and musical voices I have ever heard.

In those days actors kept to their own artistic set, and were not eager to rush into society. This was true even of Charles Kean—an old Etonian and a most scholarly man—Alfred Wigan, Charles Mathews, and others who would certainly have graced what are termed the most polite circles.

In these reminiscences of my juvenile theatre-going I must not forget to mention the Haymarket, then the home of comedy. That, with Drury Lane, which, until E. T. Smith took it, was rarely open for theatrical purposes, and the St. James's, which, after Braham's time, seemed to be pursued by some demon of ill-luck, pretty well exhausts the list of the principal theatres of that day.

When I first made the acquaintance of the Haymarket the lessee was Benjamin Webster, who was managing the Adelphi at the same time. I, however, knew very little of the Haymarket until it passed into the hands of that prince of low comedians, John Baldwin Buckstone. Besides being a genuine comedian, Buckstone was a first-rate dramatic author, as such dramas as "The Green Bushes," "The Dream at Sea," and several successful farces prove. He was always backed up by a very good company, some of the principal members of which remained with him for years. Among these was Compton, best of Shakespearian clowns and the driest of dry comedians, and others were little Clark, William Farren, and Chippendale. It was at this house that I saw the best piece of acting, in what I believe would be called the juvenile line, that it has been my good fortune to witness. It was that of Miss Blanche Fane as Gertrude in "The Little Treasure," Buckstone playing Captain Walter Maydenblush, a performance once seen never to be forgotten. It was about this time, too, that that excellent comédienne, Miss Reynolds, delighted the Haymarket audiences, which were always the most fashionable in London.

Afterwards came "The Overland Route," one of the best pieces ever put upon the stage. It was produced after Charles Mathews's return from America, whence he brought his second wife. What visitor to the theatre at that time will ever forget Compton, when the ship is on the sands, walking about in despair searching for his lost false teeth? This was as well cast and acted a piece as could be desired.

Then came an entirely new style of entertainment. A stranger from a distant shore, Edward Sothern, introduced us to Lord Dundreary. All London—nay, all England—went mad over it. The box-office was besieged, places were booked months in advance, and the questions asked you on all hands were: "Have you seen Lord Dundreary? Have you heard him tell that story of brother Sam?" The plot itself was of the barest construction, and extremely bad; but as a novelty I confess I am not surprised that the eccentric representation of this remarkable comedian commanded one of the longest runs known on the English stage.

After the withdrawal of "Our American Cousin," Sothern remained on at the Haymarket. Several pieces were tried, notably "David Garrick," but I very much doubt if any of them were genuine successes.

After I married and settled permanently in London, it was my habit, if my health and business pursuits permitted, always to attend "first nights," that is, the inaugural representations of fresh pieces. In this practice I was by no means singular. It is the custom of a great many literary, artistic, and professional people to be present at "first nights." The attendance of the same individuals is so regular that, so far as the stalls and private boxes are concerned, one can count with tolerable certainty upon whom one will see at the theatre. Naturally the audience, which of course includes the critics, is in the nature of a happy family. Everybody knows everybody else, and a buzz of conversation goes on between the acts. Of late years the tendency has been for these gatherings to become more and more fashionable.

In my early days there were not nearly so many critics as there are now. Their numbers have increased with the growth of journalism and the multiplication of theatres. It is not an uncommon thing in the present day for two or three new pieces to be presented at different theatres on the same night.

John Oxenford and afterwards Tom Taylor, represented *The Times*, E. L. Blanchard *The Daily Telegraph*, and Shirley Brooks, Bayle Bernard ("Billy" Bernard, Céleste used to call him), Stirling Coyne, Heraud, Tomlin, and Chorley attended on behalf of various other papers.

In my early days I very seldom went to the opera, but I have had the pleasure of hearing Jenny Lind, Piccolomini, Patti, and Albani. On one occasion, too, if I remember aright, I was privileged to hear Grisi, Mario, Lablache, Tamburini, and Persiani in the same opera. I was at Mario's last appearance on the London stage, which was on July 19th, 1871. It was in Donizetti's opera of "La Favorita." At the beginning he was evidently keeping his voice under, but in the fighting scene he sang as well as he had ever sung in his life. What a voice and what an actor!

In the present day theatres are rearing their heads in every direction, and it is difficult to believe that so many are required. I have known a number of theatrical managers, but I scarcely ever heard of one of them making a fortune. Of course, some have achieved great successes, notably Boucicault (with the "Colleen Bawn" at the Adelphi), Sothern, Chatterton, and Falconer; but, in every case, after the triumph came a series of failures.

The number of theatres already in existence is very large, and at the present moment three or four others are in process of erection. Can it be possible, I ask, that there is room for them all? In the early days of which I have been speaking there were no music halls and theatres of variety; now they are to be found almost all over London. That these establishments are well patronised is proved by the large crowds to be seen standing outside before the doors are opened. A great many people like ballets, and prefer what is termed a "variety show" to an ordinary theatrical performance. Thousands of people flock to the Alhambra and the Empire, and almost within a stone's throw of these places are the Trocadéro, the London Pavilion, and the Tivoli, which are nightly crammed from floor to ceiling.

Make what allowance you will for the increase of population, the greater craving for amusement, and the better times—if

N

indeed they exist—how is it possible to suppose that so many theatres can pay? Pay? Well, they certainly pay those responsible for their construction. You only have to run up a block of buildings in any part of the West End, and call it a theatre, to be able to command an enormous rent. But what about the individuals who pay the rent, engage the artistes, and run the show? Well, of course, those responsible for the control do not themselves find the money. The capital is provided by men of fortune who remain in the background, waiting for profits. But it is to be presumed that the patience of these gentlemen is limited, and that they will some day realise that, as investments, theatres are nowhere in the competition with soap and hotels.

Look at the salaries that are paid nowadays to actors and actresses, and look at the remuneration received by the authors. Poor Albert Smith used to make the remark, for which there was some ground, that the only person connected with a theatre of lower grade than the call-boy was the playwright. In former days an author was glad to receive his fifty pounds an act, and that sum covered country, American, and all other rights. Now he demands, and obtains, a portion of the nightly receipts, and one melodramatic writer is said to have recently received, at the end of the run of his piece at the Princess's, a sum considerably in excess of ten thousand pounds.

In several other directions, too, theatrical expenditure is much larger to-day than it was in my youth. The posting and advertising have become much more extensive, the scenery and stage decorations are more costly, and considerably more money is spent on the costumes, especially those of the actresses. Well, if the lessee or proprietor could not make his fortune fifty years ago, I cannot for the life of me see how he can do so now.

The old question as between theatres and music halls has lately been revived. I know as much about it as most men, for when the music halls were first started, an association of theatrical managers was formed to prevent the proprietors of the new concerns trespassing on their ground, and I was appointed standing counsel to the organisation. Benjamin Webster was the chairman, and Messrs. Webster and Graham were the solicitors. A number of summonses were heard at Marlborough Street Police Court, before Mr. Knox, and finally a case was taken to the Queen's Bench to determine what was a stage play, or, rather, what could be produced at a music hall and what could not. The upshot of the case was that spectacular ballet was practically prohibited, and, in consequence, the Middlesex magistrates temporarily put an end to the dancing licenses of some of the principal music halls. It is now suggested that farces, and other short pieces that can be performed within a certain limit of time, should be permitted at the halls; and I, for my part, cannot see why this suggestion should not be carried out. A good little comedietta or farce could not possibly work more mischief than at present results from allowing the audience to contemplate a paucity of costume and the gyrations of a number of bare legs. The particular attraction of a music hall is that smoking and drinking are permitted in the auditorium, and possibly alcohol and nicotine would assist the appreciation of the farce writer's jokes and quips. The innovation would no doubt be a good thing for the joint-stock companies that run the halls, but I question whether it would be hailed with satisfaction by theatrical lessees.

It has struck me that it might be a good thing if, now that there are so many places of amusement, some change were made in the character of the performance at a few of the theatres. Why should not some of the old farces be written up to date and revived, and why should not a manager of to-day do what Vestris did at the Lyceum in times gone by, and let the bill be composed of three or four short pieces, such as farces and comediettas?

The experiment has lately been tried by Mr. Weedon Grossmith and Mr. Brandon Thomas, with "The Pantomime Rehearsal," etc., and found to exceed their most sanguine expectations. Why should not some of the theatres not only try such a programme, but also go back to the half-price system? How pleasant it used to be, after dining at one's club, to saunter round to the theatre at nine o'clock, and, for instance, see Robson in "Retained for the Defence," "The Thumping Legacy," or one or other of the little pieces in which he was so entertaining!

Again, why not, in some of the new theatres at all events, adopt the Parisian system of allowing ladies to wear their bonnets in the stalls? How much more often would they go to the theatre were they not under the necessity of arranging their hair and dressing elaborately! Besides, what a convenience this would be to ladies living in the suburbs!

These are only some ideas that have occurred to one who has, throughout his life, derived much pleasure from theatrical performances, and who numbers among his friends many members of the dramatic profession.

CHAPTER IX

COVENT GARDEN

The flower hawkers—Counter attractions to bed—Short history of "Convent Garden"—Distinguished residents—Reminiscences—Murder of Martha Ray—Hackman hanged—Ceaseless stream of traffic—Din of voices—Scene in the market—The man in blue—Flower sellers—Plant sellers—A hard case—I am able to assist.

"ALL a-growing and a-blowing!" Of all the sounds that reach my ears during the year, none gives me greater pleasure than this, the cry of the flower sellers. It brings glad tidings of sunshine, it is an assurance that fogs are a thing of the past, and it bids you watch for the coming of the swallow.

To the hard-working professional man the advent of spring brings new life, and its first pulsations are often induced by the sight of the daffodils on the street barrows.

It may not be generally known that the flower hawkers are an extremely industrious class. Their day commences at the earliest dawn, or even before, in Covent Garden Market, or one of the other centres whither the grower consigns his produce.

In my early days it was no uncommon thing for young gentlemen, after passing the night in a somewhat dissipated manner, to wend their way, in the small hours of the morning, to Covent Garden Market in order to have a cup of coffee at the stall by the church, and, as they expressed it, "to see life with the costers."

There were many counter attractions to bed in those days. Among the popular resorts that kept open almost all night were Jessop's, at the bottom of Catherine Street, Strand; the "Coal Hole," down the dark arches of the Adelphi; the Cider Cellars in the immediate neighbourhood; the "Garrick's Head," opposite Covent Garden Theatre, where Baron Nicholson sat with his jury; and, last but not least, Evans's.

It has been said, and with a good deal of truth, that the district known as Covent Garden has more literary, and, indeed, human interest than any other spot in modern or ancient London.

"Covent Garden" is, as every one knows, a corruption of "Convent Garden." Some six hundred years ago the ground covered by the present market and the surrounding buildings was an enclosure belonging to the Abbots of Westminster. One part of the area was used by them as a kitchen garden, and another part as a place of burial. At the dissolution of the religious houses—so we learn from Thornbury—the property passed into the hands of the Duke of Somerset, on whose attainder in 1552 it was given by the Crown to John Russell, Earl of Bedford, under the description of "Covent Garden, lying in the parish of St. Martin's in the Fields, next Charing Cross, with seven acres called Long Acre, of the yearly value of six pounds six shillings and eightpence." The value of the land, I am informed, has since increased.

In 1630, or thereabouts, the large square was laid out, from the designs of Inigo Jones, by Francis, fourth Earl of Bedford. On the north was the Piazza that still exists, on the east another that has long since been destroyed by fire, on the south the blank wall bounding the garden of Bedford House, and on the vest the church of St. Paul, which was also designed by Inigo Jones, and which is a familiar building in the present day. Along the southern wall stood a number of trees, and it was beneath their foliage that the fruit and vegetable market had its first beginnings. In 1689 Strype wrote: "The south side of Covent Garden Square l.eth open to Bedford Garden, where there is a small grotto of trees, most pleasant in the summer season; and on this side there is kept a market for fruits, herbs, roots, and flowers every Tuesday, Thursday, and Saturday—which is grown to a considerable account—and well served with choice goods, which makes it much resorted to."

I may be forgiven for quoting another writer in reference to the change that time wrought on this spot. Walter Savage Landor put the matter thus: "The garden formal and quiet, where a salad was cut for a lady abbess, and flowers were gathered to adorn images, became a market, noisy and full of life, distributing thousands of fruits and flowers to a vicious population."

The market gradually developed, and in 1671 it was formally established under a charter granted by the King to the Earl of Bedford. Wooden stalls and sheds, and other makeshift erections, met the requirements of the salesmen and women for a long time, and it was not until 1830 that the present market was erected. It was built by John, sixth Duke of Bedford, the architect being Mr. William Fowler; and an interesting circumstance in connection with its construction was that, while excavating for the foundations, some navvies came upon a quantity of human remains, which no doubt dated from the time when the Abbots used the ground as their place of burial.

In days gone by, Covent Garden was a very fashionable quarter. We read that, between 1666 and 1700, the following, among other distinguished persons, resided in the Piazzas: Lord Hollis, Lord Brownlow, the Bishop of Durham, Lord Newport, the Duke of Richmond, Lord Lucas, the Earl of Oxford, Sir Godfrey Kneller, Sir Kenelm Digby, the Marquis of Winchester, Benjamin West, and Sir Peter Lely. King Street, Henrietta Street, and other thoroughfares in the immediate neighbourhood, were also crowded with "persons of quality," as the phrase runs.

Many and various are the memories that cling to Covent Garden. Looking back through a long vista of years, one can see, with the mind's eye, two monster conflagrations, separated by an interval of some five decades, in which former Covent Garden Theatres were totally destroyed. Again, to go still further back in the distance of time, it was on the Piazzas that Powell set up his famous peep-show, to which, a wit of the period declared, large congregations were attracted by the ringing of the bell at the neighbouring church.

At one end of the existing Piazza stood the Bedford Coffee Tavern, an establishment with which are intimately associated the names of Garrick, Foote, Quin, and many other notabilities; and in the immediate vicinity was Sheridan's resort, the "Piazza Hotel." Then, too, at the north-west corner of Covent Garden was Evans's, that famous meeting-place for men of wit and fashion, where, before clubs were known, it is stated that as many as nine dukes have dined on one evening.

Passing from gay to grave, I cannot help referring to a most remarkable murder of which this locality was the scene. Over a hundred years ago the Earl of Sandwich, a member of Lord North's Administration, was one day passing through

Covent Garden when, in the window of No 4, a house standing at the corner of Tavistock Street, he caught sight of a very beautiful girl. Her name was Martha Ray, and she was a milliner by trade; her parents being, it is believed, staymakers of Holywell Street. She excited the nobleman's interest to such a degree that he had her removed from the shop, made arrangements for the completion of her education, and became her guardian.

A few years later, Martha made the acquaintance of a Captain in the army named Hackman, who fell passionately in love with her and asked her to become his wife. She refused, observing that she would never "marry a knapsack." This remark the Captain took very much to heart, and, in order to remove the disability to which it pointed, he resolved to change his profession. Hoping that a black coat would succeed where a red one had failed, he entered the Church, and, as Vicar of Wyverton, in Norfolk, once more offered his hand where he had already given his heart. This time Martha seemed more disposed to yield; but she raised some question of a settlement, and misunderstandings appear to have resulted.

The sequence of events in this sad story is a little difficult to trace, and I may pass at once to the tragic episode with which they culminated.

In the evening of the seventh of April, 1779, Martha Ray, after having refused earlier in the day to inform Hackman of her intended movements, proceeded, with a female attendant, to Covent Garden Theatre, there to witness "Love in a Village." Her lover, it appears, followed her thither, and we learn that, during the performance, he was seen drinking a glass of brandy and water in the Bedford Coffee Tavern.

Hackman posted himself in the roadway when the audience began to stream out of the theatre, and, as Martha was being handed by a gentleman to her carriage, he rushed forward, drew a pistol and shot her dead. He pointed another pistol to his own head and fired, but the bullet merely grazed the skin. Next he tried to beat out his brains with the butt-end of the weapon; but, before he could effect his desperate purpose, he was seized and handed over to two Bow Street runners, who conveyed him to the Bridewell on Tothill Fields.

In due course Hackman was tried for the murder, found guilty, and sentenced to death. He was hanged at Tyburn, and it is recorded that he was accompanied in the coach to the scaffold by Lord Carlisle and Mr. James Boswell.

But I must turn from the past to the present.

The Strand and its environments never seem to go to bed. The stream of traffic flows on without intermission throughout every hour in the twenty-four, and it would be very difficult to say when the work of the night ends and the work of the day commences. The omnibuses of course stop running at a given hour; but before all the other passenger conveyances have vanished from the streets, vans laden with fruit, vegetables, hay, and other spoils from the country, come lumbering along. Early rising is the rule with labouring London.

Any of my readers who may visit Covent Garden Market in the small hours of the morning will see very much the same sights as those that were to be witnessed twenty or thirty years ago. On entering Wellington Street from the Strand you find the roadway choked with vans, carts of all shapes and sizes, and barrows. Every other street leading to the market is in the same congested condition. Who would have thought the world contained so many cabbages and potatoes as are to be seen here? Men bearing baskets and cases on their heads pass hither and thither, dodging each other with a dexterity born of long experience.

The shouts and oaths so freely exchanged are responsible for a deal of the prevailing din; but other than human throats contribute to it largely. I refer to those of the costers' donkeys. One of these animals, elated it may be by meeting so many fellow-creatures, gives utterance to a prolonged and well-executed bray. Others at once raise their voices in response, and in a moment all the donkeys in all the streets are exercising those vocal powers with which Providence, in its inscrutable wisdom, has seen fit to endow them. One cannot help feeling very sorry for such of the occupants of the neighbouring houses as desire to sleep.

The manner in which the vegetables are packed in the huge market carts is extraordinary. You see loads of lettuces and cabbages ten feet high, roped and netted down so tightly that, when unloosened, you marvel how so many could have been pressed into the space.

The market itself is, of course, the scene of scenes. For incessant industry it is a veritable bee-hive. If you are disposed to stand about and watch what is going on, you must have a care for your head and your shins. The buyers, salesmen, and porters are no respecters of persons. With them it is work first and politeness afterwards.

If it is summer-time, the air is loaded with the fragrance of flowers, and the market is made beautiful with their colours.

"Now then for your dollars," shouts the eager seller; "we come here to sell, so make your choice and be sharp about it." You turn to see by whom these words are spoken, when thump! you are nearly knocked off your feet by a burly, perspiring porter bending under a load of cauliflowers. "Why don't yer git out of the blooming way?" is his substitute for an apology.

There are plenty of beggars and loafers standing about, and, oddly enough, a little group of Sisters of Mercy and hospital nurses. What on earth are they doing here at such an hour? The answer is very simple—they are buying flowers, at market prices, to gladden the hearts of poor sufferers laid on beds of sickness.

Who is that individual in blue, standing in the middle avenue? He looks like a butcher—but no; what could a butcher be doing there? Well, absurd as it may seem at first sight, the supposition is correct. There he stands, steel on belt, with a basket of steaks and other pieces of meat. He shouts: "Buy! buy! buy!" On drawing closer you will find that the good man is doing a very brisk trade, and rapidly disposing of his stock. The market habitués, it appears, buy his meat, and take it to neighbouring coffee-shops and public-houses, where they either have it cooked for them or perform the operation themselves.

Not the least interesting among those who every morning flock to Covent Garden are the women who sell buttonholes and nosegays in the street. Theirs is a most laborious life. They have to rise in time to attend the early morning market, and it sometimes takes them the whole of the day to dispose of their stock. While they are laying out their few shillings on roses, carnations, geraniums, and maidenhair, they have to beware of the market thieves, who are always ready to pounce down upon goods that are left unguarded. Quite recently, I am informed, a poor woman, on bringing the last of her purchases from the salesman to the spot where she had left her barrow, found that the vehicle and its contents had been spirited away.

There are any number of costers who post themselves in various parts of the metropolis with barrows laden with plants, seedlings, roots, and bulbs purchased at Covent Garden. A remarkable characteristic of these individuals is the conscientious manner in which they safeguard their "stock money." It may be that, after the toils of the day, they will pass a good deal of the evening in public-houses, treating themselves and their pals to pots of beer; but, even when under the influence of drink, they may be trusted not to spend any part of the sum that has been set apart for the purchase of the following day's stock.

A few weeks ago a case came before me in which one plant coster charged another with assault. It appeared that they had had a disagreement, which had led to blows, and that one of the combatants, finding himself getting the worst of the conflict, ran forward and overturned his antagonist's barrow, thereby destroying its contents.

After dealing with the case of assault, I turned to the man who had lost his goods, and said:

"Are you married?"

"Yes," he replied.

"Have you any children?"

"Six," said he with a grin.

"Have you anything in the world to support them with, now that your stock is destroyed?"

"No, nothing."

"Then you stand there a pauper?"

"Yes, sir," he said, "that's quite right."

"What do you propose to do?"

"That's just what I don't know," he returned, scratching his head.

I thought the case so hard that I resolved to assist the man out of a little fund that had been placed at my disposal by private friends for the relief of those whose needs I might find to be pressing.

I observed:

"Well, I fancy you are an honest fellow, and I don't think you ought to go to ruin because of this misfortune. I'm therefore going to give you money to get a fresh stock. What was your stock worth?"

"Well, sir, a matter of three pound or three pound ten."

"Very well. I'll let you have it—that is, you shan't have it, but an officer shall. I'll let him off his duty, or rather, I'll see that the authorities at Scotland Yard do so, in order that he may proceed with you in the morning for the purpose of buying a stock equivalent to the one you have lost."

When the women and girl flower sellers return to their

lodgings after attending the market, they proceed to sort their stock and make up their buttonholes. It is extraordinary with what quickness and ability the latter operation is performed. A few flowers are placed together so as to form a dainty little spray, and they are then nimbly bound together with wire.

Strangely enough, the flower seller, as a rule, has no love for flowers. She knows that her customers like them, and appreciate a well-arranged buttonhole, but where the great attraction lies she herself cannot understand. How seldom you see a flower girl wearing a flower! That her male associates should be insensible to the charm of their goods is less surprising. Probably the only personal use a coster ever made of a flower was to put the stalk in his mouth and chew it.

The number of male and female street flower sellers in London is very large. Several will often congregate together at a street corner, competing for the patronage of the public with great good-nature. The women are nearly all dressed alike, with the same sort of hat and feathers, the same tartan shawls, short cotton dresses, and high-heeled lace-up boots, and the same kind of gold ear-rings.

Taking them as a whole, the flower sellers—men and women alike—are a very worthy class.

CHAPTER X

FLOSS AND FLOSS

The office in Lincoln's Inn—The partners—Their home-life—Unfortunate clients—The confidential clerk—His methodical habits—Time brings changes — Appearances deceptive —The old circus proprietor — An amazing discovery—A desperate expedient—Ugly rumours—A terrible blow—Left alone—The alternative—The choice—Flight—The arrest.

THE house of Floss and Floss had existed for generations. It was the oldest firm of solicitors in Lincoln's Inn ; nay, it was, with one exception, the oldest in the metropolis. The name had always been " Floss and Floss." Sometimes the partners had been father and son, once uncle and nephew, and frequently—as at the time of which I am writing—two brothers.

The building in which the business was carried on was one of the most ornamental and conspicuous in Lincoln's Inn. Its windows were of the picturesque type in vogue two or three centuries ago.

The two partners were George and Henry Floss. They had succeeded their father some five-and-twenty years ago, and so far they had apparently maintained the high reputation of the firm.

George was considerably older than Henry, who had become a partner at the age of twenty-one. The brothers were unlike one another in character no less than in appearance. George was of a serious turn and of austere habits, while his brother was light-hearted and genial, fond of sport, an excellent shot, and as good a cross-country rider as you could wish to see. Again, whereas George dressed in black, Henry invariably wore smart clothes, made by one of the best tailors in London, and was rather fond of colour.

The premises of the firm were divided into two departments, each of which was controlled by one of the partners. Their private rooms were on the first floor. A client reached either of them by passing up a staircase on the right-hand side of the building, and he quitted the apartment by an opposite door, and passed down a staircase on the left-hand side of the building.

Each partner had his own staff of clerks, many of whom had been in the firm's employment for a great many years. When once, indeed, a man had been fortunate enough to mount a stool in that office, there he usually remained for a very long time.

The practice itself was for the most part of a non-contentious kind, though occasionally the partners had to carry through heavy Chancery suits. Floss and Floss had, in a word, a fine old family business, and it included the management of some large estates and properties.

People from all parts of the country brought large sums of money to these solicitors in order that it might be wisely invested. Such individuals were quite satisfied, after an interview with one of the partners, to leave their wealth in his hands on the understanding that he should place it in whatever securities he thought best, and arrange for the dividends to be forwarded as they fell due. The client was informed by letter of the name of the investment selected, and he afterwards received the proceeds thereof by the firm's cheque.

The home-life of the two brothers differed very considerably. George inhabited one of the large mansions at Lancaster Gate. He was a widower, and had one child, a girl of nineteen, to whom he was very much attached. For many years past she had been his sole companion. They kept several horses and carriages, and a large staff of domestics. George Floss was very religious. He was a constant church-goer, and read family prayers every morning and evening. Anything but a cheerful man, I do not think he was a particularly happy one; but everybody with whom he came in contact unhesitatingly attributed his solemn and reserved manner to his anxiety for his clients' welfare. People pitied him as a man who carried his business cares into his domestic life. The young girl tried hard to dissipate the gloom in her father's life, and often of an evening she would put her arms coaxingly about his neck and entreat him to forget his musty old law, and give some thoughts to his darling Ada. Such moments were the happiest, and yet the bitterest, in his life.

The younger brother, who was a single man, had a small house in Mayfair, where he lived during the greater part of the year, a country mansion in Surrey, and a hunting-box at Melton Mowbray. He was a director of several public companies, and as a rule transacted the business of the younger clients. Among these were many noblemen between twenty-one and thirty years of age, who desired to raise money on mortgage, to sell their properties, or to invest their capital in securities more remunerative, if less safe, than the Three Per Cents. Their investments were not always fortunate, and more than one noble client of Henry Floss became a ruined man. The circumstance did not greatly disturb the equanimity of the young lawyer.

"Your own fault entirely," he would observe to the unhappy individual. "You would speculate so rashly, on your broker's advice, that the result is no more than I expected."

Curiously enough, if these investments were closely enquired into, they would often prove to be some of those in which Mr. Henry Floss was himself interested, and of which, as often as not, he had been a large seller.

A most interesting figure at the establishment in Lincoln's Inn was the confidential clerk. He had been with the firm for fifty years, having started as the office-boy. Possessing considerable intelligence, great industry, and high integrity, he had gradually ascended the ladder of promotion, and was appointed to the position of confidential clerk by the late head of the firm, the father of the present partners. Old Clamp, indeed, had dandled George and Henry as infants, and, in later years, had held their ponies when, as was often the case, they rode down to the office to see their father.

Clamp's office was between the private rooms of the two partners, by whom he was held in the highest esteem. He seemed to pass the whole of his days poring over, and making entries in, the books of the firm, which were in his sole care and custody. He was wholly devoted to the interests of the firm, which he always referred to as "we," or as "my principals, you know, Floss and Floss."

Clamp was the oddest little fellow conceivable. He was so small and thin as to suggest the idea that, at some time or other, he must have passed through a process of shrivelling; he had little black sparkling eyes, a wee nose, and other diminutive features to correspond, and he was quite bald. The little fellow never seemed to walk, he was always on the trot. He allowed himself just half an hour every day for dinner, and twenty minutes for tea.

For forty years Clamp had dined at a small chop-house in a thoroughfare leading out of Serle Street. Every day he entered the establishment at the same time, hung his hat on the same peg, and occupied the same seat, which was always kept for him. Having ordered his chop or steak, he would take the daily paper out of his coat-tail pocket and peruse it in silence until his repast was placed before him. His invariable beverage was half a pint of porter. Every one about the premises respected him, and wished him good day when he made his appearance.

Twenty minutes was the exact time this curious little individual took over his meal. The remaining ten minutes were devoted to what he termed "trotting about the Fields"; no matter what was the state of the weather, or the time of the year, he always took his digestive ramble round the square. This accomplished, he returned to his office, removed his tail-coat, put on a jacket and skull-cap, and once more buried himself in his books. At about five o'clock he brewed himself a pot of tea.

During the past ten or fifteen years Clamp had been the last to leave the offices at night. After enquiring of "Master George" and "Master Henry" whether they had any instructions for him before they left, he proceeded to put away the books, and, having satisfied himself that everything was shipshape, he waited to see the last of the clerks off the premises, and then locked up the offices and took his departure. At the bottom of Chancery Lane he got into an omnibus, which conveyed him within a stone's throw of his humble lodging on Islington Green. On arriving there he once more took the newspaper from his pocket, and read on until it was time for supper and bed.

It is safe to say that in days gone by no inhabitant of Islington Green slept so soundly as the confidential clerk of Floss and Floss. Time brings its changes, however, and it came to pass that every night after retiring to rest the little form on the iron bedstead tossed and turned for many an hour, and when at last weariness was succeeded by sleep, fitful sighs and sobs came from beneath the blankets. Had any one crept to the door at dead of night and put his ear to the key-hole, he might have heard, in a sleeper's guttural, such words as these: "Ah, Master Hal, Master Hal—the old house, the old house—ruin and disgrace!"

The truth is, little as the world suspected such a thing, that the firm of Floss and Floss had become an imposture and a sham. Apparently prosperous, the partners were in reality hopelessly ruined. Almost at any moment a terrible exposure might come about, and they would then be branded by the world as a pair of arrant knaves. Clamp knew all. No wonder, therefore, that he could not get much sleep.

Shortly after the younger brother had joined the firm he had become connected with a firm of stockbrokers, by whom he had been persuaded to speculate. His first ventures had been small ones, but as time went on they became more extensive, as is usually the case in this, as in every other, kind of gambling. He was sucked deeper and deeper into the vortex, and he dragged his brother with him. Thousands of pounds were lost, and at last the entire resources of the brothers had disappeared. Then came the next step in the downward path. In the hope of retrieving his fortune, Henry Floss had employed the money of his clients to speculate with. This led to the forging of transfers and other fraudulent acts.

The younger brother obtained complete control over the elder, who gave him a free hand to do whatever he desired. The actual manipulation of the accounts, and the exchanging of one client's securities for another, was done by Henry, his brother's attitude being one of passive consent.

Besides the partners, the only person in the office who was aware of what was going on was Clamp. It required all his book-keeping experience, and unceasing industry, to prevent the awful secret from leaking out.

Among the numerous clients of the firm was an old man who had been for many years a circus proprietor. He was, indeed, if I am not mistaken, successor to the celebrated Ducrow. Though very ignorant, and unable to read or write, he was an excellent business man, and had amassed no less a sum than fifteen thousand pounds. Being anxious to invest it, he had, on the advice of a friend, paid a visit to the famous firm of solicitors in Lincoln's Inn. It so happened that he was shown into the presence of the junior partner, whose pleasant manners at once inspired him with boundless confidence. The upshot of the interview was that, on the following

O

day, he paid a second visit to the office and took with him his fifteen thousand pounds, in the form of bank-notes, tied up in a handkerchief. Addressing Henry Floss, he said:

"You see I am but a poor man in learning. The stocks you mentioned yesterday will do beautiful; and if you wouldn't mind, I'll get you to do all the business part of it, and just send me along the dividends every half-year. But perhaps this would be troubling you too much?"

"Not at all," was the reply. "I shall be only too delighted to serve you in any way. You can give me a power of attorney to receive the dividends, and I'll purchase the stock and deposit the certificates in my strong box. But business is business; so as soon as I have effected the purchase I will send you the numbers of the share certificates."

In due course the stock was purchased and the numbers forwarded. This transaction occurred at the time when the firm was beginning to get into difficulties; and these bonds were among the first to be misappropriated. The transfers were forged, and the stock was sold.

Years went by, the dividends were punctually forwarded, and the fraud was not discovered. One day, however, the old man called at the office for the purpose of arranging for his property to be realised, he having resolved, on the advice of his son-in-law, who was a speculative builder, to "put his money in houses." On arriving at Lincoln's Inn, he learnt that Mr. Henry Floss was away from town, and was not expected to return until the following week. Having taken the precaution to put in his pocket before leaving home the memorandum stating the numbers of his stock, he walked from Lincoln's Inn to the office of the company concerned, with a view to at once setting in motion the necessary machinery for releasing his money. To his amazement he there learnt that the shares specified on the memorandum were standing in another name.

Hurrying back to the solicitors' office, the terrified client had an interview with the senior partner, who assured him that there must be some mistake, and undertook to wire for his brother to return to town immediately. In response to the telegram, Henry Floss left Melton Mowbray the same day, and in the evening a long and somewhat stormy interview took place between the partners.

It was arranged that a letter should be sent to their client, informing him that, by a clerical error, incorrect particulars of the stock had been originally supplied to him; that the mistake, though greatly to be regretted, was of no importance; and that, if he desired it, his property should be at once realised. This was all very well, but how was fifteen thousand pounds to be raised at a moment's notice?

Although the hour was late, a cab was sent to Islington Green to fetch Clamp. The little clerk had retired to rest when the messenger arrived, but, on hearing of the summons, he got up and hurriedly dressed.

Half an hour later, tortured with the most dismal forebodings, he entered the drawing-room of the mansion in Lancaster Gate. His principals asked him to state the exact financial position of the firm, and the poor fellow, with tears streaming down his face, explained that their defalcations amounted to over a quarter of a million sterling. There were still a number of securities left, and Henry Floss insisted that a portion of them must be sacrificed in order that the fifteen thousand pounds might be raised. George refused for a long time to consent to this proposal, but his opposition was eventually overborne by his brother's arguments. The matter having thus been settled, it was resolved that Clamp should work out a complete statement of the firm's accounts, and that the partners should decide at the end of the week what course should be adopted with reference to the future. Meanwhile, Henry Floss returned to his hunting-box at Melton Mowbray.

How suspicion was aroused it is difficult to say, but on the following day ugly rumours were afloat with regard to the old-established firm of Floss and Floss. The senior partner was at his post as usual, and saw a number of clients, none of whom, however, expressed or betrayed any uneasiness.

A close observer might have been struck by the repeated appearance in and about Lincoln's Inn that afternoon of two men who, though there seemed to be no connection between them, apparently had two things in common, namely, ample leisure, and a desire to spend it in that particular area. In appearance they were not unlike, both being rather stout and of florid complexion. One might have been a well-to-do publican, the other a gentleman farmer. But even the fascinations of Lincoln's Inn seemed at last to pall upon the latter, for at about six o'clock he quitted the neighbourhood, and spent the remainder of the evening strolling about Lancaster Gate.

A terrible blow awaited George Floss on his arrival home at about half-past six. As he entered the hall, the butler handed him a telegram that ran as follows:

"Mr. Henry Floss met with a fatal accident on the hunting field this morning. He was thrown from his horse and killed on the spot."

The wretched man stood for a moment as though paralysed. His partner in crime was dead, and he was left to bear the burden of their sins alone. It would be impossible to describe the sufferings of the unfortunate and guilty man.

Of course all business was suspended at the office pending the funeral, which was fixed to take place on the following Saturday. What would come afterwards? Monday morning would reveal all.

To outward appearance George Floss passed the Sunday much in his usual way, attending church both in the morning and evening. He was somewhat paler than usual, but his friends recognised in this circumstance only a natural outcome of the bereavement he had just sustained.

At two o'clock on the Monday morning the house at Lancaster Gate was wrapped in sleep. George Floss sat in his study alone. He had for some hours been busy writing, and before him lay the fruits of his labour—a packet securely sealed and addressed to his daughter. He had decided early in the day that he could not stand his ground and face his disgrace. There was the alternative before him—flight or death. Not being able to decide which he should choose, he had provided for both. Explaining that he had a long journey to take on the following day, he had instructed his valet to pack his portmanteau, and take it to the booking-office at Charing Cross Station. This had been done, and I may mention that as the luggage was being carried to the cab, the stout individual I have likened to a gentleman farmer stepped up to the driver, exchanged a few casual remarks with him, and then, wishing him good-day, passed on.

For some time George Floss remained seated in the study with his face buried in his hands. Rousing himself at last, he opened a drawer in the table, took out a little wooden case and lifted the lid. It contained a six-chambered revolver. Next he took a double locket from his pocket, and gazed long at the faces depicted therein; one being that of his daughter, the other that of his brother Henry. There was no anger in his eyes as he looked at the latter, only an expression of affection and sorrow. On the table stood a miniature of his dead wife. He took it up, and, after pressing it to his lips, placed it in his vest.

Passing out of the room, the wretched man went noiselessly upstairs to the apartment where his daughter slept. Drawing the curtains gently on one side he gazed upon her unconscious features, stooped and kissed her lightly upon the forehead and then hurried from the room.

When he regained the study, daylight was already breaking in through the chinks in the shutters. There lay the pistol on the table. He stood still with his eyes fixed upon the weapon; advancing a couple of steps he took it up and toyed with it irresolutely. This action lasted for some moments; then, on a sudden, he put the pistol back in the case, shut the lid, and replaced it in the drawer. He had made up his mind at last— it was to be flight.

Looking at his watch, George Floss was startled to find the hour so much later than he had supposed. In fifty minutes the early mail started for Dover. Having put on his hat and coat in the hall, he quietly let himself out at the front door. A night cab was passing, and he hailed it, stepped inside, and told the driver to take him to Charing Cross.

Ten minutes before the fugitive arrived at the railway station, the two men I have previously alluded to drove up and proceeded to the booking-office. It was a bitterly cold morning, and they were well wrapped up, their features being half concealed by their fur caps and comforters.

One of the men sat opposite George Floss on the journey to the coast; the other travelled in a neighbouring compartment.

When the train arrived at its destination the passengers at once began to stream down the gangway leading to the boat, the absconding solicitor being one of the foremost in the throng. Before he had gone a dozen steps some one touched him on the shoulder. He found a stout man on either side of him. The next moment were uttered the fatal words:

" George Floss, we hold a warrant for your apprehension ! "

The wretched man's companions were Brett and Bull, two City police officers, of whom I formed a very high opinion while I was practising at the Bar.

CHAPTER XI

THE ROAD TO RUIN

List betting—Its temptations—Centres for betting—Monotony of the evening papers—Betting in the West End—Racing clubs—Betting on the increase—The "commission agent"—What is his crime?—An old client—A plunger—Police raid on a West End club—Playing baccarat declared illegal—Decision upheld on appeal—The son of an Indian officer—Becomes popular in society—Does not know poker—Nor loo—My remark thereon—Justified by the result—A similar case in Paris—Prompt detection.

It was thought, when "lists" were done away with, that gambling on the turf, at any rate among the humbler members of the community, would be, as a consequence, practically stamped out; but events have proved that this assumption was a totally erroneous one.

It was urged, and very convincingly urged, as a reason for abolishing list betting, that it afforded a direct temptation to shop lads, office boys, and others to rob their employers; and the advocates of the reform contended that the crime of embezzlement was greatly increasing, owing to the existence of this temptation. They made out a direct case of cause and effect, but experience has shown that there was a flaw in their reasoning. It cannot be doubted that gambling on the turf is a primary cause of embezzlement among youths, but unfortunately the abolition of list betting did not remove that cause.

Statistics prove that there is more gambling at the present time among the class in question than there ever was before. The truth is that there are almost as great facilities to-day for wagering in small sums as there were forty years ago.

Nearly half the public-houses in London are centres for betting on the turf. If the landlord himself does not make a book, some constant habitué of the place does, and is willing to lay the odds on every event in the racing calendar. The money of the backer is deposited with him at the time the bet is made, and in return he gives a written voucher. Settlements take place either during the evening of the day on which the race is run, or on the following morning. In the event of any suspicious-looking individual, suggestive of an officer of the law, being present in the bar, those concerned in the transaction tip one another the wink, walk out, and settle round the corner.

This class of business is not even confined to public-houses. It is carried on in the shops of small tradesmen all over the metropolis. Barbers' shops in particular are used for the purpose, and many a shop lad or young clerk who has entered such premises merely for the purpose of getting a shave is induced, ere he leaves, to invest a shilling or half-crown on the Chester Cup, the City and Suburban, or some other race. Numerous tobacconists', too, are haunted by bookmakers and their clients.

Many youthful embezzlers are brought before me at the police court, and in ninety-nine cases out of a hundred I find that the breach of fidelity had its origin in betting.

The evening papers, or at all events the smaller ones, seem almost to live on racing news. From one o'clock in the afternoon till late at night the streets of London resound with the cry of "Winner! All the winners!" and the monotony of the announcement becomes such a nuisance that the occasional "'Orrible Murder at 'Ampstead!" or "Shocking Outrage at Regent's Park!" affords quite a pleasant relief to the ear.

Of course every now and then a licensed victualler who allows his premises to be used for the purpose of betting is summoned by the police, and taken before a magistrate, by whom he is duly fined. As, however, the business is very lucrative, this does not represent a very great punishment; and if the licensing authorities take no notice of the matter, the culprit soon returns to his evil ways. If, on the other hand, the license seems to be in jeopardy, a new tenant is found for the house at the last moment, and a transfer effected, in which case it will very likely happen that things go from bad to worse.

The small tradesman, such as the barber or tobacconist, is very seldom prosecuted, owing to the difficulty of bringing the offence home to him. This I very much regret.

In the West End, betting is carried on in shops of quite a superior kind. Very large commissions are worked on these premises, and the backer can be accommodated to the tune of several hundred pounds. Then of course there are the clubs, with which the law does not, and cannot, interfere. Here the "tape" can be consulted, so that members of the upper and middle classes, without attending the course, can back their fancies, from hour to hour, for any amount they choose.

The proprietor of a racing club usually makes a very good thing out of it, and it not infrequently happens that one of these individuals, who has commenced business with little or no capital, becomes in time a comparatively rich man. Needless to say, when this is the case, most of those who have ventured their money against him have sunk lower and lower, until very likely their end has been absolutely ruin. In fact, backing horses always has been, and always will be, one of the most ruinous of pastimes.

If, however, betting is on the increase among the lower classes, it is still more on the increase in the upper regions of society. The wonder is how some well-to-do persons manage to pursue this disastrous form of recreation for so long a period. One explanation of this singular phenomenon is to be found, I fear, in the fact that many of them continue to bet after they have become defaulters.

There can be no doubt that the sums risked on race-courses, in the recognised rings, are far larger now than in the days of our forefathers. Moreover, the number of race meetings has greatly increased of late years. Flat-racing goes on every day from the end of February to the middle or end of November, and it sometimes happens that several meetings take place on the same date.

I have always thought that it is manifestly unfair, while betting at clubs and on race-courses is permitted, to abuse the bookmaker and treat him as a sort of social pariah. This is, however, precisely what is done by a great many persons. Have my readers ever observed what advantage is taken of this feeling in a court of law?

A man steps into the witness-box, and counsel or a solicitor puts the question:

"What are you?"

Fearing something unpleasant, the witness assumes the defensive, and replies:

"A commission agent."

"Indeed," is the retort; "and pray what is that? What sort of a commission agent are you?"

"On the turf," is the dogged reply.

"Oh, now I begin to understand," observes the cross-examiner triumphantly. "You are in fact a bookmaker?"

The witness mutters an affirmative reply, and his tormentor, it may be, resumes his seat with the air of a man who has laid bare so gross a case of human depravity that any further questioning would be wholly superfluous. The witness having been proved in open court to be none other than a bookmaker, the magistrate or jury is, in effect, invited to regard his credit as damned through all eternity.

What is the bookmaker's crime? What evil can be attributed to him which has not as its fountain-head the system which has given him birth? If you hear a member of the upper classes declaiming against bookmakers, and you ask him what he can charge against them, you will receive some such answer as this:

"Oh, they are such pinchers; they give such shabbily low prices."

My reply to this would be that the price need not be accepted; that its acceptance is quite a voluntary act on the part of the backer; and that, whatever else may be said against the bookmakers, no one would deny that they pay when they lose. As a matter of fact, they are bound to do so. If they did not settle every Monday morning after a race meeting, their credit would be irretrievably lost, and they could no longer pursue their calling. Absolutely no grace is allowed to them. Moreover, those who complain of the short prices given by the bookmaker seem quite to forget the thousands of pounds these individuals lose through not being paid.

I very well remember an occasion on which I was at Ascot, standing in the Royal enclosure and looking over into Tattersall's ring. While I was thus engaged, my eye chanced to fall upon an old client of mine who had been one of the largest bookmakers in London, but who, a few years back, having realised a considerable fortune, had retired from business and gone to live in the country. He had a horse or two in training, and the year before had been fortunate enough to win one of the classic races; otherwise he took no active concern in the turf.

Observing that this gentleman was looking very intently

over the rails, I went up to him and, after shaking him by the hand, said :

"Why on earth are you studying people in the enclosure so closely?"

"Why, Mr. Montagu," he replied, "I was thinking to myself what an odd world this is. You know I am a fairly rich man, but if I had all the money that gentlemen owe me who are standing in the enclosure where you are, I should be pretty near a millionaire. Look at that young gentleman over there," he continued, pointing to a smart-looking sprig who was standing not far off; "he's new—since my time—but I know all about him. His income all told isn't over five hundred a year, and yet he's always putting himself down for a monkey [five hundred pounds] on a race, and he plays whist at his club for pony [twenty-five pounds] points. That's been going on for some time now; yet, as you know, people turn up their noses at bookmakers, who honestly pay every shilling that they lose."

Now, as of yore, large sums of money are lost, both by owners of horses and others, and as a rule these sums pass into the pockets of the bookmakers. Yet it must be borne in mind that it is the backer who goes to the bookmaker, and not the bookmaker to the backer.

Very instructive was the career of a gentleman who, a year or two back, made his appearance on the turf and at pigeon shooting, another species of gambling much indulged in at the present day. I forget the exact sum he started with, but it was a considerable fortune; and in a book he published he described how it was gambled away. Well, racing all day and baccarat all night would no doubt in time break the Bank of England. Yet both are flourishing in our midst at the present time.

As may be remembered, some time ago the police made a raid upon an establishment, situated not a hundred miles from St. James's Street, which was carried on under the guise of a proprietary club. The gentlemen who were found playing—and there were many of them—the proprietor, and some of the officials, were arrested, brought before a magistrate, and convicted, but the matter was taken before Her Majesty's Judges, who were called upon to decide whether the playing of baccarat, under the conditions stated, was, or was not, illegal. The point was argued by the greatest talent at the Bar; but their Lordships upheld the decision of the Court below, and

THE ROAD TO RUIN

refused to quash the conviction. The consequence was that the establishment in question was closed; but it is no secret that similar places have since been opened, and have, so far, not been interfered with by the authorities.

A great deal of gambling at cards goes on in men's rooms and at private houses, in the West End and elsewhere; and in some cases the player has not only to contend with the slings and arrows of outrageous fortune, but also with the hands that wield the slings. Owing to the loose way in which society is organised, and to the facility with which admission to clubs can be obtained in these days by individuals about whom nothing is known, gentlemen constantly run the risk of making the acquaintance of, and subsequently playing with, men who are nothing more nor less than professional sharpers.

A few years ago a rather nice-mannered fellow, apparently of about thirty, put in an appearance at the West End, and became personally known to one or two men of fashion. He dressed well, had rooms in one of the most fashionable thoroughfares, and was apparently a man of considerable means. He was reported to be the son of a distinguished officer in the Indian Army. Well, India is a long way from London, and this was probably the reason why the story was credited without any attempt being made to verify it.

The new arrival became very popular, and in a little while, after being duly proposed and seconded, became a member of a fashionable West End club. I may mention that its proprietor had been an officer in the Guards, and was an old friend of mine. When the club was formed he had invited me to become an original member, and I had accepted the invitation. I did not use the establishment much, however, and only dined there three or four times a year, on occasions when I was going to a neighbouring theatre. As, however, the premises lay directly in my route from the Temple to Upper Brook Street, I used occasionally to drop in there for a brief stay on my walk home. It was upon one of these occasions that I, for the first time, saw the individual to whom I have alluded, and I own that my early impression of him was that he was a very agreeable fellow.

The gaming establishment in the neighbourhood was at that time in full swing, and from a conversation that was taking place when I entered the morning-room I learnt that the stranger was a nightly visitor there. It appeared, however, that he was pursued by some demon of ill-luck, and that he always rose from the baccarat table a poorer man than when he had sat down. The staggering accounts that he gave of his losses suggested the idea that he must be descended from some Nabob or Nizam instead of from a mere officer in the Indian service. I confess that, as the new member conversed in his airy way of hundreds and thousands of pounds, I began to have my suspicions regarding him.

This man rapidly increased in favour with the members of the club, some of whom soon learnt to address him by his Christian name. He was invited to several country houses for shooting, and proved himself a very popular guest.

Among others who took the stranger up was a certain north country Baronet, who had the reputation of being very particular and exclusive in his choice of acquaintance. One day Sir L—— happened to mention his new protégé to me, which was not remarkable, as the Baronet and I were old friends, having gone to Eton at the same time and passed through the school together. Sir L——'s observations took the form of enthusiastic praise, and I presume he gathered from my expression that I did not endorse all he was saying, for he suddenly stopped short and exclaimed:

"Don't you like him? Why, he's one of the nicest fellows I ever met. We were delighted with him down at ——."

"Oh, yes," I returned, "he seems a pleasant enough chap; but have you any idea where he came from, or who is he?"

"Yes," was the confident reply; "his father is an Indian general—made a lot of money out there in indigo or something of that sort, which money Master ——," mentioning his Christian name, "seems quite able to spend."

I changed the subject, and a few minutes later Sir L—— left the club. Oddly enough, a very short time after his departure an incident occurred that strengthened the suspicions which had entered my mind.

Two young fellows, who were, I think, members of the Stock Exchange, and who had just arrived, passed through the card-room and entered the billiard saloon. It was clear that they had contemplated having a game; but finding the tables engaged, they retraced their steps, and resolved to while away the time before dinner with a game of poker. Having secured a third man, they proceeded to look about for a fourth, and, as luck would have it, while they were thus occupied, in walked the son of the Indian officer. One of the young fellows asked him to join them, and he replied very affably:

"I should be delighted, but, to tell you the truth, I'm quite ignorant of the game. I could, however, make one in a rubber or two of écarté, if you care about it."

Écarté was not fancied by the young men, who persisted in their preference for poker, and it was ultimately decided that the three proficients should instruct the novice.

I am no card-player myself, though I happen to know poker fairly well, having been privileged to watch General Schenk—one of the finest players in the States—play on more than one occasion at the time when he was Minister over here; and so it not unnaturally occurred to me to step into the other room and watch the game that was about to commence.

The rapidity with which the new player acquired a knowledge of the intricacies of poker fairly took away my breath. When, in about half an hour's time, I took my departure, he was playing as skilfully as if he had known the game from his infancy.

As I sauntered up St. James's Street I ruminated upon what I had just seen, and I confess that the suspicion that had entered my mind tended to deepen.

My next meeting with this individual was under somewhat peculiar circumstances. At that time I had some very good shooting and a shooting-box, about five-and-twenty miles from London and adjoining the estate of the Squire of the place— an intimate friend of mine. It was at the end of September, or beginning of October, and, having stolen a Saturday off, I had invited three friends down for some sport.

During the morning I received a note from my neighbour, saying that he, too, had a small shooting-party, and suggesting that, as we were going to walk partridges, we might as well finish up his way, arrange for our dress-clothes to be sent over, and join him and his friends at dinner. This seemed a very good arrangement, and we agreed to it.

On arriving at —— Park, we found that the Squire's party had just returned, and who should I see, standing in the hall and sipping a glass of curaçoa, but the gentleman who had proved so apt a pupil at the poker table. I looked him well over when I thought I was unobserved, and noticed that everything he wore was brand-new. The conversation turned upon guns, and he mentioned, among other things, that he always had his made by Grant, of St. James's Street, adding that there was no finer maker in England—a proposition no one would, I think, venture to dispute. I craved permission to examine his weapon, whereupon I found that that also was perfectly new.

Nothing more of any note occurred until we were seated round my friend's hospitable board. The stranger, who, if I remember aright, had taken the lady of the house in to dinner, occupied a seat directly opposite to me, and I must plead guilty to keeping a critical eye upon him throughout the meal.

The subject of cards cropped up during dessert, and upon some one expressing a very high opinion of loo, my *vis-à-vis* observed that he did not know the game, and had never seen it played.

What possessed me I do not know, but, looking him straight in the face, I remarked, somewhat brusquely, I'm afraid:

"I heard you say that the other day about poker, and I watched you playing, and I never saw a better game in my life."

Apparently there was something peculiar in my manner of saying this, for an awkward pause followed, and then the conversation was changed.

When we were in the smoking-room, my old friend the host took me on one side and said:

"You shouldn't have made that remark at dinner. You made that poor fellow quite uncomfortable."

"I'm very sorry," said I. "How did you fall in with the man, and where does he come from?"

"Oh," was the reply, "he's a man of excellent family. He's just been staying with Sir L——, partridge shooting in the north. I've asked him to spend a few days with us, and we all like him exceedingly."

Months passed by, and the winter had well set in when, while walking one afternoon down Bond Street, I met Sir L——, who excitedly exclaimed:

"Have you heard the news? We have had the deuce to pay at the —— Club this morning. You know that nice fellow—son of an Indian officer, as he described himself? Well, he's been caught cheating at cards, and the matter was before the committee of the club. We had him in the room, and he admitted the whole thing. On his own showing, the fellow has been a sharper for years. You don't seem surprised about it?" added my friend.

"Well, no," I returned, " I am not surprised. I suspected him almost from the first."

Upon enquiring subsequently, I heard how the rogue had been discovered. He had, some weeks before, made the acquaintance of a young, and not particularly clever, officer in the Dragoons, who was a constant habitué of the baccarat establishment previously alluded to. While this young subaltern —who, I should state, was the son of an enormously rich man —was quartered with his regiment at a large provincial town, he received a visit one morning from his new acquaintance, who stated that he was staying for a day or two at the " Grand Hotel " with his friends, Colonel —— and Admiral ——, and that they would all be very pleased if he would come round and join them at dinner, and have a little game afterwards. The pigeon was caught, and, to make a long story short, they gambled all night, and the young officer returned to his quarters, at five o'clock in the morning, a poorer man by some sixteen or seventeen thousand pounds than when he had left them a few hours before. The occurrence got hinted abroad, the dupe's comrades took the matter up, and the employment of detectives led to the knowledge that the "Colonel" and " Admiral " were two well-known card-sharpers, and that the so-called son of an Indian officer was, and had been for years, their "bonnet." The exposure at the club was the immediate result of the detectives' discoveries.

The facts that I have laid before the reader by no means stand alone. Only a few months ago, a case of a similar character was brought to light in Paris. Two young Frenchmen of fortune and position were travelling abroad, I think in Italy, when they made the acquaintance of one M——, apparently a most delightful man. He was travelling in the best style, and spent money with the greatest freedom. The acquaintance quickly ripened into friendship, and the three moved from town to town together, going finally to Monte Carlo, where they nightly frequented the gaming establishments. M—— always seemed to lose, but his bad luck never affected his temper or spirits.

The two Parisians belonged to the club that is familiarly known as " L'Epatant " (Ancien Cercle Impérial), and not long after their return to the capital they put down the name of their new friend for membership. He was duly elected, and at once became very popular.

M—— went in a great deal for gambling, and for the first few months persistently lost; then, on a sudden, his luck changed, and night after night he won largely. One morning he carried home several thousand pounds.

The French are not so dull in these cases as we phlegmatic Britons. The very next night M—— was closely watched, and caught in the act of cheating. Two lacqueys were promptly called in, and bidden to kick him out into the street—an operation they performed with enthusiasm and skill.

On the following day, M——'s proposer and seconder were summoned before the committee of the club. They were honourably acquitted of any knowledge of the rogue's doings, but, for having nominated a man of whom they knew absolutely nothing, they were requested to remove their names from the list of members.

CHAPTER XII

MONEY LENT

The money-lender—His style of living—His victims—The regular course of events—"The —— Bank of Deposit"—Its rules and manner of conducting its business—An illegal act connived at—A case in point—The jury stops the case—Discounting tailors—Experiences of a comrade—Leviathan money-lenders—A good-natured act.

ALTHOUGH conducted on slightly altered lines, the trade of the usurer is carried on as extensively to-day as it was half a century ago. The possibilities of profit being great, the supply continues to keep well abreast of the demand, which is, always has been, and probably always will be, very considerable.

The modern borrower is not asked to take half the proceeds of his bills in coal or paving-stones, and the other half in cash; but I do not think that his experiences are, on the whole, much more pleasant than were those of his predecessor.

As a rule the young heir to property, be he nobleman or commoner, passes through the hands of the small bill-discounter before he has recourse to the money-lender. His bills have been met at maturity by the discounting of others for larger amounts, and the latter have subsequently been dishonoured. That is the history of events in the generality of cases; and, matters being thus brought to a crisis, the unhappy debtor, acting on the advice of a friend—who is not always a disinterested party—goes for accommodation to the financier. "Put yourself entirely in his hands," says the friend, "and give him the whole control of your affairs, and he'll be sure to pull you through, don't you know." This course is agreed to, and an introduction is at once arranged.

It may be interesting to pause for a moment to enquire what manner of man this financier is. To begin with, he occupies fine offices in a fashionable quarter of London; he has an attractive place in the country, with good shooting; he drives a four-in-hand; and, in a word, he keeps up rather imposing appearances. He has been engaged in his usurious calling during the best part of his life, and from time to time has embarked in speculations that have not always turned out well, as his appearance more than once in the Bankruptcy Court, for very large amounts of debt, has testified.

The financier's victims are for the most part young gentlemen possessed of large reversionary properties, or noblemen whose estates are much encumbered. They are informed that there is somebody in the background possessed of considerable resources, and they are told of schemes or companies in course of developement which are represented as being sure in the end to yield magnificent returns. They are financed partly in cash and partly in shares, and the roseate prospect is held out to them, not only of their being freed from temporary embarrassment, but also of their debts and other encumbrances being eventually spirited away. The flies look upon the spider as their best friend. In other words, the young gentlemen invite the financier to their rooms or houses, take him to their clubs, and generally introduce him into society, thereby, of course, bringing fresh victims within his reach.

It is almost unnecessary to indicate the course that events take. The reversions having become mortgaged up to the hilt, the properties are ultimately brought to the hammer and disposed of at the most ruinous sacrifice. Like the three-card trick, this sort of thing is continually going on, though it has been exposed times out of mind.

I have been engaged as counsel in many money-lending cases of which the facts were of a kind to come within the purview of a criminal court. The prosecution, however, rarely succeeded, the parties defrauded being content to recover a portion of their money, and the defendants, fearing the verdict of the jury, being equally content to avoid penal servitude by disgorging a portion of their ill-gotten gains.

There is perhaps even a worse blood-sucker than the financier just described. I allude to the money-lender who finds his victims in the middle and poorer classes. As a rule he opens, in some busy part of the town, an establishment on which he causes to be inscribed, in large gilt letters: "The

—— Bank of Deposit." On a brass-plate or board appears the following announcement: "Money lent on bills of sale, notes of hand, etc., on the easiest terms. Enquire within."

Those members of the British public who act upon the invitation conveyed in the last two words of the above announcement, are furnished with a book of rules, questioned as to the nature of the securities they have to offer, requested to pay a small sum to cover the cost of preliminary enquiries, and finally informed that their business will be promptly attended to. On subsequently reading the book of rules they will learn that the money can be advanced on a bill of sale on all their worldly goods, the loan being repayable by monthly instalments of principal and interest; and if they will make a little independent calculation for themselves, they will find that the latter comes out at something over one hundred per cent. The rules also set forth the fines that will be imposed if the instalments are not paid on the day they fall due.

On the premises are needy solicitors, or parties practising as solicitors, who, in most cases, are paid by salary. When the bill of sale is put in force, and the wretched debtors are deprived of all their goods, the worthy banker receives, not only the amount of his loan, but also a considerable sum for costs, which are charged on the most exorbitant scale. As a rule, too, a broker is attached to the offices, and a similarly heavy charge is made for his services.

When a person of the better class falls into the clutches of these worthies, they bind him hand and foot. Very frequently they get him completely into their power by causing him, almost unconsciously, to commit an illegal act. Let us suppose that there is a reversion payable at the death of the borrower's father or mother, of, say, ten thousand pounds. In the first place the usurer makes an advance thereon of a few hundred pounds, charging interest at the rate of from sixty to a hundred per cent., and he then sets himself to find out something about the antecedents of his client. It may be that the latter has already mortgaged his reversion for a small sum, and, if so, the fact is likely to be promptly discovered by the usurer by means of a sort of freemasonry that exists between men of his calling.

In due time the borrower, having spent the money that has been advanced to him, will apply for a second loan, whereupon the man of finance will casually remark:

"Before lending you any further sums, of course I under-

P 2

stand that you have never raised money on this security before from anybody else?"

Anxious above all things to secure the loan, the borrower will reply:

"Oh, that's all right; you may be quite easy on that score."

"Very well," says the money-lender, smiling complacently, "then the matter can be very easily arranged. I shall, however, want you to make a statutory declaration to that effect. It is a mere matter of form. Just step with me next door, where there is a commissioner for taking oaths and declarations. It can all be arranged in five minutes, and then you shall have the money. They have, I know, printed forms on the premises for this purpose. One of these can be filled up while we are smoking a couple of cigarettes in the private office; and then all you've got to do is to sign your name."

The borrower overcomes any scruples that may trouble him, the office is entered, the signature is duly appended, and a few minutes afterwards the second loan is advanced.

What has happened is this: the borrower, by attaching his signature to this document, has placed himself within the grasp of the criminal law, for an Act of Parliament has been passed which enacts that any person making a false statutory declaration is guilty of a misdemeanour, and liable, upon conviction, to a long term of imprisonment.

Further advances are made, and for some little while everything goes quite smoothly. At length, however, comes a time of friction. It may be that the wretched man attempts to break the chains which bind him, either by borrowing money elsewhere or by refusing to pay the enormous interest he is charged; or, again, it may be that the money-lender, considering the security already sufficiently mortgaged, refuses to make some further loan that is desired. The crisis having arrived, the usurer's course of action is simplicity itself. Pretending to be extremely indignant, he accuses his victim of fraud, and threatens to take him before a magistrate on a charge of obtaining money by false pretences—a course which, having regard to the untruth contained in the statutory declaration, is quite open to him. This threat, however, is very rarely carried into effect, for the borrower usually has wealthy relatives, who, in order to avoid the disgrace of a public exposure, will, in nine cases out of ten, come forward and pecuniarily assist him.

Some few people, of course, when they have landed themselves into the embarrassing position I have indicated, have the courage to stand their ground and face the worst.

In my professional career at the Bar I was connected with many cases in which the usurer and his debtor figured, and though in the majority of instances a settlement was arrived at between the committal for trial and the preferring of the indictment, it did occasionally happen that the case went to a jury.

The prosecution of R——, a lieutenant in a regiment of Dragoons, was a case in point. He had fallen into the hands of one of the pseudo-bankers, and had gone through precisely the experiences I have described. The reversion was a large one, and the advances had been considerable. A rupture having taken place between the parties, an application was made at Marlborough Street, before the late Mr. Knox, who committed the defendant for trial, but, on my application, admitted him to bail on his own recognisances.

During the interval before the date fixed for the trial at the Central Criminal Court, the prosecution made repeated overtures with a view to bring about a private settlement. In each case the purport of these negotiations was reported to me, but my invariable answer was that, the matter having been treated as a crime, it should not be trifled with; that I would be no party to a compromise; and that if anything of the kind were contemplated, I must insist upon the brief being taken elsewhere.

The accused was the heir of his grandfather, an elderly Baronet, and, a few days before the Sessions commenced, the solicitor instructing me asked whether I had any objection to the old gentleman attending the consultation, he being, I was informed, very desirous of doing so. I raised no opposition, and accordingly, when the conference took place, the Baronet was present.

The old ground was gone over again, and once more suggestions for a settlement were considered. Upon my giving my experiences of the particular individual we had to deal with, and reiterating my determination to be no party to a compromise, the old gentleman suddenly jumped up, and, seizing me by the hand, energetically exclaimed:

"You are right, sir, you are right. We will fight the rascal to the death."

"Not quite that, sir, I think," remarked the solicitor, a

quiet, bland, gentlemanly little man. "Having regard to the information I have prepared for Mr. Williams respecting the prosecutor, and bearing in mind that Mr. Williams already knows a good deal about him, I doubt very much, when it comes to the point, whether we shall see him in the box at all."

"You are wrong there, for once in your life," said I. "I know this man, and his assurance is his strong point. I shall be much obliged to you for any materials you may have for cross-examination, though they will be scarcely necessary, for this man and I have met before in courts of justice."

Other matters having been discussed, and I having given the solicitor particular instructions to give the prosecutor the necessary notices to produce all his books, the conference came to an end.

In due course the trial took place. As I had prophesied, the prosecutor did not shirk the ordeal of cross-examination. He was, indeed, the first witness called. With a genial smile upon his face, this young man, faultlessly attired and wearing a flower in his button-hole, leapt gaily into the witness-box, yet not so quickly as he afterwards tumbled out again, after undergoing about as bad a quarter of an hour as ever a witness experienced. Suffice it to say, without wearying the reader with details, that the jury stopped the case, and acquitted the prisoner, before my cross-examination was half concluded.

This happened a great many years ago. The last I heard of my antagonist was that he had migrated to the West End, where he had established a large and lucrative money-lending business, and that, so far as personal management was concerned, he had recently retired from it. I further learnt that he had bought a large stud of race-horses, and had very nearly succeeded in getting into one of the first training establishments at Newmarket. It appeared, however, that, some particulars of his early career having leaked out, he had been baulked in this, among other efforts to get into smart society.

There is another class of money-lenders, though I believe they are not nearly so numerous in the present day as they were when I was a young man and in the Army. I allude to the subalterns' friends, the discounting tailors. They were always willing to oblige young fellows who ordered uniforms from them, and who were good customers in other ways. Of course it would never have done, in the event of a bill being dishonoured, for the tailor to sue, as he would inevitably thereby have lost his customer and got into bad odour with the regiment; therefore the paper was always endorsed away, the discounter usually urging, as his reason for the transfer, that he was momentarily pressed for money.

In my time there was a tailor in Jermyn Street who did a large business in this way, and who, in his financial as well as in his sartorial capacity, was greatly patronised by the officers in the regiment of which I was a member. I shall never forget the monetary experiences of a comrade of mine named G——, who was of a very simple and trusting disposition. He had a bill discounted for a hundred and fifty pounds, and just before it reached maturity he wrote to the tailor asking for three months' renewal, stating that he was quite unable, for the time being, to pay the money. The tailor, in reply, wrote that he had been forced to endorse the bill away, but that the present holder would probably raise no objection to a renewal.

One morning G—— burst into my room wearing a very doleful expression of countenance. He had communicated with the holder of the bill, whose reply he now held in his hand.

"What the deuce is to be done?" exclaimed G——. "He won't hear about a renewal, and I can't possibly pay at present. He says that if the money isn't forthcoming by return of post, proceedings will at once be taken."

The letter was signed by a doctor (a quack, as we afterwards found) who resided in Albemarle Street.

We discussed the matter at considerable length, and G—— ultimately decided, very much against my advice, to run up to town and see his new creditor for the purpose of arranging matters. This he did with a vengeance, and his description of what took place was very amusing.

"On knocking at the door in Albemarle Street," he said, "I was received by a footman in livery, who showed me into a gorgeously furnished drawing-room on the first floor. I was kept waiting some little time, and then a man of Jewish appearance and very fashionably dressed came in. I didn't care for the job at all, as you can understand, and I felt pretty nervous and shaky. The fellow said he was Dr. —— and asked me what I was suffering from. I couldn't imagine what in the world he meant, and began to stammer out some sort of answer, when it suddenly occurred to me that he took me for a patient, and so I did what I could in the way of a laugh, and told him there was nothing the matter with my bodily health, but that I was suffering from temporary impecuniosity. He put on a puzzled expression, though, 'pon my word, I believe he knew what I was after all the time. He must have recognised my name, don't you see, because I had sent in my card. I told him about the renewal I wanted, and then he said: 'Oh, yes, you are Mr. G—— of the ——th regiment; I remember now. But you know I never interfere with these matters myself, leaving them all to my lawyers. If you'll get into a hansom with me, and drive round to Messrs. ——, in Bedford Row, I've no doubt whatever the matter can be arranged in five minutes.'"

It appeared that the two at once got into a cab and drove to the lawyers' office, the Doctor being excessively talkative and pleasant on the journey. When they reached their destination, G—— was accommodated with a chair in an outer office, his companion passing into an inner apartment in order to see one of the partners. Half an hour went by, and the poor subaltern was beginning to feel very unhappy and fidgety, when a clerk appeared, carrying a piece of paper, and requested him to be so good as to sign it. Never doubting that the document was a renewal of the bill, my ingenuous comrade, without troubling to read one single word contained therein, at once appended his signature. The clerk retook possession of the document, and, producing another from his pocket, handed it to the visitor, together with a slip of paper on which the following was written:

"My client, Dr. ——, sends his compliments, and wishes me to say that there is no necessity for detaining you any further. He has other business to transact here, and trusts therefore you will excuse him. You can peruse the accompanying paper as you drive home in the cab, which is still at the door."

Delighted to be released from the stuffy office, and being overjoyed at what he believed to be so successful an outcome of his visit, my friend seized his hat, ran downstairs, and telling the Jehu to drive to the Rag, jumped into the cab and was driven off. Imagine his horror when, some five minutes later, on casually glancing at the document that had been given to him, he read these words: "Victoria, by the Grace of God." The truth immediately flashed upon him—he had been served with a copy of a writ. What, then, was the other paper he had signed? He could not guess, and was too frightened to go back to the lawyers' office and enquire.

My friend returned to Walmer the same night, and lost no time in seeking me out and informing me of the latest phase that his troubles had entered. In those days I was as ignorant of such matters as a man well could be, and so it was in vain that we both puzzled our brains as to the meaning of what had taken place. We were, however, not long left in doubt. Two days afterwards, as he was proceeding from the barrack square to his quarters, my friend was arrested for debt at the suit of Dr. ——, of Albemarle Street. It appeared that the document he had signed at the office was a judgement by confession, and from the moment his pen had left the paper he had been liable to be taken by the Sheriff's officer.

The money was paid without much difficulty, and the victim released, but not before the creditor had received the hundred and fifty pounds, together with interest at the rate of sixty per cent., and a considerable additional sum for costs.

There have been from time immemorial, and always no doubt will be, one or two Leviathan money-lenders who transact business on a gigantic scale. Notable among these was the late Mr. P——, so well known for many years on the turf. He employed as a sort of jackal a well-known London solicitor, who usually arranged the loans in the first instance. As soon, however, as the nobleman or landed proprietor had been well secured, the principal discovered himself, and thenceforth conducted the business in person. Some of the largest estates in the country passed into his hands, and were manipulated by him.

Then, again, there was Mr. Leopold Sampson, a really remarkable man. It was his boast that he enjoyed every moment of his life, and denied himself none of the good things of this world. He lived in a large mansion not a hundred miles from Park Lane, and rode the best horses that money could procure. His wife's equipages were among the very smartest to be seen in London. When enjoying good health, he would never miss his morning ride in the Row, which he seemed to enjoy very thoroughly.

Everybody knew him, at any rate by sight, and he would often rein up to exchange a word or two with a passing acquaintance. It might be, for instance, an officer in the Life Guards, whom he would, perhaps, address in some such words as these:

'I had a piece of luck yesterday, of which I know, Captain,

you will be glad to hear. Mr. ——, of yours, who went such a dreadful mucker over last year's Derby and had to send in his papers, was nine thousand pounds in my debt, and I never expected to see a penny of the money again. Imagine my surprise, then, yesterday morning, when I received a cheque from him for seven thousand on account. But then, you see, usurer as I am, I pride myself on generally dealing with gentlemen, and I flatter myself that I rarely make a mistake."

When away from his business Mr. Sampson was a confirmed gambler. He visited Newmarket at nearly all the meetings, and was a familiar figure on nearly every racecourse in England. His bets were never small ones. A constant visitor at Spa and Monte Carlo, he once succeeded, I believe, at the latter place, in breaking the bank.

Mr. Sampson was never ashamed of his trade, regarding which he was wont to remark :

"I conduct it in the best and fairest way I believe it can be conducted. I don't seek people out; it's their own doing, and their own fault, if they come to me."

Few, if any, persons were ever heard to speak ill of him, and some anecdotes that were told of him reflected greatly to his credit. Here is one, the facts of which came within my own knowledge.

A professional man, who was extremely clever in his own vocation, but little versed in the ways of the world, once got into temporary difficulties, and needed a loan of two hundred pounds. Having heard of Mr. Sampson, he called at his office, and requested him to discount a bill for that amount. The financier received him very courteously, and said :

"I should be delighted, Mr. ——, to oblige you in this or any other way, but you have somewhat mistaken the nature of my business. I don't touch these small matters, and if I did I should be obliged to charge you an amount of interest which in the end might place you in greater difficulties than you have to face at present. I am sure you could take the b.ll up at the end of three months, or, as a gentleman, you would never have called here and represented that you would be able to do so. I'll tell you what I will do. I'll exchange cheques with you for that period. Here," he added, taking pen in hand and writing in his cheque-book, "is one for two hundred pounds. You let me have yours for a similar amount dated this day three months. Not a word of thanks, my dear sir. Good morning."

Of course there are a number of money-lenders who send out circulars and advertise in the newspapers, but they have been so repeatedly shown up lately that I do not propose to treat of them here.

After all, I think that the most straightforward members of the calling are those whose scale of interest is regulated by Act of Parliament, whose symbol is the three balls, and whose motto, appearing in large gilt letters, is " Money Lent."

CHAPTER XIII

TALENT IN TATTERS

The sandwich man—Changes of costume—His remuneration—Keen competition—A true story—Sudden disappearance—Reappearance as a successful author—Terrible news at the zenith of success—I visit my dying friend—His history—Writes for the stage—"Returned with thanks"—Goes on the stage—Not unsuccessful—Marries—Out of employment—Has typhoid fever—From bad to worse—Desperate poverty—The doctor orders fresh air and wine!—He becomes a sandwich man—His wife dies—The end.

I KNOW of no more wearisome occupation than that of the sandwich man. In fair weather and foul, in sunshine and snow, in clouds of dust and storms of rain, he has to jog along throughout the dreary day, attracting public notice to the strong woman at the Aquarium, the performing elephants at the Crystal Palace, or the latest Ceylon blend at the sign of the Golden Cannister.

From time to time the boardsman has to don some descriptive costume. Should he be retained on behalf of the Army and Navy Hair-Cutting Saloon, he may appear in an old regimental tunic and cocked hat, accompanied by a mate who stalks the world in the guise of a British Admiral. Again, should his boards illustrate "The Convict's Doom," the latest melodramatic success at the Princess's Theatre, he will very likely walk abroad in knickerbockers and a jacket plentifully embellished with the broad arrow.

The remuneration of sandwich men varies from one shilling to one and eightpence per day. To earn this paltry amount the poor fellows have to tramp through the streets from ten in the morning to ten at night. Once during the day a halt is called for a meal, or, if that is not forthcoming, for a pipe.

In spite of the badness of the pay, the long hours, and the degradation involved, there is keen competition for the sandwich boards. The regular hands, who are known to the advertising contractors, are tolerably sure of obtaining employment, but the case is very different with the occasional men. Of such there are often fifty to every board that has to be carried. I know of no more striking illustration of the struggle for existence than is afforded by the exterior of the contractors' offices when men are being engaged. It is painful to see the eager and anxious faces of the applicants during the distribution of boards, and still more painful afterwards to see the unsuccessful ones filing dejectedly away, some to seek work elsewhere, and others to betake themselves to the parks, the day nurseries of poor wretches who have not had the means, on the previous evening, to procure a night's lodging in a "doss-house."

The sandwich men are drawn from nearly every class and calling. Almost any one can carry boards; hence the desperate fight for the work.

Few men sink any lower than this employment, for the simple reason that they do not long survive it. For the most part they end their days in the workhouse infirmary or the hospital, whither they are taken when stricken by ague or other disease induced by exposure to the cold and wet.

I am only acquainted with one case of a man who, after being reduced to this employment, has been able to regain a position in life; and the facts of this case I propose to lay before the reader. Though I shall do my best to conceal the identity of the person concerned, it will be my endeavour to reproduce his story in the language in which he himself told it to me.

It was a few days after Christmas in the year 188—, the *locus in quo* one of the small houses in Curzon Street, Mayfair, a thoroughfare then known as Bolton Row. The houses there were, for the most part, bachelor residences, and the occupier of one of them was my old friend and schoolfellow George M———. We had lost sight of one another for many years; in point of fact, shortly after leaving Eton, my friend had mysteriously disappeared. He had not been seen or heard of until a few years before the date of which I am speaking, when he suddenly burst upon the world as one of the most brilliant and successful authors of the day. His name was in everybody's mouth, that is, it was after being announced, for his first work was produced anonymously. It was on a most interesting social subject, and, getting into the hands of one of the shrewdest publishers in London, it had a great vogue, so much so, indeed, that everybody went about asking "Who wrote the —— Papers?" The author's name was soon known, and his reputation was secure. Book succeeded book, each one meeting with, if possible, a greater success than its predecessor. The new writer turned his attention to the stage, and produced one or two plays that yielded a considerable fortune for himself and for the manager of the fashionable West End theatre where they were brought out.

M—— was in the zenith of his success when he received the terrible news from his medical man that he was suffering from an incurable malady, of which the seeds had been latent in his system for some time, and that his end was rapidly approaching. It was about a fortnight after this great blow had fallen upon him that I was seated by his bedside in the little house in Bolton Row. The only other occupant of the room was the hospital nurse who was in attendance upon him. He had been quietly dozing for about half an hour, and I had been watching his pale, worn features, my mind wandering back to the old Eton days when "Sunny," as he was called, was the brightest and merriest boy in the whole school. I remembered what a terrible change I had noticed, when we had met again a few years before, in my friend's manner, spirits, and general bearing.

I was aroused from my reverie by feeling a pressure on my arm, and on looking down I saw that the invalid was awake, and watching me narrowly.

"Turn the lamp down a little lower, please, nurse," said he; "the light somehow seems to hurt my eyes. Thanks. And now will you leave us alone for an hour or so, as I want to have a private talk with my old friend."

As soon as the door was closed, he continued, addressing me:

"I know what you were thinking of just now—of old times, and school, and how changed I am from the merry little companion you used to know. You do not suppose I have not read your thoughts before. You have a tell-tale face, you know—you always had—and I noticed at our first meeting, after I became somewhat of a celebrity, how critically you observed my prematurely grey hair, furrowed cheeks, and joyless manner; and, with all the admiration you have expressed for my works, how often have you said, in your old, easy way, 'Sunny, old man, how I do wish you had not turned quite so cynical!' You have never asked me the reason why—that is like you; you thought you might give me pain. But I am going to tell you the reason to-night, for I know that nobody could feel more sorry for an old friend than you."

He paused, passed his hand over his forehead, and then continued:

"You remember just after I left school hearing of my poor father's ruin, although, I have no doubt, you were unaware of the details, and of how terrible a crash it was. From wealth he was reduced to absolute poverty. He had not long to bear it, though, for his health, which had never been very good, quickly broke up; and I, who had been brought up in the lap of luxury, and had never known what it was to have a wish ungratified, was left without a relative in the world, and, what was worse, without a sixpence in my pocket. What was to be done? I was young, and not without energy, and so I determined to try my luck at literature. I wrote two or three little things, which I hawked about from place to place, but nobody would deign to cast an eye upon them.

"I had always been very fond of acting, as you will remember, and I next turned my attention to writing for the stage. I had managed to make the acquaintance of a very poor and humble friend, who was connected with an evening paper, and who was very nearly in as straitened circumstances as myself. Through his assistance I obtained sufficient journalistic work to keep me from actual starvation while I was completing my literary attempt. At length it was finished, and I hurried, manuscript in hand, to my friend, who, when I read it to him, although not usually a demonstrative man, was loud in its praises and sanguine of its success. Through him I obtained an introduction to one or two theatrical managers, to whom I submitted my manuscript for approval, but always with the same result—'returned with thanks,' and from its outward appearance I should say they had not even looked at it. This was the second play I produced in London after the success of my books. You were there on the first night, and you will remember the enthusiastic reception it met with. And yet this was the very work that had been treated with scorn many years before, by nearly every theatre in London!"

He was sitting up in bed and getting very excited. I begged him to be calm.

"Calm!" he exclaimed, "wait until you have heard the rest. I saw at once that, as an unknown man, there was no chance for me in this particular groove. 'Well,' said I to myself, 'if I cannot succeed in having my own work interpreted, suppose I try interpreting the works of others,' and I determined to go upon the stage. There were no travelling provincial companies in those days, and I think only one regular theatrical agent, Mr. Anson. Through him I succeeded in obtaining an engagement in a company in the north of England, the manager of which was proprietor of two theatres in the district. I was not unsuccessful, and perhaps this was the reason why I committed the most selfish act of my life, an act which has since seemed to me to have amounted almost to a crime. I dared to love. I, a penniless wretch without a sixpence to call my own, ventured to say: 'With all my worldly goods I thee endow.' But I did love with all my heart and with all my soul.

"The object of my affections was a clergyman's daughter. He was the father of a large family, and Mildred—that was her name—was one of the youngest children. Anxious to relieve the burden of the household expenses, she had taken an engagement as a governess in the household of a wealthy tradesman in the place where I was acting. We met, loved, became secretly engaged, and were ultimately married in a sequestered corner of the town. My wife, on writing to her relatives, who looked upon the stage as a hotbed and sink of iniquity, received the answer she expected. They told her never to venture across her father's threshold again, and added that from henceforth her name would never be mentioned in the family circle. My wife soon recovered from the shock of the news. What cared we? Were we not flesh of one flesh, bone of one bone, loving as two creatures had never loved before?

"I don't think I ever pictured such great happiness as fell to my lot in that and a few succeeding years. For a considerable time we three—for my wife had given birth to a little boy—struggled on, doing our best on the small salary I was earning. Suddenly our manager died, the company was disbanded, and I was thrown out of employment. With the little money I had saved we came to London, and took a small lodging near Covent Garden, it being my intention to seek another provincial engagement. While endeavouring to do so, however, I was seized with typhoid fever, my poor little boy contracted the disease, and when I awoke from my delirium, which lasted several days, I learnt from my heart-broken wife that he was dead. She tried to comfort me, and nursed me like a ministering angel. I knew not how we had existed during the time I had been ill, but was not long in making the discovery. When I was well enough to cast my eyes round the room, I found that it had been stripped of the few little articles of comfort we had managed to gather about us. My wife, too, had scarcely a garment to her back. With what patience and with what fortitude she had borne up! Poor darling Mildred, to what misery my selfish love had brought her!

"Things went from bad to worse. I had no strength left, and was barely able to walk, when one morning the landlady made her appearance, and stated that she depended on the rent of the apartments for her own livelihood, and that, much as she regretted it and pitied us, we must leave on the following day, as she had re-let the rooms. I could not complain, for I knew that what she said was true; and so next morning we were outcasts, waifs on the pitiless streets of London."

"But surely you had some friends!" I interrupted. "Had you appealed to me, poor as I was then myself, something could have been done."

"Friends!" he replied bitterly. "I tell you I was lost—lost in this great world of ours—lost like thousands of others are lost, either through their own faults, or, as in my case, through misfortune. Their identity destroyed, their names forgotten, their features distorted and unrecognisable through want and disease, their very existence blotted out—who stops to notice them in their rags and tatters?

"I will not weary you with any detailed account of our sufferings. Suffice it to say that we found ourselves in a low lodging-house in Spitalfields, which was the only shelter we could pay for. Fancy for a moment my sweet, gently-nurtured darling amid such surroundings! The air was polluted with foul oaths and language too horrible to describe, and the place was packed with thieves and women of the lowest and most degraded class. We were there for two nights, and then, ill as I was, I managed to obtain some temporary employment in Spitalfields Market, which enabled me to take a small room in Bethnal Green. All this time I saw that my darling's health was giving way. My lion-hearted girl, who had suffered so much for me, patiently and without a murmur, was gradually breaking down. Day by day a terrible change came over her. The parish doctor, who was very kind, and who sees thousands of such cases every year, in answer to my anxious enquiries, shook his head. She required fresh air, he said, and wine and nourishment. Fresh air in that foul court! Wine and nourishment, when we couldn't afford any fire, though the pitiless snow was oozing through the roof! My God! I nearly went mad. The doctor, moved by the desperate state I was in, bade me follow him to his dispensary, and there gave me a small quantity of port wine. The next day was the last of my employment at the market, and with the money I received I obtained some nourishing food. I sat watching all night by the mattress on which my darling lay, every now and then moistening her parched lips. When day broke I slipped my hand from hers, and having visited a neighbour, who promised to look in once or twice during my absence—for the poor never fail to help the poor—I crept downstairs into the street.

"I enquired in vain for work until nearly nine o'clock, when I thought of the yard where I had heard that sandwich men were engaged. It seemed but a slender chance, but I resolved to try my luck. I was reduced to the utmost state of weakness by semi-starvation and distress, but I knew it was necessary to put on a bold front if I were to succeed; so, pulling myself together as well as I could, I took my stand in the crowd of applicants and tremblingly awaited the result. It so happened that an extra number of men were required that day, and I was engaged. For the twelve hours I was to receive the sum of one shilling.

"When I got between those boards, what with shame, disgrace, and hunger, I thought I should have dropped. I passed through the streets, but saw nothing distinctly. The faces and forms of passers-by were all lost in one blurred mass. I hung my head on my chest, and moved forward mechanically in the wake of my comrades.

"How I prayed for night throughout that long, weary day! It came at last, and I received my shilling and hurried home. As our task finished at Regent Circus, I did not get back to Bethnal Green until nearly eleven o'clock, when I rushed upstairs to find that my poor wife was dying. The doctor had called, my neighbour told me, and gave no hope. A faint voice came from the bed:

"'George, dear, thank Heaven you've come; I thought you would have been too late. What will become of you, darling, without me?'

"I seized her in my arms, and kissed her brow, damp with the chill of death.

"'My love, my angel!' I cried, 'it is I—I—who have brought you to this. It has been all my selfish folly.'

"By way of answer she pressed me more closely to her heart.

"'Give me a little air,' she gasped.

"I ran to the window and opened it, and as I did so the sound of a Christmas carol from a neighbouring street fell upon my ears. What hollow mockery it was! I cursed the waits, I cursed myself, and staggered back to the bed.

"'Mildred—wife!' I sobbed, and the next minute she lay lifeless before me.

"I fell senseless over her prostrate form, and when I recovered my reason I was an altered man.

"They say there is no such thing as a broken heart. Be it so, but hearts can die though this wretched frame may still live on. It was so with me, for from that moment my heart was dead."

"She knew your worth, George, as I do now, and always did!" I exclaimed, the tears pouring down my cheeks. "She loved you, and died in the arms of the man she had devoted her whole young life to. Had she lived, think how proud she would have been of you."

"Think!" he murmured. "Yes, think that if one-fiftieth part of a night's share of one of my plays had been mine that day, her life might—nay, would—have been saved. Oh, Heaven! what had I done? What had I done?"

I noticed now for the first time that a change had come over my suffering friend. I hastily summoned the nurse to the room, and she raised him gently in her arms. He clutched me convulsively by the hand, and a smile stole over his hollowed cheeks.

"Mildred," he murmured, "Mildred, the waits——"

Then he sank back upon the pillow, my hand fell from his grasp, and I knew that the gentle spirit of my long-suffering schoolfellow had passed peacefully away.

CHAPTER XIV

THE LONDON SEASON

The last day of the season—Its beginning—Ladies at the races—The Fourth of June at Eton—Eton in my young days—The procession of boats—Reminiscences of Ascot—The Master of the Buckhounds—Amusing scene at Ascot Races—A contemptible manœuvre—A funny story of this year's race meeting—His lordship outwitted—Falling off in political entertainments—How marriages are "knocked up"—The Row on a Sunday morning—Coaching Club meets—The July Meeting at Newmarket—Goodwood—Exclusiveness of Cowes society—The river forty years ago—A complete change for the worse—All is vanity.

THE twenty-eighth of July—the first day of glorious Goodwood, and practically the last of the London season! The private omnibuses, laden outside with luggage and inside with domestics, are already to be seen in the West End thoroughfares. The few people of the *monde* who are not able to leave the metropolis, at any rate for the time being, have shut up the front part of their houses, and are leading a sort of secret life in some other portion of the premises.

For my part, I am of opinion that London is never more pleasant to live in than when it is what is called unfashionable, that is, when the season is practically over. Over? By the way, when does it actually commence?

Matters have changed very much since my young days, and I suppose the beginning of the season is now somewhere about Derby week. Of course I am leaving out of account the short Easter season, when in these days there are so many smart parties.

Ladies never, or very seldom, went to the Derby forty years ago. They were content with gracing the Epsom gradients on the "ladies' day," when the Oaks was run. I don't suppose that, as late as Hermit's year, half-a-dozen representatives of the fashionable female world would have been seen on the entire course on Derby Day. True, the date I specify is not altogether an appropriate one, for there was more than one snowstorm that year.

Things are very different now. In the present day the boxes and stands are crowded with ladies. Indeed, since the institution of Sandown, Kempton, Hurst Park, and other meetings near London, racing has become almost as great an amusement for fashionable women as for fashionable men, and though the former do not wager in such high figures as the latter, they are pretty universally imbued with the spirit of gambling.

Thus it comes about that London is pretty well filled by the week in which the carnival of the English turf takes place.

There is nothing very much in the way of fashionable gatherings between Epsom and Royal Ascot, excepting, of course, the ordinary dinner-parties, dances, and receptions, and also excepting, of course, the pleasant jaunt to Eton for the popular Fourth of June. This gathering is naturally pretty much confined to the relatives of the boys, but as there are now over a thousand of the latter, representing all the aristocracy and wealth of the country, there are few more patrician and fashionable assemblages than that to be seen, on the date in question, in the Upper School at "Speeches" in the morning, in the Playing Fields after the declamatory entertainment is over, and at the fireworks and procession of boats in the evening.

Dear old Eton! things have greatly changed since my day. The aquatic gathering then generally took place in Ascot week, and that, in my opinion, was a much better arrangement than the present one. During race week fashionable London occupied the Windsor hotels—the "White Hart," the "Castle," and all the available furnished country houses in the immediate neighbourhood, and the result was a splendid attendance at the Eton Festival.

There were under six hundred boys only then. The boats were of very different build and calibre to those of the present day. First in the procession came the ten-oared *Monarch*, and a good old barge she was. The "eight" and the Upper and Lower boats followed. Nearly every craft had for steerer an old Etonian, whose privilege it was to provide the champagne, which was securely packed in a hamper and placed in the stern. He it was who afterwards headed the table at the supper at Surley.

During my time one of the most popular providers of the juice of the grape was the Duke of Newcastle—the grandfather of the present Duke—whose eldest son was in my remove. I suppose that the Fourth of June gathering will continue as long as this fine old school exists, which no doubt will be until the end of time.

Ascot, too, has undergone some changes. My first appearance on the Royal course was, I fancy, when Van Tromp, Cossack, and Chanticleer raced for the Emperor's Vase, and a splendid trio they were. Chanticleer, who belonged to Mr. Merry, was ridden by the "boy in yellow," and was, I believe, last, but I remember for a certainty that he was a grey. I subsequently saw the Flying Dutchman contend with Canezou, the former gaining an easy victory. The gold vase was the yearly gift of the Emperor of Russia, but this gift was discontinued after the Crimean War.

As I have said, the Ascot of those days was very different from the Ascot of to-day. It will be remembered that at that time there had been no domestic loss to overshadow the life of our Imperial and Gracious Queen. The presence of Royalty on the course used to be the occasion of a most gorgeous pageant.

At the time of which I am speaking, the Great Western had not opened to Windsor, Slough being the nearest station. There was a branch of the South-Western to Windsor, the terminus being in Datchet Lane, but there was no actual line to Ascot, Virginia Water, and Sunningdale. People bent on having a week's racing usually hired one of the extremely pretty houses in the immediate neighbourhood of the Park. The Grand Stand was not so large and gorgeous as at present, and there was no Royal enclosure to excite the jealousy and envy of the plutocrats, *nouveaux riches*, and arrant snobs who are never tired of using every kind of trickery and meanness to elbow their way into society.

It has often occurred to me that, during the week or ten days immediately preceding the festive gathering, the life of the Master of the Buckhounds can scarcely be a happy one. The holders of that office for many years have been two old Etonians, schoolfellows of mine, who, as is usually the case, having been known as the best of boys, turned out the most amiable and popular of men.

It is not of much use trying to race if you are staying down at a house in the neighbourhood. When you get into the enclosure you find there are many things beside horses to engage your attention. There are chairs, cloaks, race-glasses, and so forth, to be looked after, greetings to be exchanged, and general conversation to be indulged in, while he would indeed be a monster who could spare no time to scrutinise the pretty faces and exquisite costumes to be seen on every side.

One year at Ascot I witnessed a sight that caused me much amusement. There appeared at the gate, wh'ch opens directly into the course, and at which one of the keepers in green and gold is always stationed, a little man in a grey suit and bright scarlet tie, who was accompanied by his wife, a very stout lady, and his daughter, both of whom were arrayed in all the colours of the rainbow. Their appearance very forcibly put me in mind of a whimsical communication that was once made to me by an individual of Eastern origin, whose great weakness was a belief—Heaven knows whence derived—that his family, who always dressed in the most vulgar manner possible, were remarkably *distingué* and patrician-looking people. In relating their holiday experiences, he said to me:

"You know my sisters dress beautifully, don't you?"

Well, I knew they dressed, and I knew their eye for colour was alarming; so I vouchsafed an affirmative reply.

"Well," he continued, "they have been a tour in Germany, and they couldn't go down the streets without being mobbed. The German inhabitants took them for English Royalty."

I had no doubt as to the mobbing; but I could not help shaking my head over the alleged cause.

But to return to the three visitors to Ascot. The gentleman presented his tickets to the doorkeeper, who eyed them rather suspiciously, but was ultimately satisfied. The trio then marched down the centre of the enclosure—which was pretty well deserted, as everybody had passed into the paddock to see the horses saddled—and stopped immediately underneath the Prince of Wales's box, a part which, out of respect, is never used, save by His Royal Highness and his intimate friends. Into this part of the enclosure the three new arrivals promptly scrambled, and, throwing themselves back, they blew themselves out as much as to say: "Now, my good friends, what do you think of this?"

The bell rang for clearing the course, the horses left the paddock, and the people poured back into the enclosure. It was immensely funny to note the sensation that the new-comers caused. I recognised the little man at the first glance. He was a City magnate, and of some little importance in the Corporation. All eyes were turned on the box, pince-nez went up, glasses were levelled, a general titter passed through the throng, and some tolerably loud whispers were exchanged. People walked backwards and forwards, as if they could never tire of the sight before them. There the trio remained, looking just as happy and pleased as if they were sitting for their photographs, and I have not the slightest doubt that there was floating through their minds some such idea as that which took possession of my friend whose relatives were mobbed in Germany.

The three waited to see a race or two, and then quitted the enclosure by the gate at which they had entered. Ten minutes later I saw the little man return through another gate, accompanied by his daughter and eldest son, the latter being, if possible, a more vulgar-looking dog than his papa. This was breaking the rules with a vengeance, it being distinctly understood that tickets of admission to the enclosure are in no way transferable.

There is rather a funny story told in connection with the Royal enclosure this year. Mrs. B——, a lady hailing from the Colonies, had been introduced into a certain section of London society by a noble lord who had the reputation of possessing a sensitive and gallant heart. Among other places where he had lancéd the lady was the house of a well-known City man. She stayed there with his lordship, and not only became extremely popular, but was of great assistance to the City dame in entertaining and getting to the house certain celebrated society people. The lady's dress was simply perfect. All that wealth could procure, that Doucet or Worth could design, and that a rather seductive figure could show off, was "en évidence"; but it subsequently turned out, much to the horror of the hostess, that for months past the accounts for the dresses had been defrayed by the master of the establishment.

While staying at the house the lady became acquainted with Lord S——, the husband of a very charming lady greatly admired in society. His lordship at once struck up a friendship of the most intimate character with Mrs. B——, and they visited together many popular resorts, including the "Star and Garter," at Richmond, the "Ship," at Greenwich, Bushey Park, and Hampton Court. It was upon one of these jaunts that Mrs. B—— informed his lordship that ever since she had been in England the darling wish of her heart had been to visit the

Royal enclosure at Ascot, and she went on to request him to take steps to gratify her desire. Now, Lord S—— had been noted from his school-days for being one of the most careful and particular of men. Here, then, was a pretty dilemma for him to be placed in! To ask for a pass in the lady's name was out of the question, as he would bring himself into unpleasant notoriety by the request, which, moreover, would certainly be refused. He did his best to dissuade the lady from her project, but all to no purpose. One day, however, his lordship made his appearance at the " Grosvenor Hotel," where Mrs. B—— was staying, and, with his face beaming with delight, exclaimed:

"It is all right; you can go with me to Ascot, and be in the Royal enclosure on the Hunt Cup day—all day long, if you please—and that day, you know, is one of the most fashionable of the week. We can go down quietly together by the train, and have a regular day of it. And how do you think I've managed it? Why, simply by cross-examining her ladyship, and going over with her all her engagements and plans for the week. I asked her whether it would not tire her too much to go to and from Ascot every day, and sit out the races, especially as she was not over strong. She seemed quite delighted at my being so thoughtful on her account, and determined that she would stop in town on the Cup day. So you see my pass for two will do for us both, and with the official at the door you will pass as Lady S——."

Mrs. B—— was in the seventh heaven of delight, and profusely complimented his lordship on his ready wit.

The day arrived, and the pair took a train from Vauxhall, and arrived in due course at Ascot. His lordship's confusion, however, was great when the man at the door, after looking at the card, became very confused and stammered out:

" I am afraid there must be some mistake, my lord. Her ladyship arrived only an hour ago. She said she expected your lordship by the next train, and that your lordship was in possession of a pass for you both. Knowing her ladyship well by sight, of course I admitted her at once. Your lordship will find her on the lawn."

The biters had been bit, and the pair did the best thing possible under the circumstances, beat a hasty retreat.

After Ascot there is very little stirring in the fashionable world except the ordinary dinner-parties, dances, and receptions. By receptions I mean such entertainments as are given by the

Marchioness of Salisbury, Lady Stanhope, and the wives of other political leaders. Of course these gatherings are most successful during the time the Tories are in office, for they have both the houses and the money necessary for entertaining. In the matter of hospitality there has been of late years a noticeable falling off among those who are in authority as Liberals, or rather, as Home Rulers and Radicals. Mr. Gladstone, of course, has his official residence in Downing Street, but Lord Rosebery is a widower, and Lady Hayter does not now entertain to the extent she did formerly. Political entertainments on the Liberal side are, indeed, practically things of the past. This is not, however, much loss, for what, after all, are these entertainments, to obtain cards for which some people put themselves to so much trouble? They are neither useful nor interesting. The Foreign Office is certainly an extremely pretty sight, to see once and have done with it; it certainly does not repay a second visit.

As for the balls and parties of society in the present day, they are nothing. Men don't dance now, at least the young men don't. It is too much of a bore, and it is always too hot. They prefer to "sit out." A man takes up a young girl for the evening, and they pass the time in quiet nooks and corners. What a change from the good old robust English society of fifty years ago!

It is at these entertainments that most of the marriages of the year are knocked up. I say "knocked up" because that expression fittingly describes what takes place. It may be that some wretched girl has been hawked about for three or four seasons, and has come to be regarded as a drug in the matrimonial market. Her mother, who should be her protectress and well-wisher, is never tired of reproaching her. The cost of her dresses is thrown in her face, and she is constantly reminded that Lilian So-and So and Gertrude So-and-So, without half her looks or figure, have married rent-rolls of thousands a year. At last the girl becomes callous, and, utterly regardless of all that should bring two hearts together, allows herself to be sold to the highest bidder, in nine cases out of ten not caring sixpence halfpenny for the bargain.

Not an uninteresting place during the season is the Row on a Sunday morning. You see some curious sights there. Whether the people who carry prayer-books have all been to a place of worship I cannot say. To judge by their doings, I should think it rather doubtful. Here can be seen youth that has been sacrificed to age. It is true, you are told that that old gentleman—some noble earl, it may be—is devotedly attached to his fair young companion, and that she returns his affection. Well, it doesn't look much like it, to judge by the way she gazes wistfully around, heedless of the nonsense he is pouring into her ear.

Then there are the Coaching Club meets, which are always fashionably attended; the trooping of the colours on the Queen's birthday, and other entertainments "ejusdem generis."

But I must not forget one attraction of the season, notable for being free from all the nonsense and humbug of society—I mean the week behind the ditch at Newmarket, the July Meeting. Now, this really is a glorious time. In my humble judgement —and I love a horse almost as keenly as does a Yorkshireman— this is by far the pleasantest race meeting of the year.

Head-quarters, as they call it, is, after all, the only place at which to race. The whole town thinks of nothing but racing and dreams of nothing but racing; it is plunged in racing from six o'clock in the morning to twelve o'clock at night. The entire life of the place is different from that which you live elsewhere. If you are staying at a nice house— and the owners of nice houses at Newmarket are the most hospitable people in the world—you have nothing but sport and enjoyment from morning to night.

Getting up early you go out on to the Limekilns, where you see strings of race-horses brought out by their owners to be exercised. If you last year felt a little "hit" it would have restored your spirits in no time to see Tom Jennings, on an honest cob and with a piece of broom in his mouth, watching Prince Soltykoff's Sheen, Gold, or Mephisto, doing an early morning gallop; and if, just before the Cesarewitch, you had been standing by his side and heard him whistle and cry "Sheen!" between his teeth, as the old horse went by, you would have felt you had a good tip for the coming race.

What visitor to Newmarket does not know "the Captain," and his faithful trainer, Jewitt? Then there are other trainers too numerous to mention.

I was very much amused one morning when, on strolling away from my host, a popular trainer of race-horses, who was engaged on the Limekilns watching his favourites go through their paces, I came upon a sign-post, on which some one had written the following: "Robert S—— is a d—n fraud. He never tells his —— boys nothink." The allusion was to a well-known trainer, who, I believe, is not celebrated for imparting his secrets to other persons.

After Newmarket comes Goodwood, and then Cowes, which is the last "go" of the year. Cowes has always been rather a puzzler for people trying to wedge their way into society. If you are not in the set on the lawn, at the fireworks, etc., you might just as well be at home in London.

After Cowes, unless there is cholera on the Continent, or some other startling preventive, everybody goes abroad, save, of course, those who affect the river.

The river, also, is not what it was. I am now fifty-seven years of age, and at the present moment I am casting my mind back to the time when I was fifteen. In those days there were scarcely any boats to be seen between Boveney Lock and Maidenhead Bridge, and none at all further up, between Maidenhead and Cookham. There were, moreover, no filthy house-boats and no steam launches to wash away the banks of the river, and place the angler's life, or rather soul, in jeopardy —for the number is unknown of the oaths he utters, day by day, at being unloosened and washed away from his moorings. Those unable to afford a boat could fish from the bank with a fair prospect of good sport; and their more prosperous comrades could row down to Water Oakley and Bray, and catch their thirty or forty dozen gudgeon a day.

What has the river become now? The banks are stuccoed, and there is no chub fishing, no barbel fishing, and scarcely any gudgeon fishing to be had. The whole tning has been completely ruined. Look at Boulter's Lock on a Sunday afternoon; turn your eyes towards the lovely woods of Clive-den, formerly the property of Lord Orkney, and now owned by the Duke of Westminster; think of Skindle's, the "Orkney Arms," kept then by the original proprietor himself; and lastly, look across the river at the new hotel, where some skirt-dancer is indulging her admirers in a corner with a suddenly-inspired rehearsal of "Ta-ra-ra-Boom-de-ay."

And then a word as to the occupants of the punts, with their Japanese umbrellas as screens, who moor their craft in the nooks of Cliveden Reach on a Sunday afternoon. I am not a particular man, but I cannot help taking exception to the behaviour of these people.

One season runs its course, there is a brief interlude; and then the gay crowds reassemble for their frolics. There are changes in the programme, but the vanity of the thing is immortal.

INDEX

Abuse, Venomous, 82.
Acol, Rector of, 154.
Act, A kindly, 218.
Adelphi Theatre, The, 172, 177.
Albini, Madame, 177.
Albemarle Street, 215.
Albert Square, 75.
Albert Street, 75.
"Alderman," The, 99.
Aldgate, 21, 102.
Alexandra wing of London Hospital, 47.
Alhambra, The, 177.
"Amok! amok!" 77.
Anson, Mr., 224.
Aquarium, The, 220.
Argyll Rooms, 66.
Artillery Lane, 88.
Ascot, 133, 201, 229, 230; horses running at, 230; an amusing sight at, 231.
Athletes, 6.
Attractions of Ramsgate, 109.
Authors, Remuneration of, 178.
Avona, The, 109.

Babel, A modern, 75.
Baccarat playing declared illegal, 202.
Baker Street Station, 21, 78.
Baker, Thomas, 10.
Baldwin, Joe, 143.
Ballantine, Serjeant, 65.
Baroda Place, 75..
Bath-chair men, 110.
Battersea Park, 90.
Bedford Coffee Tavern, The, 183, 184.
Bedford, Earls of, 182, 183.
Bedford House, 182.
Bedford, Paul, 172.
Bedford Row, 216.
Belgrave Square, 115, 118, 122, 123.
Bell Lane, 25.

Bell's match manufactory, 15.
Bennett, Sir John, 80.
Bernard, Bayle, 177.
Bethnal Green, 29, 36, 85, 87, 225, 226.
Betting, 198; on the increase, 198; in the West End, 200.
Bignell, Mr., 66.
Bill-discounter, The, 209, 214.
Bird-fanciers, 27; language of, 27.
Birds in the East End, 22.
Biters bit, The, 233.
"Black-eyed Susan," 174.
Blanchard, E. L., 177.
Blind, Jem, 173.
Blankets on the brain, 31; to be stamped, 32; and not grey ones, 33.
Bloomsbury, 117.
Bluegate Fields, 76.
Board of Trade officials, 82.
Bodkin, Sir William, 65, 70, 71.
Bolton Row, 221, 222.
Bond Street, 206.
Bookmaker, The, unfairly treated, 200.
Borough, The, 42.
Boswell, Mr. James, 184.
Boucicault, Dion, 177.
Boulter's Lock, 236.
Boundary Street, 33, 34.
Boveney Lock, 236.
Bow Road, 96.
"Boxer," 24.
Bray, 236.
Brennan, Inspector, 96.
Brett, the police officer, 197.
Brewertons, The, 95, 96.
Brick Lane, 90.
Bridewell, The, 184.
"Bridge of Sighs," The, 77.
Brooks, Shirley, 177; verses in *Punch* by, 101.
Brough, William and Robert, 173.
Brown, Mr., 25.

INDEX

Brownlow, Lord, 183.
Bryant & May's match manufactory, 12, 18.
Buck's Row, 6, 107.
Buckhounds, Master of the, 230.
Buckstone, John Baldwin, 175; as Captain Walter Maydenblush, 175.
Bull, the police officer, 197.
Burglar, A remarkable, 94.
Burglarious Bill, 93.
Burglary, Description of a, 97.
Burnand, Frank, 174.
Bushey Park, 143, 232.
Bushey, Our cottage at, 143.
Butcher, A, in Covent Garden Market, 186.
Byron, Henry J., 173.
Bythesea, Lord, 127; is arrested, 128; we visit him, 129; his high spirits, 130; he marries, 132; his daughter, 132; arranges for her marriage, 135; the sequel, 136; his solitary death, 136.

Café Royal, The, 160.
Cambridge, Duke of, 48.
Cambridge Heath, 35.
Canezou, 230.
Cannon Street, 103.
"Captain," The, 235.
Carlingford, Lady, 143.
Carlisle, Lord, 184.
Carlsbad, 124.
Carlton House Terrace, 149, 151.
Caseley, Thomas, 95, 96; sentence upon, 97; gives evidence, 97.
Cases, a few distressing, 34-37.
"Castle," The, at Windsor, 229.
Casuals, Various classes of, 61; concealing money, 63; and stone-breaking, 59-61.
Catherine Street, 181.
Cave, Mr., 111.
Céleste, 172.
Central Criminal Court, 168, 213.
Cesarewitch, The, 235.
Chancery Lane, E., 75.
Chancery Lane, E.C., 131, 192.
Chanticleer, 230.
Chapel Royal, The, Savoy, 136.
Charing Cross, 103, 196, 197.
Chatterton, 177.
Chaunting, 41.
Chestnuts, The avenue of, in Bushey Park, 143.
Chinamen and their knives, 78.
Chinese quarter, The, 76.
Chingford, 16.
Chippendale, 175.

Chislehurst, 105.
Chorley, 177.
Cider Cellars, The, 181.
"Citizen," The, 99.
"Citizen's Friend," The, 99.
City magnate, A, 232.
Clark, 175.
Clarke, Johnnie, 174.
Clerkenwell Green, 64.
Clerkenwell Sessions House, 68, 71.
Clifden House Institute, 18.
Climbing the ladder, 115-126.
Cliveden, 236.
Cliveden Reach, 236.
Clothing distributed, 34.
Clubs, East End, 91.
Coaching Club meets, 235.
"Coal Hole," The, 181.
Cockburn, Lord Chief Justice, 168.
"Colleen Bawn," The, 177.
Colony, An Italian, 64.
Colours, Trooping the, 235.
Commercial Road, 4, 76, 106.
Commercial Street, 21.
Common lodging-houses, 38.
Compton, 173, 175, 176.
Conference at Medland Hall, 57; resolutions at, 57, 58; speeches by casuals at, 58.
Congregational Union, London, 56.
Conversation in a public-house, 26.
Cookham, 235.
Coombs Street, 30.
Cork Street, 128.
Cornhill burglary, The, 95.
"Corsican Brothers," The, 175.
Cossack, 230.
Coster, A, and his bride, 104.
County Council, The London, 65, 72.
County of London, Sessions of the, 72.
Court of Queen's Bench, 168, 179.
Covent Garden, 181, 224; origin of, 182; distinguished residents in, 183.
Covent Garden Market, 181; in the early morning, 185.
Covent Garden Theatre, 182; murder near, 184.
Cowes, 133; exclusiveness of, 236.
Coyne, Stirling, 177.
Cremorne Gardens, 66, 67.
Cricket at the East End, 85.
Cricketers, Some famous, 84.
Criminal advocate, My first appearance as a, 65.
Critics, Increase in numbers of, 176.
Cromwell, Canon, 67.
Crossley's, Sir Charles, 97, 98.
Crowded trains, 103.

INDEX

Crystal Palace, The, 220.
Cursitor Street, 131.
Curzon Street, 221.

Daily News, My letter to the, 30.
Daily Telegraph, The, 108, 177.
Dance, Charles, 173.
"Daniel the Dutchman," 8.
"David Garrick," 176.
Davis, Silas, 147, 154, 157.
Depôt, My, 29; opened, 31.
Deptford, 38.
Derby week, 228.
Descending the ladder, 127-136.
Detectives from the West End, 82; in Lincoln's Inn, 195.
Devonshire Street, 76.
Dickinson, Jimmy, 128.
Dietary in the London Hospital, 52.
Digby, Sir Kenelm, 183.
Dinner-parties, Conversation at modern, 142.
Discounting tailors, 214.
District served by the London Hospital, 48.
Ditch, The, at Newmarket, 235.
Dobbs, Madeline, 146-153; ineffectual remonstrance with, 151.
Dobbs, Maria, 149.
Dobbs, Ralph, 146, 147, 148.
Docks, The London, 74.
Donizetti, 177.
Donkeys, Chorus of, 185.
"Doss-houses," 38.
Doucet, 232.
Dover, 197.
Downing Street, 234.
Draper's stock interesting, 33.
"Dream at Sea," The, 175.
Dress and fashion in the East End, 17.
Drunkenness on Sunday, 90; England and Scotland compared, 90, 91.
Drury Lane Theatre, The, 67, 175.
Ducrow, 193.
Duke Street, St. James's, 128.
Dummett, Mr. Robert, 32.
Durham, Bishop of, 183.
Dwarf, A black, 6.

"Eagle," The, 16.
Early marriages, 17.
East End deficient in recreation grounds, 84.
East End hats, 4.
East End shows, 3.
East End to Ramsgate, 102.
East Mount Street, 47.
Eaton, Alfred, 10.
Eaton Square, 115, 147, 154.

Edgware, 21, 23, 94.
Edlin, Sir Peter, 72.
Ellis, Mr. William, 32.
Ely Terrace, 96.
Empire, The, 177.
Enadine, The, 109.
Eton, Reminiscences of, 84; the Fourth of June at, 229.
Evans's, 182, 183.
Executions, Scenes in the days of public, 169.
Experience of three street singers, 43.

"Fair One with the Golden Locks," The, 173.
Falconer, 177.
Families assisted, 34-37.
Family, A Jewish, 103; I make room for them, 104; their pets, 104.
Fane, Miss Blanche, 175.
Farren, William, 175.
Fat Lady, A, 6.
"Favorita," La, 177.
Fechter, 175.
Female athlete, 7.
"Fences," 100.
Financier, The, 210; his victims, 210.
"First nights," 176.
Firth, Mr. Bottomley, 67.
Fish, Cold fried, 105, 107, 109.
Fisher, of Eton, 20.
Floss & Floss, 189; the partners, 189; their practice and high reputation, 190; their home-life, 190; the confidential clerk, 191; fraudulent acts, 193; the discovery, 194; enormous defalcations, 195; death, flight, and arrest, 196, 197.
Flower sellers, 186, 188.
"Flowers of the Forest," The, 172.
Flying Dutchman, The, 230.
Foote, 183.
Foreign Office, The, 234.
Foresters' Music Hall, 16.
"Forty Thieves," The, 75, 173.
Foulger, Thomas, 96.
Fowler, Mr. William, 183.
Fuller & Co., Messrs., 149.

Gaming-houses a century ago, 116.
Garrick, the actor, 183.
Garrick Club, The, 174.
"Garrick's Head," The, 181.
"Gate," Winning a, 27.
Gates, Mr., 57.
Gladstone, Mr., 234.
Goff, Billy, 40.
Gold, 235.
Gold Vase, The, at Ascot, 230.

"Golden Branch," The, 173.
Golf links, 109.
Goodwood, 228, 236.
Gordon Square, 142.
Gotelee, Mr. George, 32.
Grand Stand, The, at Ascot, 230.
Grange, The, 143.
Great Western Railway, 230.
"Green Bushes," The, 175.
Greenwich, 90, 232.
Greenwich Police Court, 60.
Griddlers, 38; their répertoire, 45.
Grisi, Madame, 177.
Grocers' Company's wing of London Hospital, 47.
Grossmith, Mr. Weedon, 179.
"Grosvenor Hotel," The, 233.
Grosvenor Square, 115, 163.
Guildhall, The, 97.
Gull Mine, The, 165-167.

Hackman, Captain, 184; enters the Church, 184; shoots Martha Ray, 184; is hanged, 184.
Halifax, Mr. Sydney, 56, 57.
Halliday, Andrew, 173.
Hampstead Heath, 16.
Hampton Court, 90, 232.
Happiest days, My, 143.
Hare Court, 34.
Hats in the East End, 4.
Haverstock Street, 30.
Hawker, An inspector's experience of a, 62.
Haymarket Theatre, The, 173, 175, 176.
Hayter, Lady, 234.
Henrietta Street, 183.
Heraud, 177.
"Hicks's Hall," 64.
High Street, Shoreditch, 31, 33.
Holker, Lord Chief Justice, 65; Sir John, 67.
Hollis, Lord, 183.
Holloway, 42.
Holverston Hall, 152.
Holywell Street, 184.
Homburg, 124, 157.
Hornsey Road, 23.
Hospital experiences, 52.
Hospital nurses in Covent Garden Market, 186.
Houndsditch, 102, 107.
Hours of work in match manufactory, 13.
House-boats, Before the days of, 236.
Houses to let, 3.
Howe, Mrs., 72.
Hoxton, 102.

Huckstering Hymen, 146-162.
Hudson, George, 137.
"Hudson's Hotel," 129.
Hunt Cup, The, 233.
Hurst Park, 229.
Hyde Park, 21.

Improvement in Ratcliff Highway, 82, 74.
Incident, A humorous, 54.
Ind, Mr. Edward Murray, 48.
Indian Army, Son of an officer in the, 203.
Irving, Mr. Henry, 174.
Isaacs, Mr., 106.
Islington Green, 192, 195.
Italian Colony, An, 64.

James, Sir Henry, 65.
"Janet Pride," 172.
Jennings, Tom, 235.
Jermyn Street, 215.
Jessop's, 181.
Jewitt, 235.
Jews at the London Hospital, 49.
"Johnnies," 158; their favourite songs, 159.
Jonas, The late Mr., 169.
Jones, Inigo, 182.
Journalist, A celebrated, 69.
Juanita, Miss, 7.
"Julks," 27.
July meeting, The, at Newmarket, 235.
Juryman, the long-suffering, 68.

Kean, Charles, and Mrs., 174.
Keeley, Mr. and Mrs., 172, 173.
Kemp, the fisherman, 143; his son William, 143.
Kempton, 229.
"Kenilworth," 173.
Kenny, Charlie, 173.
Kensington, 163.
Kilburn, 21.
"Kips," 38.
"King of the Peacocks," The, 173.
King Street, Ramsgate, 107.
King Street, W.C., 183.
Kneller, Sir Godfrey, 183.
Knox, Mr., 178, 213.
Kosher meat, 107.

Lablache, 177.
Lacy, Walter, 174.
Lamson, 170.
Lancaster Gate, 190, 195, 196.
Landor, Walter Savage, Quotation from, 182.
Langford, Joe, 174.

INDEX

Lawful and unlawful tools, 99.
Lawson, Mr. and Mrs. Edward, 143.
Leclercq, Carlotta, 174.
Lely, Sir Peter, 183.
Leman Street, 76, 78.
L'Estrange, Lord, 156.
Leviathan money-lenders, 217.
Liberal spirit, 32.
License, A hawker's, 62.
Licenses, 65.
Limehouse, 48.
Limehouse Board of Works, 57.
Limekilns, The, 235, 235.
Limelight Theatre, The, 158–160.
Lincoln's Inn, 189.
Lind, Jenny, 177.
List betting, 198.
Little Tower Hill, 74.
" Little Treasure," The, 175.
Liver brigade, 141.
Lockyer, the Sessions officer, 71.
Lodging-house keeper, A vindictive, 81.
Lodging-houses, Inmates of, 39 ; at Ramsgate, 110.
Lombard, The Hon. Allan, 156.
Lombard & Throgmorton, Messrs., 156.
London Bridge, 103.
London County Council, 33, 65, 72.
London Hospital, 3, 6, 9, 47, 78 ; staff of, 48 ; arrangements at, 48 ; Jews in, 49 ; on Saturday night, 50 ; admission to, 48 ; nurses at, 48 ; district served by, 48 ; out-patients at, 51 ; daily routine at, 52.
London and Westminster Bank, 96.
London Pavilion, The, 177.
London Police Court Mission, 30.
Long Acre, 182.
Lord Chancellor, The late, 65.
" Love in a Village," 184.
Lucas, Lord, 183.
Ludgate Hill, 168.
Ludgate Hill Station, 53.
Lyceum Theatre, The, 173.

Magistrate, A choleric, 67.
" Maid and the Magpie," The, 173.
Maiden speech, A, 58, 59.
Maidenhead Bridge, 236.
Malicious prosecution, A, 81 ; its collapse, 82.
Mannings, The, 170.
Mansion House, 168.
Margate, 102, 107.
Marienbad, 109.
Mario, Signor, 177 ; his last appearance on the London stage, 177.
Marketing on Sunday morning, 22.

Marlborough Street Police Court, 178, 213.
Marriages, where made ? 146–161.
Marsden, Lady Ethel, 131, 135.
Martin, Maria, 9.
Marylebone Theatre, 111.
Massey, Mr., 30, 34.
Match girls, 12.
Match manufactories, 12.
Mathews, Charles, 173, 175, 17.
Maurice, Herbert, Esq., 118 ; his wife and children, 119 ; his son and heir, 119 ; he becomes a Liberal Unionist, 121 ; his reason, 121 ; his entertainments, 123 ; his country seat, 124 ; the ruined nobleman, 126.
Mayfair, 191.
Meadows, 174.
" Medea," 173.
Medland Hall, 56; conference at, 57; its objects, 63.
Melton Mowbray, 191, 194, 195.
Mephisto, 235.
Merrivale, Marquis of, 146, 150.
Merry, Mr., 230.
Messenger's boat-house, 144.
Michael Angelo Taylor's Act, summonses under, 28.
Middlesex Sessions House, 64.
Mile End, 36, 59.
Millbank, 171.
Millington, Viscount, 147, 160.
Mill Lane, Deptford, 38.
Milner, Messrs., 95, 97.
Misterton, Claude, 134–136.
Mitchell, Mr., 95.
Monarch, The, 229.
Money-lender, The, 209; keeps up an imposing appearance, 210; opens what he calls a " Bank of Deposit," 211; his manner of conducting business, 211; a case in point, 213; a kindly act, 218.
Monte Carlo, 109, 207, 218.
Morning Post, The, 146, 157.
Morris, Mordecai, 116; his early life, 117; his will, 117; his son's good fortune, 117.
Moses, Mr. Marcus, 110.
Moss, Sergeant, 96.
Murderous affray, A, 78.
Murray, Leigh, 172.
Music-halls *versus* theatres, 178.
Music-halls, The attraction of, 179.

Nash, Miss, 18.
Newcastle, Duke of, 230.
Newgate, 168.
Newmarket, 128, 133, 214, 218, 235.

R

INDEX

Newport, Lord, 183.
Nichols, Mary Ann, 6.
Nicholson, Baron, 181.
"Nipper," The East End, 85.
North, Lord, 183.
Notting Hill, 40, 42, 45.
Novelty dealer, A, 10.
Nurses require strength, 51.

Oath, Curious way of taking an, 78.
Old Bailey, 73, 168, 169, 170; public-houses in the, 169; scenes in the court, 170.
Old Jewry, 110.
Oliver, Martha, 174.
Olympic Theatre, The, 173.
Opium-dens, 76; I try a cigarette, 77.
"Orkney Arms," The, 236.
Orkney, Lord, 235.
Ott, Dr., 109.
"Our American Cousin," 176
Out-patients at the London Hospital, 51.
"Overland Route," The, 176.
Oxenford, John, 177.
Oxford, Earl of, 183.
Oxford Street, E., 47.

"Paddy's Goose," 76.
Pall Mall, 151.
"Pantomime Rehearsal," The, 179.
Paragon Music Hall, 16.
Park Lane, 21, 115, 133, 217.
Parry, Serjeant, 65.
Patti, Madame, 177.
Payment of matchbox-makers, 14.
Payne, Mr., 65.
Peace, Charles, 8.
Pegwell Bay, 110.
Penny, Stephen, 109.
Penny gaff, 6.
Pereira Street, 14.
Persiani, 177.
Philpott Street, 47.
"Phossy jaw," 13.
"Piazza Hotel," The, 183.
Piazzas, The, of Covent Garden, 182.
Piccolomini, 177.
Pickpockets, 8.
Planché, 173.
Plant costers, A quarrel between, 187.
Playing Fields, The, 229.
Plunger, A, 202.
"Pluto and Proserpine," 173.
Plutocracy, The reign of, 115.
Poland, Mr., Q.C., 65.
Police regulation re street singers, 45.
Potter, Inspector, 96.

Powell's peep-show, 183.
"Prisoners' friends,' 68.
Princess's Theatre, The, 174, 175, 178.
Prince of Wales's box, The, at Ascot, invaded, 231.
Promoter, The, 163.
Public-house, An extraordinary, 88; conversation in a, 26.
Pugilism, 6, 7, 8.

Queen's Bench Prison, The, 128; we inspect, 129; its inmates, 129; racquet courts in, 129; its "poor side," 129; the "Tap," 130
Queen's birthday, Trooping the colours on the, 235.
Quin, 183.

Races Ladies at the, 229.
Ramsgate, Lodging-houses at, 110; old habitués of, 110; amusements at, 108; why the Jews go to, 107; attractions of, 109.
"Raspberry Nose," 24.
Ratcliff Highway, 74, 76, 78, 83; its former condition, 74; public-houses in, 75; my last visit to, 76; its character improved, 82.
Rawson, Miss, 18.
Ray, Martha, 184; shot, 184.
Receivers, 100.
Receptions, Decrease in number of, 234.
Recent Circus, 226.
Remarkable collection of hats, 4.
"Retained for the Defence," 179.
Revengeful design frustrated, A, 81.
Reynolds, Miss, 176.
Richmond, Duke of, 183.
Richmond, 160, 232.
River, Changes in the appearance of the, 236.
Robson, 179; as Shylock, 173.
Rogers, Jemmy, as the Widow Twankey, 173.
Roose, Dr. Robson, 109.
Rosebery, Lord, 234.
Rotherham & Co., 31, 32, 33.
Rotherhithe casual ward, 60.
Rotten Row, 118, 217.
Routine, Daily, in the London Hospital, 52.
Row, The, on Sunday morning, 234.
Royal Enclosure, The, at Ascot, 201 a funny story, 232.
Rumbelow, 71.
"Runner," The, 138; his manner of conducting business, 139.
Russell, Sir Charles, 65.

INDEX 243

Russia, Emperor of, 230.
Ryder, John, 174.

Safe, The easiest, 99.
St. James's Street, 205, 206; police raid on a club near, 202.
St. James's Theatre, The, 175.
St. Martin's-in-the-Fields, 182.
St. Peter's, Eaton Square, 147, 154, 158.
Salisbury, The Marchioness of, 234.
Salvation Army match manufactory, 13.
Sampson, Mr. Leopold, 217.
Samson, A female, 7.
Sandown, 229.
Sandwich, 109.
Sandwich, Earl of, 183.
Sandwich man, The, 220; his remuneration, 220; keen competition, 221; a sad story, 222.
Saturday night at the London Hospital, 50.
Saunders, Charlotte, 174.
Scarborough, Miss, 159, 160.
Schenk, General, 205.
Schoolfellow, An old, 221.
Sclater Street, 21, 22, 26, 28.
"Sea of Ice," The, 172.
Season, The London, 228; the Ramsgate, 109.
Sebright Music Hall, 16.
Separate lives, 152.
Serle Street, 192.
Set-to, An informal, 7.
Seven Dials, 25.
Shadwell, 74, 78.
Sharpers, Professional, 203; mixing in polite society, 203; a similar case in Paris, 207.
Sheen, 235.
Sheppard, Jack, 8.
Shepperton, 143.
Sheridan, 183.
"Ship and Turtle," The, 76.
"Ship," The, 232.
Shoreditch, 4, 21, 22, 25, 29, 35, 87, 102.
Shoreditch casual ward, 58.
Signalling by burglars, Method of, 99.
Simpson, Mr., 66.
Sisters of Mercy in Covent Garden Market, 186.
Skindle's, 236.
Skin-dresser, A, 106.
Skirt-dancer, A successful, 159.
"Slaughter House," The, 71.
Sleigh, Serjeant, 65.
Slough, 230.

Slowman's sponging-house, 131; charges at, 131.
Smith, Albert, 173, 178.
Smith, Mr. E. T., 67, 175.
Smith, O., 172.
Smithfield, 169.
Smoking in self-defence, 106.
Snowden, Mr. Frederick, 32.
Society, A great change in, 234.
Society touts, 161.
Soltykoff, Prince, 235.
Somerset, Duke of, 182.
Sothern, Edward, 176, 177.
South-Western Railway, 230.
Spa, 124, 218.
Spa Road, 104.
Spitalfields, 42, 225.
Spitalfields Market, 21, 225.
Stables at Messrs. Rotherham's, 33.
Staff of London Hospital, 48.
Stanhope, Lady, 234.
Staplehurst, 107.
Stapley, Mr., 57.
"Star and Garter," The, 232.
Statutory declaration, A, 212.
Stauntons, The, 170.
"Stiff," A, 62.
Stiff, Leopold, 164; scene at his office, 166; dinner-party given by, 167; arrested, 168; trial of, 170; sentence, 171.
Stockbrokers, Modern, 137.
Stockbroking, Changes in, 138; a fresh arrangement, 144.
Strand, The, 185.
Strand Theatre, The, 173.
Strawberry Hill, 143.
Strype, Quotation from, 182.
Stuckey & Co., Messrs., 4.
Suez Canal, The, 82.
Sufferings of the poor, 34-37.
Sullivan, Mog, 40.
Summonses, A curious batch of, 82.
Sun Court, 97.
Sunday at the East End, 84.
Sunday closing, 90.
Sunday drives in the East End, 87.
Sunday morning in the East End, 22.
Sunday morning marketing, 28.
Sunningdale, 230.
Surley, 229.
Surrey Sessions House, 64.
Swallows Fields, 133.
Swanborough, Miss, 173.
Sympathy among the match girls, 17.

Talent in tatters, 220.
Talfourd, Frank, 173.
Tamburini, 177

INDEX

Tattersall's ring at Ascot, 201.
Tavistock Street, 184.
Taylor, Tom, 173, 177.
Teddington, 143, 144.
Temple, The, 164, 203.
Terry, Miss Kate, 174.
Thames Police Court, 4, 14, 47, 78, 79, 90.
Thames Tunnel, The, 75.
Thanet, Countess of, 155-157.
Thanet, Earl of, 147, 154, 155
Thanet, The Isle of, 102, 110, 111.
Theatres, New, 177; is there room for so many? 178.
Theatrical expenditure, 178.
Theatrical managers, Association of, 178.
Thomas, Mr. Brandon, 179.
Thomas Street, 10.
Thornbury, 182.
"Thumping Legacy," The, 179.
Times, The, 177; my letter to, 30.
Tivoli, The, 177.
Tomlin, 177.
Tothill Fields, 184.
Tottenham, 23.
Tramp, The life of a, a merry one, 63.
Trocadéro, The, 177.
Turner, Matilda, 6.
Turner Street, 47.
Twickenham, 143.
Tyburn, 184.

Understanding, A clear, 152.
Upper Brook Street, 203.
Upper School, The, at Eton, 229.
Upper Shooting Fields, The, 84.

"Valentine and Orson," 173.
Valuable stock, A, 33.
Van Tromp, 230.
Vaux'all, 233.
Vegetables, Enormous supply of, 185.
Verinder, Hon. Louisa, 147, 154-157.
Vestris, Madame, 173.
Victoria, 21, 104.
Victoria Street, 75, 133, 136.
Virginia Water, 230.
Visit to a common lodging-house, 39.

Waldegrave, Countess of, 143.
Walker, Mr., 95, 97; brings an action against Messrs. Milner, 97; verdict against, 100.
Walmer, 217.
Wa'ton, 143.
Warner Street, 10.
Waterloo Station, 143.
Water Oakley, 236.
Watney Street, 78, 79.
Waxwork exhibition, 6.
Webster & Graham, Messrs., 178.
Webster, Benjamin, 172, 175, 178.
Weight-lifter, A female, 7.
Weir Bank, 144.
Wellington Street, Strand, 185.
"Welshman," The, 8.
Wesleyan Methodist Home Mission Hall, 76.
West, Benjamin, 183.
West Cliff The, of Ramsgate, 109.
Westminster, 25, 42.
Westminster, The Abbots of, 182; the Duke of, 236.
Whimsical incident, A, 69.
Whitechapel, 4, 42, 107.
Whitechapel casual ward, 59.
Whitechapel murders, 6, 8.
Whitechapel Road, 3, 5, 7, 10, 11, 47, 96.
"White Hart," The, at Windsor, 229
"White Swan," The, 76.
Wholesale correction, 11.
Wigan, Alfred, 172; as Chateau Renaud, 175.
Wilson, Catherine, 170.
Wilton, Miss Marie, 173.
Winchester, Marquis of, 183.
Windmill Street, 66.
Windsor, 230.
Woking, The Earl of, 127.
Woolgar, Miss, 172, 173.
Worship Street Police Court, 4, 14, 16, 29, 36, 47, 90, 92.
Worth, 232.
"Wreck Ashore," The, 172.
Wright, 172.
Wyverton, in Norfolk, 184.

Zulus, Performing, 9.

CHARLES DICKENS AND EVANS, CRYSTAL PALACE PRESS.

MACMILLAN'S THREE-AND-SIXPENNY SERIES

OF

WORKS BY POPULAR AUTHORS.

In Crown 8vo. Cloth extra. Price 3s. 6d. each.

By Sir SAMUEL BAKER.
True Tales for My Grandsons.
Reprinted from the "TIMES."
Annual Summaries. In 2 vols. | Biographies of Eminent Persons. In 4 vols.

By ROLF BOLDREWOOD.
SATURDAY REVIEW.—"Mr. Boldrewood can tell what he knows with great point and vigour, and there is no better reading than the adventurous parts of his books."
PALL MALL GAZETTE.—"The volumes are brimful of adventure, in which gold, gold-diggers, prospectors, claim-holders, take an active part."

Robbery under Arms. | The Squatter's Dream.
The Miner's Right. | A Sydney-Side Saxon.
A Colonial Reformer. | Nevermore.

By FRANCES HODGSON BURNETT.
Louisiana; and That Lass o' Lowrie's.

By HUGH CONWAY.
MORNING POST.—"Life-like, and full of individuality."
DAILY NEWS.—"Throughout written with spirit, good feeling, and ability, and a certain dash of humour."

Living or Dead? | A Family Affair.

By Mrs. CRAIK.
(The Author of "JOHN HALIFAX, GENTLEMAN.")

Olive. With Illustrations by G. BOWERS. | The Laurel Bush.
The Ogilvies. With Illustrations. | My Mother and I. With Illustrations.
Agatha's Husband. With Illustrations. | Miss Tommy: A Mediæval Romance.
Head of the Family. With Illustrations. | Illustrated.
Two Marriages. | King Arthur: Not a Love Story.
Sermons out of Church.

By F. MARION CRAWFORD.
SPECTATOR.—"With the solitary exception of Mrs. Oliphant we have no living novelist more distinguished for variety of theme and range of imaginative outlook than Mr. Marion Crawford."

Mr. Isaacs: A Tale of Modern India. | Paul Patoff.
Portrait of Author. | With the Immortals
Dr. Claudius: A True Story. | Greifenstein. | Sant' Ilario.
A Roman Singer. | A Cigarette-Maker's Romance.
Zoroaster. | Marzio's Crucifix. | Khaled. | The Three Fates.
A Tale of a Lonely Parish. | The Witch of Prague.

By Sir HENRY CUNNINGHAM, K.C.I.E.
ST. JAMES'S GAZETTE.—"Interesting as specimens of romance, the style of writing is so excellent—scholarly and at the same time easy and natural—that the volumes are worth reading on that account alone. But there is also masterly description of persons, places, and things; skilful analysis of character; a constant play of wit and humour; and a happy gift of instantaneous portraiture."

The Cœruleans. | The Heriots. | Wheat and Tares.

By CHARLES DICKENS.

The Pickwick Papers. With 50 Illustrations.
Oliver Twist. With 27 Illustrations.
Nicholas Nickleby. With 44 Illustrations.
Martin Chuzzlewit. With 41 Illustrations.
The Old Curiosity Shop. With 97 Illustrations.
Barnaby Rudge. With 76 Illustrations.
Dombey and Son. With 40 Illustrations.
Christmas Books. With 65 Illustrations.
Sketches by Boz. With 44 Illustrations
David Copperfield. With 41 Illustrations.
American Notes and Pictures from Italy. With 4 Illustrations.
The Letters of Charles Dickens.

By MARY ANGELA DICKENS.
A Mere Cypher.

By LANOE FALCONER.
Cecilia de Noel.

By W. WARDE FOWLER.
A Year with the Birds. Illustrated by BRYAN HOOK.
Tales of the Birds. Illustrated by BRYAN HOOK.

By the Rev. JOHN GILMORE.
Storm Warriors.

By THOMAS HARDY.

TIMES.—" There is hardly a novelist, dead or living, who so skilfully harmonises the poetry of moral life with its penury. Just as Millet could in the figure of a solitary peasant toiling on a plain, convey a world of pathetic meaning, so Mr. Hardy with his yeomen and villagers. Their occupations in his hands wear a pathetic dignity, which not even the encomiums of a Ruskin could heighten."

| The Woodlanders. | Wessex Tales. |

By BRET HARTE.

SPEAKER.—"The best work of Mr. Bret Harte stands entirely alone. . . . marked on every page by distinction and quality. . . . Strength and delicacy, spirit and tenderness, go together in his best work."

| Cressy. | The Heritage of Dedlow Marsh. |
A First Family of Tasajara.

By the Author of "Hogan, M.P."
Hogan, M.P.

By THOMAS HUGHES.
Tom Brown's Schooldays. With Illustrations by A. HUGHES and S. P. HALL.
Tom Brown at Oxford. With Illustrations by S. P. HALL.
The Scouring of the White Horse, and The Ashen Faggot. With Illustrations by RICHARD DOYLE.

By HENRY JAMES.

SATURDAY REVIEW.—"He has the power of seeing with the artistic perception of the few, and of writing about what he has seen, so that the many can understand and feel with him."

WORLD.—" His touch is so light, and his humour, while shrewd and keen, so free from bitterness."

| A London Life. | The Aspern Papers. | The Tragic Muse. |

By ANNIE KEARY.

SPECTATOR.—" In our opinion there have not been many novels published better worth reading. The literary workmanship is excellent, and all the windings of the stories are worked with patient fulness and a skill not often found."

| Castle Daly. | A Doubting Heart. |
| A York and a Lancaster Rose. | Janet's Home. |
Oldbury.

By PATRICK KENNEDY.
Legendary Fictions of the Irish Celts.

By CHARLES KINGSLEY.

Westward Ho!
Hypatia.
Yeast.
Alton Locke.
Two Years Ago.
Hereward the Wake.
Poems.
The Heroes.
The Water Babies.
Madam How and Lady Why.
At Last.
Prose Idylls.
Plays and Puritans, &c.
The Roman and the Teuton.
Sanitary and Social Lectures and Essays.
Historical Lectures and Essays.
Scientific Lectures and Essays.
Literary and General Lectures.
The Hermits.
Glaucus; or The Wonders of the Seashore. With Coloured Illustrations.
Village and Town and Country Sermons.
The Water of Life, and other Sermons.
Sermons on National Subjects, and the King of the Earth.
Sermons for the Times.
Good News of God.
The Gospel of the Pentateuch, and David.
Discipline, and other Sermons.
Westminster Sermons.
All Saints' Day, and other Sermons.

By HENRY KINGSLEY.
Tales of Old Travel.

By MARGARET LEE.
Faithful and Unfaithful.

By AMY LEVY.
Reuben Sachs.

By S. R. LYSAGHT.
The Marplot.

By the EARL OF LYTTON.
The Ring of Amasis.

By MALCOLM M'LENNAN.
Muckle Jock, and other Stories of Peasant Life.

By LUCAS MALET.
Mrs. Lorimer.

By GUSTAVE MASSON.
Dictionary of the French Language.

By A. B. MITFORD.
Tales of Old Japan. Illustrated.

By D. CHRISTIE MURRAY.

SPECTATOR.—"Mr. Christie Murray has more power and genius for the delineation of English rustic life than any half-dozen of our surviving novelists put together."

SATURDAY REVIEW.—"Few modern novelists can tell a story of English country life better than Mr. D. Christie Murray."

Aunt Rachel.
John Vale's Guardian.
Schwartz.
The Weaker Vessel.
He Fell among Thieves. By D. C. MURRAY and H. HERMAN.

The New Antigone: A Romance.

By Mrs. OLIPHANT.

ACADEMY.—"At her best she is, with one or two exceptions, the best of living English novelists."

SATURDAY REVIEW.—"Has the charm of style, the literary quality and flavour that never fails to please."

A Beleaguered City.
Joyce.
Neighbours on the Green.
Kirsteen.
Hester.
He that Will Not when he May.
The Railway Man and his Children.
The Marriage of Elinor.
Sir Tom.
The Heir Presumptive and the Heir Apparent.

By W. CLARK RUSSELL.

TIMES.—"Mr. Clark Russell is one of those writers who have set themselves to revive the British sea story in all its glorious excitement. Mr. Russell has made a considerable reputation in this line. His plots are well conceived, and that of *Marooned* is no exception to this rule."

Marooned. | A Strange Elopement.

By J. H. SHORTHOUSE.

ANTI-JACOBIN—"Powerful, striking, and fascinating romances."

John Inglesant. | The Countess Eve.
Sir Percival. | A Teacher of the Violin.
The Little Schoolmaster Mark.

By THE MARCHESA THEODOLI.

Under Pressure.

Tim.

By WALTER C. RHOADES.

John Trevennick.

By JOHN ROY.

Helen Treveryan.

By MRS. HUMPHRY WARD.

Miss Bretherton.

By MONTAGU WILLIAMS, Q.C.

Leaves of a Life. | Later Leaves.

By Miss CHARLOTTE M. YONGE.

The Heir of Redclyffe. | Unknown to History.
Heartsease. | Stray Pearls.
Hopes and Fears. | The Armourer's 'Prentices.
Dynevor Terrace. | The Two Sides of the Shield.
The Daisy Chain. | Nuttie's Father.
The Trial: More Links of the Daisy Chain. | Scenes and Characters.
 | Chantry House.
Pillars of the House. Vol. I. | A Modern Telemachus.
Pillars of the House. Vol. II. | Bye-Words.
The Young Stepmother. | Beechcroft at Rockstone.
The Clever Woman of the Family. | More Bywords.
The Three Brides. | A Reputed Changeling.
My Young Alcides. | The Little Duke.
The Caged Lion. | The Lances of Lynwood.
The Dove in the Eagle's Nest. | The Prince and the Page.
The Chaplet of Pearls. | P's and Q's, and Little Lucy's Wonderful Globe.
Lady Hester, and the Danvers Papers. |
Magnum Bonum. | The Two Penniless Princesses.
Love and Life. | That Stick.
An Old Woman's Outlook.

By ARCHDEACON FARRAR.

Seekers after God. | Saintly Workers.
Eternal Hope. | Ephphatha.
The Fall of Man. | Mercy and Judgment.
The Witness of History to Christ. | Sermons and Addresses Delivered in America.
The Silence and Voices of God. |
In the Days of thy Youth.

By FREDERICK DENISON MAURICE.

Sermons Preached in Lincoln's Inn Chapel. In 6 vols.

Christmas Day and Other Sermons. | Epistle of St. John.
Theological Essays. | Lectures on the Apocalypse.
Prophets and Kings. | Friendship of Books.
Patriarchs and Lawgivers. | Social Morality.
The Gospel of the Kingdom of Heaven. | Prayer Book and Lord's Prayer.
Gospel of St. John. | The Doctrine of Sacrifice.

**MACMILLAN & CO., BEDFORD STREET,
STRAND, LONDON.**

50-7-93.

January, 1894.

A CLASSIFIED
CATALOGUE OF BOOKS
IN GENERAL LITERATURE
PUBLISHED BY
MACMILLAN AND CO.
BEDFORD STREET, STRAND, LONDON, W.C.

For purely Educational Works see MACMILLAN AND CO.'S *Educational Catalogue*

AGRICULTURE.

(*See also* BOTANY; GARDENING.)

FRANKLAND (Prof. P. F.).—A HANDBOOK OF AGRICULTURAL CHEMICAL ANALYSIS. Cr. 8vo. 7s. 6d.

LAURIE (A. P.).—THE FOOD OF PLANTS. Pott 8vo. 1s.

NICHOLLS (H. A. A.).—TEXT BOOK OF TROPICAL AGRICULTURE. Cr. 8vo. 6s.

TANNER (Henry).—ELEMENTARY LESSONS IN THE SCIENCE OF AGRICULTURAL PRACTICE. Fcp. 8vo. 3s. 6d.
— FIRST PRINCIPLES OF AGRICULTURE. Pott 8vo. 1s.
— THE PRINCIPLES OF AGRICULTURE. For Use in Elementary Schools. Ext. fcp. 8vo.— THE ALPHABET OF THE PRINCIPLES OF AGRICULTURE. 6d.—FURTHER STEPS IN THE PRINCIPLES OF AGRICULTURE. 1s.— ELEMENTARY SCHOOL READINGS ON THE PRINCIPLES OF AGRICULTURE FOR THE THIRD STAGE. 1s.
— THE ABBOT'S FARM; or, Practice with Science. Cr. 8vo. 3s. 6d.

ANATOMY, Human. (*See* PHYSIOLOGY.)

ANTHROPOLOGY.

BROWN (J. Allen).—PALÆOLITHIC MAN IN NORTH-WEST MIDDLESEX. 8vo. 7s. 6d.

DAWKINS (Prof. W. Boyd).—EARLY MAN IN BRITAIN AND HIS PLACE IN THE TERTIARY PERIOD. Med. 8vo. 25s.

FINCK (Henry T.).—ROMANTIC LOVE AND PERSONAL BEAUTY. 2 vols. Cr. 8vo. 18s.

FISON (L.) and HOWITT (A. W.).—KAMILAROI AND KURNAI GROUP. Group-Marriage and Relationship, and Marriage by Elopement. 8vo. 15s.

FRAZER (J. G.).—THE GOLDEN BOUGH: A Study in Comparative Religion. 2 vols. 8vo. 28s.

GALTON (Francis).—ENGLISH MEN OF SCIENCE: THEIR NATURE AND NURTURE. 8vo. 8s. 6d.
— INQUIRIES INTO HUMAN FACULTY AND ITS DEVELOPMENT. 8vo. 16s.
— LIFE-HISTORY ALBUM : Being a Personal Note-book, combining Diary, Photograph Album, a Register of Height, Weight, and other Anthropometrical Observations, and a Record of Illnesses. 4to. 3s. 6d.—Or with Cards of Wool for Testing Colour Vision. 4s. 6d.

GALTON (Francis).—NATURAL INHERITANCE. 8vo. 9s.
— RECORD OF FAMILY FACULTIES. Consisting of Tabular Forms and Directions for Entering Data. 4to. 2s. 6d.
— HEREDITARY GENIUS: An Enquiry into its Laws and Consequences. Ext. cr. 8vo. 7s. net.
— FINGER PRINTS. 8vo. 6s. net.
— BLURRED FINGER PRINTS. 8vo. 2s. 6d. net.

M'LENNAN (J. F.).—THE PATRIARCHAL THEORY. Edited and completed by DONALD M'LENNAN, M.A. 8vo. 14s.
— STUDIES IN ANCIENT HISTORY. Comprising "Primitive Marriage." 8vo. 16s.

MONTELIUS—WOODS.—THE CIVILISATION OF SWEDEN IN HEATHEN TIMES. By Prof. OSCAR MONTELIUS. Translated by Rev. F. H. WOODS. Illustr. 8vo. 14s.

ORR (H. B.).—THEORY OF DEVELOPMENT AND HEREDITY. Cr. 8vo. 6s. net.

TURNER (Rev. Geo.).—SAMOA, A HUNDRED YEARS AGO AND LONG BEFORE. Cr. 8vo. 9s.

TYLOR (E. B.).—ANTHROPOLOGY. With Illustrations. Cr. 8vo. 7s. 6d.

WESTERMARCK (Dr. Edward).—THE HISTORY OF HUMAN MARRIAGE. With Preface by Dr. A. R. WALLACE. 8vo. 14s. net.

WILSON (Sir Daniel).—PREHISTORIC ANNALS OF SCOTLAND. Illustrated. 2 vols. 8vo. 36s.
— PREHISTORIC MAN: Researches into the Origin of Civilisation in the Old and New World. Illustrated. 2 vols. 8vo. 36s.
— THE RIGHT HAND: LEFT-HANDEDNESS. Cr. 8vo. 4s. 6d.

ANTIQUITIES.

(*See also* ANTHROPOLOGY.)

ATKINSON (Rev. J. C.).—FORTY YEARS IN A MOORLAND PARISH. Ext. cr. 8vo. 8s. 6d. net.—*Illustrated Edition.* 12s. net.

BURN (Robert).—ROMAN LITERATURE IN RELATION TO ROMAN ART. With Illustrations. Ext. cr. 8vo. 14s.

DILETTANTI SOCIETY'S PUBLICATIONS.
ANTIQUITIES OF IONIA. Vols. I.—III. 2l. 2s. each, or 5l. 5s. the set, net.—Vol. IV. Folio half morocco, 3l. 13s. 6d. net.
AN INVESTIGATION OF THE PRINCIPLES OF ATHENIAN ARCHITECTURE. By F. C. PENROSE. Illustrated. Folio. 7l. 7s. net.
SPECIMENS OF ANCIENT SCULPTURE: EGYPTIAN, ETRUSCAN, GREEK, AND ROMAN. Vol. II. Folio. 5l. 5s. net.

ANTIQUITIES—ASTRONOMY.

ANTIQUITIES—*continued.*

DYER (Louis).—STUDIES OF THE GODS IN GREECE AT CERTAIN SANCTUARIES RECENTLY EXCAVATED. Ext. cr. 8vo. 8s. 6d. net.

FOWLER (W. W.).—THE CITY-STATE OF THE GREEKS AND ROMANS. Cr. 8vo. 5s.

GARDNER (Percy).—SAMOS AND SAMIAN COINS: An Essay. 8vo. 7s. 6d.

GOW (J., Litt.D.).—A COMPANION TO SCHOOL CLASSICS. Illustrated. 3rd Ed. Cr. 8vo. 6s.

HARRISON (Miss Jane) and VERRALL (Mrs.).—MYTHOLOGY AND MONUMENTS OF ANCIENT ATHENS. Illustrated. Cr. 8vo. 16s.

HELLENIC SOCIETY'S PUBLICATIONS
— EXCAVATIONS AT MEGALOPOLIS, 1890–1891. By Messrs. E. A. GARDNER, W. LORING, G. C. RICHARDS, and W. J. WOODHOUSE. With an Architectural Description by R. W. SCHULTZ. 4to. 25s.
— ECCLESIASTICAL SITES IN ISAURIA (CILICIA TRACHEA). By the Rev. A. C. HEADLAM. Imp. 4to. 5s.

LANCIANI (Prof. R.).—ANCIENT ROME IN THE LIGHT OF RECENT DISCOVERIES. 4to. 24s.
— PAGAN AND CHRISTIAN ROME. 4to. 24s.

MAHAFFY (Prof. J. P.).—A PRIMER OF GREEK ANTIQUITIES. Pott 8vo. 1s.
— SOCIAL LIFE IN GREECE FROM HOMER TO MENANDER. 6th Edit. Cr. 8vo. 9s.
— RAMBLES AND STUDIES IN GREECE. Illustrated. 3rd Edit. Cr. 8vo. 10s. 6d.
(*See also* HISTORY, p. 11.)

NEWTON (Sir C. T.).—ESSAYS ON ART AND ARCHÆOLOGY. 8vo. 12s. 6d.

SCHUCHHARDT (C.).—DR. SCHLIEMANN'S EXCAVATIONS AT TROY, TIRYNS, MYCENAE, ORCHOMENOS, ITHACA, IN THE LIGHT OF RECENT KNOWLEDGE. Trans. by EUGENIE SELLERS. Preface by WALTER LEAF, Litt.D. Illustrated. 8vo. 18s. net.

STRANGFORD. (*See* VOYAGES & TRAVELS.)

WALDSTEIN (C.).—CATALOGUE OF CASTS IN THE MUSEUM OF CLASSICAL ARCHÆOLOGY, CAMBRIDGE. Crown 8vo. 1s. 6d.—Large Paper Edition. Small 4to. 5s.

WHITE (Gilbert). (*See* NATURAL HISTORY.)

WILKINS (Prof. A. S.).—A PRIMER OF ROMAN ANTIQUITIES. Pott 8vo. 1s.

ARCHÆOLOGY. (*See* ANTIQUITIES.)

ARCHITECTURE.

FREEMAN (Prof. E. A.).—HISTORY OF THE CATHEDRAL CHURCH OF WELLS. Cr. 8vo. 3s. 6d.

HULL (E.).—A TREATISE ON ORNAMENTAL AND BUILDING STONES OF GREAT BRITAIN AND FOREIGN COUNTRIES. 8vo. 12s.

MOORE (Prof. C. H.).—THE DEVELOPMENT AND CHARACTER OF GOTHIC ARCHITECTURE. Illustrated. Med. 8vo. 18s.

PENROSE (F. C.). (*See* ANTIQUITIES.)

STEVENSON (J. J.).—HOUSE ARCHITECTURE. With Illustrations. 2 vols. Roy. 8vo. 18s. each.—Vol. I. ARCHITECTURE; Vol. II. HOUSE PLANNING.

ART.
(*See also* MUSIC.)

ART AT HOME SERIES. Edited by W. J. LOFTIE, B.A. Cr. 8vo.
THE BEDROOM AND BOUDOIR. By Lady BARKER. 2s. 6d.
NEEDLEWORK. By ELIZABETH GLAISTER. Illustrated. 2s. 6d.
MUSIC IN THE HOUSE. By JOHN HULLAH. 4th edit. 2s. 6d.
THE DINING-ROOM. By Mrs. LOFTIE. With Illustrations. 2nd Edit. 2s. 6d.
AMATEUR THEATRICALS. By WALTER H. POLLOCK and LADY POLLOCK. Illustrated by KATE GREENAWAY. 2s. 6d.

ATKINSON (J. B.).—AN ART TOUR TO NORTHERN CAPITALS OF EUROPE. 8vo. 12s.

BURN (Robert). (*See* ANTIQUITIES.)

CARR (J. C.)—PAPERS ON ART. Cr. 8vo. 8s. 6d.

COLLIER (Hon. John).—A PRIMER OF ART. Pott 8vo. 1s.

COOK (E. T.).—A POPULAR HANDBOOK TO THE NATIONAL GALLERY. Including Notes collected from the Works of Mr. RUSKIN. 4th Edit. Cr. 8vo, half morocco. 14s.—Large paper Edition, 250 copies. 2 vols. 8vo.

DELAMOTTE (Prof. P. H.).—A BEGINNER'S DRAWING-BOOK. Cr. 8vo. 3s. 6d.

ELLIS (Tristram).—SKETCHING FROM NATURE. Illustr. by H. STACY MARKS, R.A., and the Author. 2nd Edit. Cr. 8vo. 3s. 6d.

HAMERTON (P. G.).—THOUGHTS ABOUT ART. New Edit. Cr. 8vo. 8s. 6d.

HOOPER (W. H.) and PHILLIPS (W. C.).—A MANUAL OF MARKS ON POTTERY AND PORCELAIN. 16mo. 4s. 6d.

HUNT (W.).—TALKS ABOUT ART. With a Letter from Sir J. E. MILLAIS, Bart., R.A. Cr. 8vo. 3s. 6d.

HUTCHINSON (G. W. C.).—SOME HINTS ON LEARNING TO DRAW. Roy. 8vo. 8s. 6d.

LECTURES ON ART. By REGD. STUART POOLE, Professor W. B. RICHMOND, E. J. POYNTER, R.A., J. T. MICKLETHWAITE, and WILLIAM MORRIS. Cr. 8vo. 4s. 6d

NEWTON (Sir C. T.).—(*See* ANTIQUITIES.)

PALGRAVE (Prof. F. T.).—ESSAYS ON ART. Ext. fcp. 8vo. 6s.

PATER (W.).—THE RENAISSANCE: Studies in Art and Poetry. 5th Edit. Cr. 8vo. 10s. 6d.

PROPERT (J. Lumsden).—A HISTORY OF MINIATURE ART. Illustrated. Super roy. 4to. 3l. 13s. 6d.—Bound in vellum. 4l. 14s. 6d.

TAYLOR (E. R.).—DRAWING AND DESIGN. Ob. cr. 8vo. 2s. 6d.

TURNER'S LIBER STUDIORUM: A DESCRIPTION AND A CATALOGUE. By W. G. RAWLINSON. Med. 8vo. 12s. 6d.

TYRWHITT (Rev. R. St. John).—OUR SKETCHING CLUB. 5th Edit. Cr. 8vo. 7s. 6d.

WYATT (Sir M. Digby).—FINE ART: A Sketch of its History, Theory, Practice, and Application to Industry. 8vo. 5s.

ASTRONOMY.

AIRY (Sir G. B.).—POPULAR ASTRONOMY. Illustrated. 7th Edit. Fcp. 8vo. 4s. 6d.
— GRAVITATION. An Elementary Explanation of the Principal Perturbations in the Solar System. 2nd Edit. Cr. 8vo. 7s. 6d.

ATLASES—BIOGRAPHY. 3

BLAKE (J. F.).—Astronomical Myths. With Illustrations. Cr. 8vo. 9s.
CHEYNE (C. H. H.).—An Elementary Treatise on the Planetary Theory. Cr. 8vo. 7s. 6d.
CLARK (L.) and SADLER (H.).—The Star Guide. Roy. 8vo. 5s.
CROSSLEY (E.), GLEDHILL (J.), and WILSON (J. M.).—A Handbook of Double Stars. 8vo. 21s.
—— Corrections to the Handbook of Double Stars. 8vo. 1s.
FORBES (Prof. George).—The Transit of Venus. Illustrated. Cr. 8vo. 3s. 6d.
GODFRAY (Hugh).—An Elementary Treatise on the Lunar Theory. 2nd Edit. Cr. 8vo. 5s. 6d.
—— A Treatise on Astronomy, for the use of Colleges and Schools. 8vo. 12s. 6d.
LOCKYER (J. Norman, F.R.S.).—A Primer of Astronomy. Illustrated. Pott 8vo. 1s.
—— Elementary Lessons in Astronomy. Illustr. New Edition. Fcp. 8vo. 5s. 6d.
—— Questions on the same. By J. Forbes Robertson. Fcp. 8vo. 1s. 6d.
—— The Chemistry of the Sun. Illustrated. 8vo. 14s.
—— The Meteoritic Hypothesis of the Origin of Cosmical Systems. Illustrated. 8vo. 17s. net.
—— The Evolution of the Heavens and the Earth. Illustrated. Cr. 8vo.
—— Star-Gazing Past and Present. Expanded from Notes with the assistance of G. M. Seabroke. Roy. 8vo. 21s.
LODGE (O. J.).—Pioneers of Science. Ex. cr. 8vo. 7s. 6d.
MILLER (R. Kalley).—The Romance of Astronomy. 2nd Edit. Cr. 8vo. 4s. 6d.
NEWCOMB (Prof. Simon).—Popular Astronomy. Engravings and Maps. 8vo. 18s.
RADCLIFFE (Charles B.).—Behind the Tides. 8vo. 4s. 6d.
ROSCOE—SCHUSTER. (See Chemistry.)

ATLASES.

(See also Geography).
BARTHOLOMEW (J. G.).—Elementary School Atlas. 4to. 1s.
—— Physical and Political School Atlas. 80 maps. 4to. 8s. 6d.; half mor. 10s. 6d.
—— Library Reference Atlas of the World. With Index to 100,000 places. Folio. 52s. 6d. net.—Also in 7 parts. 5s. net; Geographical Index. 7s. 6d. net.
LABBERTON (R. H.).—New Historical Atlas and General History. 4to. 15s.

BIBLE. (See under Theology, p. 33.)

BIBLIOGRAPHY.
A BIBLIOGRAPHICAL CATALOGUE OF MACMILLAN AND CO.'S PUBLICATIONS, 1843—89. Med. 8vo. 10s. net.

BIBLIOGRAPHY—continued.
MAYOR (Prof. John E. B.).—A Bibliographical Clue to Latin Literature. Cr. 8vo. 10s. 6d.
RYLAND (F.).—Chronological Outlines of English Literature. Cr. 8vo. 6s.

BIOGRAPHY.

(See also History.)
For other subjects of Biography, see English Men of Letters, English Men of Action, Twelve English Statesmen.
ABBOTT (E. A.).—The Anglican Career of Cardinal Newman. 2 vols. 8vo. 25s. net.
AGASSIZ (Louis): His Life and Correspondence. Edited by Elizabeth Cary Agassiz 2 vols. Cr. 8vo. 18s.
ALBEMARLE (Earl of).—Fifty Years of My Life. 3rd Edit., revised. Cr. 8vo. 7s. 6d.
ALFRED THE GREAT. By Thomas Hughes. Cr. 8vo. 6s.
AMIEL (H. F.)—The Journal Intime. Trans. Mrs. Humphry Ward. 2nd Ed. Cr. 8vo. 6s.
ANDREWS (Dr. Thomas). (See Physics.)
ARNAULD, ANGELIQUE. By Frances Martin. Cr. 8vo. 4s. 6d.
ARTEVELDE. James and Philip van Artevelde. By W. J. Ashley. Cr. 8vo. 6s.
BACON (Francis): An Account of his Life and Works. By E. A. Abbott. 8vo. 14s.
BARNES. Life of William Barnes, Poet and Philologist. By his Daughter, Lucy Baxter ("Leader Scott"). Cr. 8vo. 7s. 6d.
BERLIOZ (Hector): Autobiography of. Trns. by R. & E. Holmes. 2 vols. Cr. 8vo. 21s.
BERNARD (St.). The Life and Times of St. Bernard, Abbot of Clairvaux. By J. C. Morison, M.A. Cr. 8vo. 6s.
BLACKBURNE. Life of the Right Hon. Francis Blackburne, late Lord Chancellor of Ireland, by his Son, Edward Blackburne. With Portrait. 8vo. 12s.
BLAKE. Life of William Blake. With Selections from his Poems, etc. Illustr. from Blake's own Works. By Alexander Gilchrist. 2 vols. Med. 8vo. 42s.
BOLEYN (Anne): A Chapter of English History, 1527—36. By Paul Friedmann. 2 vols. 8vo. 28s.
BROOKE (Sir Jas.), The Raja of Sarawak (Life of). By Gertrude L. Jacob. 2 vols. 8vo. 25s.
BURKE. By John Morley. Globe 8vo. 5s.
CALVIN. (See Select Biography, p. 6.)
CAMPBELL (Sir G.).—Memoirs of my Indian Career. Edited by Sir C. E. Bernard. 2 vols. 8vo. 21s. net.
CARLYLE (Thomas). Edited by Charles E. Norton. Cr. 8vo.
—— Reminiscences. 2 vols. 12s.
—— Early Letters, 1814—26. 2 vols. 18s.
—— Letters, 1826—36. 2 vols. 18s.
—— Correspondence between Goethe and Carlyle. 9s.

BIOGRAPHY.

BIOGRAPHY—*continued.*

CARSTARES (Wm.): A CHARACTER AND CAREER OF THE REVOLUTIONARY EPOCH (1649—1715). By R. H. STORY. 8vo. 12s.

CAVOUR. (*See* SELECT BIOGRAPHY, p. 6.)

CHATTERTON: A STORY OF THE YEAR 1770. By Prof. DAVID MASSON. Cr. 8vo. 5s.
— A BIOGRAPHICAL STUDY. By Sir DANIEL WILSON. Cr. 8vo. 6s. 6d.

CLARK. MEMORIALS FROM JOURNALS AND LETTERS OF SAMUEL CLARK, M.A. Edited by HIS WIFE. Cr. 8vo. 7s. 6d.

CLEVELAND (Duchess of).—TRUE STORY OF KASPAR HAUSER. Cr. 8vo. 4s. 6d.

CLOUGH (A. H.). (*See* LITERATURE, p. 21.)

COMBE. LIFE OF GEORGE COMBE. By CHARLES GIBBON. 2 vols. 8vo. 32s.

CROMWELL. (*See* SELECT BIOGRAPHY, p. 6.)

DAMIEN (Father): A JOURNEY FROM CASHMERE TO HIS HOME IN HAWAII. By EDWARD CLIFFORD. Portrait. Cr. 8vo. 2s. 6d.

DANTE: AND OTHER ESSAYS. By Dean CHURCH. Globe 8vo. 5s.

DARWIN (Charles): MEMORIAL NOTICES, By T. H. HUXLEY, G. J. ROMANES, Sir ARCH. GEIKIE, and W. THISELTON DYER. With Portrait. Cr. 8vo. 2s. 6d.

DEAK (Francis): HUNGARIAN STATESMAN. A Memoir. 8vo. 12s. 6d.

DRUMMOND OF HAWTHORNDEN. By Prof. D. MASSON. Cr. 8vo. 10s. 6d.

EADIE. LIFE OF JOHN EADIE, D.D. By JAMES BROWN, D.D. Cr. 8vo. 7s. 6d.

ELLIOTT. LIFE OF H. V. ELLIOTT, OF BRIGHTON. By J. BATEMAN. Cr. 8vo. 6s.

EMERSON. LIFE OF RALPH WALDO EMERSON. By J. L. CABOT. 2 vols. Cr. 8vo. 18s.

ENGLISH MEN OF ACTION. Cr. 8vo. With Portraits. 2s. 6d. each.
CLIVE. By Colonel Sir CHARLES WILSON.
COOK (CAPTAIN). By WALTER BESANT.
DAMPIER. By W. CLARK RUSSELL.
DRAKE. By JULIAN CORBETT.
GORDON (GENERAL). By Col. Sir W. BUTLER.
HASTINGS (WARREN). By Sir A. LYALL.
HAVELOCK (SIR HENRY). By A. FORBES.
HENRY V. By the Rev. A. J. CHURCH.
LAWRENCE (LORD). By Sir RICH. TEMPLE.
LIVINGSTONE. By THOMAS HUGHES.
MONK. By JULIAN CORBETT.
MONTROSE. By MOWBRAY MORRIS.
MOORE(SIR JOHN). By Col. MAURICE.[*In prep.*
NAPIER (SIR CHARLES). By Colonel Sir WM. BUTLER.
PETERBOROUGH. By W. STEBBING.
RODNEY. By DAVID HANNAY.
SIMON DE MONTFORT. By G. W. PROTHERO. [*In prep.*
STRAFFORD. By H. D. TRAILL.
WARWICK, THE KING-MAKER. By C. W. OMAN.
WELLINGTON. By GEORGE HOOPER.

ENGLISH MEN OF LETTERS. Edited by JOHN MORLEY. Cr. 8vo. 2s. 6d. each. Cheap Edition, 1s. 6d.; sewed, 1s.
ADDISON. By W. J. COURTHOPE.

ENGLISH MEN OF LETTERS—*contd.*
BACON. By Dean CHURCH.
BENTLEY. By Prof. JEBB.
BUNYAN. By J. A. FROUDE.
BURKE. By JOHN MORLEY.
BURNS. By Principal SHAIRP.
BYRON. By JOHN NICHOL.
CARLYLE. By JOHN NICHOL.
CHAUCER. By Prof. A. W. WARD.
COLERIDGE. By H. D. TRAILL.
COWPER. By GOLDWIN SMITH.
DEFOE. By W. MINTO.
DE QUINCEY. By Prof. MASSON.
DICKENS. By A. W. WARD.
DRYDEN. By G. SAINTSBURY.
FIELDING. By AUSTIN DOBSON.
GIBBON. By J. COTTER MORISON.
GOLDSMITH. By WILLIAM BLACK.
GRAY. By EDMUND GOSSE.
HAWTHORNE. By HENRY JAMES.
HUME. By T. H. HUXLEY.
JOHNSON. By LESLIE STEPHEN.
KEATS. By SIDNEY COLVIN.
LAMB. By Rev. ALFRED AINGER.
LANDOR. By SIDNEY COLVIN.
LOCKE. By Prof. FOWLER.
MACAULAY. By J. COTTER MORISON.
MILTON. By MARK PATTISON.
POPE. By LESLIE STEPHEN.
SCOTT. By R. H. HUTTON.
SHELLEY. By J. A. SYMONDS.
SHERIDAN. By Mrs. OLIPHANT.
SIDNEY. By J. A. SYMONDS.
SOUTHEY. By Prof. DOWDEN.
SPENSER. By Dean CHURCH.
STERNE. By H. D. TRAILL.
SWIFT. By LESLIE STEPHEN.
THACKERAY. By ANTHONY TROLLOPE.
WORDSWORTH. By F. W. H. MYERS.

ENGLISH STATESMEN, TWELVE. Cr. 8vo. 2s. 6d. each.
WILLIAM THE CONQUEROR. By EDWARD A. FREEMAN, D.C.L., LL.D.
HENRY II. By Mrs. J. R. GREEN.
EDWARD I. By T. F. TOUT, M.A.
HENRY VII. By JAMES GAIRDNER.
CARDINAL WOLSEY. By Bp. CREIGHTON.
ELIZABETH. By E. S. BEESLY.
OLIVER CROMWELL. By F. HARRISON.
WILLIAM III. By H. D. TRAILL.
WALPOLE. By JOHN MORLEY.
CHATHAM. By JOHN MORLEY. [*In the Press.*
PITT. By LORD ROSEBERY.
PEEL. By J. R. THURSFIELD.

EPICTETUS. (*See* SELECT BIOGRAPHY, p. 6.)

FAIRFAX. LIFE OF ROBERT FAIRFAX OF STEETON, Vice-Admiral, Alderman, and Member for York, A.D. 1666-1725. By CLEMENTS R. MARKHAM, C.B. 8vo. 12s. 6d.

FITZGERALD (Edward). (*See* LITERATURE, p. 21.)

FORBES (Edward): MEMOIR OF. By GEORGE WILSON, M.P., and Sir ARCHIBALD GEIKIE, F.R.S., etc. 8vo. 14s.

FORBES MITCHELL(W.)-REMINISCENCES OF THE GREAT MUTINY. Cr. 8vo. 8s. 6d. net.

FRANCIS OF ASSISI. By Mrs. OLIPHANT. Cr. 8vo. 6s.

FRASER. JAMES FRASER, SECOND BISHOP OF MANCHESTER: A Memoir. By T. HUGHES. Cr. 8vo. 6s.

GARIBALDI. (*See* SELECT BIOGRAPHY, p. 6.)

BIOGRAPHY.

GOETHE: LIFE OF. By Prof. HEINRICH DÜNTZER. Translated by T. W. LYSTER. 2 vols. Cr. 8vo. 21s.

GOETHE AND CARLYLE. (See CARLYLE.)

GORDON (General): A SKETCH. By REGINALD H. BARNES. Cr. 8vo. 1s.
—— LETTERS OF GENERAL C. G. GORDON TO HIS SISTER, M. A. GORDON. 4th Edit. Cr. 8vo. 3s. 6d.

HANDEL: LIFE OF. By W. S. ROCKSTRO. Cr. 8vo. 10s. 6d.

HOBART. (See COLLECTED WORKS, p. 22.)

HODGSON. MEMOIR OF REV. FRANCIS HODGSON, B.D. By his Son, Rev. JAMES T. HODGSON, M.A. 2 vols. Cr. 8vo. 18s.

JEVONS (W. Stanley).—LETTERS AND JOURNAL. Edited by HIS WIFE. 8vo. 14s.

KAVANAGH (Rt. Hon. A. McMurrough): A BIOGRAPHY. From papers chiefly unpublished, compiled by his Cousin, SARAH L. STEELE. With Portrait. 8vo. 14s. net.

KINGSLEY: HIS LETTERS, AND MEMORIES OF HIS LIFE. Edited by HIS WIFE. 2 vols. Cr. 8vo. 12s.—Cheap Edition. 1 vol. 6s.

LAMB. THE LIFE OF CHARLES LAMB. By Rev. ALFRED AINGER, M.A. Globe 8vo. 5s.

LETHBRIDGE (Sir R.).—GOLDEN BOOK OF INDIA. Royal 8vo. 40s.

LOUIS (St.). (See SELECT BIOGRAPHY, p 6.)

MACMILLAN (D.). MEMOIR OF DANIEL MACMILLAN. By THOMAS HUGHES, Q.C. With Portrait. Cr. 8vo. 4s. 6d.—Cheap Edition. Cr. 8vo, sewed. 1s.

MALTHUS AND HIS WORK. By JAMES BONAR. 8vo. 12s. 6d.

MARCUS AURELIUS. (See SELECT BIOGRAPHY, p. 6.)

MATHEWS. THE LIFE OF CHARLES J. MATHEWS. Edited by CHARLES DICKENS. With Portraits. 2 vols. 8vo. 25s.

MAURICE. LIFE OF FREDERICK DENISON MAURICE. By his Son, FREDERICK MAURICE. Two Portraits. 2 vols. 8vo. 36s.—Popular Edit. (4th Thousand). 2 vols. Cr. 8vo. 16s.

MAXWELL. PROFESSOR CLERK MAXWELL, A LIFE OF. By Prof. L. CAMPBELL, M.A., and W. GARNETT, M.A. Cr. 8vo. 7s. 6d.

MAZZINI. (See SELECT BIOGRAPHY, p. 6.)

MELBOURNE. MEMOIRS OF VISCOUNT MELBOURNE. By W. M. TORRENS. With Portrait. 2nd Edit. 2 vols. 8vo. 32s.

MILTON. THE LIFE OF JOHN MILTON. By Prof. DAVID MASSON. Vol. I., 21s.; Vol. III., 18s.; Vols. IV. and V., 32s.; Vol. VI., with Portrait, 21s. (See also p. 16.)

MILTON, JOHNSON'S LIFE OF. With Introduction and Notes by K. DEIGHTON. Globe 8vo. 1s. 9d.

NAPOLEON I., HISTORY OF. By P. LANFREY. 4 vols. Cr. 8vo. 30s.

NELSON. SOUTHEY'S LIFE OF NELSON. With Introduction and Notes by MICHAEL MACMILLAN, B.A. Globe 8vo. 3s. 6d.

NORTH (M.).—RECOLLECTIONS OF A HAPPY LIFE. Being the Autobiography of MARIANNE NORTH. Ed. by Mrs. J. A. SYMONDS. 2nd Edit. 2 vols. Ex. cr. 8vo. 17s. net.
—— SOME FURTHER RECOLLECTIONS OF A HAPPY LIFE. Cr. 8vo. 8s. 6d. net.

OXFORD MOVEMENT, THE, 1833—45. By Dean CHURCH. Gl. 8vo. 5s.

PARKER (W. K.)—A BIOGRAPHICAL SKETCH. By HIS SON. Cr. 8vo. 4s. net.

PATTESON. LIFE AND LETTERS OF JOHN COLERIDGE PATTESON, D.D., MISSIONARY BISHOP. By C. M. YONGE. 2 vols. Cr. 8vo. 12s. (See also BOOKS FOR THE YOUNG, p. 41.)

PATTISON (M.).—MEMOIRS. Cr. 8vo. 8s. 6d.

PITT. (See SELECT BIOGRAPHY, p. 6.)

POLLOCK (Sir Frdk., 2nd Bart.).—PERSONAL REMEMBRANCES. 2 vols. Cr. 8vo. 16s.

POOLE, THOS., AND HIS FRIENDS. By Mrs. SANDFORD. 2nd edit. Cr. 8vo. 6s.

RENAN (Ernest).—IN MEMORIAM. By Sir M. E. GRANT DUFF. Cr. 8vo. 6s.

RITCHIE (Mrs.).—RECORDS OF TENNYSON, RUSKIN, AND BROWNING. Globe 8vo. 5s.

ROBINSON (Matthew): AUTOBIOGRAPHY OF. Edited by J. E. B. MAYOR. Fcp. 8vo. 5s.

ROSSETTI (Dante Gabriel): A RECORD AND A STUDY. By W. SHARP. Cr. 8vo. 10s. 6d.

RUMFORD. (See COLLECTED WORKS, p. 24.)

SCHILLER, LIFE OF. By Prof. H. DÜNTZER. Trans. by P. E. PINKERTON. Cr. 8vo. 10s. 6d.

SHELBURNE. LIFE OF WILLIAM, EARL OF SHELBURNE. By Lord EDMOND FITZMAURICE. In 3 vols.—Vol. I. 8vo. 12s.—Vol. II. 8vo. 12s.—Vol. III. 8vo. 16s.

SIBSON. (See MEDICINE.)

SMETHAM (Jas.).: LETTERS OF. Ed. by SARAH SMETHAM and W. DAVIES. Portrait. Globe 8vo. 5s.
—— THE LITERARY WORKS. Gl. 8vo. 5s.

TAIT. THE LIFE OF ARCHIBALD CAMPBELL TAIT, ARCHBISHOP OF CANTERBURY. By the BISHOP OF ROCHESTER and Rev. W. BENHAM, B.D. 2 vols. 8vo. 10s. net.
—— CATHARINE AND CRAWFORD TAIT, WIFE AND SON OF ARCHIBALD CAMPBELL, ARCHBISHOP OF CANTERBURY: A Memoir. Ed. by Rev. W. BENHAM, B.D. Cr. 8vo. 6s. —Popular Edit., abridged. Cr. 8vo. 2s. 6d.

THRING (Edward): A MEMORY OF. By J. H. SKRINE. Cr. 8vo. 6s.

TUCKWELL (W.).—THE ANCIENT WAYS: WINCHESTER FIFTY YEARS AGO. Globe 8vo. 4s. 6d.

VICTOR EMMANUEL II., FIRST KING OF ITALY. By G. S. GODKIN. Cr. 8vo. 6s.

WARD. WILLIAM GEORGE WARD AND THE OXFORD MOVEMENT. By his Son, WILFRID WARD. With Portrait. 8vo. 14s.
—— WILLIAM GEORGE WARD AND THE CATHOLIC REVIVAL. 8vo. 14s.

WATSON. A RECORD OF ELLEN WATSON. By ANNA BUCKLAND. Cr. 8vo. 6s.

WHEWELL. DR. WILLIAM WHEWELL, late Master of Trinity College, Cambridge. An Account of his Writings, with Selections from his Literary and Scientific Correspondence. By I. TODHUNTER, M.A. 2 vols. 8vo. 25s.

WILLIAMS (Montagu).—LEAVES OF A LIFE. Cr. 8vo. 3s. 6d.
—— LATER LEAVES. Being further Reminiscences. With Portrait. Cr. 8vo. 3s. 6d.
—— ROUND LONDON, DOWN EAST AND UP WEST. Cr. 8vo. 3s. 6d.

BIOGRAPHY—BOTANY.

WILSON. MEMOIR OF PROF. GEORGE WILSON, M.D. By HIS SISTER. With Portrait. 2nd Edit. Cr. 8vo. 6s.

WORDSWORTH. DOVE COTTAGE, WORDSWORTH'S HOME 1800—8. Gl. 8vo, swd. 1s.

Select Biography.

BIOGRAPHIES OF EMINENT PERSONS. Reprinted from the *Times*. 4 vols. Cr. 8vo. 3s. 6d. each.

FARRAR (Archdeacon).—SEEKERS AFTER GOD. Cr. 8vo. 3s. 6d.

FAWCETT (Mrs. H.). — SOME EMINENT WOMEN OF OUR TIMES. Cr. 8vo. 2s. 6d.

GUIZOT.—GREAT CHRISTIANS OF FRANCE: ST. LOUIS AND CALVIN. Cr. 8vo. 6s.

HARRISON (Frederic).—THE NEW CALENDAR OF GREAT MEN. Ex. cr. 8vo. 7s. 6d. net.

MARRIOTT (J. A. R.).—THE MAKERS OF MODERN ITALY: MAZZINI, CAVOUR, GARIBALDI. Cr. 8vo. 1s. 6d.

MARTINEAU (Harriet). — BIOGRAPHICAL SKETCHES, 1852—75. Cr. 8vo. 6s.

NEW HOUSE OF COMMONS, JULY, 1892. Reprinted from the *Times*. 16mo. 1s.

SMITH (Goldwin).—THREE ENGLISH STATESMEN: CROMWELL, PYM, PITT. Cr. 8vo. 5s.

STEVENSON (F. S.).—HISTORIC PERSONALITY. Cr. 8vo. 4s. 6d.

WINKWORTH (Catharine). — CHRISTIAN SINGERS OF GERMANY. Cr. 8vo. 4s. 6d.

YONGE (Charlotte M.).—THE PUPILS OF ST. JOHN. Illustrated. Cr. 8vo. 6s.

—— PIONEERS AND FOUNDERS; or, Recent Workers in the Mission Field. Cr. 8vo. 6s.

—— A BOOK OF WORTHIES. Pott 8vo. 2s. 6d. net.

—— A BOOK OF GOLDEN DEEDS. Pott 8vo. 2s. 6d. net.—*Globe Readings Edition*. Globe 8vo. 2s.—*Abridged Edition*. Pott 8vo. 1s.

BIOLOGY.

(*See also* BOTANY; NATURAL HISTORY; PHYSIOLOGY; ZOOLOGY.)

BALFOUR (F. M.).—COMPARATIVE EMBRYOLOGY. Illustrated. 2 vols. 8vo. Vol. I. 18s. Vol. II. 21s.

BALL (W. P.).—ARE THE EFFECTS OF USE AND DISUSE INHERITED? Cr. 8vo. 3s. 6d.

BASTIAN (H. Charlton).—THE BEGINNINGS OF LIFE. 2 vols. Crown 8vo. 28s.

—— EVOLUTION AND THE ORIGIN OF LIFE. Cr. 8vo. 6s. 6d.

BATESON (W.).—MATERIALS FOR THE STUDY OF VARIATION IN ANIMALS. Part I. DISCONTINUOUS VARIATION. Illustr. 8vo.

BERNARD (H. M.).—THE APODIDAE. Cr. 8vo. 7s. 6d.

BIRKS (T. R.).—MODERN PHYSICAL FATALISM, AND THE DOCTRINE OF EVOLUTION. Including an Examination of Mr. Herbert Spencer's "First Principles." Cr. 8vo. 6s.

CALDERWOOD (H.). — EVOLUTION AND MAN'S PLACE IN NATURE. Cr. 8vo. 7s. 6d.

DE VARIGNY (H.).—EXPERIMENTAL EVOLUTION. Cr. 8vo. 5s.

EIMER (G. H. T.).—ORGANIC EVOLUTION AS THE RESULT OF THE INHERITANCE OF ACQUIRED CHARACTERS ACCORDING TO THE LAWS OF ORGANIC GROWTH. Translated by J. T. CUNNINGHAM, M.A. 8vo. 12s. 6d.

FISKE (John).—OUTLINES OF COSMIC PHILOSOPHY, BASED ON THE DOCTRINE OF EVOLUTION. 2 vols. 8vo. 25s.

—— MAN'S DESTINY VIEWED IN THE LIGHT OF HIS ORIGIN. Cr. 8vo. 3s. 6d.

FOSTER (Prof. M.) and BALFOUR (F. M.).—THE ELEMENTS OF EMBRYOLOGY. Ed. A. SEDGWICK, and WALTER HEAPE. Illus. 3rd Edit., revised and enlarged. Cr. 8vo. 10s. 6d.

HUXLEY (T. H.) and MARTIN (H. N.).—(*See under* ZOOLOGY, p. 43.)

KLEIN (Dr. E.).—MICRO-ORGANISMS AND DISEASE. With 121 Engravings. 3rd Edit. Cr. 8vo. 6s.

LANKESTER (Prof. E. Ray).—COMPARATIVE LONGEVITY IN MAN AND THE LOWER ANIMALS. Cr. 8vo. 4s. 6d.

LUBBOCK (Sir John, Bart.). — SCIENTIFIC LECTURES. Illustrated. 2nd Edit. 8vo. 8s. 6d.

MURPHY (J. J.).—NATURAL SELECTION. Gl. 8vo. 5s.

PARKER (T. Jeffery).—LESSONS IN ELEMENTARY BIOLOGY. Illustr. Cr. 8vo. 10s. 6d.

ROMANES (G. J.).—SCIENTIFIC EVIDENCES OF ORGANIC EVOLUTION. Cr. 8vo. 2s. 6d.

WALLACE (Alfred R.).—DARWINISM: An Exposition of the Theory of Natural Selection. Illustrated. 3rd Edit. Cr. 8vo. 9s.

—— CONTRIBUTIONS TO THE THEORY OF NATURAL SELECTION, AND TROPICAL NATURE: and other Essays. New Ed. Cr. 8vo. 6s.

—— THE GEOGRAPHICAL DISTRIBUTION OF ANIMALS. Illustrated. 2 vols. 8vo. 42s.

—— ISLAND LIFE. Illustr. Ext. Cr. 8vo. 6s.

BIRDS. (*See* ZOOLOGY; ORNITHOLOGY.)

BOOK-KEEPING.

THORNTON (J.).—FIRST LESSONS IN BOOKKEEPING. New Edition. Cr. 8vo. 2s. 6d.

—— KEY. Oblong 4to. 10s. 6d.

—— PRIMER OF BOOK-KEEPING. Pott 8vo. 1s.

—— KEY. Demy 8vo. 2s. 6d.

—— EXERCISES IN BOOK-KEEPING. Pott 8vo. 1s.

BOTANY.

(*See also* AGRICULTURE; GARDENING.)

ALLEN (Grant). — ON THE COLOURS OF FLOWERS. Illustrated. Cr. 8vo. 3s. 6d.

BALFOUR (Prof. J. B.) and WARD (Prof. H. M.).—A GENERAL TEXT-BOOK OF BOTANY. 8vc. [*In preparation*.

BETTANY (G. T.).—FIRST LESSONS IN PRACTICAL BOTANY. Pott 8vo. 1s.

BOWER (Prof. F. O.).—A COURSE OF PRACTICAL INSTRUCTION IN BOTANY. Cr. 8vo. 10s. 6d.—Abridged Edition. [*In preparation*.

CHURCH (Prof. A. H.) and VINES (S. H.).—MANUAL OF VEGETABLE PHYSIOLOGY. Illustrated. Crown 8vo. [*In preparation*.

GOODALE (Prof. G. L.).—PHYSIOLOGICAL BOTANY.—1. OUTLINES OF THE HISTOLOGY OF PHÆNOGAMOUS PLANTS; 2. VEGETABLE PHYSIOLOGY. 8vo. 10s. 6d.

GRAY (Prof. Asa).—STRUCTURAL BOTANY; or, Organography on the Basis of Morphology. 8vo. 10s. 6d.

—— THE SCIENTIFIC PAPERS OF ASA GRAY. Selected by C. S. SARGENT. 2 vols. 8vo. 21s.

HANBURY (Daniel). — SCIENCE PAPERS, CHIEFLY PHARMACOLOGICAL AND BOTANICAL. Med. 8vo. 14s.

HARTIG (Dr. Robert).—TEXT-BOOK OF THE DISEASES OF TREES. Transl. by Prof. WM. SOMERVILLE, B.Sc. With Introduction by Prof. H. MARSHALL WARD. 8vo.

HOOKER (Sir Joseph D.).—THE STUDENT'S FLORA OF THE BRITISH ISLANDS. 3rd Edit. Globe 8vo. 10s. 6d.

—— A PRIMER OF BOTANY. Pott 8vo. 1s.

LASLETT (Thomas).—TIMBER AND TIMBER TREES, NATIVE AND FOREIGN. Cr. 8vo 8s. 6d.

LUBBOCK (Sir John, Bart.).—ON BRITISH WILD FLOWERS CONSIDERED IN RELATION TO INSECTS. Illustrated. Cr. 8vo. 4s. 6d.

—— FLOWERS, FRUITS, AND LEAVES. With Illustrations. Cr. 8vo. 4s. 6d.

MÜLLER–THOMPSON.—THE FERTILISATION OF FLOWERS. By Prof. H. MÜLLER. Transl. by D'ARCY W. THOMPSON. Preface by CHARLES DARWIN, F.R.S. 8vo. 21s.

NISBET (J.).—BRITISH FOREST TREES AND THEIR SYLVICULTURAL CHARACTERISTICS AND TREATMENT. Cr. 8vo. 6s. net.

OLIVER (Prof. Daniel).—LESSONS IN ELEMENTARY BOTANY. Illustr. Fcp. 8vo. 4s. 6d.

—— FIRST BOOK OF INDIAN BOTANY. Illustrated. Ext. fcp. 8vo. 6s. 6d.

PETTIGREW (J. Bell).—THE PHYSIOLOGY OF THE CIRCULATION IN PLANTS, IN THE LOWER ANIMALS, AND IN MAN. 8vo. 12s

SMITH (J.).—ECONOMIC PLANTS; DICTIONARY OF POPULAR NAMES OF; THEIR HISTORY, PRODUCTS, AND USES. 8vo. 14s.

SMITH (W. G.).—DISEASES OF FIELD AND GARDEN CROPS, CHIEFLY SUCH AS ARE CAUSED BY FUNGI. Illust. Fcp. 8vo. 4s. 6d.

WARD (Prof. H. M.).—TIMBER AND SOME OF ITS DISEASES. Illustrated. Cr. 8vo. 6s.

YONGE (C. M.).—THE HERB OF THE FIELD. New Edition, revised. Cr. 8vo. 5s.

BREWING AND WINE.

PASTEUR – FAULKNER. — STUDIES ON FERMENTATION: THE DISEASES OF BEER, THEIR CAUSES, AND THE MEANS OF PREVENTING THEM. By L. PASTEUR. Translated by FRANK FAULKNER. 8vo. 21s.

CHEMISTRY.

(See also METALLURGY.)

BRODIE (Sir Benjamin).—IDEAL CHEMISTRY. Cr. 8vo. 2s.

COHEN (J. B.). — THE OWENS COLLEGE COURSE OF PRACTICAL ORGANIC CHEMISTRY. Fcp. 8vo. 2s. 6d.

COOKE (Prof. J. P., jun.).—PRINCIPLES OF CHEMICAL PHILOSOPHY. New Ed. 8vo. 19s.

DOBBIN (L.) and WALKER (Jas.) —CHEMICAL THEORY FOR BEGINNERS. Pott 8vo. 2s. 6d.

FLEISCHER (Emil).—A SYSTEM OF VOLUMETRIC ANALYSIS. Transl. with Additions, by M. M. P. MUIR, F.R.S.E. Cr. 8vo. 7s. 6d.

FRANKLAND (Prof. P. F.). (See AGRICULTURE.)

GLADSTONE (J. H.) and TRIBE (A.).— THE CHEMISTRY OF THE SECONDARY BATTERIES OF PLANTÉ AND FAURE. Cr. 8vo. 2s. 6d.

HARTLEY (Prof. W. N.).—A COURSE OF QUANTITATIVE ANALYSIS FOR STUDENTS. Globe 8vo. 5s.

HEMPEL (Dr. W.). — METHODS OF GAS ANALYSIS. Translated by L. M. DENNIS. Cr. 8vo. 7s. 6d.

HOFMANN (Prof. A. W.).—THE LIFE WORK OF LIEBIG IN EXPERIMENTAL AND PHILOSOPHIC CHEMISTRY. 8vo. 5s.

JONES (Francis).—THE OWENS COLLEGE JUNIOR COURSE OF PRACTICAL CHEMISTRY. Illustrated. Fcp. 8vo. 2s. 6d.

—— QUESTIONS ON CHEMISTRY. Fcp. 8vo. 3s.

LANDAUER (J.). — BLOWPIPE ANALYSIS. Translated by J. TAYLOR. Gl. 8vo. 4s. 6d.

LOCKYER (J. Norman, F.R.S.). — THE CHEMISTRY OF THE SUN. Illustr. 8vo. 14s.

LUPTON (S.). — CHEMICAL ARITHMETIC. With 1200 Problems. Fcp. 8vo. 4s. 6d.

MANSFIELD (C. B.).—A THEORY OF SALTS. Cr. 8vo. 14s.

MELDOLA (Prof. R.).—THE CHEMISTRY OF PHOTOGRAPHY. Illustrated. Cr. 8vo. 6s.

MEYER (E. von).—HISTORY OF CHEMISTRY FROM EARLIEST TIMES TO THE PRESENT DAY. Trans. G. McGOWAN. 8vo. 14s. net.

MIXTER (Prof. W. G.).—AN ELEMENTARY TEXT-BOOK OF CHEMISTRY. Cr. 8vo. 7s. 6d.

MUIR (M. M. P.).—PRACTICAL CHEMISTRY FOR MEDICAL STUDENTS (First M. B. Course). Fcp. 8vo. 1s. 6d.

MUIR (M. M. P.) and WILSON (D. M.).— ELEMENTS OF THERMAL CHEMISTRY. 12s. 6d.

OSTWALD (Prof.).—OUTLINES OF GENERAL CHEMISTRY. Trans. Dr. J. WALKER. 10s. net.

RAMSAY (Prof. William).—EXPERIMENTAL PROOFS OF CHEMICAL THEORY FOR BEGINNERS. Pott 8vo. 2s. 6d.

REMSEN (Prof. Ira).—THE ELEMENTS OF CHEMISTRY. Fcp. 8vo. 2s. 6d.

—— AN INTRODUCTION TO THE STUDY OF CHEMISTRY (INORGANIC CHEMISTRY). Cr 8vo. 6s. 6d.

—— A TEXT-BOOK OF INORGANIC CHEMISTRY. 8vo. 16s.

—— COMPOUNDS OF CARBON; or, An Introduction to the Study of Organic Chemistry Cr. 8vo. 6s. 6d.

ROSCOE (Sir Henry E., F.R.S.).—A PRIMER OF CHEMISTRY. Illustrated. Pott 8vo. 1s.

—— LESSONS IN ELEMENTARY CHEMISTRY, INORGANIC AND ORGANIC. Fcp. 8vo. 4s. 6d.

ROSCOE (Sir H. E.) and SCHORLEMMER (Prof. C.).—A COMPLETE TREATISE ON INORGANIC AND ORGANIC CHEMISTRY. Illustr. 8vo.—Vols. I. and II. INORGANIC CHEMISTRY: Vol. I. THE NON-METALLIC ELEMENTS, 2nd Edit., 21s. Vol. II. Parts I. and II. METALS, 18s. each.—Vol. III. ORGANIC CHEMISTRY: THE CHEMISTRY OF THE HYDRO-CARBONS AND THEIR DERIVATIVES. Parts I. II. IV. and VI. 21s.; Parts III. and V. 18s. each.

DICTIONARIES—EDUCATION.

ROSCOE (Sir H. E.) and SCHUSTER (A.).—SPECTRUM ANALYSIS. By Sir HENRY E. ROSCOE. 4th Edit., revised by the Author and A. SCHUSTER, F.R.S. With Coloured Plates. 8vo. 21s.

THORPE (Prof. T. E.) and TATE (W.).— A SERIES OF CHEMICAL PROBLEMS. With KEY. Fcp. 8vo. 2s.

THORPE (Prof. T. E.) and RÜCKER (Prof. A. W.).—A TREATISE ON CHEMICAL PHYSICS. Illustrated. 8vo. [In preparation.

WURTZ (Ad.).—A HISTORY OF CHEMICAL THEORY. Transl. by H. WATTS. Cr. 8vo. 6s.

CHRISTIAN CHURCH, History of the.
(See under THEOLOGY, p. 34.)

CHURCH OF ENGLAND, The.
(See under THEOLOGY, p. 35.)

COLLECTED WORKS.
(See under LITERATURE, p. 20.)

COMPARATIVE ANATOMY.
(See under ZOOLOGY, p. 43.)

COOKERY.
(See under DOMESTIC ECONOMY, below.)

DEVOTIONAL BOOKS.
(See under THEOLOGY, p. 35.)

DICTIONARIES AND GLOSSARIES.

AUTENRIETH (Dr. G.).—AN HOMERIC DICTIONARY. Translated from the German, by R. P. KEEP, Ph.D. Cr. 8vo. 6s.

BARTLETT (J.).—FAMILIAR QUOTATIONS. Cr. 8vo. 12s. 6d.

GROVE (Sir George).—A DICTIONARY OF MUSIC AND MUSICIANS. (See MUSIC.)

HOLE (Rev. C.).—A BRIEF BIOGRAPHICAL DICTIONARY. 2nd Edit. Pott 8vo. 4s. 6d.

MASSON (Gustave).—A COMPENDIOUS DICTIONARY OF THE FRENCH LANGUAGE. Cr. 8vo. 3s. 6d.

PALGRAVE (R. H. I.).—A DICTIONARY OF POLITICAL ECONOMY. (See POLITICAL ECONOMY.)

WHITNEY (Prof. W. D.).—A COMPENDIOUS GERMAN AND ENGLISH DICTIONARY. Cr. 8vo. 5s.—German-English Part separately. 3s. 6d.

WRIGHT (W. Aldis).—THE BIBLE WORD-BOOK. 2nd Edit. Cr. 8vo. 7s. 6d.

YONGE (Charlotte M.).—HISTORY OF CHRISTIAN NAMES. Cr. 8vo. 7s. 6d.

DOMESTIC ECONOMY.
Cookery—Nursing—Needlework.

Cookery.

BARKER (Lady).—FIRST LESSONS IN THE PRINCIPLES OF COOKING. 3rd Edit. Pott 8vo. 1s.

BARNETT (E. A.) and O'NEILL (H. C.).—PRIMER OF DOMESTIC ECONOMY. Pott 8vo. 1s.

MIDDLE-CLASS COOKERY BOOK, THE. Compiled for the Manchester School of Cookery. Pott 8vo. 1s. 6d.

TEGETMEIER (W. B.).—HOUSEHOLD MANAGEMENT AND COOKERY. Pott 8vo. 1s.

WRIGHT (Miss Guthrie).—THE SCHOOL COOKERY-BOOK. Pott 8vo. 1s.

Nursing.

CRAVEN (Mrs. Dacre).—A GUIDE TO DISTRICT NURSES. Cr. 8vo. 2s. 6d.

FOTHERGILL (Dr. J. M.).—FOOD FOR THE INVALID, THE CONVALESCENT, THE DYSPEPTIC, AND THE GOUTY. Cr. 8vo. 3s. 6d.

JEX-BLAKE (Dr. Sophia).—THE CARE OF INFANTS. Pott 8vo. 1s.

RATHBONE (Wm.).—THE HISTORY AND PROGRESS OF DISTRICT NURSING, FROM 1859 TO THE PRESENT DATE. Cr. 8vo. 2s. 6d.

RECOLLECTIONS OF A NURSE. By E. D. Cr. 8vo. 2s.

STEPHEN (Caroline E.).—THE SERVICE OF THE POOR. Cr. 8vo. 6s. 6d.

Needlework.

GLAISTER (Elizabeth).—NEEDLEWORK. Cr. 8vo. 2s. 6d.

GRAND'HOMME. — CUTTING OUT AND DRESSMAKING. From the French of Mdlle. E. GRAND'HOMME. Pott 8vo. 1s.

GRENFELL (Mrs.)—DRESSMAKING. Pott 8vo. 1s.

ROSEVEAR (E.).—NEEDLEWORK, KNITTING, AND CUTTING OUT. Cr. 8vo. 6s.

DRAMA, The.
(See under LITERATURE, p. 14.)

ELECTRICITY.
(See under PHYSICS, p. 29.)

EDUCATION.

ARNOLD (Matthew).—HIGHER SCHOOLS AND UNIVERSITIES IN GERMANY. Cr. 8vo. 6s.

—— REPORTS ON ELEMENTARY SCHOOLS, 1852-82. Ed. by Lord SANDFORD. 8vo. 3s. 6d.

—— A FRENCH ETON : OR MIDDLE CLASS EDUCATION AND THE STATE. Cr. 8vo. 6s.

BLAKISTON (J. R.).—THE TEACHER: HINTS ON SCHOOL MANAGEMENT. Cr. 8vo. 2s. 6d.

CALDERWOOD (Prof. H.).—ON TEACHING. 4th Edit. Ext. fcp. 8vo. 2s. 6d.

COMBE (George).—EDUCATION : ITS PRINCIPLES AND PRACTICE AS DEVELOPED BY GEORGE COMBE. Ed. by W. JOLLY. 8vo. 15s.

CRAIK (Henry).—THE STATE IN ITS RELATION TO EDUCATION. Cr. 8vo. 2s. 6d.

FEARON (D. R.).—SCHOOL INSPECTION. 6th Edit. Cr. 8vo. 2s. 6d.

FITCH (J. G.).—NOTES ON AMERICAN SCHOOLS AND TRAINING COLLEGES. Reprinted by permission. Globe 8vo. 2s. 6d.

GLADSTONE (J. H.).—SPELLING REFORM FROM AN EDUCATIONAL POINT OF VIEW. 3rd Edit. Cr. 8vo. 1s. 6d.

ENGINEERING—GEOLOGY.

[H]ERTEL (Dr.).—OVERPRESSURE IN HIGH SCHOOLS IN DENMARK. With Introduction by Sir J. CRICHTON-BROWNE. Cr. 8vo. 3s. 6d.

[K]INGSLEY (Charles).—HEALTH AND EDUCATION. Cr. 8vo. 6s.

[L]UBBOCK (Sir John, Bart.).—POLITICAL AND EDUCATIONAL ADDRESSES. 8vo. 8s. 6d.

[M]AURICE (F. D.).—LEARNING AND WORKING. Cr. 8vo. 4s. 6d.

[R]ECORD OF TECHNICAL AND SECONDARY EDUCATION. Crown 8vo. Sewed, 2s. net. No. I. Nov. 1891.

[T]HRING (Rev. Edward).—EDUCATION AND SCHOOL. 2nd Edit. Cr. 8vo. 6s.

ENGINEERING.

[A]LEXANDER (T.) and THOMSON (A. W.)—ELEMENTARY APPLIED MECHANICS. Part II. TRANSVERSE STRESS. Cr. 8vo. 10s. 6d.

[C]HALMERS (J. B.).—GRAPHICAL DETERMINATION OF FORCES IN ENGINEERING STRUCTURES. Illustrated. 8vo. 24s.

[C]OTTERILL (Prof. J. H.).—APPLIED MECHANICS: An Elementary General Introduction to the Theory of Structures and Machines. 3rd Edit. 8vo. 18s.

[C]OTTERILL (Prof. J. H.) and SLADE (J. H.).—LESSONS IN APPLIED MECHANICS. Fcp. 8vo. 5s. 6d.

[K]ENNEDY (Prof. A. B. W.).—THE MECHANICS OF MACHINERY. Cr. 8vo. 8s. 6d.

[L]ANGMAID (T.) and GAISFORD (H.).—STEAM MACHINERY. 8vo. 6s. net.

[P]EABODY (Prof. C. H.).—THERMODYNAMICS OF THE STEAM ENGINE AND OTHER HEAT-ENGINES. 8vo. 21s.

[S]HANN (G.).—AN ELEMENTARY TREATISE ON HEAT IN RELATION TO STEAM AND THE STEAM-ENGINE. Illustrated. Cr. 8vo. 4s. 6d.

[W]EISBACH (J.) and HERRMANN (G.).—MECHANICS OF HOISTING MACHINERY. Transl. K. P. DAHLSTROM. 8vo. 12s. 6d. net.

[W]OODWARD (C. M.).—A HISTORY OF THE ST. LOUIS BRIDGE. 4to. 2l. 2s. net.

[Y]OUNG (E. W.).—SIMPLE PRACTICAL METHODS OF CALCULATING STRAINS ON GIRDERS, ARCHES, AND TRUSSES. 8vo. 7s. 6d.

ENGLISH CITIZEN SERIES.
(See POLITICS.)

ENGLISH MEN OF ACTION.
(See BIOGRAPHY.)

ENGLISH MEN OF LETTERS.
(See BIOGRAPHY.)

ENGLISH STATESMEN, Twelve.
(See BIOGRAPHY.)

ENGRAVING. (See ART.)

ESSAYS. (See under LITERATURE, p. 20.)

ETCHING. (See ART.)

ETHICS. (See under PHILOSOPHY, p. 27.)

FATHERS, The.
(See under THEOLOGY, p. 36.)

FICTION, Prose.
(See under LITERATURE, p. 18.)

GARDENING.
(See also AGRICULTURE; BOTANY.)

BLOMFIELD (R.) and THOMAS (F. I.).—THE FORMAL GARDEN IN ENGLAND. Illustrated. Ex. cr. 8vo. 7s. 6d. net.

BRIGHT (H. A.).—THE ENGLISH FLOWER GARDEN. Cr. 8vo. 3s. 6d.
— A YEAR IN A LANCASHIRE GARDEN. Cr. 8vo. 3s. 6d.

HOBDAY (E.).— VILLA GARDENING. A Handbook for Amateur and Practical Gardeners. Ext. cr. 8vo. 6s.

HOPE (Frances J.).—NOTES AND THOUGHTS ON GARDENS AND WOODLANDS. Cr. 8vo. 6s.

WRIGHT (J.).—A PRIMER OF PRACTICAL HORTICULTURE. Pott 8vo. 1s.

GEOGRAPHY.
(See also ATLASES.)

BLANFORD (H. F.).—ELEMENTARY GEOGRAPHY OF INDIA, BURMA, AND CEYLON. Globe 8vo. 2s. 6d.

CLARKE (C. B.).—A GEOGRAPHICAL READER AND COMPANION TO THE ATLAS. Cr. 8vo. 2s.
— A CLASS-BOOK OF GEOGRAPHY. With 18 Coloured Maps. Fcp. 8vo. 3s.; swd., 2s. 6d.

DAWSON (G. M.) and SUTHERLAND (A.).—ELEMENTARY GEOGRAPHY OF THE BRITISH COLONIES. Globe 8vo. 3s.

ELDERTON (W. A.).—MAPS AND MAP-DRAWING. Pott 8vo. 1s.

GEIKIE (Sir Archibald).—THE TEACHING OF GEOGRAPHY. A Practical Handbook for the use of Teachers. Globe 8vo. 2s.
— GEOGRAPHY OF THE BRITISH ISLES. Pott 8vo. 1s.

GREEN (J. R. and A. S.).—A SHORT GEOGRAPHY OF THE BRITISH ISLANDS. Fcp. 8vo. 3s. 6d.

GROVE (Sir George).—A PRIMER OF GEOGRAPHY. Maps. Pott 8vo. 1s.

KIEPERT (H.).—MANUAL OF ANCIENT GEOGRAPHY. Cr. 8vo. 5s.

MILL (H. R.).—ELEMENTARY CLASS-BOOK OF GENERAL GEOGRAPHY. Cr. 8vo. 3s. 6d.

SIME (James).—GEOGRAPHY OF EUROPE. With Illustrations. Globe 8vo. 3s.

STRACHEY (Lieut.-Gen. R.).—LECTURES ON GEOGRAPHY. Cr. 8vo. 4s. 6d.

SUTHERLAND (A.).—GEOGRAPHY OF VICTORIA. Pott 8vo. 1s.

TOZER (H. F.).—A PRIMER OF CLASSICAL GEOGRAPHY. Pott 8vo. 1s.

GEOLOGY AND MINERALOGY.

BLANFORD (W. T.). — GEOLOGY AND ZOOLOGY OF ABYSSINIA. 8vo. 21s.

COAL: ITS HISTORY AND ITS USES. By Profs. GREEN, MIALL, THORPE, RÜCKER, and MARSHALL. 8vo. 12s. 6d.

DAWSON (Sir J. W.).—THE GEOLOGY OF NOVA SCOTIA, NEW BRUNSWICK, AND PRINCE EDWARD ISLAND; or, Acadian Geology. 4th Edit. 8vo. 21s.

GEIKIE (Sir Archibald).—A PRIMER OF GEOLOGY. Illustrated. Pott 8vo. 1s.
— CLASS-BOOK OF GEOLOGY. Illustrated. Cr. 8vo. 4s. 6d.

HISTORY.

GEOLOGY AND MINERALOGY—*contd.*

GEIKIE (Sir A.).—GEOLOGICAL SKETCHES AT HOME AND ABROAD. Illus. 8vo. 10s. 6d.
—— OUTLINES OF FIELD GEOLOGY. With numerous Illustrations. Gl. 8vo. 3s. 6d.
—— TEXT-BOOK OF GEOLOGY. Illustrated. 3rd Edit. Med. 8vo. 28s.
—— THE SCENERY OF SCOTLAND. Viewed in connection with its Physical Geology. 2nd Edit. Cr. 8vo. 12s. 6d.

HULL (E.).—A TREATISE ON ORNAMENTAL AND BUILDING STONES OF GREAT BRITAIN AND FOREIGN COUNTRIES. 8vo. 12s.

PENNINGTON (Rooke).—NOTES ON THE BARROWS AND BONE CAVES OF DERBYSHIRE. 8vo. 6s.

RENDU—WILLS.—THE THEORY OF THE GLACIERS OF SAVOY. By M. LE CHANOINE RENDU. Trans. by A. WILLS, Q.C. 8vo. 7s. 6d.

WILLIAMS (G. H.).—ELEMENTS OF CRYSTALLOGRAPHY. Cr. 8vo. 6s.

GLOBE LIBRARY. (*See* LITERATURE, p. 21.)

GLOSSARIES. (*See* DICTIONARIES.)

GOLDEN TREASURY SERIES. (*See* LITERATURE, p. 21.)

GRAMMAR. (*See* PHILOLOGY.)

HEALTH. (*See* HYGIENE.)

HEAT. (*See under* PHYSICS, p. 29.)

HISTOLOGY. (*See* PHYSIOLOGY.)

HISTORY.
(*See also* BIOGRAPHY.)

ANDREWS (C. M.).—THE OLD ENGLISH MANOR: A STUDY IN ECONOMIC HISTORY. Royal 8vo. 6s. net.

ANNALS OF OUR TIME. A Diurnal of Events, Social and Political, Home and Foreign. By JOSEPH IRVING. 8vo.—Vol. I. June 20th, 1837, to Feb. 28th, 1871, 18s.; Vol. II. Feb. 24th, 1871, to June 24th, 1887, 18s. Also Vol. II. in 3 parts: Part I. Feb. 24th, 1871, to March 19th, 1874, 4s. 6d.; Part II. March 20th, 1874, to July 22nd, 1878, 4s. 6d.; Part III. July 23rd, 1878, to June 24th, 1887, 9s. Vol. III. By H. H. FYFE. Part I. June 25th, 1887, to Dec. 30th, 1890. 4s. 6d.; sewed, 3s. 6d. Part II. 1891, 1s. 6d.; sewed, 1s.

ANNUAL SUMMARIES. Reprinted from the *Times*. 2 Vols. Cr. 8vo. 3s. 6d. each.

ARNOLD (T.).—THE SECOND PUNIC WAR. By THOMAS ARNOLD, D.D. Ed. by W. T. ARNOLD, M.A. With 8 Maps. Cr. 8vo. 5s.

ARNOLD (W. T.).—A HISTORY OF THE EARLY ROMAN EMPIRE. Cr. 8vo. [*In prep.*

BEESLY (Mrs.).—STORIES FROM THE HISTORY OF ROME. Fcp. 8vo. 2s. 6d.

BLACKIE (Prof. John Stuart).—WHAT DOES HISTORY TEACH? Globe 8vo. 2s. 6d.

BRETT (R. B.).—FOOTPRINTS OF STATESMEN DURING THE EIGHTEENTH CENTURY IN ENGLAND. Cr. 8vo. 6s.

BRYCE (James, M.P.).—THE HOLY ROMAN EMPIRE. 8th Edit. Cr. 8vo. 7s. 6d.— *Library Edition.* 8vo. 14s.

BUCKLEY (Arabella).—HISTORY OF ENGLAND FOR BEGINNERS. Globe 8vo. 3s.
—— PRIMER OF ENGLISH HISTORY. Pott 8vo. 1s.

BURKE (Edmund). (*See* POLITICS.)

BURY (J. B.).—A HISTORY OF THE LATER ROMAN EMPIRE FROM ARCADIUS TO IRENE, A.D. 390—800. 2 vols. 8vo. 32s.

CASSEL (Dr. D.).—MANUAL OF JEWISH HISTORY AND LITERATURE. Translated by Mrs. HENRY LUCAS. Fcp. 8vo. 2s. 6d.

COX (G. V.).—RECOLLECTIONS OF OXFORD 2nd Edit. Cr. 8vo. 6s.

ENGLISH STATESMEN, TWELVE. (*See* BIOGRAPHY, p. 4.)

FISKE (John).—THE CRITICAL PERIOD IN AMERICAN HISTORY, 1783—89. Ext. cr 8vo. 10s. 6d.
—— THE BEGINNINGS OF NEW ENGLAND; or, The Puritan Theocracy in its Relations to Civil and Religious Liberty. Cr. 8vo. 7s. 6d.
—— THE AMERICAN REVOLUTION. 2 vols. Cr. 8vo. 18s.
—— THE DISCOVERY OF AMERICA. 2 vols. Cr. 8vo. 18s.

FRAMJI (Dosabhai).—HISTORY OF THE PARSIS, INCLUDING THEIR MANNERS, CUSTOMS, RELIGION, AND PRESENT POSITION. With Illustrations. 2 vols. Med. 8vo. 36s.

FREEMAN (Prof. E. A.).—HISTORY OF THE CATHEDRAL CHURCH OF WELLS. Cr. 8vo. 3s. 6d.
—— OLD ENGLISH HISTORY. With 3 Coloured Maps. 9th Edit., revised. Ext. fcp. 8vo. 6s.
—— HISTORICAL ESSAYS. First Series. 4th Edit. 8vo. 10s. 6d.
—— —— Second Series. 3rd Edit., with Additional Essays. 8vo. 10s. 6d.
—— —— Third Series. 8vo. 12s.
—— —— Fourth Series. 8vo. 12s. 6d.
—— THE GROWTH OF THE ENGLISH CONSTITUTION FROM THE EARLIEST TIMES. 5th Edit. Cr. 8vo. 5s.
—— COMPARATIVE POLITICS. Lectures at the Royal Institution. To which is added "The Unity of History." 8vo. 14s.
—— SUBJECT AND NEIGHBOUR LANDS OF VENICE. Illustrated. Cr. 8vo. 10s. 6d.
—— ENGLISH TOWNS AND DISTRICTS. A Series of Addresses and Essays. 8vo. 14s.
—— THE OFFICE OF THE HISTORICAL PROFESSOR. Cr. 8vo. 2s.
—— DISESTABLISHMENT AND DISENDOWMENT; WHAT ARE THEY? Cr. 8vo. 2s.
—— GREATER GREECE AND GREATER BRITAIN: GEORGE WASHINGTON THE EXPANDER OF ENGLAND. With an Appendix on IMPERIAL FEDERATION. Cr. 8vo. 3s. 6d.
—— THE METHODS OF HISTORICAL STUDY. Eight Lectures at Oxford. 8vo. 10s. 6d.
—— THE CHIEF PERIODS OF EUROPEAN HISTORY. With Essay on "Greek Cities under Roman Rule." 8vo. 10s. 6d.
—— FOUR OXFORD LECTURES, 1887; FIFTY YEARS OF EUROPEAN HISTORY; TEUTONIC CONQUEST IN GAUL AND BRITAIN. 8vo. 5s.
—— HISTORY OF FEDERAL GOVERNMENT IN GREECE AND ITALY. New Edit. by J. B. BURY, M.A. Ex. crn. 8vo. 12s. 6d.

FRIEDMANN (Paul). (*See* BIOGRAPHY.)

GIBBINS (H. de B.).—HISTORY OF COMMERCE IN EUROPE. Globe 8vo. 3s. 6d.

HISTORY.

GREEN (John Richard).—A SHORT HISTORY OF THE ENGLISH PEOPLE. New Edit., revised. 159th Thousand. Cr. 8vo. 8s. 6d.—Also in Parts, with Analysis. 3s. each.—Part I. 607—1265; II. 1204—1553; III. 1540—1689; IV. 1660—1873.—*Illustrated Edition*, in Parts. Super roy. 8vo. 1s. each net.—Part I. Oct. 1891. Vols. I. II. III. 12s. each net.
—— HISTORY OF THE ENGLISH PEOPLE. In 4 vols. 8vo. 16s. each.
—— THE MAKING OF ENGLAND. 8vo. 16s.
—— THE CONQUEST OF ENGLAND. With Maps and Portrait. 8vo. 18s.
—— READINGS IN ENGLISH HISTORY. In 3 Parts. Fcp. 8vo. 1s. 6d. each.
GREEN (Alice S.).—THE ENGLISH TOWN IN THE 15TH CENTURY. 2 vols. 8vo.
GUEST (Dr. E.).—ORIGINES CELTICÆ. Maps. 2 vols. 8vo. 32s.
GUEST (M. J.).—LECTURES ON THE HISTORY OF ENGLAND. Cr. 8vo. 6s.
HISTORY PRIMERS. Edited by JOHN RICHARD GREEN. Pott 8vo. 1s. each.
EUROPE. By E. A. FREEMAN, M.A.
GREECE. By C. A. FYFFE, M.A.
ROME. By Bishop CREIGHTON.
FRANCE. By CHARLOTTE M. YONGE.
ENGLISH HISTORY. By A. B. BUCKLEY.
HISTORICAL COURSE FOR SCHOOLS. Ed. by E. A. FREEMAN, D.C.L. Pott 8vo.
GENERAL SKETCH OF EUROPEAN HISTORY. By E. A. FREEMAN. Maps. 3s. 6d.
HISTORY OF ENGLAND. By EDITH THOMPSON. Coloured Maps. 2s. 6d.
HISTORY OF SCOTLAND. By MARGARET MACARTHUR. 2s.
HISTORY OF ITALY. By the Rev. W. HUNT, M.A. With Coloured Maps. 3s. 6d.
HISTORY OF GERMANY. By JAMES SIME, M.A. 3s.
HISTORY OF AMERICA. By J. A. DOYLE. With Maps. 4s. 6d.
HISTORY OF EUROPEAN COLONIES. By E. J. PAYNE, M.A. Maps. 4s. 6d.
HISTORY OF FRANCE. By CHARLOTTE M. YONGE. Maps. 3s. 6d.
HOLE (Rev. C.).—GENEALOGICAL STEMMA OF THE KINGS OF ENGLAND AND FRANCE. On a Sheet. 1s.
INGRAM (T. Dunbar).—A HISTORY OF THE LEGISLATIVE UNION OF GREAT BRITAIN AND IRELAND. 8vo. 10s. 6d.
—— TWO CHAPTERS OF IRISH HISTORY: 1. The Irish Parliament of James II.; 2. The Alleged Violation of the Treaty of Limerick. 8vo. 6s.
JEBB (Prof. R. C.).—MODERN GREECE. Two Lectures. Crown 8vo. 5s.
JENNINGS (A. C.).—CHRONOLOGICAL TABLES OF ANCIENT HISTORY. 8vo. 5s.
KEARY (Annie).—THE NATIONS AROUND ISRAEL. Cr. 8vo. 3s. 6d.
KINGSLEY (Charles).—THE ROMAN AND THE TEUTON. Cr. 8vo. 3s. 6d.
—— HISTORICAL LECTURES AND ESSAYS. Cr. 8vo. 3s. 6d.
LABBERTON (R. H.). (*See* ATLASES.)
LEGGE (Alfred O.).—THE GROWTH OF THE TEMPORAL POWER OF THE PAPACY. Cr. 8vo. 8s. 6d.

LETHBRIDGE (Sir Roper).—A SHORT MANUAL OF THE HISTORY OF INDIA. Cr. 8vo. 5s.
—— THE WORLD'S HISTORY. Cr. 8vo, swd. 1s.
—— HISTORY OF INDIA. Cr. 8vo. 2s.; sewed, 1s. 6d.
—— HISTORY OF ENGLAND. Cr.8vo, swd. 1s.6d.
—— EASY INTRODUCTION TO THE HISTORY AND GEOGRAPHY OF BENGAL. Cr.8vo. 1s.6d.
LYTE (H. C. Maxwell).—A HISTORY OF ETON COLLEGE, 1440—1884. Illustrated. 8vo. 21s.
—— A HISTORY OF THE UNIVERSITY OF OXFORD, FROM THE EARLIEST TIMES TO THE YEAR 1530. 8vo. 16s.
MAHAFFY (Prof. J. P.).—GREEK LIFE AND THOUGHT, FROM THE AGE OF ALEXANDER TO THE ROMAN CONQUEST. Cr. 8vo. 12s. 6d.
—— SOCIAL LIFE IN GREECE, FROM HOMER TO MENANDER. 6th Edit. Cr. 8vo. 9s.
—— THE GREEK WORLD UNDER ROMAN SWAY, FROM POLYBIUS TO PLUTARCH. Cr. 8vo. 10s. 6d.
—— PROBLEMS IN GREEK HISTORY. Crown 8vo. 7s. 6d.
MARRIOTT (J. A. R.). (*See* SELECT BIOGRAPHY, p. 6.)
MICHELET (M.).—A SUMMARY OF MODERN HISTORY. Translated by M. C. M. SIMPSON. Globe 8vo. 4s. 6d.
MULLINGER (J. B.).—CAMBRIDGE CHARACTERISTICS IN THE SEVENTEENTH CENTURY. Cr. 8vo. 4s. 6d.
NORGATE (Kate).—ENGLAND UNDER THE ANGEVIN KINGS. In 2 vols. 8vo. 32s.
OLIPHANT (Mrs. M. O. W.).—THE MAKERS OF FLORENCE: DANTE, GIOTTO, SAVONAROLA, AND THEIR CITY. Illustr. Cr. 8vo. 10s. 6d.—*Edition de Luxe*. 8vo. 21s. net.
—— THE MAKERS OF VENICE: DOGES, CONQUERORS, PAINTERS, AND MEN OF LETTERS. Illustrated. Cr. 8vo. 10s. 6d.
—— ROYAL EDINBURGH: HER SAINTS, KINGS, PROPHETS, AND POETS. Illustrated by Sir G. REID, R.S.A. Cr. 8vo. 10s. 6d.
—— JERUSALEM, ITS HISTORY AND HOPE. Illust. Cr. 8vo. 10s. 6d.—Large Paper Edit. 50s. net.
OTTÉ (E. C.).—SCANDINAVIAN HISTORY. With Maps. Globe 8vo. 6s.
PALGRAVE (Sir F.).—HISTORY OF NORMANDY AND OF ENGLAND. 4 vols. 8vo. 4l. 4s.
PARKMAN (Francis). — MONTCALM AND WOLFE. Library Edition. Illustrated with Portraits and Maps. 2 vols. 8vo. 12s. 6d. each.
—— THE COLLECTED WORKS OF FRANCIS PARKMAN. Popular Edition. In 10 vols. Cr. 8vo. 7s. 6d. each; or complete, 3l. 13s. 6d.—PIONEERS OF FRANCE IN THE NEW WORLD, 1 vol.; THE JESUITS IN NORTH AMERICA, 1 vol.; LA SALLE AND THE DISCOVERY OF THE GREAT WEST, 1 vol.; THE OREGON TRAIL, 1 vol.; THE OLD RÉGIME IN CANADA UNDER LOUIS XIV., 1 vol.; COUNT FRONTENAC AND NEW FRANCE UNDER LOUIS XIV., 1 vol.; MONTCALM AND WOLFE, 2 vols.; THE CONSPIRACY OF PONTIAC, 2 vols.
—— A HALF CENTURY OF CONFLICT. 2 vols. 8vo. 25s.
—— THE OREGON TRAIL. Illustrated. Med. 8vo. 21s.
PERKINS (J. B.).—FRANCE UNDER THE REGENCY. Cr. 8vo. 8s. 6d.

HISTORY—ILLUSTRATED BOOKS.

HISTORY—*continued.*

POOLE (R. L.).—A HISTORY OF THE HUGUENOTS OF THE DISPERSION AT THE RECALL OF THE EDICT OF NANTES. Cr. 8vo. 6s.

RHODES (J. F.).—HISTORY OF THE UNITED STATES FROM THE COMPROMISE OF 1850 TO 1880. 2 vols. 8vo. 24s.

ROGERS (Prof. J. E. Thorold).—HISTORICAL GLEANINGS. Cr. 8vo.—1st Series. 4s. 6d.—2nd Series. 6s.

SAYCE (Prof. A. H.).—THE ANCIENT EMPIRES OF THE EAST. Cr. 8vo. 6s.

SEELEY (Prof. J. R.). — LECTURES AND ESSAYS. 8vo. 10s. 6d.
— THE EXPANSION OF ENGLAND. Two Courses of Lectures. Cr. 8vo. 4s. 6d.
— OUR COLONIAL EXPANSION. Extracts from the above. Cr. 8vo. 1s.

SEWELL (E. M.) and YONGE (C. M.).—EUROPEAN HISTORY, NARRATED IN A SERIES OF HISTORICAL SELECTIONS FROM THE BEST AUTHORITIES. 2 vols. 3rd Edit. Cr. 8vo. 6s. each.

SHUCKBURGH (E. S.).—A SCHOOL HISTORY OF ROME. Cr. 8vo. [*In preparation.*

SMITH (G.). (*See under* POLITICS, p. 32.)

STEPHEN (Sir J. Fitzjames, Bart.).—THE STORY OF NUNCOMAR AND THE IMPEACHMENT OF SIR ELIJAH IMPEY. 2 vols. Cr. 8vo. 15s.

TAIT (C. W. A.).—ANALYSIS OF ENGLISH HISTORY, BASED ON GREEN'S "SHORT HISTORY OF THE ENGLISH PEOPLE." Cr. 8vo. 3s. 6d.

TOUT (T. F.).—ANALYSIS OF ENGLISH HISTORY. Pott 8vo. 1s.

TREVELYAN (Sir Geo. Otto).—CAWNPORE. Cr. 8vo. 6s.

WHEELER (J. Talboys).—PRIMER OF INDIAN HISTORY, ASIATIC AND EUROPEAN. Pott 8vo. 1s.
— COLLEGE HISTORY OF INDIA, ASIATIC AND EUROPEAN. Cr. 8vo. 3s.; swd. 2s. 6d.
— A SHORT HISTORY OF INDIA. With Maps. Cr. 8vo. 12s.
— INDIA UNDER BRITISH RULE. 8vo. 12s. 6d.

WOOD (Rev. E. G.).—THE REGAL POWER OF THE CHURCH. 8vo. 4s. 6d.

YONGE (Charlotte).—CAMEOS FROM ENGLISH HISTORY. Ext. fcp. 8vo. 5s. each.—Vol. 1. FROM ROLLO TO EDWARD II.; Vol. 2. THE WARS IN FRANCE; Vol. 3. THE WARS OF THE ROSES; Vol. 4. REFORMATION TIMES; Vol. 5. ENGLAND AND SPAIN; Vol. 6. FORTY YEARS OF STEWART RULE (1603—43); Vol. 7. THE REBELLION AND RESTORATION (1642—1678).
— THE VICTORIAN HALF-CENTURY. Cr. 8vo. 1s. 6d.; sewed, 1s.
— THE STORY OF THE CHRISTIANS AND MOORS IN SPAIN. Pott 8vo. 2s. 6d. net

HORTICULTURE. (*See* GARDENING.)

HYGIENE.

BERNERS (J.).—FIRST LESSONS ON HEALTH. Pott 8vo. 1s.

BLYTH (A. Wynter).—A MANUAL OF PUBLIC HEALTH. 8vo. 17s. net.
— LECTURES ON SANITARY LAW. 8vo. 8s. 6d. net.

BROWNE (J. H. Balfour).—WATER SUPPLY. Cr. 8vo. 2s. 6d.

CORFIELD (Dr. W. H.).—THE TREATMENT AND UTILISATION OF SEWAGE. 3rd Edit. Revised by the Author, and by LOUIS C. PARKES, M.D. 8vo. 16s.

GOODFELLOW (J.).—THE DIETETIC VALUE OF BREAD. Cr. 8vo. 6s.

KINGSLEY (Charles).—SANITARY AND SOCIAL LECTURES. Cr. 8vo. 3s. 6d.
— HEALTH AND EDUCATION. Cr. 8vo. 6s.

MIERS (H. A.) and CROSSKEY (R.).—THE SOIL IN RELATION TO HEALTH. Cr. 8vo. 3s. 6d.

REYNOLDS (Prof. Osborne).—SEWER GAS, AND HOW TO KEEP IT OUT OF HOUSES. 3rd Edit. Cr. 8vo. 1s. 6d.

RICHARDSON (Dr. B. W.).—HYGEIA: A CITY OF HEALTH. Cr. 8vo. 1s.
— THE FUTURE OF SANITARY SCIENCE. Cr. 8vo. 1s.
— ON ALCOHOL. Cr. 8vo. 1s.

WILLOUGHBY (E. F.).—PUBLIC HEALTH AND DEMOGRAPHY. Fcp. 8vo. 4s. 6d.

HYMNOLOGY.

(*See under* THEOLOGY, p. 36.)

ILLUSTRATED BOOKS.

BALCH (Elizabeth). — GLIMPSES OF OLD ENGLISH HOMES. Gl. 4to. 14s.

BLAKE. (*See* BIOGRAPHY, p. 3.)

BOUGHTON (G. H.) and ABBEY (E. A.). (*See* VOYAGES AND TRAVELS.)

CHRISTMAS CAROL (A). Printed in Colours, with Illuminated Borders. 4to. 21s.

DAYS WITH SIR ROGER DE COVERLEY. From the *Spectator.* Illustrated by HUGH THOMSON. Cr. 8vo. 6s.—Also with uncut edges, paper label. 6s.

DELL (E. C.).—PICTURES FROM SHELLEY. Engraved by J. D. COOPER. Folio. 21s. net.

GASKELL (Mrs.).—CRANFORD. Illustrated by HUGH THOMSON. Cr. 8vo. 6s.—Also with uncut edges paper label. 6s.

GOLDSMITH (Oliver). — THE VICAR OF WAKEFIELD. New Edition, with 182 Illustrations by HUGH THOMSON. Preface by AUSTIN DOBSON. Cr. 8vo. 6s.—Also with Uncut Edges, paper label. 6s.

GREEN (John Richard). — ILLUSTRATED EDITION OF THE SHORT HISTORY OF THE ENGLISH PEOPLE. In Parts. Sup. roy. 8vo. 1s. each net. Oct. 1891. Vols. I. II. and III. 12s. each net.

GRIMM. (*See* BOOKS FOR THE YOUNG, p. 41.)

HALLWARD (R. F.).—FLOWERS OF PARADISE. Music, Verse, Design, Illustration. 6s.

HAMERTON (P. G.).—MAN IN ART. With Etchings and Photogravures. 3l. 13s. 6d. net. —Large Paper Edition. 10l. 10s. net.

HARRISON (F.).—ANNALS OF AN OLD MANOR HOUSE, SUTTON PLACE, GUILDFORD. 4to. 42s. net.

HOOD (Thomas).—HUMOROUS POEMS. Illustrated by C. E. BROCK. Cr. 8vo. 6s.—Also with uncut edges, paper label. 6s.

LAW—LIFE-BOAT.

IRVING (Washington).—OLD CHRISTMAS. From the Sketch Book. Illustr. by RANDOLPH CALDECOTT. Gilt edges. Cr. 8vo. 6s.—Also with uncut edges, paper label. 6s.—Large Paper Edition. 30s. net.
— BRACEBRIDGE HALL. Illustr. by RANDOLPH CALDECOTT. Gilt edges. Cr. 8vo. 6s.—Also with uncut edges, paper label. 6s.
— OLD CHRISTMAS AND BRACEBRIDGE HALL. Edition de Luxe. Roy. 8vo. 21s.
— RIP VAN WINKLE AND THE LEGEND OF SLEEPY HOLLOW. Illustr. by G. H. BOUGHTON. Cr. 8vo. 6s.—Also with uncut edges, paper label. 6s.—Edition de Luxe. Roy. 8vo. 30s. net.

KINGSLEY (Charles).—THE WATER BABIES. (See BOOKS FOR THE YOUNG.)
— THE HEROES. (See BOOKS for the YOUNG.)
— GLAUCUS. (See NATURAL HISTORY.)

LANG (Andrew).—THE LIBRARY. With a Chapter on Modern English Illustrated Books, by AUSTIN DOBSON. Cr. 8vo. 4s. 6d. —Large Paper Edition. 21s. net.

LYTE (H. C. Maxwell). (See HISTORY.)

MAHAFFY (Rev. Prof. J. P.) and ROGERS (J. E.). (See VOYAGES AND TRAVELS.)

MEREDITH (L. A.).—BUSH FRIENDS IN TASMANIA. Native Flowers, Fruits, and Insects, with Prose and Verse Descriptions. Folio. 52s. 6d. net.

MITFORD (M. R.).—OUR VILLAGE. Illustrated by HUGH THOMSON. Cr. 8vo. 6s.— Also with uncut edges, paper label. 6s.

OLD SONGS. With Drawings by E. A. ABBEY and A. PARSONS. 4to, mor. gilt. 31s. 6d.

PROPERT (J. L.). (See ART.)

STUART, RELICS OF THE ROYAL HOUSE OF. Illustrated by 40 Plates in Colours drawn from Relics of the Stuarts by WILLIAM GIBB. With an Introduction by JOHN SKELTON, C.B., LL.D., and Descriptive Notes by W. ST. JOHN HOPE. Folio, half morocco, gilt edges. 10l. 10s. net.

TENNYSON (Lord).—JACK AND THE BEAN-STALK. English Hexameters. Illustrated by R. CALDECOTT. Fcp. 4to. 3s. 6d.

TRISTRAM (W. O.).—COACHING DAYS AND COACHING WAYS. Illust. H. RAILTON and HUGH THOMSON. Cr. 8vo. 6s.—Also with uncut edges, paper label, 6s.—Large Paper Edition. 30s. net.

TURNER'S LIBER STUDIORUM: A DESCRIPTION AND A CATALOGUE. By W. G. RAWLINSON. Med. 8vo. 12s. 6d.

WALTON and COTTON—LOWELL.—THE COMPLETE ANGLER. With Introduction by JAS. RUSSELL LOWELL. 2 vols. Ext. cr. 8vo. 52s. 6d. net.

WINTER (W.).—SHAKESPEARE'S ENGLAND. 80 Illustrations. Cr. 8vo. 6s.

LANGUAGE. (See PHILOLOGY.)

LAW.

BERNARD (M.).—FOUR LECTURES ON SUBJECTS CONNECTED WITH DIPLOMACY. 8vo. 9s.

BIGELOW (M. M.).—HISTORY OF PROCEDURE IN ENGLAND FROM THE NORMAN CONQUEST, 1066-1204. 8vo. 16s.

BOUTMY (E.).—STUDIES IN CONSTITUTIONAL LAW. Transl. by Mrs. DICEY. Preface by Prof. A. V. DICEY. Cr. 8vo. 6s.
— THE ENGLISH CONSTITUTION. Transl. by Mrs. EADEN. Introduction by Sir F. POLLOCK, Bart. Cr. 8vo. 6s.

CHERRY (R. R.).—LECTURES ON THE GROWTH OF CRIMINAL LAW IN ANCIENT COMMUNITIES. 8vo. 5s. net.

DICEY (Prof. A. V.).—INTRODUCTION TO THE STUDY OF THE LAW OF THE CONSTITUTION. 4th Edit. 8vo. 12s. 6d.

ENGLISH CITIZEN SERIES, THE. (See POLITICS.)

HOLLAND (Prof. T. E.).—THE TREATY RELATIONS OF RUSSIA AND TURKEY, FROM 1774 TO 1853. Cr. 8vo. 2s.

HOLMES (O. W., jun.).—THE COMMON LAW. 8vo. 12s.

LIGHTWOOD (J. M.).—THE NATURE OF POSITIVE LAW. 8vo. 12s. 6d.

MAITLAND (F. W.).—PLEAS OF THE CROWN FOR THE COUNTY OF GLOUCESTER, A.D. 1221. 8vo. 7s. 6d.
— JUSTICE AND POLICE. Cr. 8vo. 3s. 6d.

MONAHAN (James H.).—THE METHOD OF LAW. Cr. 8vo. 6s.

MUNRO (J. E. C.)—COMMERCIAL LAW. Globe 8vo. 3s. 6d.

PATERSON (James).—COMMENTARIES ON THE LIBERTY OF THE SUBJECT, AND THE LAWS OF ENGLAND RELATING TO THE SECURITY OF THE PERSON. 2 vols. Cr. 8vo. 21s.
— THE LIBERTY OF THE PRESS, SPEECH, AND PUBLIC WORSHIP. Cr. 8vo. 12s.

PHILLIMORE (John G.).—PRIVATE LAW AMONG THE ROMANS. 8vo. 6s.

POLLOCK (Sir F., Bart.).—ESSAYS IN JURISPRUDENCE AND ETHICS. 8vo. 10s. 6d.
— THE LAND LAWS. Cr. 8vo. 2s. 6d.
— LEADING CASES DONE INTO ENGLISH. Cr. 8vo. 3s. 6d.

RICHEY (Alex. G.).—THE IRISH LAND LAWS. Cr. 8vo. 3s. 6d.

STEPHEN (Sir J. F., Bart.).—A DIGEST OF THE LAW OF EVIDENCE. 6th Ed. Cr. 8vo. 6s.
— A DIGEST OF THE CRIMINAL LAW: CRIMES AND PUNISHMENTS. 4th Ed. 8vo. 16s.
— A DIGEST OF THE LAW OF CRIMINAL PROCEDURE IN INDICTABLE OFFENCES. By Sir J. F., Bart., and HERBERT STEPHEN, LL.M. 8vo. 12s. 6d.
— A HISTORY OF THE CRIMINAL LAW OF ENGLAND. 3 vols. 8vo. 48s.
— A GENERAL VIEW OF THE CRIMINAL LAW OF ENGLAND. 2nd Edit. 8vo. 14s.

STEPHEN (J. K.).—INTERNATIONAL LAW AND INTERNATIONAL RELATIONS. Cr. 8vo. 6s.

WILLIAMS (S. E.).—FORENSIC FACTS AND FALLACIES. Globe 8vo. 4s. 6d.

LETTERS. (See under LITERATURE, p. 20.)

LIFE-BOAT.

GILMORE (Rev. John).—STORM WARRIORS; or, Life-Boat Work on the Goodwin Sands. Cr. 8vo. 3s. 6d.

LEWIS (Richard).—HISTORY OF THE LIFE-BOAT AND ITS WORK. Cr. 8vo. 5s.

LITERATURE.

LIGHT. (*See under* PHYSICS, p. 29.)

LITERATURE.

History and Criticism of—Commentaries, etc.—Poetry and the Drama—Poetical Collections and Selections—Prose Fiction—Collected Works, Essays, Lectures, Letters, Miscellaneous Works.

History and Criticism of.

(*See also* ESSAYS, p. 20.)

ARNOLD (M.). (*See* ESSAYS. p. 21.)

BROOKE (Stopford A.).—A PRIMER OF ENGLISH LITERATURE. Pott 8vo. 1s.—Large Paper Edition. 8vo. 7s. 6d.
— A HISTORY OF EARLY ENGLISH LITERATURE. 2 vols. 8vo. 20s. net.

CLASSICAL WRITERS. Edited by JOHN RICHARD GREEN. Fcp. 8vo. 1s. 6d. each.
DEMOSTHENES. By Prof. BUTCHER, M.A.
EURIPIDES. By Prof. MAHAFFY.
LIVY. By the Rev. W. W. CAPES, M.A.
MILTON. By STOPFORD A. BROOKE.
SOPHOCLES. By Prof. L. CAMPBELL, M.A.
TACITUS. By Messrs. CHURCH and BRODRIBB.
VERGIL. By Prof. NETTLESHIP, M.A.

ENGLISH MEN OF LETTERS. (*See* BIOGRAPHY, p. 4.)

HISTORY OF ENGLISH LITERATURE. In 4 vols. Cr. 8vo.
EARLY ENGLISH LITERATURE. By STOPFORD BROOKE, M.A. [*In preparation.*
ELIZABETHAN LITERATURE (1560—1665). By GEORGE SAINTSBURY. 7s. 6d.
EIGHTEENTH CENTURY LITERATURE (1660—1780). By EDMUND GOSSE, M.A. 7s. 6d.
THE MODERN PERIOD. By Prof. DOWDEN. [*In preparation.*

JEBB (Prof. R. C.).—A PRIMER OF GREEK LITERATURE. Pott 8vo. 1s.
— THE ATTIC ORATORS, FROM ANTIPHON TO ISAEOS. 2nd Edit. 2 vols 8vo. 25s.

JOHNSON'S LIVES OF THE POETS. MILTON, DRYDEN, POPE, ADDISON, SWIFT, AND GRAY. With Macaulay's "Life of Johnson" Ed. by M. ARNOLD. Cr. 8vo. 4s. 6d.

KINGSLEY (Charles).— LITERARY AND GENERAL LECTURES. Cr. 8vo. 3s. 6d.

MAHAFFY (Prof. J. P.).—A HISTORY OF CLASSICAL GREEK LITERATURE. 2 vols. Cr. 8vo.—Vol. 1. THE POETS. With an Appendix on Homer by Prof. SAYCE. In 2 Parts.—Vol. 2. THE PROSE WRITERS. In 2 Parts. 4s. 6d. each.

MORLEY (John). (*See* COLLECTED WORKS, p. 23.)

NICHOL (Prof. J.) and McCORMICK (Prof W. S.).—A SHORT HISTORY OF ENGLISH LITERATURE. Globe 8vo. [*In preparation.*

OLIPHANT (Mrs. M. O. W.).—THE LITERARY HISTORY OF ENGLAND IN THE END OF THE 18TH AND BEGINNING OF THE 19TH CENTURY. 3 vols. 8vo. 21s.

RYLAND (F.).—CHRONOLOGICAL OUTLINES OF ENGLISH LITERATURE. Cr. 8vo. 6s.

WARD (Prof. A. W.).—A HISTORY OF ENGLISH DRAMATIC LITERATURE, TO THE DEATH OF QUEEN ANNE. 2 vols. 8vo. 32s.

WILKINS (Prof. A. S.).—A PRIMER OF ROMAN LITERATURE. Pott 8vo. 1s.

Commentaries, etc.

BROWNING.
A PRIMER ON BROWNING. By MARY WILSON. Cr. 8vo. 2s. 6d.

CHAUCER.
A PRIMER OF CHAUCER. By A. W. POLLARD. Pott 8vo. 1s.

DANTE.
READINGS ON THE PURGATORIO OF DANTE. Chiefly based on the Commentary of Benvenuto da Imola. By the Hon. W. W. VERNON, M.A. With an Introduction by Dean CHURCH. 2 vols. Cr. 8vo. 24s.
COMPANION TO DANTE. From G A. SCARTAZZINI. By A. J. BUTLER. Cr. 8vo. 10s. 6d.

HOMER.
HOMERIC DICTIONARY. (*See* DICTIONARIES.)
THE PROBLEM OF THE HOMERIC POEMS. By Prof. W. D. GEDDES. 8vo. 14s.
HOMERIC SYNCHRONISM. An Inquiry into the Time and Place of Homer. By the Rt. Hon. W. E. GLADSTONE. Cr. 8vo. 6s.
PRIMER OF HOMER. By same. Pott 8vo. 1s.
LANDMARKS OF HOMERIC STUDY, TOGETHER WITH AN ESSAY ON THE POINTS OF CONTACT BETWEEN THE ASSYRIAN TABLETS AND THE HOMERIC TEXT. By the same. Cr. 8vo. 2s. 6d.
COMPANION TO THE ILIAD FOR ENGLISH READERS. By W. LEAF, Litt.D. Crown 8vo. 7s. 6d.

HORACE.
STUDIES, LITERARY AND HISTORICAL, IN THE ODES OF HORACE. By A. W. VERRALL, Litt.D. 8vo. 8s. 6d.

SHAKESPEARE.
A PRIMER OF SHAKSPERE. By Prof. DOWDEN. Pott 8vo. 1s.
A SHAKESPEARIAN GRAMMAR. By Rev. E. A. ABBOTT. Ext. fcp. 8vo. 6s.
SHAKESPEAREANA GENEALOGICA. By G. R. FRENCH. 8vo. 15s.
A SELECTION FROM THE LIVES IN NORTH'S PLUTARCH WHICH ILLUSTRATE SHAKESPEARE'S PLAYS. Edited by Rev. W. W. SKEAT, M.A. Cr. 8vo. 6s.
SHORT STUDIES OF SHAKESPEARE'S PLOTS. By Prof. CYRIL RANSOME. Cr. 8vo. 3s. 6d.
—Also separately : HAMLET, 9d. ; MACBETH, 9d. ; TEMPEST, 9d.
CALIBAN : A Critique on "The Tempest" and "A Midsummer Night's Dream." By Sir DANIEL WILSON. 8vo. 10s. 6d.

TENNYSON.
A COMPANION TO "IN MEMORIAM." By ELIZABETH R. CHAPMAN. Globe 8vo. 2s.
ESSAYS ON THE IDYLLS OF THE KING. By H. LITTLEDALE, M.A. Cr. 8vo. 4s. 6d.
A STUDY OF THE WORKS OF ALFRED LORD TENNYSON. By E. C. TAINSH. New Ed. Cr. 8vo. 6s.

WORDSWORTH.
WORDSWORTHIANA : A Selection of Papers read to the Wordsworth Society. Edited by W. KNIGHT. Cr. 8vo. 7s. 6d.

Poetry and the Drama.

ALDRICH (T. Bailey).—THE SISTERS' TRAGEDY ; with other Poems, Lyrical and Dramatic. Fcp. 8vo. 3s. 6d. net.

POETRY AND THE DRAMA.

AN ANCIENT CITY: AND OTHER POEMS. Ext. fcp. 8vo. 6s.
ANDERSON (A.).—BALLADS AND SONNETS. Cr. 8vo. 5s.
ARNOLD (Matthew).—THE COMPLETE POETICAL WORKS. New Edition. 3 vols. Cr. 8vo. 7s. 6d. each.
    Vol. 1. EARLY POEMS, NARRATIVE POEMS AND SONNETS.
    Vol. 2. LYRIC AND ELEGIAC POEMS.
    Vol. 3. DRAMATIC AND LATER POEMS.
—— COMPLETE POETICAL WORKS. 1 vol. Cr. 8vo. 7s. 6d.
—— SELECTED POEMS. Pott 8vo. 2s. 6d. net.
AUSTIN (Alfred).—POETICAL WORKS. New Collected Edition. 6 vols. Cr. 8vo. 5s. each.
    Vol. 1. THE TOWER OF BABEL.
    Vol. 2. SAVONAROLA, etc.
    Vol. 3. PRINCE LUCIFER.
    Vol. 4. THE HUMAN TRAGEDY.
    Vol. 5. LYRICAL POEMS.
    Vol. 6. NARRATIVE POEMS.
—— SOLILOQUIES IN SONG. Cr. 8vo. 6s.
—— AT THE GATE OF THE CONVENT: and other Poems. Cr. 8vo. 6s.
—— MADONNA'S CHILD. Cr. 4to. 3s. 6d.
—— ROME OR DEATH. Cr. 4to. 9s.
—— THE GOLDEN AGE. Cr. 8vo. 5s.
—— THE SEASON. Cr. 8vo. 5s.
—— LOVE'S WIDOWHOOD. Cr. 8vo. 6s.
—— ENGLISH LYRICS. Cr. 8vo. 3s. 6d.
—— FORTUNATUS THE PESSIMIST. Cr. 8vo. 6s.
BETSY LEE: A FO'C'S'LE YARN. Ext. fcp. 8vo. 3s. 6d.
BLACKIE (John Stuart).—MESSIS VITAE: Gleanings of Song from a Happy Life. Cr. 8vo. 4s. 6d.
—— THE WISE MEN OF GREECE. In a Series of Dramatic Dialogues. Cr. 8vo. 9s.
—— GOETHE'S FAUST. Translated into English Verse. 2nd Edit. Cr. 8vo. 9s.
BLAKE. (*See* BIOGRAPHY, p. 3.)
BROOKE (Stopford A.).—RIQUET OF THE TUFT: A Love Drama. Ext. cr. 8vo. 6s.
—— POEMS. Globe 8vo. 6s.
BROWN (T. E.).—THE MANX WITCH: and other Poems. Cr. 8vo. 6s.
—— OLD JOHN, AND OTHER POEMS. Crown 8vo. 6s.
BURGON (Dean).—POEMS. Ex.fcp.8vo. 4s.6d.
BURNS. THE POETICAL WORKS. With a Biographical Memoir by ALEXANDER SMITH. In 2 vols. Fcp. 8vo. 10s. (*See also* GLOBE LIBRARY, p. 21.)
BUTLER (Samuel).—HUDIBRAS. Edit. by ALFRED MILNES. Fcp. 8vo.—Part I. 3s. 6d.; Parts II. and III. 4s. 6d.
BYRON. (*See* GOLDEN TREASURY SERIES, p. 22.)
CALDERON.—SELECT PLAYS. Edited by NORMAN MACCOLL. Cr. 8vo. 14s.
CAUTLEY (G. S.).—A CENTURY OF EMBLEMS. With Illustrations by Lady MARION ALFORD. Small 4to. 10s. 6d.
CLOUGH (A. H.).—POEMS. Cr. 8vo. 7s. 6d.
COLERIDGE: POETICAL AND DRAMATIC WORKS. 4 vols. Fcp. 8vo. 31s. 6d.—Also an Edition on Large Paper, 2l. 12s. 6d.
—— COMPLETE POETICAL WORKS. With Introduction by J. D. CAMPBELL, and Portrait. Cr. 8vo. 7s. 6d.

COLQUHOUN.—RHYMES AND CHIMES. By F. S. COLQUHOUN (*née* F. S. FULLER MAITLAND). Ext. fcp. 8vo. 2s. 6d.
COWPER. (*See* GLOBE LIBRARY, p. 21; GOLDEN TREASURY SERIES, p. 22.)
CRAIK (Mrs.).—POEMS. Ext. fcp. 8vo. 6s.
DAWSON (W. J.).—POEMS AND LYRICS. Fcp. 8vo. 4s. 6d.
DE VERE (A.).—POETICAL WORKS. 7 vols. Cr. 8vo. 5s. each.
DOYLE (Sir F. H.).—THE RETURN OF THE GUARDS: and other Poems. Cr. 8vo. 7s. 6d.
DRYDEN. (*See* GLOBE LIBRARY, p. 21.)
EMERSON. (*See* COLLECTED WORKS, p. 21.)
EVANS (Sebastian).—BROTHER FABIAN'S MANUSCRIPT: and other Poems. Fcp. 8vo. 6s.
—— IN THE STUDIO: A Decade of Poems. Ext. fcp. 8vo. 5s.
FITZ GERALD (Caroline).—VENETIA VICTRIX: and other Poems. Ext. fcp. 8vo. 3s. 6d.
FITZGERALD (Edward).—THE RUBÁIYÁT OF OMAR KHÁYYÁM. Ext. cr. 8vo. 10s. 6d.
FOAM. Pott 8vo. 2s. 6d. net.
FO'C'SLE YARNS, including "Betsy Lee," and other Poems. Cr. 8vo. 6s.
FRASER-TYTLER. — SONGS IN MINOR KEYS. By C. C. FRASER-TYTLER (Mrs. EDWARD LIDDELL). 2nd Edit. Pott 8vo. 6s.
FURNIVALL (F. J.).—LE MORTE ARTHUR. Edited from the Harleian MSS. 2252, in the British Museum. Fcp. 8vo. 7s. 6d.
GARNETT (R.).—IDYLLS AND EPIGRAMS. Chiefly from the Greek Anthology. Fcp. 8vo. 2s. 6d.
GOETHE.—FAUST. (*See* BLACKIE.)
—— REYNARD THE FOX. Transl. into English Verse by A. D. AINSLIE. Cr. 8vo. 7s. 6d.
GOLDSMITH.—THE TRAVELLER AND THE DESERTED VILLAGE. With Introduction and Notes, by ARTHUR BARRETT, B.A. 1s. 9d.; sewed, 1s. 6d.—THE TRAVELLER (separately), sewed, 1s.—By J. W. HALES. Cr. 8vo. 6d. (*See also* GLOBE LIBRARY, p. 21.)
GRAHAM (David).—KING JAMES I. An Historical Tragedy. Globe 8vo. 7s.
GRAY.—POEMS. With Introduction and Notes, by J. BRADSHAW, LL.D. Gl. 8vo. 1s. 9d.; sewed, 1s. 6d. (*See also* COLLECTED WORKS, p. 22.)
HALLWARD. (*See* ILLUSTRATED BOOKS.)
HAYES (A.).—THE MARCH OF MAN: and other Poems. Fcp. 8vo. 3s. 6d. net.
HERRICK. (*See* GOLDEN TREASURY SERIES, p. 22.)
HOPKINS (Ellice).—AUTUMN SWALLOWS: A Book of Lyrics. Ext. fcp. 8vo. 6s.
HOSKEN (J. D.).—PHAON AND SAPPHO, AND NIMROD. Fcp. 8vo. 5s.
JONES (H. A.).—SAINTS AND SINNERS. Ext. fcp. 8vo. 3s. 6d.
—— THE CRUSADERS. Fcp. 8vo. 2s. 6d.
KEATS. (*See* GOLDEN TREASURY SERIES, p. 22.)

LITERATURE.

Poetry and the Drama—*continued*.

KINGSLEY (Charles).—POEMS. Cr. 8vo. 3s. 6d.—*Pocket Edition*. Pott 8vo. 1s. 6d.—*Eversley Edition*. 2 vols. Cr. 8vo. 10s.

LAMB. (*See* COLLECTED WORKS, p. 23.)

LANDOR. (*See* GOLDEN TREASURY SERIES, p. 22.)

LONGFELLOW. (*See* GOLDEN TREASURY SERIES, p. 22.)

LOWELL (Jas. Russell).—COMPLETE POETICAL WORKS. Pott 8vo. 4s. 6d.
— With Introduction by THOMAS HUGHES, and Portrait. Cr. 8vo. 7s. 6d.
— HEARTSEASE AND RUE. Cr. 8vo. 5s.
— OLD ENGLISH DRAMATISTS. Cr. 8vo. 5s.
(*See also* COLLECTED WORKS, p. 23.)

LUCAS (F.).—SKETCHES OF RURAL LIFE. Poems. Globe 8vo. 5s.

MEREDITH (George).— A READING OF EARTH. Ext. fcp. 8vo. 5s.
— POEMS AND LYRICS OF THE JOY OF EARTH. Ext. fcp. 8vo. 6s.
— BALLADS AND POEMS OF TRAGIC LIFE. Cr. 8vo. 6s.
— MODERN LOVE. Ex. fcap. 8vo. 5s.
— THE EMPTY PURSE. Fcp. 8vo. 5s.

MILTON.—POETICAL WORKS. Edited, with Introductions and Notes, by Prof. DAVID MASSON, M.A. 3 vols. 8vo. 2l. 2s.—[Uniform with the Cambridge Shakespeare.]
— Edited by Prof. MASSON. 3 vols. Globe 8vo. 15s.
— — *Globe Edition*. Edited by Prof. MASSON. Globe 8vo. 3s. 6d.
— PARADISE LOST, BOOKS 1 and 2. Edited by MICHAEL MACMILLAN, B.A. 1s. 9d.; sewed, 1s. 6d.—BOOKS 1 and 2 (separately), 1s. 3d. each; sewed, 1s. each.
— L'ALLEGRO, IL PENSEROSO, LYCIDAS, ARCADES, SONNETS, ETC. Edited by WM. BELL, M.A. 1s. 9d.; sewed, 1s. 6d.
— COMUS. By the same. 1s. 3d.; swd. 1s.
— SAMSON AGONISTES. Edited by H. M. PERCIVAL, M.A. 2s.; sewed, 1s. 9d.

MOULTON (Louise Chandler). — IN THE GARDEN OF DREAMS: Lyrics and Sonnets. Cr. 8vo. 6s.
— SWALLOW FLIGHTS. Cr. 8vo. 6s.

MUDIE (C. E.).—STRAY LEAVES: Poems. 4th Edit. Ext. fcp. 8vo. 3s. 6d.

MYERS (E.).—THE PURITANS: A Poem. Ext. fcp. 8vo. 2s. 6d.
— POEMS. Ext. fcp. 8vo. 4s. 6d.
— THE DEFENCE OF ROME; and other Poems. Ext. fcp. 8vo. 5s.
— THE JUDGMENT OF PROMETHEUS: and other Poems. Ext. fcp. 8vo. 3s. 6d.

MYERS (F. W. H.).—THE RENEWAL OF YOUTH: and other Poems. Cr. 8vo. 7s. 6d.
— ST. PAUL: A Poem. Ext. fcp. 8vo. 2s. 6d.

NORTON (Hon. Mrs.).—THE LADY OF LA GARAYE. 9th Edit. Fcp. 8vo. 4s. 6d.

PALGRAVE (Prof. F. T.).—ORIGINAL HYMNS. 3rd Edit. Pott 8vo. 1s. 6d.
— LYRICAL POEMS. Ext. fcp. 8vo. 6s.
— VISIONS OF ENGLAND. Cr. 8vo. 7s. 6d.
— AMENOPHIS. Pott 8vo. 4s. 6d.

PALGRAVE (W. G.).—A VISION OF LIFE: SEMBLANCE AND REALITY. Cr. 8vo. 7s. net.

PEEL (Edmund).—ECHOES FROM HOREB ! and other Poems. Cr. 8vo. 3s. 6d

POPE. (*See* GLOBE LIBRARY, p. 21.)

RAWNSLEY (H. D.).—POEMS, BALLADS, AND BUCOLICS. Fcp. 8vo. 5s.

ROSCOE (W. C.).—POEMS. Edit. by E. M. ROSCOE. Cr. 8vo. 7s. net.

ROSSETTI (Christina).—POEMS. New Collected Edition. Globe 8vo. 7s. 6d.
— SING-SONG: A Nursery Rhyme Book. Small 4to. Illustrated. 4s. 6d.

SCOTT.—THE LAY OF THE LAST MINSTREL, and THE LADY OF THE LAKE. Edited by Prof. F. T. PALGRAVE. 1s.
— THE LAY OF THE LAST MINSTREL. By G. H. STUART, M.A., and E. H. ELLIOT, B.A. Globe 8vo. 2s.; sewed, 1s. 9d.—Canto I. 9d.—Cantos I.—III. and IV.—VI. 1s. 3d. each; sewed, 1s. each.
— MARMION. Edited by MICHAEL MACMILLAN, B.A. 3s.; sewed, 2s. 6d.
— MARMION, and THE LORD OF THE ISLES. By Prof. F. T. PALGRAVE. 1s.
— THE LADY OF THE LAKE. By G. H. STUART, M.A. Gl. 8vo. 2s. 6d.; swd. 2s.
— ROKEBY. By MICHAEL MACMILLAN, B.A. 3s.; sewed, 2s. 6d.
(*See also* GLOBE LIBRARY, p. 21.)

SHAIRP (John Campbell).—GLEN DESSERAY: and other Poems, Lyrical and Elegiac. Ed. by F. T. PALGRAVE. Cr. 8vo. 6s.

SHAKESPEARE.—THE WORKS OF WILLIAM SHAKESPEARE. *Cambridge Edition*. New and Revised Edition, by W. ALDIS WRIGHT, M.A. 9 vols. 8vo. 10s. 6d. each.—*Edition de Luxe*. 40 vols Sup. roy. 8vo. 6s. each net.
— *Victoria Edition*. In 3 vols.—COMEDIES; HISTORIES; TRAGEDIES. Cr. 8vo. 6s. each.
— THE TEMPEST. With Introduction and Notes, by K. DEIGHTON.. Gl. 8vo. 1s. 9d.; sewed, 1s. 6d.
— MUCH ADO ABOUT NOTHING. 2s.; sewed, 1s. 9d.
— A MIDSUMMER NIGHT'S DREAM. 1s. 9d.; sewed, 1s. 6d.
— THE MERCHANT OF VENICE. 1s. 9d.; sewed, 1s. 6d.
— AS YOU LIKE IT. 1s. 9d.; sewed, 1s. 6d.
— TWELFTH NIGHT. 1s. 9d.; sewed, 1s. 6d
— THE WINTER'S TALE. 2s.; sewed, 1s. 9d
— KING JOHN. 1s. 9d.; sewed, 1s. 6d.
— RICHARD II. 1s. 9d.; sewed, 1s. 6d.
— HENRY IV. Part I. 2s. 6d.; sewed, 2s.
— HENRY IV. Part II. 2s. 6d.; sewed, 1s.
— HENRY V. 1s. 9d.; sewed, 1s. 6d.
— RICHARD III. By C. H. TAWNEY, M.A. 2s. 6d.; sewed, 2s.
— CORIOLANUS. By K. DEIGHTON. 2s. 6d. sewed, 2s.
— ROMEO AND JULIET. 2s. 6d.; sewed 2s.
— JULIUS CÆSAR. 1s. 9d.; sewed, 1s. 6d.
— MACBETH. 1s. 9d.; sewed, 1s. 6d.
— HAMLET. 2s. 6d.; sewed, 2s.
— KING LEAR. 1s. 9d.; sewed, 1s. 6d.
— OTHELLO. 2s.; sewed, 1s. 9d.
— ANTONY AND CLEOPATRA. 2s. 6d.; swd. 2s.
— CYMBELINE. 2s. 6d.; sewed, 2s.

(*See also* GLOBE LIBRARY, p. 21; GOLDEN TREASURY SERIES, p. 22.)

POETRY AND THE DRAMA. 17

SHELLEY.—COMPLETE POETICAL WORKS. Edited by Prof. DOWDEN. Portrait. Cr. 8vo. 7s. 6d. (See GOLDEN TREASURY SERIES, p. 22.)
SMITH (C. Barnard).—POEMS. Fcp. 8vo. 5s.
SMITH (Horace).—POEMS. Globe 8vo. 5s.
—— INTERLUDES. Cr. 8vo. 5s.
SPENSER.—FAIRIE QUEENE. Book I. By H. M. PERCIVAL, M.A. Gl. 8vo. 3s.; swd., 2s. 6d. (See also GLOBE LIBRARY, p. 21.)
STEPHENS (J. B.).—CONVICT ONCE: and other Poems. Cr. 8vo. 7s. 6d.
STRETTELL (Alma).—SPANISH AND ITALIAN FOLK SONGS. Illustr. Roy.16mo. 12s.6d.
SYMONS (Arthur).— DAYS AND NIGHTS. Globe 8vo. 6s.
TENNYSON (Lord).—COMPLETE WORKS. New and Enlarged Edition, with Portrait. Cr. 8vo. 7s. 6d.—*School Edition.* In Four Parts. Cr. 8vo. 2s. 6d. each.
—— POETICAL WORKS. *Pocket Edition.* Pott 8vo, morocco, gilt edges. 7s. 6d. net.
—— WORKS. *Library Edition.* In 9 vols. Globe 8vo. 5s. each. [Each volume may be had separately.]—POEMS, 2 vols.—IDYLLS OF THE KING.—THE PRINCESS, and MAUD.—ENOCH ARDEN, and IN MEMORIAM.—BALLADS, and other Poems.—QUEEN MARY, and HAROLD.—BECKET, and other Plays.—DEMETER, and other Poems.
—— WORKS. *Ext. fcp. 8vo. Edition,* on Handmade Paper. In 10 vols. (supplied in sets only). 5l. 5s. 0d.—EARLY POEMS.—LUCRETIUS, and other Poems.—IDYLLS OF THE KING.—THE PRINCESS, and MAUD.—ENOCH ARDEN, and IN MEMORIAM.—QUEEN MARY, and HAROLD.—BALLADS, and other Poems. —BECKET, THE CUP.—THE FORESTERS, THE FALCON, THE PROMISE OF MAY.—TIRESIAS, and other Poems.
—— WORKS. *Miniature Edition,* in 16 vols., viz. THE POETICAL WORKS. 12 vols. in a box. 25s.—THE DRAMATIC WORKS. 4 vols. in a box. 10s. 6d.
—— WORKS. *Miniature Edition on India Paper.* POETICAL AND DRAMATIC WORKS. 8 vols. in a box. 40s. net.
—— *The Original Editions.* Fcp. 8vo.
POEMS. 6s.
MAUD: and other Poems. 3s. 6d.
THE PRINCESS. 3s. 6d.
THE HOLY GRAIL: and other Poems. 4s.6d.
BALLADS: and other Poems. 5s.
HAROLD: A Drama. 6s.
QUEEN MARY: A Drama. 6s.
THE CUP, and THE FALCON. 5s.
BECKET. 6s.
TIRESIAS: and other Poems. 6s.
LOCKSLEY HALL SIXTY YEARS AFTER, etc. 6s.
DEMETER: and other Poems. 6s.
THE FORESTERS: ROBIN HOOD AND MAID MARIAN. 6s.
THE DEATH OF OENONE, AKBAR'S DREAM, AND OTHER POEMS. 6s.
—— POEMS BY TWO BROTHERS. Fcp. 8vo. 6s.
—— MAUD. *Kelmscott Edition.* Small 4to, vellum. 42s. net.
—— POEMS. Reprint of 1857 Edition. Original Illustrations. 4to. 21s.—*Edition de Luxe.* Roy. 8vo. 42s. net.
—— *The Royal Edition.* 1 vol. 8vo. 16s.
—— THE TENNYSON BIRTHDAY BOOK. Edit. by EMILY SHAKESPEAR. Pott 8vo. 2s. 6d.

TENNYSON (Lord).—BECKET. As arranged for the Stage by H. IRVING. 8vo. swd. 2s. net.
—— THE BROOK. With 20 Illustrations by A. WOODRUFF. 32mo. 2s. 6d.
—— SONGS FROM TENNYSON'S WRITINGS. Square 8vo. 2s. 6d.
—— SELECTIONS FROM TENNYSON. With Introduction and Notes, by F. J. ROWE, M.A., and W. T. WEBB, M.A. Globe 8vo. 3s. 6d. Or Part I. 2s. 6d.; Part II. 2s. 6d.
—— ENOCH ARDEN. By W. T. WEBB, M.A. Globe 8vo. 2s. 6d.
—— AYLMER'S FIELD. By W. T. WEBB, M.A. Globe 8vo. 2s. 6d.
—— THE COMING OF ARTHUR, and THE PASSING OF ARTHUR. By F. J. ROWE. Gl. 8vo. 2s.6d.
—— THE PRINCESS. By P. M. WALLACE, M.A. Globe 8vo. 3s. 6d.
—— GARETH AND LYNETTE. By G. C. MACAULAY, M.A. Globe 8vo. 2s. 6d.
—— GERAINT AND ENID. By G. C. MACAULAY, M.A. Globe 8vo. 2s. 6d.
—— THE HOLY GRAIL. By G. C. MACAULAY, M.A. Globe 8vo. 2s. 6d.
—— TENNYSON FOR THE YOUNG. By Canon AINGER. Pott 8vo. 1s. net.—Large Paper, uncut, 3s. 6d.; gilt edges, 4s. 6d.
TENNYSON (Frederick).—THE ISLES OF GREECE: SAPPHO AND ALCAEUS. Cr. 8vo. 7s. 6d.
—— DAPHNE: and other Poems. Cr.8vo. 7s.6d.
TENNYSON (Lord). (*See* ILLUSTRATED BOOKS.)
TRUMAN (Jos.).—AFTER-THOUGHTS: Poems. Cr. 8vo. 3s. 6d.
TURNER (Charles Tennyson).—COLLECTED SONNETS, OLD AND NEW. Ext.fcp.8vo. 7s.6d.
TYRWHITT (R. St. John).—FREE FIELD. Lyrics, chiefly Descriptive. Gl. 8vo. 3s. 6d.
—— BATTLE AND AFTER, CONCERNING SERGEANT THOMAS ATKINS, GRENADIER GUARDS: and other Verses. Gl. 8vo. 3s.6d.
WARD (Samuel).—LYRICAL RECREATIONS. Fcp. 8vo. 6s.
WATSON (W.).—POEMS. Fcap. 8vo. 5s.
—— LACHRYMAE MUSARUM. Fcp.8vo. 4s.6d. (*See also* GOLDEN TREASURY SERIES, p. 21.)
WEBSTER (A.).—PORTRAITS. Fcp. 8vo. 5s.
—— SELECTIONS FROM VERSE. Fp. 8vo. 4s. 6d.
—— Disguises: A Drama. Fcp. 8vo. 5s.
—— IN A DAY: A Drama. Fcp. 8vo. 2s. 6d.
—— THE SENTENCE: A Drama. Fcp. 8vo. 3s. 6d.
WHITTIER.—COMPLETE POETICAL WORKS OF JOHN GREENLEAF WHITTIER. With Portrait. Pott 8vo. 4s. 6d. (*See also* COLLECTED WORKS, p. 24.)
WILLS (W. G.).—MELCHIOR. Cr. 8vo. 9s.
WOOD (Andrew Goldie).—THE ISLES OF THE BLEST: and other Poems. Globe 8vo. 5s.
WOOLNER (Thomas). — MY BEAUTIFUL LADY. 3rd Edit. Fcp. 8vo. 5s.
—— PYGMALION. Cr. 8vo. 7s. 6d.
—— SILENUS. Cr. 8vo. 6s.
WORDSWORTH. — COMPLETE POETICAL WORKS. Copyright Edition. With an Introduction by JOHN MORLEY, and Portrait. Cr. 8vo. 7s. 6d.
—— THE RECLUSE. Fcp. 8vo. 2s. 6d.—Large Paper Edition. 8vo. 10s. 6d.
(*See also* GOLDEN TREASURY SERIES, p. 22.)

LITERATURE.

Poetical Collections and Selections.

(*See also* GOLDEN TREASURY SERIES, p. 21 ; BOOKS FOR THE YOUNG, p. 41.)

HALES (Prof. J. W.).—LONGER ENGLISH POEMS. With Notes, Philological and Explanatory, and an Introduction on the Teaching of English. Ext. fcp. 8vo. 4s. 6d.

MACDONALD (George).—ENGLAND'S ANTIPHON. Cr. 8vo. 4s. 6d.

MARTIN (F.). (*See* BOOKS FOR THE YOUNG p. 42.)

MASSON (R. O. and D.).—THREE CENTURIES OF ENGLISH POETRY. Being Selections from Chaucer to Herrick. Globe 8vo. 3s. 6d.

PALGRAVE (Prof. F. T.).—THE GOLDEN TREASURY OF THE BEST SONGS AND LYRICAL POEMS IN THE ENGLISH LANGUAGE. Large Type. Cr. 8vo. 10s. 6d. (*See also* GOLDEN TREASURY SERIES, p. 22; BOOKS FOR THE YOUNG, p. 42.)

SMITH (G.).—BAY LEAVES. Translations from Latin Poets. Globe 8vo. 5s.

WARD (T. H.).—ENGLISH POETS. Selections, with Critical Introductions by various Writers, and a General Introduction by MATTHEW ARNOLD. Edited by T. H. WARD, M.A. 4 vols. 2nd Edit. Cr. 8vo. 7s. 6d. each.—Vol. I. CHAUCER TO DONNE; II. BEN JONSON TO DRYDEN; III. ADDISON TO BLAKE; IV. WORDSWORTH TO ROSSETTI.

WOODS (M. A.).—A FIRST POETRY BOOK. Fcp. 8vo. 2s. 6d.
— A SECOND POETRY BOOK. 2 Parts. Fcp. 8vo. 2s. 6d. each.—Complete, 4s. 6d.
— A THIRD POETRY BOOK. Fcp. 8vo. 4s. 6d.

WORDS FROM THE POETS. With a Vignette and Frontispiece. 12th Edit. 18mo. 1s.

Prose Fiction.

BIKELAS (D.).—LOUKIS LARAS; or, The Reminiscences of a Chiote Merchant during the Greek War of Independence. Translated by J. GENNADIUS. Cr. 8vo. 7s. 6d.

BJÖRNSON (B.).—SYNNÖVË SOLBAKKEN. Translated by JULIE SUTTER. Cr. 8vo. 6s.

BOLDREWOOD (Rolf).—*Uniform Edition*. Cr. 8vo. 3s. 6d. each.
ROBBERY UNDER ARMS.
THE MINER'S RIGHT.
THE SQUATTER'S DREAM.
A SYDNEY-SIDE SAXON.
A COLONIAL REFORMER.
NEVERMORE.

BURNETT (F. H.).—HAWORTH'S. Gl. 8vo. 2s.
— LOUISIANA, and THAT LASS O' LOWRIE'S. Illustrated. Cr. 8vo. 3s. 6d.

CALMIRE. 2 vols. Cr. 8vo. 21s.

CARMARTHEN (Marchioness of).—A LOVER OF THE BEAUTIFUL. Cr. 8vo. 6s.

CONWAY (Hugh).—A FAMILY AFFAIR. Cr. 8vo. 3s. 6d.
— LIVING OR DEAD. Cr. 8vo. 3s. 6d.

COOPER (E. H.).—RICHARD ESCOTT. Cr. 8vo. 6s.

CORBETT (Julian).—THE FALL OF ASGARD: A Tale of St. Olaf's Day. 2 vols. Gl. 8vo. 12s.
— FOR GOD AND GOLD. Cr. 8vo. 6s.
— KOPHETUA THE THIRTEENTH. 2 vols. Globe 8vo. 12s.

CRAIK (Mrs.).—*Uniform Edition*. Cr. 8vo. 3s. 6d. each.
OLIVE.
THE OGILVIES. Also Globe 8vo, 2s.
AGATHA'S HUSBAND. Also Globe 8vo, 2s.
THE HEAD OF THE FAMILY.
TWO MARRIAGES. Also Globe 8vo, 2s.
THE LAUREL BUSH.
MY MOTHER AND I.
MISS TOMMY: A Mediæval Romance.
KING ARTHUR: Not a Love Story.

CRAWFORD (F. Marion).—*Uniform Edition*. Cr. 8vo. 3s. 6d. each.
MR. ISAACS: A Tale of Modern India.
DR. CLAUDIUS.
A ROMAN SINGER.
ZOROASTER.
A TALE OF A LONELY PARISH.
MARZIO'S CRUCIFIX.
PAUL PATOFF.
WITH THE IMMORTALS.
GREIFENSTEIN.
SANT' ILARIO.
A CIGARETTE MAKER'S ROMANCE.
KHALED: A Tale of Arabia.
THE WITCH OF PRAGUE.
THE THREE FATES.
— DON ORSINO. Cr. 8vo. 6s.
— CHILDREN OF THE KING. Cr. 8vo. 6s.
— PIETRO GHISLERI. 3 vols. Cr. 8vo. 31s. 6d.
— MARION DARCHE. 2 vols. Gl. 8vo. 12s.

CUNNINGHAM (Sir H. S.).—THE CŒRULEANS: A Vacation Idyll. Cr. 8vo. 3s. 6d.
— THE HERIOTS. Cr. 8vo. 3s. 6d.
— WHEAT AND TARES. Cr. 8vo. 3s. 6d.

DAGONET THE JESTER. Cr. 8vo. 4s. 6d

DAHN (Felix).—FELICITAS. Translated by M. A. C. E. Cr. 8vo. 4s. 6d.

DAY (Rev. Lal Behari).—BENGAL PEASANT LIFE. Cr. 8vo. 6s.
— FOLK TALES OF BENGAL. Cr. 8vo. 4s. 6d.

DEFOE (D.). (*See* GLOBE LIBRARY, p. 21 : GOLDEN TREASURY SERIES, p. 22.)

DEMOCRACY: AN AMERICAN NOVEL. Cr 8vo. 4s. 6d.

DICKENS (Charles). — *Uniform Edition*. Cr. 8vo. 3s. 6d. each.
THE PICKWICK PAPERS.
OLIVER TWIST.
NICHOLAS NICKLEBY.
MARTIN CHUZZLEWIT.
THE OLD CURIOSITY SHOP.
BARNABY RUDGE.
DOMBEY AND SON.
CHRISTMAS BOOKS.
SKETCHES BY BOZ.
DAVID COPPERFIELD.
AMERICAN NOTES, AND PICTURES FROM ITALY.
— THE POSTHUMOUS PAPERS OF THE PICKWICK CLUB. Illust. Edit. by C. DICKENS, Jun. 2 vols. Ext. cr. 8vo. 21s.

DICKENS (M. A.).—A MERE CYPHER. Cr. 8vo. 3s. 6d.

DILLWYN (E. A.).—JILL. Cr. 8vo. 6s.
— JILL AND JACK. 2 vols. Globe 8vo. 12s.

DUNSMUIR (Amy).—VIDA: Study of a Girl. 3rd Edit. Cr. 8vo. 6s.
DURAND (Sir M.).—HELEN TREVERYAN. Cr. 8vo. 3s. 6d.
EBERS (Dr. George).—THE BURGOMASTER'S WIFE. Transl. by C. BELL. Cr. 8vo. 4s. 6d.
— ONLY A WORD. Translated by CLARA BELL. Cr. 8vo. 4s. 6d.
"ESTELLE RUSSELL" (The Author of).—HARMONIA. 3 vols. Cr. 8vo. 31s. 6d.
FALCONER (Lanoe).—CECILIA DE NOËL. Cr. 8vo. 3s. 6d.
FLEMING (G.).—A NILE NOVEL. Gl. 8vo. 2s.
— MIRAGE: A Novel. Globe 8vo. 2s.
— THE HEAD OF MEDUSA. Globe 8vo. 2s.
— VESTIGIA. Globe 8vo. 2s.
FRATERNITY: A Romance. 2 vols. Cr. 8vo. 21s.
"FRIENDS IN COUNCIL" (The Author of).—REALMAH. Cr. 8vo. 6s.
GRAHAM (John W.).—NEÆRA: A Tale of Ancient Rome. Cr. 8vo. 6s.
HARBOUR BAR, THE. Cr. 8vo. 6s.
HARDY (Arthur Sherburne).—BUT YET A WOMAN: A Novel. Cr. 8vo. 4s. 6d.
— THE WIND OF DESTINY. 2 vols. Gl. 8vo. 12s.
HARDY (Thomas).—THE WOODLANDERS. Cr. 8vo. 3s. 6d.
— WESSEX TALES. Cr. 8vo. 3s. 6d.
HARTE (Bret).—CRESSY. Cr. 8vo. 3s. 6d.
— THE HERITAGE OF DEDLOW MARSH and other Tales. Cr. 8vo. 3s. 6d.
— A FIRST FAMILY OF TASAJARA. Cr. 8vo. 3s. 6d.
"HOGAN, M.P." (The Author of).—HOGAN, M.P. Cr. 8vo. 3s. 6d.
— THE HON. MISS FERRARD. Gl. 8vo. 2s.
— FLITTERS, TATTERS, AND THE COUNSELLOR, ETC. Globe 8vo. 2s.
— CHRISTY CAREW. Globe 8vo. 2s.
— ISMAY'S CHILDREN. Globe 8vo. 2s.
HOPPUS (Mary).—A GREAT TREASON: A Story of the War of Independence. 2 vols. Cr. 8vo. 9s.
HUGHES (Thomas).—TOM BROWN'S SCHOOL DAYS. By AN OLD BOY.—Golden Treasury Edition. 2s. 6d. net.—Uniform Edit. 3s. 6d.—People's Edition. 2s.—People's Sixpenny Edition. Illustr. Med. 4to. 6d.—Uniform with Sixpenny Kingsley. Med. 8vo. 6d.
— TOM BROWN AT OXFORD. Cr. 8vo. 3s. 6d.
— THE SCOURING OF THE WHITE HORSE, and THE ASHEN FAGGOT. Cr. 8vo. 3s. 6d.
IRVING (Washington). (See ILLUSTRATED BOOKS, p. 12.)
JACKSON (Helen).—RAMONA. Gl. 8vo. 2s.
JAMES (Henry).—THE EUROPEANS: A Novel. Cr. 8vo. 6s.; Pott 8vo, 2s.
— DAISY MILLER: and other Stories. Cr. 8vo. 6s.; Globe 8vo, 2s.
— THE AMERICAN. Cr. 8vo. 6s.—Pott 8vo. 2 vols. 4s.
— RODERICK HUDSON. Cr. 8vo. 6s.; Gl. 8vo, 2s.; Pott 8vo, 2 vols. 4s.

JAMES (Henry).—THE MADONNA OF THE FUTURE: and other Tales. Cr. 8vo. 6s.; Globe 8vo, 2s.
— WASHINGTON SQUARE, THE PENSION BEAUREPAS. Globe 8vo. 2s.
— THE PORTRAIT OF A LADY. Cr. 8vo. 6s. Pott 8vo, 3 vols. 6s.
— STORIES REVIVED. In Two Series. Cr. 8vo. 6s. each.
— THE BOSTONIANS. Cr. 8vo. 6s.
— NOVELS AND TALES. Pocket Edition. Pott 8vo. 2s. each volume.
CONFIDENCE. 1 vol.
THE SIEGE OF LONDON; MADAME DE MAUVES. 1 vol.
AN INTERNATIONAL EPISODE; THE PENSION BEAUREPAS; THE POINT OF VIEW. 1 vol.
DAISY MILLER, a Study; FOUR MEETINGS; LONGSTAFF'S MARRIAGE; BENVOLIO. 1 vol.
THE MADONNA OF THE FUTURE; A BUNDLE OF LETTERS; THE DIARY OF A MAN OF FIFTY; EUGENE PICKERING. 1 vol.
— TALES OF THREE CITIES. Cr. 8vo. 4s. 6d.
— THE PRINCESS CASAMASSIMA. Cr. 8vo. 6s.; Globe 8vo, 2s.
— THE REVERBERATOR. Cr. 8vo. 6s.
— THE ASPERN PAPERS; LOUISA PALLANT; THE MODERN WARNING. Cr. 8vo. 3s. 6d.
— A LONDON LIFE. Cr. 8vo. 3s. 6d.
— THE TRAGIC MUSE. Cr. 8vo. 3s. 6d.
— THE LESSON OF THE MASTER, AND OTHER STORIES. Cr. 8vo. 6s.
— THE REAL THING, AND OTHER TALE Cr. 8vo. 6s.
KEARY (Annie).—JANET'S HOME. Cr. 8vo. 3s. 6d.
— CLEMENCY FRANKLYN. Globe 8vo. 2s.
— OLDBURY. Cr. 8vo. 3s. 6d.
— A YORK AND A LANCASTER ROSE. Cr. 8vo. 3s. 6d.
— CASTLE DALY. Cr. 8vo. 3s. 6d.
— A DOUBTING HEART. Cr. 8vo. 3s. 6d
KENNEDY (P.).—LEGENDARY FICTIONS OF THE IRISH CELTS. Cr. 8vo. 3s. 6d.
KINGSLEY (Charles).—*Eversley Edition.* 13 vols. Globe 8vo. 5s. each.—WESTWARD HO! 2 vols.—TWO YEARS AGO. 2 vols.—HYPATIA. 2 vols.—YEAST. 1 vol.—ALTON LOCKE. 2 vols.—HEREWARD THE WAKE. 2 vols.
— *Complete Edition.* Cr. 8vo. 3s. 6d. each. —WESTWARD HO! With a Portrait.—HYPATIA.—YEAST.—ALTON LOCKE.—TWO YEARS AGO.—HEREWARD THE WAKE.
— *Sixpenny Edition.* Med. 8vo. 6d. each. — WESTWARD HO! — HYPATIA. — YEAST.—ALTON LOCKE.—TWO YEARS AGO. — HEREWARD THE WAKE.
KIPLING (Rudyard).—PLAIN TALES FROM THE HILLS. Cr. 8vo. 6s.
— THE LIGHT THAT FAILED. Cr. 8vo. 6s.
— LIFE'S HANDICAP: Being Stories of mine own People. Cr. 8vo. 6s.
— MANY INVENTIONS. Cr. 8vo. 6s.
LAFARGUE (Philip).—THE NEW JUDGMENT OF PARIS. 2 vols. Globe 8vo. 12s.

LITERATURE.

Prose Fiction—*continued.*

LEE (Margaret).—FAITHFUL AND UNFAITHFUL. Cr. 8vo. 3s. 6d.

LEVY (A.).—REUBEN SACHS. Cr. 8vo. 3s.6d.

LITTLE PILGRIM IN THE UNSEEN, A. 24th Thousand. Cr. 8vo. 2s. 6d.

"LITTLE PILGRIM IN THE UNSEEN, A" (Author of).—THE LAND OF DARKNESS. Cr. 8vo. 5s.

LYSAGHT (S. R.).—THE MARPLOT. Cr. 8vo. 3s. 6d.

LYTTON (Earl of).—THE RING OF AMASIS: A Romance. Cr. 8vo. 3s. 6d.

McLENNAN (Malcolm).—MUCKLE JOCK; and other Stories of Peasant Life in the North. Cr. 8vo. 3s. 6d.

MACQUOID (K. S.).—PATTY. Gl. 8vo. 2s.

MADOC (Fayr).—THE STORY OF MELICENT. Cr. 8vo. 4s. 6d.

MALET (Lucas).—MRS. LORIMER: A Sketch in Black and White. Cr. 8vo. 3s. 6d.

MALORY (Sir Thos.). (*See* GLOBE LIBRARY, p. 21.)

MINTO (W.).—THE MEDIATION OF RALPH HARDELOT. 3 vols. Cr. 8vo. 31s. 6d.

MITFORD (A. B.).—TALES OF OLD JAPAN. With Illustrations. Cr. 8vo. 3s. 6d.

MIZ MAZE (THE); OR, THE WINKWORTH PUZZLE. A Story in Letters by Nine Authors. Cr. 8vo. 4s. 6d.

MURRAY (D. Christie). — AUNT RACHEL. Cr. 8vo. 3s. 6d.
—— SCHWARTZ. Cr. 8vo. 3s 6d.
—— THE WEAKER VESSEL. Cr. 8vo. 3s. 6d.
—— JOHN VALE'S GUARDIAN. Cr. 8vo. 3s. 6d.

MURRAY (D. Christie) and HERMAN (H.). —HE FELL AMONG THIEVES. Cr. 8vo. 3s.6d.

NEW ANTIGONE, THE: A ROMANCE. Cr. 8vo. 3s. 6d.

NOEL (Lady Augusta).—HITHERSEA MERE. 3 vols. Cr. 8vo. 31s. 6d.

NORRIS (W. E.).—MY FRIEND JIM. Globe 8vo. 2s.
—— CHRIS. Globe 8vo. 2s.

NORTON (Hon. Mrs.).—OLD SIR DOUGLAS. Cr. 8vo. 6s.

OLIPHANT (Mrs. M. O. W.).—A SON OF THE SOIL. Globe 8vo. 2s.
—— THE CURATE IN CHARGE. Globe 8vo. 2s.
—— YOUNG MUSGRAVE. Globe 8vo. 2s.
—— HE THAT WILL NOT WHEN HE MAY. Cr. 8vo. 3s. 6d.—Gl. 8vo. 2s.
—— SIR TOM. Cr. 8vo. 3s. 6d.—Gl. 8vo. 2s.
—— HESTER. Cr. 8vo. 3s. 6d.
—— THE WIZARD'S SON. Globe 8vo. 2s.
—— THE COUNTRY GENTLEMAN AND HIS FAMILY. Globe 8vo. 2s.
—— THE SECOND SON. Globe 8vo. 2s.
—— NEIGHBOURS ON THE GREEN. Cr. 8vo. 3s. 6d.
—— JOYCE. Cr. 8vo. 3s. 6d.
—— A BELEAGUERED CITY. Cr. 8vo. 3s. 6d.
—— KIRSTEEN. Cr. 8vo. 3s. 6d.
—— THE RAILWAY MAN AND HIS CHILDREN. Cr. 8vo. 3s. 6d.

OLIPHANT (Mrs. M. O. W.).—THE MARRIAGE OF ELINOR Cr. 8vo. 3s. 6d.
—— THE HEIR-PRESUMPTIVE AND THE HEIR-APPARENT. Cr. 8vo. 3s. 6d.

PALMER (Lady Sophia).—MRS. PENICOTT'S LODGER; and other Stories. Cr. 8vo. 2s. 6d.

PARRY (Gambier).—THE STORY OF DICK. Cr. 8vo. 3s. 6d.

PATER (Walter).—MARIUS THE EPICUREAN: HIS SENSATIONS AND IDEAS. 3rd Edit. 2 vols. 8vo. 12s.

RHOADES (J.).—THE STORY OF JOHN TREVENNICK. Cr. 8vo. 3s. 6d.

ROSS (Percy).—A MISGUIDIT LASSIE. Cr. 8vo. 4s. 6d.

RUSSELL (W. Clark).—MAROONED. Cr. 8vo. 3s. 6d.
—— A STRANGE ELOPEMENT. Cr. 8vo. 3s.6d.

ST. JOHNSTON (A.). — A SOUTH SEA LOVER: A Romance. Cr. 8vo. 6s.

SHORTHOUSE (J. Henry).—*Uniform Edition.* Cr. 8vo. 3s. 6d. each.
JOHN INGLESANT: A Romance.
SIR PERCIVAL: A Story of the Past and of the Present.
THE LITTLE SCHOOLMASTER MARK: A Spiritual Romance.
THE COUNTESS EVE.
A TEACHER OF THE VIOLIN; and other Tales.
—— BLANCHE, LADY FALAISE. Cr. 8vo. 6s.

SLIP IN THE FENS, A. Globe 8vo. 2s.

STEEL (Mrs. F. A.).—MISS STUART'S LEGACY. 3 vols. Cr. 8vo. 31s. 6d.

THEODOLI (Marchesa)—UNDER PRESSURE. Cr. 8vo. 3s. 6d.

TIM. Cr. 8vo. 3s. 6d.

TOURGÉNIEF.—VIRGIN SOIL. Translated by ASHTON W. DILKE. Cr. 8vo. 6s.

VELEY (Margaret).—A GARDEN OF MEMORIES; MRS. AUSTIN; LIZZIE'S BARGAIN. Three Stories. 2 vols. Globe 8vo. 12s.

VICTOR (H.).—MARIAM; OR TWENTY-ONE DAYS. Cr. 8vo. 6s.

VOICES CRYING IN THE WILDERNESS: A NOVEL. Cr. 8vo. 7s. 6d.

WARD (Mrs. T. Humphry).—MISS BRETHERTON. Cr. 8vo. 3s. 6d.

WEST (M.).—A BORN PLAYER. Cr. 8vo. 6s.

WORTHEY (Mrs.).—THE NEW CONTINENT: A Novel. 2 vols. Globe 8vo. 12s.

YONGE (C. M.).—GRISLY GRISELL. 2 vols. Cr. 8vo. 12s. (*See also* p. 24.)

YONGE (C. M.) and COLERIDGE (C. R.) —STROLLING PLAYERS. Cr. 8vo. 6s.

Collected Works; Essays; Lectures; Letters; Miscellaneous Works.

ADDISON.—SELECTIONS FROM THE "SPECTATOR." With Introduction and Notes by K. DEIGHTON. Globe 8vo. 3s. 6d.

AN AUTHOR'S LOVE. Being the Unpublished Letters of PROSPER MÉRIMÉE'S "Inconnue." 2 vols. Ext. cr. 8vo. 12s.

COLLECTED WORKS.

ARNOLD (Matthew).—Essays in Criticism. 6th Edit. Cr. 8vo. 9s.
—— Essays in Criticism. Second Series. Cr. 8vo. 7s. 6d.
—— Discourses in America. Cr. 8vo. 4s. 6d.

BACON.—Essays. With Introduction and Notes, by F. G. Selby, M.A. Gl. 8vo. 3s.; swd., 2s. 6d.
—— Advancement of Learning. By the same. Gl. 8vo. Book I. 2s. Book II. 3s. 6d. (See also Golden Treasury Series, p. 22)

BATES(K. L.).—English Religious Drama. Cr. 8vo. 6s. 6d. net.

BLACKIE(J. S.).—Lay Sermons. Cr. 8vo. 6s.

BRIDGES (John A.).—Idylls of a Lost Village. Cr. 8vo. 7s. 6d.

BRIMLEY (George).—Essays. Globe 8vo. 5s.

BUNYAN (John).—The Pilgrim's Progress from this World to that which is to Come. Pott 8vo. 2s. 6d. net.

BUTCHER (Prof. S. H.)—Some Aspects of the Greek Genius. Cr. 8vo. 7s. net

CARLYLE (Thomas). (See Biography.)

CHURCH (Dean).—Miscellaneous Writings. Collected Edition. 6 vols. Globe 8vo. 5s. each.—Vol. I. Miscellaneous Essays.—II. Dante: and other Essays. —III. St. Anselm.—IV. Spenser.—V. Bacon.—VI. The Oxford Movement, 1833—45.

CLIFFORD (Prof. W. K.). Lectures and Essays. Edited by Leslie Stephen and Sir F. Pollock. Cr. 8vo. 8s. 6d.

CLOUGH (A. H.).—Prose Remains. With a Selection from his Letters, and a Memoir by His Wife. Cr. 8vo. 7s. 6d.

COLLINS (J. Churton).—The Study of English Literature. Cr. 8vo. 4s. 6d.

CRAIK (H.).—English Prose Selections. With Critical Introductions by various writers, and General Introductions to each Period. Edited by H. Craik, C.B. Vol. I. Crown 8vo. 7s. 6d.

CRAIK (Mrs.).—Concerning Men: and other Papers. Cr. 8vo. 3s. 6d.
—— About Money: and other Things. Cr. 8vo. 3s. 6d.
—— Sermons out of Church. Cr. 8vo. 3s. 6d.

CRAWFORD (F. M.).—The Novel: what it is. Pott 8vo. 3s.

CUNLIFFE (J. W.).—The Influence of Seneca on Elizabethan Tragedy. 4s. net.

DE VERE (Aubrey).—Essays Chiefly on Poetry. 2 vols. Globe 8vo. 12s.
—— Essays, Chiefly Literary and Ethical. Globe 8vo. 6s.

DICKENS.—Letters of Charles Dickens. Edited by his Sister-in-Law and Mary Dickens. Cr. 8vo. 3s. 6d.

DRYDEN, Essays of. Edited by Prof. C. D. Yonge. Fcp. 8vo. 2s. 6d. (See also Globe Library, below.)

DUFF (Rt. Hon. Sir M. E. Grant).—Miscellanies, Political and Literary. 8vo. 10s. 6d.

EMERSON(Ralph Waldo).—The Collected Works. 6 vols. Globe 8vo. 5s. each.— I. Miscellanies. With an Introductory Essay by John Morley.—II. Essays.— III. Poems.—IV. English Traits; Representative Men.—V. Conduct of Life; Society and Solitude.—VI. Letters; Social Aims, etc.

FINLAYSON (T. C.).—Essays, Addresses, and Lyrical Translations. Cr. 8vo. 7s. 6d.

FITZGERALD (Edward): Letters and Literary Remains of. Ed. by W. Aldis Wright, M.A. 3 vols. Cr. 8vo. 31s. 6d.

GLOBE LIBRARY. Gl. 8vo. 3s. 6d. each: Boswell's Life of Johnson. Introduction by Mowbray Morris.
Burns.—Complete Poetical Works and Letters. Edited, with Life and Glossarial Index, by Alexander Smith.
Cowper.—Poetical Works. Edited by the Rev. W. Benham, B.D.
Defoe.—The Adventures of Robinson Crusoe. Introduction by H. Kingsley.
Dryden.—Poetical Works. A Revised Text and Notes. By W. D. Christie, M.A.
Goldsmith. — Miscellaneous Works. Edited by Prof. Masson.
Horace.—Works. Rendered into English Prose by James Lonsdale and S. Lee.
Malory.—Le Morte d'Arthur. Sir Thos. Malory's Book of King Arthur and of his Noble Knights of the Round Table. The Edition of Caxton, revised for modern use. By Sir E. Strachey, Bart.
Milton.—Poetical Works. Edited, with Introductions, by Prof. Masson.
Pope.—Poetical Works. Edited, with Memoir and Notes, by Prof. Ward.
Scott.—Poetical Works. With Essay by Prof. Palgrave.
Shakespeare.—Complete Works. Edit. by W. G. Clark and W. Aldis Wright. India Paper Edition. Cr. 8vo, cloth extra, gilt edges. 10s. 6d. net.
Spenser.—Complete Works Edited by R. Morris. Memoir by J. W. Hales, M.A.
Virgil.—Works. Rendered into English Prose by James Lonsdale and S. Lee.

GOETHE. — Maxims and Reflections. Trans. by T. B. Saunders. Gl. 8vo. 5s.
—— Nature Aphorisms. Transl. by T. B. Saunders. Pott 8vo. 6d. net.

GOLDEN TREASURY SERIES.—Uniformly printed in Pott 8vo, with Vignette Titles by Sir J. E. Millais, Sir Noel Paton, T. Woolner W. Holman Hunt, Arthur Hughes, etc. 2s. 6d. net each.
Balladen und Romanzen. Being a Selection of the best German Ballads and Romances. Edited, with Introduction and Notes, by Dr. Buchheim.
Children's Treasury of Lyrical Poetry. By F. T. Palgrave.
Deutsche Lyrik. The Golden Treasury of the best German Lyrical Poems. Selected by Dr. Buchheim.
La Lyre Française. Selected and arranged, with Notes, by G. Masson.
Lyric Love: An Anthology. Edited by W. Watson.
The Ballad Book. A Selection of the Choicest British Ballads. Edited by William Allingham.

LITERATURE.

Collected Works; Essays; Lectures; Letters; Miscellaneous Works—contd.

GOLDEN TREASURY SERIES—contd.

BOOK OF GOLDEN THOUGHTS, A. By Sir HENRY ATTWELL.
BOOK OF PRAISE, THE. From the Best English Hymn Writers. Selected by ROUNDELL, EARL OF SELBORNE.
CHILDREN'S GARLAND FROM THE BEST POETS THE. Selected by COVENTRY PATMORE.
FAIRY BOOK, THE: THE BEST POPULAR FAIRY STORIES. Selected by Mrs. CRAIK, Author of "John Halifax, Gentleman."
GOLDEN TREASURY OF THE BEST SONGS AND LYRICAL POEMS IN THE ENGLISH LANGUAGE, THE. Selected and arranged, with Notes, by Prof. F. T. PALGRAVE.—Large Type. Cr. 8vo. 10s. 6d.—Large Paper Edition. 8vo. 10s. 6d. net.
GOLDEN TREASURY PSALTER. By Four Friends.
SCOTTISH SONG. Compiled by MARY CARLYLE AITKEN.
SONG BOOK, THE. Words and Tunes selected and arranged by JOHN HULLAH.
SUNDAY BOOK OF POETRY FOR THE YOUNG, THE. Selected by C. F. ALEXANDER.
THEOLOGIA GERMANICA. By S. WINKWORTH.

MATTHEW ARNOLD.—SELECTED POEMS.
ADDISON.—ESSAYS. Chosen and Edited by JOHN RICHARD GREEN.
BACON.—ESSAYS, AND COLOURS OF GOOD AND EVIL. With Notes and Glossarial Index by W. ALDIS WRIGHT, M.A.—Large Paper Edition. 8vo. 10s. 6d. net.
BUNYAN.—THE PILGRIM'S PROGRESS FROM THIS WORLD TO THAT WHICH IS TO COME.—Large Paper Edition. 8vo. 10s. 6d. net.
BYRON.—POETRY. Chosen and arranged by M. ARNOLD.—Large Paper Edit. 9s.
COWPER.—LETTERS. Edited, with Introduction, by Rev. W. BENHAM.
— SELECTIONS FROM POEMS. With an Introduction by Mrs. OLIPHANT.
DEFOE.—THE ADVENTURES OF ROBINSON CRUSOE. Edited by J. W. CLARK, M.A.
GRACIAN (BALTHASAR).—ART OF WORLDLY WISDOM. Translated by J. JACOBS.
HERRICK.—CHRYSOMELA. Edited by Prof. F. T. PALGRAVE.
HUGHES.—TOM BROWN'S SCHOOL DAYS.
KEATS.—THE POETICAL WORKS. Edited by Prof. F. T. PALGRAVE.
LAMB.—TALES FROM SHAKSPEARE. Edited by Rev. ALFRED AINGER, M.A.
LANDOR.—SELECTIONS. Ed. by S. COLVIN.
LONGFELLOW. — BALLADS, LYRICS, AND SONNETS.
MOHAMMAD.—SPEECHES AND TABLE-TALK. Translated by STANLEY LANE-POOLE.
NEWCASTLE.—THE CAVALIER AND HIS LADY. Selections from the Works of the First Duke and Duchess of Newcastle. With Introductory Essay by E. JENKINS.
PLATO.—THE REPUBLIC. Translated by J. LL. DAVIES, M.A., and D. J. VAUGHAN.—Large Paper Edition. 8vo. 10s. 6d. net.
— THE TRIAL AND DEATH OF SOCRATES. Being the Euthyphron, Apology, Crito and Phaedo of Plato. Trans. by F. J. CHURCH.

GOLDEN TREASURY SERIES—contd.

PLATO.—THE PHAEDRUS, LYSIS, AND PROTAGORAS. Translated by J. WRIGHT.
SHAKESPEARE.—SONGS AND SONNETS. Ed. with Notes, by Prof. F. T. PALGRAVE.
SHELLEY.—POEMS. Edited by STOPFORD A. BROOKE.—Large Paper Edit. 12s. 6d.
SIR THOMAS BROWNE.—RELIGIO MEDICI, LETTER TO A FRIEND, &C., AND CHRISTIAN MORALS. Ed. W. A. GREENHILL.
THEOCRITUS.—BION, AND MOSCHUS. Rendered into English Prose by ANDREW LANG.—Large Paper Edition. 9s.
THE JEST BOOK. The Choicest Anecdotes and Sayings. Arranged by MARK LEMON.
WORDSWORTH.—POEMS. Chosen and Edited by M. ARNOLD.—Large Paper Edition. 10s. 6d. net.
HARE.—GUESSES AT TRUTH. By Two Brothers. 4s. 6d.
LONGFELLOW.—POEMS OF PLACES: ENGLAND AND WALES. Edited by H. W. LONGFELLOW. 2 vols. 9s.
TENNYSON.—LYRICAL POEMS. Selected and Annotated by Prof. F. T. PALGRAVE. 4s. 6d.—Large Paper Edition. 9s.
— IN MEMORIAM. 4s. 6d.—Large Paper Edition. 9s.
YONGE.—A BOOK OF GOLDEN DEEDS.
— A BOOK OF WORTHIES.
— THE STORY OF THE CHRISTIANS AND MOORS IN SPAIN.

GOLDSMITH, ESSAYS OF. Edited by C. D. YONGE, M.A. Fcp. 8vo. 2s. 6d. (See also Globe Library, p. 21; Illustrated Books, p. 12.)

GRAY (Asa).—LETTERS. Edited by J. L. GRAY. 2 vols. Cr. 8vo. 15s. net.

GRAY (Thomas).—WORKS. Edited by EDMUND GOSSE. In 4 vols. Globe 8vo. 20s.—Vol. I. POEMS, JOURNALS, AND ESSAYS.—II. LETTERS.—III. LETTERS.—IV. NOTES ON ARISTOPHANES AND PLATO.

GREEN (J. R.).—STRAY STUDIES FROM ENGLAND AND ITALY. Globe 8vo. 5s.

GREENWOOD (F.).—THE LOVER'S LEXICON. Cr. 8vo. 6s.

HAMERTON (P. G.).—THE INTELLECTUAL LIFE. Cr. 8vo. 10s. 6d.
— HUMAN INTERCOURSE. Cr. 8vo. 8s. 6d.
— FRENCH AND ENGLISH: A Comparison. Cr. 8vo. 10s. 6d.

HARRISON (Frederic).—THE CHOICE OF BOOKS. Gl. 8vo. 6s.—Large Paper Ed. 15s.

HARWOOD (George).—FROM WITHIN. Cr. 8vo. 6s.

HELPS (Sir Arthur).—ESSAYS WRITTEN IN THE INTERVALS OF BUSINESS. With Introduction and Notes, by F. J. ROWE, M.A., and W. T. WEBB, M.A. 1s. 9d.; swd. 1s. 6d.

HOBART (Lord).—ESSAYS AND MISCELLANEOUS WRITINGS. With Biographical Sketch. Ed. Lady HOBART. 2 vols. 8vo. 25s.

HUTTON (R. H.).—ESSAYS ON SOME OF THE MODERN GUIDES OF ENGLISH THOUGHT IN MATTERS OF FAITH. Globe 8vo. 5s.
— ESSAYS. 2 vols. Gl. 8vo 5s. each.—Vol. I. Literary; II. Theological.

COLLECTED WORKS.   23

HUXLEY (Prof. T. H.).—COLLECTED WORKS. Monthly Volumes, from Oct. 1893. Gl. 8vo. 5s. each.—I. METHOD AND RESULTS.—II. DARWINIANA. -III. SCIENCE AND EDUCATION.—IV. SCIENCE AND HEBREW TRADITION.—V. SCIENCE AND CHRISTIAN TRADITION.—VI. HUME.—VII. ETHICAL AND PHILOSOPHICAL ESSAYS.—VIII. MAN'S PLACE IN NATURE.—IX. ESSAYS IN SCIENCE.

—— LAY SERMONS, ADDRESSES, AND REVIEWS. 8vo. 7s. 6d.

—— CRITIQUES AND ADDRESSES. 8vo. 10s. 6d.

—— AMERICAN ADDRESSES, WITH A LECTURE ON THE STUDY OF BIOLOGY. 8vo. 6s. 6d.

—— SCIENCE AND CULTURE, AND OTHER ESSAYS. 8vo. 10s. 6d.

—— INTRODUCTORY SCIENCE PRIMER. 18mo. 1s.

—— ESSAYS UPON SOME CONTROVERTED QUESTIONS. 8vo. 14s.

IRELAND (A.).—BOOK-LOVER'S ENCHIRIDION. Fcp. 8vo. 7s.; vellum, 10s. 6d.

JAMES (Henry).—FRENCH POETS AND NOVELISTS. New Edition. Gl. 8vo. 5s.

—— PORTRAITS OF PLACES. Cr. 8vo. 7s. 6d.

—— PARTIAL PORTRAITS. Cr. 8vo. 6s.

JEBB (R. C.).—GROWTH AND INFLUENCE OF CLASSICAL GREEK POETRY. Cr. 8vo. 7s. net.

KEATS.—LETTERS. Edited by SIDNEY COLVIN. Globe 8vo. 5s.

KINGSLEY (Charles).—COMPLETE EDITION OF THE WORKS OF CHARLES KINGSLEY. Cr. 8vo. 3s. 6d. each.
WESTWARD HO! With a Portrait.
HYPATIA.
YEAST.
ALTON LOCKE.
TWO YEARS AGO.
HEREWARD THE WAKE.
POEMS.
THE HEROES; or, Greek Fairy Tales for my Children.
THE WATER BABIES: A Fairy Tale for a Land Baby.
MADAM HOW AND LADY WHY; or, First Lesson in Earth-Lore for Children.
AT LAST: A Christmas in the West Indies.
PROSE IDYLLS.
PLAYS AND PURITANS.
THE ROMAN AND THE TEUTON. With Preface by Professor MAX MÜLLER.
SANITARY AND SOCIAL LECTURES.
HISTORICAL LECTURES AND ESSAYS.
SCIENTIFIC LECTURES AND ESSAYS.
LITERARY AND GENERAL LECTURES.
THE HERMITS.
GLAUCUS; or, The Wonders of the Sea-Shore. With Coloured Illustrations.
VILLAGE AND TOWN AND COUNTRY SERMONS.
THE WATER OF LIFE, AND OTHER SERMONS.
SERMONS ON NATIONAL SUBJECTS: AND THE KING OF THE EARTH.
SERMONS FOR THE TIMES.
GOOD NEWS OF GOD.
THE GOSPEL OF THE PENTATEUCH: AND DAVID.
DISCIPLINE, AND OTHER SERMONS.
WESTMINSTER SERMONS.
ALL SAINTS' DAY, AND OTHER SERMONS.

LAMB (Charles).—COLLECTED WORKS. Ed., with Introduction and Notes, by the Rev. ALFRED AINGER, M.A. Globe 8vo. 5s. each volume.—I. ESSAYS OF ELIA.—II. PLAYS, POEMS, AND MISCELLANEOUS ESSAYS.—III. MRS. LEICESTER'S SCHOOL; THE ADVENTURES OF ULYSSES; AND OTHER ESSAYS.—IV. TALES FROM SHAKESPEARE.—V. and VI. LETTERS. Newly arranged, with additions.

—— TALES FROM SHAKESPEARE. Pott 8vo. 2s. 6d. net.

LANKESTER (Prof. E. Ray).—THE ADVANCEMENT OF SCIENCE. Occasional Essays and Addresses. 8vo. 10s. 6d.

LESLIE (G. D.).—LETTERS TO MARCO. Ex. cr. 8vo. 7s. 6d.

LETTERS FROM SOUTH AFRICA. Reprinted from the *Times*. Cr. 8vo. 2s. 6d.

LETTERS FROM QUEENSLAND. Reprinted from the *Times*. Cr. 8vo. 2s. 6d.

LODGE (Prof. Oliver).—THE PIONEERS OF SCIENCE. Illustrated. Ext. cr. 8vo. 7s. 6d.

LOWELL (Jas. Russell).—COMPLETE WORKS. 10 vols. Cr. 8vo. 6s. each.—Vols. I.—IV. LITERARY ESSAYS.—V. POLITICAL ESSAYS.—VI. LITERARY AND POLITICAL ADDRESSES. VII.—X. POETICAL WORKS.

—— POLITICAL ESSAYS. Ext. cr. 8vo. 7s. 6d.

—— LATEST LITERARY ESSAYS. Cr. 8vo. 6s.

LUBBOCK (Rt. Hon. Sir John, Bart.).—SCIENTIFIC LECTURES. Illustrated. 2nd Edit. revised. 8vo. 8s. 6d.

—— POLITICAL AND EDUCATIONAL ADDRESSES. 8vo. 8s. 6d.

—— FIFTY YEARS OF SCIENCE: Address to the British Association, 1881. 5th Edit. Cr. 8vo. 2s. 6d.

—— THE PLEASURES OF LIFE. New Edit. 60th Thousand. Gl. 8vo. Part I. 1s. 6d.; swd. 1s.—Library Edition. 3s. 6d.—Part II. 1s. 6d.; sewed, 1s.—Library Edition. 3s. 6d.—Complete in 1 vol. 2s. 6d.

—— THE BEAUTIES OF NATURE. Cr. 8vo. 6s.

—— —— Without Illustrations. Cr. 8vo. 1s. 6d.; sewed, 1s.

LYTTELTON (E.).—MOTHERS AND SONS. Cr. 8vo. 3s. 6d.

MACAULAY.—ESSAY ON WARREN HASTINGS. Ed. by K. DEIGHTON. Gl. 8vo. 2s. 6d.

—— ESSAY ON LORD CLIVE. By the same. 2s.

MACMILLAN (Rev. Hugh).—ROMAN MOSAICS, or, Studies in Rome and its Neighbourhood. Globe 8vo. 6s.

MAHAFFY (Prof. J. P.).—THE PRINCIPLES OF THE ART OF CONVERSATION. Cr. 8vo. 4s. 6d.

MAURICE (F. D.).—THE FRIENDSHIP OF BOOKS: and other Lectures. Cr. 8vo. 3s. 6d.

MORLEY (John).—WORKS. Collected Edit. In 11 vols. Globe 8vo. 5s. each.—VOLTAIRE. 1 vol.—ROUSSEAU. 2 vols.—DIDEROT AND THE ENCYCLOPÆDISTS. 2 vols.—ON COMPROMISE. 1 vol.—MISCELLANIES. 3 vols.—BURKE. 1 vol.—STUDIES IN LITERATURE. 1 vol.

MYERS (F. W. H.).—ESSAYS. 2 vols. Cr. 8vo. 4s. 6d. each.—I. CLASSICAL; II. MODERN.

—— SCIENCE AND A FUTURE LIFE. Gl. 8vo. 5s.

NADAL (E. S.).—ESSAYS AT HOME AND ELSEWHERE. Cr. 8vo. 6s.

LITERATURE.

Collected Works; Essays: Lectures; Letters Miscellaneous Works—*contd.*

OLIPHANT (T. L. Kington).—THE DUKE AND THE SCHOLAR: and other Essays. 8vo. 7s. 6d.

OWENS COLLEGE ESSAYS AND ADDRESSES. By Professors and Lecturers of the College. 8vo. 14s.

PATER (W.).—THE RENAISSANCE; Studies in Art and Poetry. 4th Ed. Cr. 8vo. 10s. 6d.
—— IMAGINARY PORTRAITS. Cr. 8vo. 6s.
—— APPRECIATIONS. With an Essay on "Style." 2nd Edit. Cr. 8vo. 8s. 6d.
—— MARIUS THE EPICUREAN. 2 vols. Cr. 8vo. 12s.
—— PLATO AND PLATONISM. Ex. cr. 8vo. 8s. 6d.

PICTON (J. A.).—THE MYSTERY OF MATTER: and other Essays. Cr. 8vo. 6s.

POLLOCK (Sir F., Bart.).—OXFORD LECTURES: and other Discourses. 8vo. 9s.

POOLE (M. E.).—PICTURES OF COTTAGE LIFE IN THE WEST OF ENGLAND. 2nd Ed. Cr. 8vo. 3s. 6d.

POTTER (Louisa).—LANCASHIRE MEMORIES. Cr. 8vo. 6s.

PRICKARD (A. O.).—ARISTOTLE ON THE ART OF POETRY. Cr. 8vo. 3s. 6d.

RUMFORD.—COMPLETE WORKS OF COUNT RUMFORD. Memoir by G. ELLIS. Portrait. 5 vols. 8vo. 4l. 14s. 6d.

SCAIFE (W. B.).—FLORENTINE LIFE DURING THE RENAISSANCE. 8vo. 6s. net.

SCIENCE LECTURES AT SOUTH KENSINGTON. Illustr. 2 vols. Cr. 8vo. 6s. each.

SMALLEY (George W.).—LONDON LETTERS AND SOME OTHERS. 2 vols. 8vo. 32s.

SMITH (G.).—GREEK TRAGEDY. 2 vols. 10s.

STEPHEN (Sir James F., Bart.).—HORAE SABBATICAE. Three Series. Gl. 8vo. 5s. each.

THRING (Edward).—THOUGHTS ON LIFE SCIENCE. 2nd Edit. Cr. 8vo. 7s. 6d.

WARD (W.).—WITNESSES TO THE UNSEEN. 8vo. 10s. 6d.

WESTCOTT (Bishop). (See THEOLOGY, p. 39.)

WILSON (Dr. George).—RELIGIO CHEMICI. Cr. 8vo. 8s. 6d.
—— THE FIVE GATEWAYS OF KNOWLEDGE. 9th Edit. Ext. fcp. 8vo. 2s. 6d.

WHITTIER (John Greenleaf). THE COMPLETE WORKS. 7 vols. Cr. 8vo. 6s. each.—Vol. I. NARRATIVE AND LEGENDARY POEMS—II. POEMS OF NATURE; POEMS SUBJECTIVE AND REMINISCENT; RELIGIOUS POEMS.—III. ANTI-SLAVERY POEMS; SONGS OF LABOUR AND REFORM.—IV. PERSONAL POEMS; OCCASIONAL POEMS; THE TENT ON THE BEACH; with the Poems of ELIZABETH H. WHITTIER, and an Appendix containing Early and Uncollected Verses.—V. MARGARET SMITH'S JOURNAL; TALES AND SKETCHES.—VI. OLD PORTRAITS AND MODERN SKETCHES; PERSONAL SKETCHES AND TRIBUTES; HISTORICAL PAPERS.—VII. THE CONFLICT WITH SLAVERY, POLITICS, AND REFORM; THE INNER LIFE, CRITICISM.

YONGE (Charlotte M.).—*Uniform Edition*. Cr. 8vo. 3s. 6d. each.
THE HEIR OF REDCLYFFE.
HEARTSEASE.
HOPES AND FEARS.
DYNEVOR TERRACE.
THE DAISY CHAIN.
THE TRIAL: More Links of the Daisy Chain.
PILLARS OF THE HOUSE. Vol. I.
PILLARS OF THE HOUSE. Vol. II.
THE YOUNG STEPMOTHER.
CLEVER WOMAN OF THE FAMILY.
THE THREE BRIDES.
MY YOUNG ALCIDES.
THE CAGED LION.
THE DOVE IN THE EAGLE'S NEST.
THE CHAPLET OF PEARLS.
LADY HESTER, and THE DANVERS PAPERS.
MAGNUM BONUM.
LOVE AND LIFE.
UNKNOWN TO HISTORY.
STRAY PEARLS.
THE ARMOURER'S PRENTICES.
THE TWO SIDES OF THE SHIELD.
NUTTIE'S FATHER.
SCENES AND CHARACTERS.
CHANTRY HOUSE.
A MODERN TELEMACHUS.
BYE WORDS.
BEECHCROFT AT ROCKSTONE.
MORE BYWORDS.
A REPUTED CHANGELING.
THE LITTLE DUKE, RICHARD THE FEARLESS.
THE LANCES OF LYNWOOD.
THE PRINCE AND THE PAGE.
P's AND Q's: LITTLE LUCY'S WONDERFUL GLOBE.
THE TWO PENNILESS PRINCESSES.
THAT STICK.
AN OLD WOMAN'S OUTLOOK.

LOGIC. (*See under* PHILOSOPHY, p. 28.)

MAGAZINES. (*See* PERIODICALS, p. 27.)

MAGNETISM. (*See under* PHYSICS, p. 29.)

MATHEMATICS, History of.

BALL (W. W. R.).—A SHORT ACCOUNT OF THE HISTORY OF MATHEMATICS. 2nd Ed. Cr. 8vo. 10s. net.
—— MATHEMATICAL RECREATIONS AND PROBLEMS. Cr. 8vo. 7s. net.
—— AN ESSAY ON NEWTON'S PRINCIPIA. Cr. 8vo. 6s. net.

MEDICINE.

(*See also* DOMESTIC ECONOMY; NURSING; HYGIENE; PHYSIOLOGY.)

ACLAND (Sir H. W.).—THE ARMY MEDICAL SCHOOL: Address at Netley Hospital. 1s.

ALLBUTT (Dr. T. Clifford).—ON THE USE OF THE OPHTHALMOSCOPE. 8vo. 15s.

ANDERSON (Dr. McCall).—LECTURES ON CLINICAL MEDICINE. Illustr. Roy. 8vo. 10s. 6d.

BALLANCE (C. A.) and EDMUNDS (Dr. W.).—LIGATION IN CONTINUITY. Illustr. Roy. 8vo. 30s. net.

BARWELL (Richard, F.R.C.S.).—THE CAUSES AND TREATMENT OF LATERAL CURVATURE OF THE SPINE. Cr. 8vo. 5s.
—— ON ANEURISM, ESPECIALLY OF THE THORAX AND ROOT OF THE NECK. 3s. 6d.

MEDICINE. 25

BASTIAN (H. Charlton).—On Paralysis from Brain Disease in its Common Forms. Cr. 8vo. 10s. 6d.

BICKERTON (T. H.).—On Colour Blindness. Cr. 8vo.

BRAIN: A Journal of Neurology. Edited for the Neurological Society of London, by A. De Watteville, Quarterly. 8vo. 3s. 6d. (Part I. in Jan. 1878.) Vols. I. to XII. 8vo. 15s. each. [Cloth covers for binding, 1s. each.]

BRUNTON (Dr. T. Lauder).—A Text-Book of Pharmacology, Therapeutics, and Materia Medica. 3rd Edit. Med. 8vo. 21s.—Or in 2 vols. 22s. 6d.—Supplement, 1s.

—— Disorders of Digestion: their Consequences and Treatment. 8vo. 10s. 6d.

—— Pharmacology and Therapeutics; or, Medicine Past and Present. Cr. 8vo. 6s.

—— Tables of Materia Medica: A Companion to the Materia Medica Museum. 8vo. 5s.

—— An Introduction to Modern Therapeutics. Croonian Lectures on the Relationship between Chemical Structure and Physiological Action. 8vo. 3s. 6d. net.

BUCKNILL (Dr.).—The Care of the Insane. Cr. 8vo. 3s. 6d.

CARTER (R. Brudenell, F.C.S.).—A Practical Treatise on Diseases of the Eye. 8vo. 16s.

—— Eyesight, Good and Bad. Cr. 8vo. 6s.

—— Modern Operations for Cataract. 8vo. 6s.

CHRISTIE (J.).—Cholera Epidemics in East Africa. 8vo. 15s.

COWELL (George).—Lectures on Cataract: Its Causes, Varieties, and Treatment. Cr. 8vo. 4s. 6d.

ECCLES (A. S.).—Sciatica. 8vo. 3s. 6d.

FLÜCKIGER (F. A.) and HANBURY (D.).—Pharmacographia. A History of the Principal Drugs of Vegetable Origin met with in Great Britain and India. 8vo. 21s.

FOTHERGILL (Dr. J. Milner).—The Practitioner's Handbook of Treatment; or, The Principles of Therapeutics. 8vo. 16s.

—— The Antagonism of Therapeutic Agents, and what it Teaches. Cr. 8vo. 6s.

—— Food for the Invalid, the Convalescent, the Dyspeptic, and the Gouty. 2nd Edit. Cr. 8vo. 3s. 6d.

FOX (Dr. Wilson).— On the Artificial Production of Tubercle in the Lower Animals. With Plates. 4to. 5s. 6d.

—— On the Treatment of Hyperpyrexia, as Illustrated in Acute Articular Rheumatism by means of the External Application of Cold. 8vo. 2s. 6d.

GRIFFITHS (W. H.).—Lessons on Prescriptions and the Art of Prescribing. New Edition. Pott 8vo. 3s. 6d.

HAMILTON (Prof. D. J.).—On the Pathology of Bronchitis, Catarrhal Pneumonia, Tubercle, and Allied Lesions of the Human Lung. 8vo. 8s. 6d.

—— A Text-Book of Pathology, Systematic and Practical. Illustrated. Vol. I. 8vo. 25s.

HANBURY (Daniel).— Science Papers, chiefly Pharmacological and Botanical. Med. 8vo. 14s.

KLEIN (Dr. E.).—Micro-Organisms and Disease. An Introduction into the Study of Specific Micro-Organisms. Cr. 8vo. 6s.

—— The Bacteria in Asiatic Cholera. Cr. 8vo. 5s.

LEPROSY INVESTIGATION COMMITTEE, JOURNAL OF THE. Edited by P. S. Abraham, M.A. Nos. 2—4. 2s. 6d. each net.

LINDSAY (Dr. J. A.).— The Climatic Treatment of Consumption. Cr. 8vo. 5s.

MACLAGAN (Dr. T.).—The Germ Theory. 8vo. 10s. 6d.

MACLEAN (Surgeon-General W. C.).—Diseases of Tropical Climates. Cr. 8vo. 10s. 6d.

MACNAMARA (C.).—A History of Asiatic Cholera. Cr. 8vo. 10s. 6d.

—— Asiatic Cholera, History up to July 15, 1892: Causes and Treatment. 8vo. 2s. 6d.

MERCIER (Dr. C.).—The Nervous System and the Mind. 8vo. 12s. 6d.

PIFFARD (H. G.).—An Elementary Treatise on Diseases of the Skin. 8vo. 16s.

PRACTITIONER, THE: A Monthly Journal of Therapeutics and Public Health. Edited by T. Lauder Brunton, F.R.S., etc.; Donald MacAlister, M.A., M.D., and J. Mitchell Bruce, M.D. 1s. 6d. monthly. Vols. I.—XLIX. Half-yearly vols. 10s. 6d. each. [Cloth covers for binding, 1s. each.]

REYNOLDS (J. R.).—A System of Medicine. Edited by J. Russell Reynolds, M.D., In 5 vols. Vols. I.—III. and V. 8vo. 25s. each.—Vol. IV. 21s.

RICHARDSON (Dr. B. W.).—Diseases of Modern Life. Cr. 8vo.

—— The Field of Disease. A Book of Preventive Medicine. 8vo. 25s.

SEATON (Dr. Edward C.).—A Handbook of Vaccination. Ext. fcp. 8vo. 8s. 6d.

SEILER (Dr. Carl).—Micro-Photographs in Histology, Normal and Pathological. 4to. 31s. 6d.

SIBSON (Dr. Francis).—Collected Works Edited by W. M. Ord, M.D. Illustrated. 4 vols. 8vo. 3l. 3s.

SPENDER (J. Kent).—Therapeutic Means for the Relief of Pain. 8vo. 8s. 6d.

SURGERY (THE INTERNATIONAL ENCYCLOPAEDIA OF). A Systematic Treatise on the Theory and Practice of Surgery by Authors of various Nations. Edited by John Ashhurst, jun., M.D. 6 vols. Roy. 8vo. 31s. 6d. each.

THORNE (Dr. Thorne).—Diphtheria. Cr. 8vo. 8s. 6d.

WHITE (Dr. W. Hale).—A Text-Book of General Therapeutics. Cr. 8vo 8s. 6d.

MEDICINE—*continued*.

ZIEGLER (Ernst).—A TEXT-BOOK OF PATHOLOGICAL ANATOMY AND PATHOGENESIS. Translated and Edited by DONALD MACALISTER, M.A., M.D. Illustrated. 8vo.—Part I. GENERAL PATHOLOGICAL ANATOMY. 12s. 6d.—Part II. SPECIAL PATHOLOGICAL ANATOMY. Sections I.—VIII. and IX.—XII. 8vo. 12s. 6d. each.

METALLURGY.
(*See also* CHEMISTRY.)

HIORNS (Arthur H.).—A TEXT-BOOK OF ELEMENTARY METALLURGY. Gl. 8vo. 4s.
—— PRACTICAL METALLURGY AND ASSAYING. Illustrated. 2nd Edit. Globe 8vo. 6s.
—— IRON AND STEEL MANUFACTURE. Illustrated. Globe 8vo. 3s. 6d.
—— MIXED METALS OR METALLIC ALLOYS Globe 8vo. 6s.
—— METAL COLOURING AND BRONZING. Globe 8vo. 5s.

PHILLIPS (J. A.).—A TREATISE ON ORE DEPOSITS. Illustrated. Med. 8vo. 25s.

METAPHYSICS.
(*See under* PHILOSOPHY, p. 27.)

MILITARY ART AND HISTORY.

ACLAND (Sir H. W.). (*See* MEDICINE.)
AITKEN (Sir W.).—THE GROWTH OF THE RECRUIT AND YOUNG SOLDIER. Cr. 8vo. 8s. 6d.
CUNYNGHAME (Gen. Sir A. T.).—MY COMMAND IN SOUTH AFRICA, 1874—78. 8vo. 12s. 6d.
DILKE (Sir C) and **WILKINSON** (S.).—IMPERIAL DEFENCE. Cr. 8vo. 3s. 6d.
HOZIER (Lieut.-Col. H. M.).—THE SEVEN WEEKS' WAR. 3rd Edit. Cr. 8vo. 6s.
—— THE INVASIONS OF ENGLAND. 2 vols. 8vo. 28s.
MARTEL (Chas.).—MILITARY ITALY. With Map. 8vo. 12s. 6d.
MAURICE (Lt.-Col.).—WAR. 8vo. 5s. net.
—— THE NATIONAL DEFENCES. Cr. 8vo.
MERCUR (Prof. J.).—ELEMENTS OF THE ART OF WAR. 8vo. 17s.
SCRATCHLEY — KINLOCH COOKE. — AUSTRALIAN DEFENCES AND NEW GUINEA. Compiled from the Papers of the late Major-General Sir PETER SCRATCHLEY, R.E., by C. KINLOCH COOKE. 8vo. 14s.
THROUGH THE RANKS TO A COMMISSION. New Edition. Cr. 8vo. 2s. 6d.
WILKINSON (S.). — THE BRAIN OF AN ARMY. A Popular Account of the German General Staff. Cr. 8vo. 2s. 6d.
WINGATE (Major F. R.).—MAHDIISM AND THE EGYPTIAN SUDAN. An Account of the Rise and Progress of Mahdiism, and of Subsequent Events in the Sudan to the Present Time. With 17 Maps. 8vo. 30s. net.
WOLSELEY (General Viscount).—THE SOLDIER'S POCKET-BOOK FOR FIELD SERVICE. 5th Edit. 16mo, roan. 5s.
—— FIELD POCKET-BOOK FOR THE AUXILIARY FORCES. 16mo. 1s. 6d.

MINERALOGY. (*See* GEOLOGY.)

MISCELLANEOUS WORKS.
(*See under* LITERATURE, p. 20.)

MUSIC.

CHAPPELL (W.).—OLD ENGLISH POPULAR MUSIC. 2 vols. 4to. 42s. net.
FAY (Amy).—MUSIC-STUDY IN GERMANY Preface by Sir GEO. GROVE. Cr. 8vo. 4s. 6d
GROVE (Sir George).—A DICTIONARY OF MUSIC AND MUSICIANS, A.D. 1450—1889. Edited by Sir GEORGE GROVE, D.C.L. In 4 vols. 8vo. 21s. each. With Illustrations in Music Type and Woodcut.—Also published in Parts. Parts I.—XIV., XIX.—XXII 3s. 6d. each; XV. XVI. 7s.; XVII. XVIII. 7s.; XXIII.—XXV., Appendix. Edited by J. A. FULLER MAITLAND, M.A. 9s. [Cloth cases for binding the volumes, 1s. each.]
—— A COMPLETE INDEX TO THE ABOVE. By Mrs. E. WODEHOUSE. 8vo. 7s. 6d.
HULLAH (John).—MUSIC IN THE HOUSE. 4th Edit. Cr. 8vo. 2s. 6d.
TAYLOR (Franklin).—A PRIMER OF PIANOFORTE PLAYING. Pott 8vo. 1s.
TAYLOR (Sedley).—SOUND AND MUSIC. 2nd Edit. Ext. cr. 8vo. 8s. 6d.
—— A SYSTEM OF SIGHT-SINGING FROM THE ESTABLISHED MUSICAL NOTATION. 8vo. 5s. net.
—— RECORD OF THE CAMBRIDGE CENTENARY OF W. A. MOZART. Cr. 8vo. 2s. 6d. net.

NATURAL HISTORY.

ATKINSON (J. C.). (*See* ANTIQUITIES, p. 1.)
BAKER (Sir Samuel W.). (*See* SPORT, p. 32.)
BLANFORD (W. T.).—GEOLOGY AND ZOOLOGY OF ABYSSINIA. 8vo. 21s.
FOWLER (W. W.).—TALES OF THE BIRDS. Illustrated. Cr. 8vo. 3s. 6d.
—— A YEAR WITH THE BIRDS. Illustrated. Cr. 8vo. 3s. 6d.
KINGSLEY (Charles).—MADAM HOW AND LADY WHY; or, First Lessons in Earth-Lore for Children. Cr. 8vo. 3s. 6d.
—— GLAUCUS; or, The Wonders of the Sea-Shore. With Coloured Illustrations. Cr. 8vo. 3s. 6d.—*Presentation Edition.* Cr. 8vo, extra cloth. 7s. 6d.
KLEIN (E.).—ETIOLOGY AND PATHOLOGY OF GROUSE DISEASE. 8vo. 7s. net.
WALLACE (Alfred Russel).—THE MALAY ARCHIPELAGO: The Land of the Orang Utang and the Bird of Paradise. Maps and Illustrations. Ext. cr. 8vo. 6s. (*See also* BIOLOGY.)
WATERTON (Charles).— WANDERINGS IN SOUTH AMERICA, THE NORTH-WEST OF THE UNITED STATES, AND THE ANTILLES. Edited by Rev. J. G. WOOD. Illustrated. Cr. 8vo. 6s.—People's Edition. 4to. 6d.
WHITE (Gilbert).—NATURAL HISTORY AND ANTIQUITIES OF SELBORNE. Ed. by FRANK BUCKLAND. With a Chapter on Antiquities by the EARL OF SELBORNE. Cr. 8vo. 6s.

NATURAL PHILOSOPHY. (See Physics.)

NAVAL SCIENCE.

KELVIN (Lord).—Popular Lectures and Addresses.—Vol. III. Navigation. Cr. 8vo. 7s. 6d.

ROBINSON (Rev. J. L.).—Marine Surveying, An Elementary Treatise on. For Younger Naval Officers. Illustrated. Cr. 8vo. 7s. 6d

SHORTLAND (Admiral).—Nautical Surveying. 8vo. 21s.

NOVELS. (See Prose Fiction, p. 18.)

NURSING.
(See under Domestic Economy, p. 8.)

OPTICS (or LIGHT). (See Physics, p. 29)

PAINTING. (See Art, p. 2.)

PATHOLOGY. (See Medicine, p. 24.)

PERIODICALS.

AMERICAN JOURNAL OF PHILOLOGY, THE. (See Philology.)
BRAIN. (See Medicine.)
CANTERBURY DIOCESAN GAZETTE. Monthly. 8vo. 2d.
ECONOMIC JOURNAL, THE. (See Political Economy.)
ECONOMICS, THE QUARTERLY JOURNAL OF. (See Political Economy.)
NATURAL SCIENCE: A Monthly Review of Scientific Progress. 8vo. 1s. net. No. 1. March 1892.
NATURE: A Weekly Illustrated Journal of Science. Published every Thursday. Price 6d. Monthly Parts, 2s. and 2s. 6d.; Current Half-yearly vols., 15s. each. Vols. I.—XLVII. [Cases for binding vols. 1s. 6d. each.]
HELLENIC STUDIES, THE JOURNAL OF. Published Half-Yearly from 1880. 8vo. 30s.; or each Part, 15s. Vol. XIII. Part I. 15s. net.
  The Journal will be sold at a reduced price to Libraries wishing to subscribe, but official application must in each case be made to the Council. Information on this point, and upon the conditions of Membership, may be obtained on application to the Hon. Sec., Mr. George Macmillan, 29, Bedford Street, Covent Garden.
LEPROSY INVESTIGATION COMMITTEE, JOURNAL OF. (See Medicine.)
MACMILLAN'S MAGAZINE. Published Monthly. 1s.—Vols. I.-LXVII. 7s. 6d. each. [Cloth covers for binding, 1s. each.]
PHILOLOGY, THE JOURNAL OF. (See Philology.)
PHYSICAL REVIEW, THE: A Journal of Experimental and Theoretical Physics 2s. 6d. net.
PRACTITIONER, THE. (See Medicine.)
RECORD OF TECHNICAL AND SECONDARY EDUCATION. (See Education, p. 8.)

PHILOLOGY.

AMERICAN JOURNAL OF PHILOLOGY, THE. Edited by Prof. Basil L. Gildersleeve. 4s. 6d. each No. (quarterly).
CORNELL UNIVERSITY STUDIES IN CLASSICAL PHILOLOGY. Edited by I. Flagg, W. G. Hale, and B. I. Wheeler. I. The CUM-Constructions: their History and Functions. Part I. Critical. 1s. 8d. net. Part II. Constructive. By W. G. Hale. 3s. 4d. net.—II. Analogy and the Scope of its Application in Language. By B. I. Wheeler. 1s. 3d. net.
GILES (P.).—A Short Manual of Philology for Classical Students. Cr. 8vo.
JOURNAL OF SACRED AND CLASSICAL PHILOLOGY. 4 vols. 8vo. 12s. 6d. each.
JOURNAL OF PHILOLOGY. New Series. Edited by W. A. Wright, M.A., I. Bywater, M.A., and H. Jackson, M.A. 4s. 6d. each No. (half-yearly).
KELLNER (Dr. L.).- Historical Outlines in English Syntax. Globe 8vo. 6s.
MORRIS (Rev. Richard, LL.D.).—Primer of English Grammar. Pott 8vo. 1s.
—— Elementary Lessons in Historical English Grammar. Pott 8vo. 2s. 6d.
—— Historical Outlines of English Accidence. Extra fcp. 8vo. 6s.
MORRIS (R.) and BOWEN (H. C.).—English Grammar Exercises. Pott 8vo. 1s.
OLIPHANT (T. L. Kington). — The Old and Middle English. Globe 8vo. 9s.
—— The New English. 2 vols. Cr. 8vo. 21s.
PEILE (John). — A Primer of Philology. Pott 8vo. 1s.
PELLISSIER (E.).—French Roots and their Families. Globe 8vo. 6s.
TAYLOR (Isaac).—Words and Places. 9th Edit. Maps. Globe 8vo. 6s.
—— Etruscan Researches. 8vo. 14s.
—— Greeks and Goths: A Study of the Runes. 8vo. 9s.
WETHERELL (J.).—Exercises on Morris's Primer of English Grammar. 18mo. 1s.
YONGE (C. M.).—History of Christian Names. New Edit., revised. Cr. 8vo. 7s. 6d.

PHILOSOPHY.
Ethics and Metaphysics—Logic—Psychology.

Ethics and Metaphysics.

BIRKS (Thomas Rawson).—First Principles of Moral Science. Cr. 8vo. 8s. 6d.
—— Modern Utilitarianism ; or, The Systems of Paley, Bentham, and Mill Examined and Compared. Cr. 8vo. 6s. 6d.
—— Modern Physical Fatalism, and the Doctrine of Evolution. Including an Examination of Mr. Herbert Spencer's "First Principles." Cr. 8vo. 6s.
CALDERWOOD (Prof. H.).—A Handbook of Moral Philosophy. Cr. 8vo. 6s.
FISKE (John).—Outlines of Cosmic Philosophy, based on the Doctrine of Evolution. 2 vols. 8vo. 25s.

PHILOSOPHY.

PHILOSOPHY.
Ethics and Metaphysics—*continued.*

FOWLER (Rev. Thomas). — PROGRESSIVE MORALITY: An Essay in Ethics. Cr. 8vo. 5s.

HARPER (Father Thomas).—THE METAPHYSICS OF THE SCHOOL. In 5 vols.—Vols. I. and II. 8vo. 18s. each.—Vol. III. Part I. 12s.

HILL (D. J.).—GENETIC PHILOSOPHY. Cr. 8vo. 7s. net.

HUXLEY (Prof. T. H.).—EVOLUTION AND ETHICS. 8vo. 2s. net.

KANT.—KANT'S CRITICAL PHILOSOPHY FOR ENGLISH READERS. By J. P. MAHAFFY, D.D., and J. H. BERNARD, B.D. 2 vols. Cr. 8vo.—Vol. I. THE KRITIK OF PURE REASON EXPLAINED AND DEFENDED. 7s. 6d. —Vol. II. THE PROLEGOMENA. Translated, with Notes and Appendices. 6s.
— KRITIK OF JUDGMENT. Translated by J. H. BERNARD, D.D. 8vo. 10s. net.

KANT—MAX MÜLLER. — CRITIQUE OF PURE REASON BY IMMANUEL KANT. Translated by F. MAX MÜLLER. With Introduction by LUDWIG NOIRÉ. 2 vols. 8vo. 16s. each (sold separately).—Vol. I. HISTORICAL INTRODUCTION, by LUDWIG NOIRÉ, etc.—Vol. II. CRITIQUE OF PURE REASON.

KNIGHT (W. A.).—ASPECTS OF THEISM. 8vo. 8s. 6d.

MAURICE (F. D.).—MORAL AND METAPHYSICAL PHILOSOPHY. 2 vols. 8vo. 16s.

McCOSH (Rev. Dr. James).—THE METHOD OF THE DIVINE GOVERNMENT, PHYSICAL AND MORAL. 8vo. 10s. 6d.
— THE SUPERNATURAL IN RELATION TO THE NATURAL. Cr. 8vo. 7s. 6d.
— INTUITIONS OF THE MIND. 8vo. 10s. 6d.
— AN EXAMINATION OF MR. J. S. MILL'S PHILOSOPHY. 8vo. 10s. 6d.
— CHRISTIANITY AND POSITIVISM. Lectures on Natural Theology and Apologetics. Cr. 8vo. 7s. 6d.
— THE SCOTTISH PHILOSOPHY FROM HUTCHESON TO HAMILTON, BIOGRAPHICAL, EXPOSITORY, CRITICAL. Roy. 8vo. 16s.
— REALISTIC PHILOSOPHY DEFENDED IN A PHILOSOPHIC SERIES. 2 vols.—Vol. I. EXPOSITORY. Vol. II. HISTORICAL AND CRITICAL. Cr. 8vo. 14s.
— FIRST AND FUNDAMENTAL TRUTHS. Being a Treatise on Metaphysics. 8vo. 9s.
— THE PREVAILING TYPES OF PHILOSOPHY: CAN THEY LOGICALLY REACH REALITY? 8vo. 3s. 6d.
— OUR MORAL NATURE. Cr. 8vo. 2s. 6d.

MASSON (Prof. David).—RECENT BRITISH PHILOSOPHY. 3rd Edit. Cr. 8vo. 6s.

SIDGWICK (Prof. Henry).—THE METHODS OF ETHICS. 5th Edit., revised. 8vo. 14s.
— A SUPPLEMENT TO THE SECOND EDITION. Containing all the important Additions and Alterations in the Fourth Edition. 8vo. 6s.
— OUTLINES OF THE HISTORY OF ETHICS FOR ENGLISH READERS. Cr. 8vo. 3s. 6d.

THORNTON (W. T.). — OLD-FASHIONED ETHICS AND COMMON-SENSE METAPHYSICS. 8vo. 10s. 6d.

WILLIAMS (C. M.)—A REVIEW OF THE SYSTEMS OF ETHICS FOUNDED ON THE THEORY OF EVOLUTION. Cr. 8vo. 12s. net.

WINDELBAND (W.).—HISTORY OF PHILOSOPHY. Translated by J. H. TUFTS. 8vo. 21s. net.

Logic.

BOOLE (George). — THE MATHEMATICAL ANALYSIS OF LOGIC. 8vo. sewed. 5s.

CARROLL (Lewis).—THE GAME OF LOGIC. Cr. 8vo. 3s. net.

JEVONS (W. Stanley).—A PRIMER OF LOGIC. Pott 8vo. 1s.
— ELEMENTARY LESSONS IN LOGIC, DEDUCTIVE AND INDUCTIVE. Pott 8vo. 3s. 6d.
— STUDIES IN DEDUCTIVE LOGIC. 2nd Edit. Cr. 8vo. 6s.
— THE PRINCIPLES OF SCIENCE: Treatise on Logic and Scientific Method. Cr. 8vo. 12s. 6d.
— PURE LOGIC: and other Minor Works. Edited by R. ADAMSON, M.A., and HARRIET A. JEVONS. 8vo. 10s. 6d.

KEYNES (J. N.).—STUDIES AND EXERCISES IN FORMAL LOGIC. 2nd Edit. Cr. 8vo. 10s. 6d.

McCOSH (Rev. Dr.).—THE LAWS OF DISCURSIVE THOUGHT. A Text-Book of Formal Logic. Cr. 8vo. 5s.

RAY (Prof. P. K.).—A TEXT-BOOK OF DEDUCTIVE LOGIC. 4th Edit. Globe 8vo. 4s. 6d.

VENN (Rev. John).—THE LOGIC OF CHANCE. 2nd Edit. Cr. 8vo. 10s. 6d.
— SYMBOLIC LOGIC. Cr. 8vo. 10s. 6d.
— THE PRINCIPLES OF EMPIRICAL OR INDUCTIVE LOGIC. 8vo. 18s.

Psychology.

BALDWIN (Prof. J. M.).—HANDBOOK OF PSYCHOLOGY: Senses and Intellect. 8vo. 10s. 6d.
— FEELING AND WILL. 8vo. 12s. 6d.
— ELEMENTS OF PSYCHOLOGY. Cr. 8vo. 7s. 6d.

CALDERWOOD (Prof. H.). — THE RELATIONS OF MIND AND BRAIN. 3rd Ed. 8vo. 8s.

CLIFFORD (W. K.).—SEEING AND THINKING. Cr. 8vo. 3s. 6d.

HÖFFDING (Prof. H.).—OUTLINES OF PSYCHOLOGY. Translated by M. E. LOWNDES. Cr. 8vo. 6s.

JAMES (Prof. William).—THE PRINCIPLES OF PSYCHOLOGY. 2 vols. Demy 8vo. 25s. net.
— TEXT-BOOK OF PSYCHOLOGY. Cr. 8vo. 7s. net.

JARDINE (Rev. Robert).—THE ELEMENTS OF THE PSYCHOLOGY OF COGNITION. 3rd Edit. Cr. 8vo. 6s. 6d.

McCOSH (Rev. Dr.).—PSYCHOLOGY. Cr. 8vo. I. THE COGNITIVE POWERS. 6s. 6d.—II. THE MOTIVE POWERS. 6s. 6d.
— THE EMOTIONS. 8vo. 9s.

MAUDSLEY (Dr. Henry).—THE PHYSIOLOGY OF MIND. Cr. 8vo. 10s. 6d.
— THE PATHOLOGY OF MIND. 8vo. 18s.
— BODY AND MIND. Cr. 8vo. 6s. 6d.

MURPHY (J. J.).—HABIT AND INTELLIGENCE. 2nd Edit. Illustrated. 8vo. 16s.

PHOTOGRAPHY.

MELDOLA (Prof. R.).—THE CHEMISTRY OF PHOTOGRAPHY. Cr. 8vo. 6s.

PHYSICS.

PHYSICS OR NATURAL PHILOSOPHY.

General—Electricity and Magnetism—Heat, Light, and Sound.

General.

ANDREWS (Dr. Thomas): THE SCIENTIFIC PAPERS OF THE LATE. With a Memoir by Profs. TAIT and CHRUM BROWN. 8vo. 18s.

BARKER (G. F.).—PHYSICS: ADVANCED COURSE. 8vo. 21s.

DANIELL (A.)—A TEXT-BOOK OF THE PRINCIPLES OF PHYSICS. Illustrated. 2nd Edit. Med. 8vo. 21s.

EVERETT (Prof. J. D.).—THE C. G. S. SYSTEM OF UNITS, WITH TABLES OF PHYSICAL CONSTANTS. New Edit. Globe 8vo. 5s.

FESSENDEN (C.).—ELEMENTS OF PHYSICS. Fcp. 8vo. 3s.

FISHER (Rev. Osmond).—PHYSICS OF THE EARTH'S CRUST. 2nd Edit. 8vo. 12s.

GORDON (H.)—PRACTICAL SCIENCE. Part I. Pott 8vo. 1s.

GUILLEMIN (Amédée).—THE FORCES OF NATURE. A Popular Introduction to the Study of Physical Phenomena. 455 Woodcuts. Roy. 8vo. 21s.

KELVIN (Lord).—POPULAR LECTURES AND ADDRESSES.—Vol. I. CONSTITUTION OF MATTER. Cr. 8vo. 7s. 6d.

KEMPE (A. B.).—HOW TO DRAW A STRAIGHT LINE. Cr. 8vo. 1s. 6d.

LOEWY (B.).—QUESTIONS AND EXAMPLES IN EXPERIMENTAL PHYSICS, SOUND, LIGHT, HEAT, ELECTRICITY, AND MAGNETISM. Fcp. 8vo. 2s.
—— A GRADUATED COURSE OF NATURAL SCIENCE. Part I. Gl. 8vo. 2s.—Part II. 2s.6d.

MOLLOY (Rev. G.).—GLEANINGS IN SCIENCE: A Series of Popular Lectures on Scientific Subjects. 8vo. 7s. 6d.

PHYSICAL REVIEW. Bi-Monthly. 8vo. 2s. 6d. net.

STEWART (Prof. Balfour).—A PRIMER OF PHYSICS. Illustrated. Pott 8vo. 1s.
—— LESSONS IN ELEMENTARY PHYSICS. Illustrated. Fcp. 8vo. 4s. 6d.
—— QUESTIONS. By T. H. CORE. Pott 8vo. 2s.

STEWART (Prof. Balfour) and GEE (W. W. Haldane).—LESSONS IN ELEMENTARY PRACTICAL PHYSICS. Illustrated.—GENERAL PHYSICAL PROCESSES. Cr. 8vo. 6s.

TAIT (Prof. P. G.).—LECTURES ON SOME RECENT ADVANCES IN PHYSICAL SCIENCE. 3rd Edit. Cr. 8vo. 9s.

Electricity and Magnetism.

CUMMING (Linnæus).—AN INTRODUCTION TO ELECTRICITY. Cr. 8vo. 8s. 6d.

DAY (R. E.).—ELECTRIC LIGHT ARITHMETIC. Pott 8vo. 2s.

GRAY (Prof. Andrew).—THE THEORY AND PRACTICE OF ABSOLUTE MEASUREMENTS IN ELECTRICITY AND MAGNETISM. 2 vols. Cr. 8vo. Vol. I. 12s. 6d.—Vol. II. 2 parts. 25s.
—— ABSOLUTE MEASUREMENTS IN ELECTRICITY AND MAGNETISM. Fcp. 8vo. 5s. 6d.

GUILLEMIN (A.).—ELECTRICITY AND MAGNETISM. A Popular Treatise. Translated and Edited by Prof. SILVANUS P. THOMPSON. Super Roy. 8vo. 31s. 6d.

HEAVISIDE (O.) — ELECTRICAL PAPERS. 2 vols. 8vo. 30s. net.

JACKSON (D. C.).—TEXT-BOOK ON ELECTRO-MAGNETISM Vol. I. Cr. 8vo. 9s. net.

KELVIN (Lord). — PAPERS ON ELECTROSTATICS AND MAGNETISM. 8vo. 18s.

LODGE (Prof. Oliver).—MODERN VIEWS OF ELECTRICITY. Illust. Cr. 8vo. 6s. 6d.

MENDENHALL (T. C.)—A CENTURY OF ELECTRICITY. Cr. 8vo. 4s. 6d.

STEWART (Prof. Balfour) and GEE (W. W. Haldane).—LESSONS IN ELEMENTARY PRACTICAL PHYSICS. Cr. 8vo. Illustrated.—ELECTRICITY AND MAGNETISM. 7s. 6d.
—— PRACTICAL PHYSICS FOR SCHOOLS. Gl. 8vo.—ELECTRICITY AND MAGNETISM. 2s.6d.

THOMPSON (Prof. Silvanus P.). — ELEMENTARY LESSONS IN ELECTRICITY AND MAGNETISM. Illustrated. Fcp. 8vo. 4s. 6d.

TURNER (H. H.).—EXAMPLES ON HEAT AND ELECTRICITY. Cr. 8vo. 2s. 6d.

Heat, Light, and Sound.

AIRY (Sir G. B.).—ON SOUND AND ATMOSPHERIC VIBRATIONS. Cr. 8vo. 9s.

CARNOT--THURSTON.--REFLECTIONS ON THE MOTIVE POWER OF HEAT, AND ON MACHINES FITTED TO DEVELOP THAT POWER. From the French of N. L. S. CARNOT. Edited by R. H. THURSTON, LL.D. Cr. 8vo. 7s. 6d.

JOHNSON (Amy).—SUNSHINE. Illustrated. Cr. 8vo. 6s.

JONES (Prof. D. E.).—HEAT, LIGHT, AND SOUND. Globe 8vo. 2s. 6d.
—— LESSONS IN HEAT AND LIGHT. Globe 8vo. 3s. 6d.

MAYER (Prof. A. M.).—SOUND. A Series of Simple Experiments. Illustr. Cr. 8vo. 3s.6d.

MAYER (Prof. A. M.) and BARNARD (C.)— LIGHT. A Series of Simple Experiments. Illustrated. Cr. 8vo. 2s. 6d.

PARKINSON (S.).—A TREATISE ON OPTICS. 4th Edit., revised. Cr. 8vo. 10s. 6d.

PEABODY (Prof. C. H.).—THERMODYNAMICS OF THE STEAM ENGINE AND OTHER HEAT-ENGINES. 8vo. 21s.

PERRY (Prof. J.).—STEAM: An Elementary Treatise. Pott 8vo. 4s. 6d.

PRESTON (T.).—THE THEORY OF LIGHT. Illustrated. 8vo. 15s. net.
—— THE THEORY OF HEAT. 8vo.

RAYLEIGH (Lord).—THEORY OF SOUND. 8vo. Vol. I. 12s. 6d.—Vol. II. 12s. 6d.

SHANN (G.).—AN ELEMENTARY TREATISE ON HEAT IN RELATION TO STEAM AND THE STEAM-ENGINE. Illustr. Cr. 8vo. 4s. 6d.

SPOTTISWOODE (W.).—POLARISATION OF LIGHT. Illustrated. Cr. 8vo. 3s. 6d.

PHYSICS—POLITICAL ECONOMY.

PHYSICS—*continued.*

STEWART (Prof. Balfour) and GEE (W. W. Haldane).—LESSONS IN ELEMENTARY PRACTICAL PHYSICS. Cr. 8vo. Illustrated.—OPTICS, HEAT, AND SOUND.
—— PRACTICAL PHYSICS FOR SCHOOLS. Gl. 8vo.—HEAT, LIGHT, AND SOUND.

STOKES (Sir George G.).—ON LIGHT. The Burnett Lectures. Cr. 8vo. 7s. 6d.

STONE (W. H.).—ELEMENTARY LESSONS ON SOUND. Illustrated. Fcp. 8vo. 3s. 6d.

TAIT (Prof. P. G.).—HEAT. With Illustrations. Cr. 8vo. 6s.

TAYLOR (Sedley).—SOUND AND MUSIC. 2nd Edit. Ext. cr. 8vo. 8s. 6d.

TURNER (H. H.). (*See* ELECTRICITY.)

WRIGHT (Lewis).—LIGHT. A Course of Experimental Optics. Illust. Cr. 8vo. 7s. 6d.

PHYSIOGRAPHY and METEOROLOGY.

ARATUS.—THE SKIES AND WEATHER FORECASTS OF ARATUS. Translated by E. POSTE, M.A. Cr. 8vo. 3s. 6d.

BLANFORD (H. F.).—THE RUDIMENTS OF PHYSICAL GEOGRAPHY FOR THE USE OF INDIAN SCHOOLS. Illustr. Cr. 8vo. 2s. 6d.
—— A PRACTICAL GUIDE TO THE CLIMATES AND WEATHER OF INDIA, CEYLON AND BURMAH, AND THE STORMS OF INDIAN SEAS. 8vo. 12s 6d.

FERREL (Prof. W.).—A POPULAR TREATISE ON THE WINDS. 2nd Ed. 8vo. 17s. net.

FISHER (Rev. Osmond).—PHYSICS OF THE EARTH'S CRUST. 2nd Edit. 8vo. 12s.

GEIKIE (Sir Archibald).—A PRIMER OF PHYSICAL GEOGRAPHY. Illustr. Pott 8vo. 1s.
—— ELEMENTARY LESSONS IN PHYSICAL GEOGRAPHY. Illustrated. Fcp. 8vo. 4s. 6d.
—— QUESTIONS ON THE SAME. 1s. 6d.

HUXLEY (Prof. T. H.).—PHYSIOGRAPHY. Illustrated. Cr. 8vo. 6s.

LOCKYER (J. Norman).—OUTLINES OF PHYSIOGRAPHY: THE MOVEMENTS OF THE EARTH. Illustrated. Cr. 8vo, swd. 1s. 6d.

MELDOLA (Prof. R.) and WHITE (Wm.).—REPORT ON THE EAST ANGLIAN EARTHQUAKE OF APRIL 22ND, 1884. 8vo. 3s. 6d.

PHYSIOLOGY.

FEARNLEY (W.).—A MANUAL OF ELEMENTARY PRACTICAL HISTOLOGY. Cr. 8vo. 7s. 6d.

FOSTER (Prof. Michael).—A TEXT-BOOK OF PHYSIOLOGY. Illustrated. 6th Edit. 8vo.—Part I. Book I. BLOOD: THE TISSUES OF MOVEMENT, THE VASCULAR MECHANISM. 10s. 6d.—Part II. Book II. THE TISSUES OF CHEMICAL ACTION, WITH THEIR RESPECTIVE MECHANISMS: NUTRITION. 10s. 6d.—Part III. Book III. THE CENTRAL NERVOUS SYSTEM. 7s. 6d.—Part IV. Book III. THE SENSES, AND SOME SPECIAL MUSCULAR MECHANISMS.—BOOK IV. THE TISSUES AND MECHANISMS OF REPRODUCTION. 10s. 6d. —Appendix, by A. S. LEA. 7s. 6d.
—— A PRIMER OF PHYSIOLOGY. Pott 8vo. 1s.

FOSTER (Prof. M.) and LANGLEY (J. N.). —A COURSE OF ELEMENTARY PRACTICAL PHYSIOLOGY AND HISTOLOGY. Cr. 8vo. 7s. 6d.

GAMGEE (Arthur).—A TEXT-BOOK OF THE PHYSIOLOGICAL CHEMISTRY OF THE ANIMAL BODY. Vol. I. 8vo. 18s. Vol. II. 18s.

HUMPHRY (Prof. Sir G. M.).—THE HUMAN FOOT AND THE HUMAN HAND. Illustrated. Fcp. 8vo. 4s. 6d.

HUXLEY (Prof. Thos. H.).—LESSONS IN ELEMENTARY PHYSIOLOGY. Fcp. 8vo. 4s. 6d.
—— QUESTIONS. By T. ALCOCK. Pott 8vo. 1s. 6d.

MIVART (St. George).—LESSONS IN ELEMENTARY ANATOMY. Fcp. 8vo. 6s. 6d.

PETTIGREW (J. Bell).—THE PHYSIOLOGY OF THE CIRCULATION IN PLANTS IN THE LOWER ANIMALS AND IN MAN. 8vo. 12s.

SEILER (Dr. Carl).—MICRO-PHOTOGRAPHS IN HISTOLOGY, NORMAL AND PATHOLOGICAL. 4to. 31s. 6d.

POETRY. (*See under* LITERATURE, p. 14.)

POLITICAL ECONOMY.

BASTABLE (Prof. C. F.).—PUBLIC FINANCE. 8vo. 12s. 6d. net.

BÖHM-BAWERK (Prof.).—CAPITAL AND INTEREST. Trans. by W. SMART. 8vo. 12s.net.
—— THE POSITIVE THEORY OF CAPITAL. By the same Translator. 8vo. 12s. net.

BOISSEVAIN (G. M.).—THE MONETARY QUESTION. 8vo, sewed. 3s. net.

BONAR (James).—MALTHUS AND HIS WORK. 8vo. 12s. 6d.

CAIRNES (J. E.).—SOME LEADING PRINCIPLES OF POLITICAL ECONOMY NEWLY EXPOUNDED. 8vo. 14s.
—— THE CHARACTER AND LOGICAL METHOD OF POLITICAL ECONOMY. Cr. 8vo. 6s.

CANTILLON. —ESSAI SUR LE COMMERCE. 12mo. 7s. net.

CLARE (G.).—A B C OF THE FOREIGN EXCHANGES. Cr. 8vo. 3s. net.

CLARKE (C. B.). — SPECULATIONS FROM POLITICAL ECONOMY. Cr. 8vo. 3s. 6d.

COMMONS (J. R.)—DISTRIBUTION OF WEALTH. Cr. 8vo. 7s. net.

COSSA (L.).—INTRODUCTION TO THE STUDY OF POLITICAL ECONOMY. Translated by L. DYER. Cr. 8vo. 8s. 6d. net.

DICTIONARY OF POLITICAL ECONOMY, A. By various Writers. Ed. R. H. I. PALGRAVE. 3s.6d. net. (Part I. July, 1891.)

ECONOMIC JOURNAL, THE. — THE JOURNAL OF THE BRITISH ECONOMIC ASSOCIATION. Edit. by Prof. F. Y. EDGEWORTH. Published Quarterly. 8vo. 5s. (Part I. April, 1891.) Vol. I. 21s. [Cloth Covers for binding Volumes, 1s. 6d. each.]

ECONOMICS: THE QUARTERLY JOURNAL OF. Vol. II. Parts II. III. IV. 2s. 6d. each. —Vol. III. 4 parts. 2s. 6d. each.—Vol. IV. 4 parts. 2s. 6d. each.—Vol. V. 4 parts. 2s. 6d. each.—Vol. VI. 4 parts. 2s. 6d. each.—Vol. VII 4 parts. 2s. 6d. each.

FAWCETT (Henry).—MANUAL OF POLITICAL ECONOMY. 7th Edit. Cr. 8vo. 12s.
—— AN EXPLANATORY DIGEST OF THE ABOVE. By C. A. WATERS. Cr. 8vo. 2s. 6d.
—— FREE TRADE AND PROTECTION. 6th Edit. Cr. 8vo. 3s. 6d.

POLITICAL ECONOMY—POLITICS.

FAWCETT (Mrs. H.).—POLITICAL ECONOMY FOR BEGINNERS, WITH QUESTIONS. 7th Edit. Pott 8vo. 2s. 6d.

FIRST LESSONS IN BUSINESS MATTERS. By A BANKER'S DAUGHTER. 2nd Edit. Pott 8vo. 1s.

GILMAN (N. P.).—PROFIT-SHARING BETWEEN EMPLOYER AND EMPLOYEE. Cr. 8vo. 7s. 6d.

GOSCHEN (Rt. Hon. George J.).—REPORTS AND SPEECHES ON LOCAL TAXATION. 8vo. 5s.

GUIDE TO THE UNPROTECTED: IN EVERY-DAY MATTERS RELATING TO PROPERTY AND INCOME. Ext. fcp. 8vo. 3s. 6d.

GUNTON (George).—WEALTH AND PROGRESS. Cr. 8vo. 6s.

HORTON (Hon. S. Dana).—THE SILVER POUND AND ENGLAND'S MONETARY POLICY SINCE THE RESTORATION. 8vo. 14s.

HOWELL (George).—THE CONFLICTS OF CAPITAL AND LABOUR. Cr. 8vo. 7s. 6d.

JEVONS (W. Stanley).—A PRIMER OF POLITICAL ECONOMY. Pott 8vo. 1s.
—— THE THEORY OF POLITICAL ECONOMY. 3rd Edit. 8vo. 10s. 6d.
—— INVESTIGATIONS IN CURRENCY AND FINANCE. Edit. by H. S. FOXWELL. 8vo. 21s.

KEYNES (J. N.).—THE SCOPE AND METHOD OF POLITICAL ECONOMY. Cr. 8vo. 7s. net.

MARSHALL (Prof. Alfred).—PRINCIPLES OF ECONOMICS. 2 vols. 8vo. Vol. I. 12s. 6d. net.
—— ELEMENTS OF ECONOMICS OF INDUSTRY. Crown 8vo. 3s. 6d.

MARTIN (Frederick).—THE HISTORY OF LLOYD'S, AND OF MARINE INSURANCE IN GREAT BRITAIN. 8vo. 14s.

PRICE (L. L. F. R.).—INDUSTRIAL PEACE: ITS ADVANTAGES, METHODS, AND DIFFICULTIES. Med. 8vo. 6s.

SIDGWICK (Prof. Henry).—THE PRINCIPLES OF POLITICAL ECONOMY. 2nd Edit. 8vo. 16s.

SMART (W.).—AN INTRODUCTION TO THE THEORY OF VALUE. Cr. 8vo. 3s. net.

THOMPSON (H. M.).—THE THEORY OF WAGES AND ITS APPLICATION TO THE EIGHT HOURS QUESTION. Cr. 8vo. 3s. 6d.

WALKER (Francis A.).—FIRST LESSONS IN POLITICAL ECONOMY. Cr. 8vo. 5s.
—— A BRIEF TEXT-BOOK OF POLITICAL ECONOMY. Cr. 8vo. 6s. 6d.
—— POLITICAL ECONOMY. 8vo. 12s. 6d.
—— THE WAGES QUESTION. Ext. cr. 8vo. 8s. 6d. net.
—— MONEY. New Edit. Ext.cr.8vo. 8s.6d.net.
—— MONEY IN ITS RELATION TO TRADE AND INDUSTRY. Cr. 8vo. 7s. 6d.
—— LAND AND ITS RENT. Fcp. 8vo. 3s. 6d.

WALLACE (A. R.).—BAD TIMES: An Essay. Cr. 8vo. 2s. 6d.

WICKSTEED (Ph. H.).—THE ALPHABET OF ECONOMIC SCIENCE.—I. ELEMENTS OF THE THEORY OF VALUE OR WORTH. Gl.8vo. 2s.6d.

WIESER (F. von).—NATURAL VALUE. Edit. by W. SMART, M.A. 8vo. 10s. net.

POLITICS.
(*See also* HISTORY, p. 10.)

ADAMS (Sir F. O.) and **CUNNINGHAM** (C.)—THE SWISS CONFEDERATION. 8vo. 14s.

BAKER (Sir Samuel W.).—THE EGYPTIAN QUESTION. 8vo, sewed. 2s.

BATH (Marquis of).—OBSERVATIONS ON BULGARIAN AFFAIRS. Cr. 8vo. 3s. 6d.

BRIGHT (John).—SPEECHES ON QUESTIONS OF PUBLIC POLICY. Edit. by J. E. THOROLD ROGERS. With Portrait. 2 vols. 8vo. 25s.
—*Popular Edition.* Ext. fcp. 8vo. 3s. 6d.
—— PUBLIC ADDRESSES. Edited by J. E. T. ROGERS. 8vo. 14s.

BRYCE (Jas., M.P.).—THE AMERICAN COMMONWEALTH. 2 vols. New Edit. Ext. cr. 8vo. Vol. I. 12s. 6d.

BUCKLAND (Anna).—OUR NATIONAL INSTITUTIONS. Pott 8vo. 1s.

BURKE (Edmund).—LETTERS, TRACTS, AND SPEECHES ON IRISH AFFAIRS. Edited by MATTHEW ARNOLD, with Preface. Cr.8vo. 6s.
—— REFLECTIONS ON THE FRENCH REVOLUTION. Ed. by F. G. SELBY. Globe 8vo. 5s.

CAIRNES (J. E.).—POLITICAL ESSAYS. 8vo. 10s. 6d.
—— THE SLAVE POWER. 8vo. 10s. 6d.

COBDEN (Richard).—SPEECHES ON QUESTIONS OF PUBLIC POLICY. Ed. by J. BRIGHT and J. E. THOROLD ROGERS. Gl. 8vo. 3s. 6d.

DICEY (Prof. A. V.).—LETTERS ON UNIONIST DELUSIONS. Cr. 8vo. 2s. 6d.

DILKE (Rt. Hon. Sir Charles W.).—GREATER BRITAIN. 9th Edit. Cr. 8vo. 6s.
—— PROBLEMS OF GREATER BRITAIN. Maps. 3rd Edit. Ext. cr. 8vo. 12s. 6d.

DONISTHORPE (Wordsworth).—INDIVIDUALISM: A System of Politics. 8vo. 14s.

DUFF (Rt. Hon. Sir M. E. Grant).—MISCELLANIES, POLITICAL AND LITERARY. 8vo. 10s.6d.

ENGLISH CITIZEN, THE.—His Rights and Responsibilities. Ed. by HENRY CRAIK, C.B. New Edit. Monthly Volumes from Oct. 1892. Cr. 8vo. 2s. 6d. each.
CENTRAL GOVERNMENT. By H. D. TRAILL.
THE ELECTORATE AND THE LEGISLATURE. By SPENCER WALPOLE.
THE LAND LAWS. By Sir F. POLLOCK, Bart. 2nd Edit.
THE PUNISHMENT AND PREVENTION OF CRIME. By Col. Sir EDMUND DU CANE.
LOCAL GOVERNMENT. By M. D. CHALMERS.
COLONIES AND DEPENDENCIES: Part I. INDIA. By J. S. COTTON, M.A.—II. THE COLONIES. By E. J. PAYNE.
THE STATE IN ITS RELATION TO EDUCATION. By HENRY CRAIK, C.B.
THE STATE AND THE CHURCH. By Hon. ARTHUR ELLIOTT, M.P.
THE STATE IN ITS RELATION TO TRADE. By Sir T. H. FARRER, Bart.
THE POOR LAW. By the Rev. T. W. FOWLE.
THE STATE IN RELATION TO LABOUR. By W. STANLEY JEVONS.
JUSTICE AND POLICE. By F. W. MAITLAND.
THE NATIONAL DEFENCES. By Colonel MAURICE, R.A. [*In the Press.*
FOREIGN RELATIONS. By S. WALPOLE.
THE NATIONAL BUDGET; NATIONAL DEBT; TAXES AND RATES. By A. J. WILSON.

POLITICS—TECHNOLOGY.

POLITICS—*continued.*

FAWCETT (Henry).—SPEECHES ON SOME CURRENT POLITICAL QUESTIONS. 8vo. 10s. 6d.
—— FREE TRADE AND PROTECTION. 6th Edit. Cr. 8vo. 3s. 6d.

FAWCETT (Henry and Mrs. H.).—ESSAYS AND LECTURES ON POLITICAL AND SOCIAL SUBJECTS. 8vo. 10s. 6d.

FISKE (John).—AMERICAN POLITICAL IDEAS VIEWED FROM THE STAND-POINT OF UNIVERSAL HISTORY. Cr. 8vo. 4s.
—— CIVIL GOVERNMENT IN THE UNITED STATES CONSIDERED WITH SOME REFERENCE TO ITS ORIGIN. Cr. 8vo. 6s. 6d.

FREEMAN (E. A.).— DISESTABLISHMENT AND DISENDOWMENT. WHAT ARE THEY? 4th Edit. Cr. 8vo. 1s.
—— THE GROWTH OF THE ENGLISH CONSTITUTION. 5th Edit. Cr. 8vo. 5s.

HARWOOD (George).—DISESTABLISHMENT; or, a Defence of the Principle of a National Church. 8vo. 12s.
—— THE COMING DEMOCRACY. Cr. 8vo. 6s.

HILL (Florence D.).—CHILDREN OF THE STATE. Edited by FANNY FOWKE. Crown 8vo. 6s.

HILL (Octavia).—OUR COMMON LAND, AND OTHER ESSAYS. Ext. fcp. 8vo. 3s. 6d.

HOLLAND (Prof. T. E.).—THE TREATY RELATIONS OF RUSSIA AND TURKEY, FROM 1774 TO 1853. Cr. 8vo. 2s.

JENKS (Prof. Edward).—THE GOVERNMENT OF VICTORIA (AUSTRALIA). 8vo. 14s.

JEPHSON (H.).—THE PLATFORM: ITS RISE AND PROGRESS. 2 vols. 8vo. 21s.

LOWELL (J. R.). (*See* COLLECTED WORKS.)

LUBBOCK (Sir J.). (*See* COLLECTED WORKS.)

PALGRAVE (W. Gifford). — ESSAYS ON EASTERN QUESTIONS. 8vo. 10s. 6d.

PARKIN (G. R.).—IMPERIAL FEDERATION. Cr. 8vo. 4s. 6d.

POLLOCK (Sir F., Bart.).—INTRODUCTION TO THE HISTORY OF THE SCIENCE OF POLITICS. Cr. 8vo. 2s. 6d.
—— LEADING CASES DONE INTO ENGLISH. Crown 8vo 3s. 6d.

PRACTICAL POLITICS. 8vo. 6s.

ROGERS (Prof. J. E. T.).—COBDEN AND POLITICAL OPINION. 8vo. 10s. 6d.

ROUTLEDGE (Jas.).—POPULAR PROGRESS IN ENGLAND. 8vo. 16s.

RUSSELL (Sir Charles).—NEW VIEWS ON IRELAND. Cr. 8vo. 2s. 6d.
—— THE PARNELL COMMISSION: THE OPENING SPEECH FOR THE DEFENCE. 8vo. 10s. 6d. —*Popular Edition.* Sewed. 2s.

SIDGWICK (Prof. Henry).—THE ELEMENTS OF POLITICS. 8vo. 14s. net.

SMITH (Goldwin).—CANADA AND THE CANADIAN QUESTION. 8vo. 8s. net.
—— THE UNITED STATES, 1492—1871. Cr. 8vo. 8s. 6d.

STATESMAN'S YEAR-BOOK, THE. (*See under* STATISTICS.)

STATHAM (R.).—BLACKS, BOERS, AND BRITISH. Cr. 8vo. 6s.

THORNTON (W. T.).--A PLEA FOR PEASANT PROPRIETORS. New Edit. Cr. 8vo. 7s. 6d.
—— INDIAN PUBLIC WORKS, AND COGNATE INDIAN TOPICS. Cr. 8vo. 8s. 6d.

TRENCH (Capt. F.).—THE RUSSO-INDIAN QUESTION. Cr. 8vo. 7s. 6d.

WALLACE (Sir Donald M.).—EGYPT AND THE EGYPTIAN QUESTION. 8vo. 14s.

PSYCHOLOGY.
(*See under* PHILOSOPHY, p. 28.)

SCULPTURE. (*See* ART.)

SOCIAL ECONOMY.

BOOTH (C.).—A PICTURE OF PAUPERISM. Cr. 8vo. 5s.—Cheap Edit. 8vo. Swd., 6d.
—— LIFE AND LABOUR OF THE PEOPLE OF LONDON. 4 vols. Cr. 8vo. 3s. 6d. each.— Maps to illustrate the above. 5s.

FAWCETT (H. and Mrs. H.). (*See* POLITICS.)

GILMAN (N. P.).—SOCIALISM AND THE AMERICAN SPIRIT. Cr. 8vo. 6s. 6d.

HILL (Octavia).—HOMES OF THE LONDON POOR. Cr. 8vo, sewed. 1s.

HUXLEY (Prof. T. H.).—SOCIAL DISEASES AND WORSE REMEDIES: Letters to the "Times." Cr. 8vo. sewed. 1s. net.

JEVONS (W. Stanley).—METHODS OF SOCIAL REFORM. 8vo. 10s. 6d.

PEARSON (C. H.).—NATIONAL LIFE AND CHARACTER: A FORECAST. 8vo. 10s. net.

STANLEY (Hon. Maude). — CLUBS FOR WORKING GIRLS. Cr. 8vo. 3s. 6d.

SOUND. (*See under* PHYSICS, p. 29.)

SPORT.

BAKER (Sir Samuel W.).—WILD BEASTS AND THEIR WAYS: REMINISCENCES OF EUROPE, ASIA, AFRICA, AMERICA, FROM 1845—88. Illustrated. Ext. cr. 8vo. 12s. 6d.

CHASSERESSE (D.).—SPORTING SKETCHES. Illustrated. Cr. 8vo. 3s. 6d.

CLARK (R.).—GOLF: A Royal and Ancient Game. Small 4to. 8s. 6d. net.

EDWARDS-MOSS (Sir J. E., Bart). — A SEASON IN SUTHERLAND. Cr. 8vo. 1s. 6d.

STATISTICS.

STATESMAN'S YEAR-BOOK, THE. Statistical and Historical Annual of the States of the World for the Year 1893. Revised after Official Returns. Ed. by J. SCOTT KELTIE. Cr. 8vo. 10s. 6d.

SURGERY. (*See* MEDICINE.)

SWIMMING.

LEAHY (Sergeant).—THE ART OF SWIMMING IN THE ETON STYLE. Cr. 8vo. 2s.

TECHNOLOGY.

BENSON (W. A. S.).—HANDICRAFT AND DESIGN. Cr. 8vo. 5s. net.

LETHABY (W. R.).—LEAD WORK. Cr. 8vo. 4s. 6d. net.

THEOLOGY.

THEOLOGY.
The Bible—History of the Christian Church—The Church of England—Devotional Books—The Fathers—Hymnology—Sermons, Lectures, Addresses, and Theological Essays.

The Bible.

History of the Bible—
THE ENGLISH BIBLE; An External and Critical History of the various English Translations of Scripture. By Prof. JOHN EADIE. 2 vols. 8vo. 28s.
THE BIBLE IN THE CHURCH. By Right Rev. Bp. WESTCOTT. 10th edit. Pott 8vo. 4s. 6d.
Biblical History—
BIBLE LESSONS. By Rev. E. A. ABBOTT. Cr. 8vo. 4s. 6d.
SIDE-LIGHTS UPON BIBLE HISTORY. By Mrs. SYDNEY BUXTON. Cr. 8vo. 5s.
STORIES FROM THE BIBLE. By Rev. A. J. CHURCH. Illust. Cr. 8vo. 2 parts. 3s. 6d. each.
BIBLE READINGS SELECTED FROM THE PENTATEUCH AND THE BOOK OF JOSHUA. By Rev. J. A. CROSS. Gl. 8vo. 2s. 6d.
THE CHILDREN'S TREASURY OF BIBLE STORIES. By Mrs. H. GASKOIN. 18mo. 1s. each.—Part I. Old Testament; II. New Testament; III. The Apostles.
THE NATIONS AROUND ISRAEL. By A. KEARY. Cr. 8vo. 3s. 6d.
A CLASS-BOOK OF OLD TESTAMENT HISTORY. By Rev. Dr. MACLEAR. Pott 8vo. 4s. 6d.
A CLASS-BOOK OF NEW TESTAMENT HISTORY. By the same. Pott 8vo. 5s. 6d.
A SHILLING BOOK OF OLD TESTAMENT HISTORY. By the same. Pott 8vo. 1s.
A SHILLING BOOK OF NEW TESTAMENT HISTORY. By the same. Pott 8vo. 1s.
The Old Testament—
SCRIPTURE READINGS FOR SCHOOLS AND FAMILIES. By C. M. YONGE. Globe 8vo. 1s. 6d. each: also with questions, 3s. 6d. each.—GENESIS TO DEUTERONOMY.—JOSHUA TO SOLOMON.—KINGS AND THE PROPHETS.—THE GOSPEL TIMES.—APOSTOLIC TIMES.
THE PATRIARCHS AND LAWGIVERS OF THE OLD TESTAMENT. By F. D. MAURICE. Cr. 8vo. 3s. 6d.
THE PROPHETS AND KINGS OF THE OLD TESTAMENT. By same. Cr. 8vo. 3s. 6d.
THE CANON OF THE OLD TESTAMENT. By Prof. H. E. RYLE. Cr. 8vo. 6s.
The Pentateuch—
AN HISTORICO-CRITICAL INQUIRY INTO THE ORIGIN AND COMPOSITION OF THE HEXATEUCH (PENTATEUCH AND BOOK OF JOSHUA). By Prof. A. KUENEN. Trans. by P. H. WICKSTEED, M.A. 8vo. 14s.
The Psalms—
THE PSALMS CHRONOLOGICALLY ARRANGED. By FOUR FRIENDS. Cr. 8vo. 5s. net.
GOLDEN TREASURY PSALTER. Student's Edition of the above. Pott 8vo. 2s. 6d. net.
THE PSALMS. With Introduction and Notes. By A. C. JENNINGS, M.A., and W. H. LOWE, M.A. 2 vols. Cr. 8vo. 10s. 6d. each.
INTRODUCTION TO THE STUDY AND USE OF THE PSALMS. By Rev. J. F. THRUPP. 2nd Edit. 2 vols. 8vo. 21s.
Isaiah—
ISAIAH XL.—LXVI. With the Shorter Prophecies allied to it. Edited by MATTHEW ARNOLD. Cr. 8vo. 5s.

Isaiah—
ISAIAH OF JERUSALEM. In the Authorised English Version, with Introduction and Notes. By MATTHEW ARNOLD. Cr. 8vo. 4s. 6d.
A BIBLE-READING FOR SCHOOLS. The Great Prophecy of Israel's Restoration (Isaiah xl.—lxvi.). Arranged and Edited for Young Learners. By the same. Pott 8vo. 1s.
COMMENTARY ON THE BOOK OF ISAIAH: Critical, Historical, and Prophetical; including a Revised English Translation. By T. R. BIRKS. 2nd Edit. 8vo. 12s. 6d.
THE BOOK OF ISAIAH CHRONOLOGICALLY ARRANGED. By T. K. CHEYNE. Cr. 8vo. 7s. 6d.
Zechariah—
THE HEBREW STUDENT'S COMMENTARY ON ZECHARIAH, Hebrew and LXX. By W. H. LOWE, M.A. 8vo. 10s. 6d.
The New Testament—
THE NEW TESTAMENT. Essay on the Right Estimation of MS. Evidence in the Text of the New Testament. By T. R. BIRKS. Cr. 8vo. 3s. 6d.
THE MESSAGES OF THE BOOKS. Discourses and Notes on the Books of the New Testament. By Archd. FARRAR. 8vo. 14s.
THE CLASSICAL ELEMENT IN THE NEW TESTAMENT. Considered as a Proof of its Genuineness, with an Appendix on the Oldest Authorities used in the Formation of the Canon. By C. H. HOOLE. 8vo. 10s. 6d.
ON A FRESH REVISION OF THE ENGLISH NEW TESTAMENT. With an Appendix on the last Petition of the Lord's Prayer. By Bishop LIGHTFOOT. Cr. 8vo. 7s. 6d.
THE UNITY OF THE NEW TESTAMENT. By F. D. MAURICE. 2 vols. Cr. 8vo. 12s.
THE SYNOPTIC PROBLEM FOR ENGLISH READERS. By A. J. JOLLEY. Cr. 8vo. 3s. net.
A GENERAL SURVEY OF THE HISTORY OF THE CANON OF THE NEW TESTAMENT DURING THE FIRST FOUR CENTURIES. By Bishop WESTCOTT. Cr. 8vo. 10s. 6d.
GREEK-ENGLISH LEXICON TO THE NEW TESTAMENT. By W. J. HICKIE, M.A. Pott 8vo. 3s.
THE NEW TESTAMENT IN THE ORIGINAL GREEK. The Text revised by Bishop WESTCOTT, D.D., and Prof. F. J. A. HORT, D.D. 2 vols. Cr. 8vo. 10s. 6d. each.—Vol. I. Text.—Vol. II. Introduction and Appendix.
SCHOOL EDITION OF THE ABOVE. Pott 8vo, 4s. 6d.; Pott 8vo, roan, 5s. 6d.; morocco, gilt edges, 6s. 6d.
The Gospels—
THE COMMON TRADITION OF THE SYNOPTIC GOSPELS. In the Text of the Revised Version. By Rev. E. A. ABBOTT and W. G. RUSHBROOKE. Cr. 8vo. 3s. 6d.
SYNOPTICON: An Exposition of the Common Matter of the Synoptic Gospels. By W. G. RUSHBROOKE. Printed in Colours. In Six Parts, and Appendix. 4to.—Part I. 3s. 6d.—Parts II. and III.—Parts IV. V. and VI., with Indices, 10s. 6d.—Appendices, 10s. 6d.—Complete in 1 vol. 35s.
INTRODUCTION TO THE STUDY OF THE FOUR GOSPELS. By Bp. WESTCOTT. Cr. 8vo. 10s. 6d.
THE COMPOSITION OF THE FOUR GOSPELS. By Rev. ARTHUR WRIGHT. Cr. 8vo. 5s.

THEOLOGY.

The Bible—*continued.*

The Gospels—
THE AKHMIM FRAGMENT OF THE APOCRYPHAL GOSPEL OF ST. PETER. By H. B. SWETE. 8vo. 5s. net.

Gospel of St. Matthew—
THE GREEK TEXT, with Introduction and Notes by Rev. A. SLOMAN. Fcp.8vo. 2s.6d.
CHOICE NOTES ON ST. MATTHEW. Drawn from Old and New Sources. Cr. 8vo. 4s.6d. (St. Matthew and St. Mark in 1 vol. 9s.)

Gospel of St. Mark—
SCHOOL READINGS IN THE GREEK TESTAMENT. Being the Outlines of the Life of our Lord as given by St. Mark, with additions from the Text of the other Evangelists. Edited, with Notes and Vocabulary, by Rev. A. CALVERT, M.A. Fcp. 8vo. 2s.6d.
CHOICE NOTES ON ST. MARK. Drawn from Old and New Sources. Cr. 8vo. 4s. 6d. (St. Matthew and St. Mark in 1 vol. 9s.)

Gospel of St. Luke—
GREEK TEXT, with Introduction and Notes by Rev. J. BOND, M.A. Fcp. 8vo. 2s.6d.
CHOICE NOTES ON ST. LUKE. Drawn from Old and New Sources. Cr. 8vo. 4s. 6d.
THE GOSPEL OF THE KINGDOM OF HEAVEN. A Course of Lectures on the Gospel of St. Luke. By F. D. MAURICE. Cr. 8vo. 3s 6d.

Gospel of St. John—
THE GOSPEL OF ST. JOHN. By F. D. MAURICE. Cr. 8vo. 3s. 6d.
CHOICE NOTES ON ST. JOHN. Drawn from Old and New Sources. Cr. 8vo. 4s. 6d.

The Acts of the Apostles—
THE OLD SYRIAC ELEMENT IN THE TEXT OF THE CODEX BEZÆ. By F. H. CHASE. 8vo. 7s. 6d. net.
GREEK TEXT, with Notes by T. E. PAGE, M.A. Fcp. 8vo. 3s. 6d.
THE CHURCH OF THE FIRST DAYS: THE CHURCH OF JERUSALEM, THE CHURCH OF THE GENTILES, THE CHURCH OF THE WORLD. Lectures on the Acts of the Apostles. By Very Rev. C. J. VAUGHAN. Cr. 8vo. 10s. 6d.

The Epistles of St. Paul—
THE EPISTLE TO THE ROMANS. The Greek Text, with English Notes. By the Very Rev. C. J. VAUGHAN. 7th Edit. Cr. 8vo. 7s. 6d.
THE EPISTLES TO THE CORINTHIANS. Greek Text, with Commentary. By Rev. W KAY. 8vo. 9s.
The EPISTLE TO THE GALATIANS. A Revised Text, with Introduction, Notes, and Dissertations. By Bishop LIGHTFOOT. 10th Edit. 8vo. 12s.
THE EPISTLE TO THE PHILIPPIANS. A Revised Text, with Introduction, Notes, and Dissertations. By the same. 8vo. 12s
THE EPISTLE TO THE PHILIPPIANS. With Translation, Paraphrase, and Notes for English Readers. By the Very Rev. C. J. VAUGHAN. Cr. 8vo. 5s.
THE EPISTLES TO THE COLOSSIANS AND TO PHILEMON. A Revised Text, with Introductions, etc. By Bishop LIGHTFOOT. 9th Edit. 8vo. 12s.

The Epistles of St. Paul—
THE EPISTLES TO THE EPHESIANS, THE COLOSSIANS, AND PHILEMON. With Introduction and Notes. By Rev. J. LL. DAVIES. 2nd Edit. 8vo. 7s. 6d.
THE FIRST EPISTLE TO THE THESSALONIANS. By Very Rev. C. J. VAUGHAN. 8vo, sewed. 1s. 6d.
THE EPISTLES TO THE THESSALONIANS. Commentary on the Greek Text. By Prof. JOHN EADIE. 8vo. 12s.

The Epistle of St. James—
THE GREEK TEXT, with Introduction and Notes. By Rev. JOSEPH B. MAYOR. 8vo. 14s.

The Epistles of St. John—
THE EPISTLES OF ST. JOHN. By F. D. MAURICE. Cr. 8vo. 3s. 6d.
— The Greek Text, with Notes, by Bishop WESTCOTT. 3rd Edit. 8vo. 12s. 6d.

The Epistle to the Hebrews—
GREEK AND ENGLISH. Edited by Rev. FREDERIC RENDALL. Cr. 8vo. 6s.
ENGLISH TEXT, with Commentary. By the same. Cr. 8vo. 7s. 6d.
THE GREEK TEXT, with Notes, by Very Rev C. J. VAUGHAN. Cr. 8vo. 7s. 6d.
THE GREEK TEXT, with Notes and Essays, by Bishop WESTCOTT. 8vo. 14s.

Revelation—
LECTURES ON THE APOCALYPSE. By F. D. MAURICE. Cr. 8vo. 3s. 6d.
THE REVELATION OF ST. JOHN. By Rev. Prof. W. MILLIGAN. Cr. 8vo. 7s. 6d.
LECTURES ON THE APOCALYPSE. By the same. Crown 8vo. 5s.
DISCUSSIONS ON THE APOCALYPSE. By the same. Cr. 8vo. 5s.
LECTURES ON THE REVELATION OF ST. JOHN. By Very Rev. C. J. VAUGHAN. 5th Edit. Cr. 8vo. 10s. 6d.

THE BIBLE WORD-BOOK. By W. ALDIS WRIGHT. 2nd Edit. Cr. 8vo. 7s. 6d.

History of the Christian Church.

CHURCH (Dean).—THE OXFORD MOVEMENT, 1833–45. Gl. 8vo. 5s.

CUNNINGHAM (Rev. John).—THE GROWTH OF THE CHURCH IN ITS ORGANISATION AND INSTITUTIONS. 8vo. 9s.

CUNNINGHAM (Rev. William). — THE CHURCHES OF ASIA: A Methodical Sketch of the Second Century. Cr. 8vo. 6s.

DALE (A. W. W.).—THE SYNOD OF ELVIRA, AND CHRISTIAN LIFE IN THE FOURTH CENTURY. Cr. 8vo. 10s. 6d.

GWATKIN (H. M.).—SELECTIONS FROM EARLY WRITERS ILLUSTRATIVE OF CHURCH HISTORY TO THE TIME OF CONSTANTINE. Cr. 8vo. 4s. net.

HARDWICK (Archdeacon).—A HISTORY OF THE CHRISTIAN CHURCH: MIDDLE AGE Edited by Bp. STUBBS. Cr. 8vo. 10s. 6d.

— A HISTORY OF THE CHRISTIAN CHURCH DURING THE REFORMATION. 9th Edit., revised by Bishop STUBBS. Cr. 8vo. 10s. 6d.

THE CHURCH OF ENGLAND—DEVOTIONAL BOOKS. 35

HORT (Dr. F. J. A.).—Two Dissertations.
I. On MONOΓENHΣ ΘEOΣ in Scripture and Tradition. II. On the "Constantinopolitan" Creed and other Eastern Creeds of the Fourth Century. 8vo. 7s. 6d.

KILLEN (W. D.).—Ecclesiastical History of Ireland, from the Earliest Date to the Present Time. 2 vols. 8vo. 25s.

SIMPSON (Rev. W.).—An Epitome of the History of the Christian Church. 7th Edit. Fcp. 8vo 3s. 6d.

VAUGHAN (Very Rev. C. J.).—The Church of the First Days: The Church of Jerusalem, The Church of the Gentiles, The Church of the World. Cr. 8vo. 10s. 6d.

WARD (W.).—William George Ward and the Oxford Movement. 8vo. 14s.
—— W. G. Ward and the Catholic Revival. 8vo. 14s.

The Church of England.

Catechism of—
Catechism and Confirmation. Pott 8vo. 1s. net.
A Class-Book of the Catechism of the Church of England. By Rev. Canon Maclear. Pott 8vo. 1s. 6d.
A First Class-Book of the Catechism of the Church of England. By the same. Pott 8vo. 6d.
The Order of Confirmation. With Prayers and Devotions. By the same. 32mo. 6d.

Collects—
Collects of the Church of England. With a Coloured Floral Design to each Collect. Cr. 8vo. 12s.

Disestablishment—
Disestablishment and Disendowment. What are they? By Prof. E. A. Freeman. 4th Edit. Cr. 8vo. 1s.
Disestablishment; or, A Defence of the Principle of a National Church. By Geo. Harwood. 8vo. 12s.
A Defence of the Church of England against Disestablishment. By Roundell, Earl of Selborne. Cr. 8vo. 2s. 6d.
Ancient Facts and Fictions concerning Churches and Tithes By the same. 2nd Edit. Cr. 8vo. 7s. 6d.

Dissent in its Relation to—
Dissent in its Relation to the Church of England. By Rev. G. H. Curteis. Bampton Lectures for 1871. Cr. 8vo. 7s. 6d.

Holy Communion—
Those Holy Mysteries. By Rev. J. C. P. Aldous. 16mo. 1s. net.
The Communion Service from the Book of Common Prayer. With Select Readings from the Writings of the Rev. F. D. Maurice. Edited by Bishop Colenso. 6th Edit. 16mo. 2s. 6d.
Before the Table: An Inquiry, Historical and Theological, into the Meaning of the Consecration Rubric in the Communion Service of the Church of England. By Very Rev. J. S. Howson. 8vo. 7s. 6d.

Holy Communion—
First Communion. With Prayers and Devotions for the newly Confirmed. By Rev. Canon Maclear. 32mo. 6d.
A Manual of Instruction for Confirmation and First Communion. With Prayers and Devotions. By the same. 32mo. 2s.

Liturgy—
An Introduction to the Creeds. By Rev. Canon Maclear. Pott 8vo. 3s. 6d.
An Introduction to the Thirty-Nine Articles. By same. Pott 8vo. [*In Press.*
A History of the Book of Common Prayer. By Rev F. Procter. 18th Edit. Cr. 8vo. 10s. 6d.
An Elementary Introduction to the Book of Common Prayer. By Rev. F. Procter and Rev. Canon Maclear. Pott 8vo. 2s. 6d.
Twelve Discourses on Subjects connected with the Liturgy and Worship of the Church of England. By Very Rev. C. J. Vaughan. Fcp. 8vo. 6s.
A Companion to the Lectionary. By Rev. W. Benham, B.D. Cr. 8vo. 4s. 6d.

Devotional Books.

EASTLAKE (Lady).—Fellowship: Letters addressed to my Sister-Mourners. Cr. 8vo. 2s. 6d.

IMITATIO CHRISTI. Libri IV. Printed in Borders after Holbein, Dürer, and other old Masters, containing Dances of Death, Acts of Mercy, Emblems, etc. Cr.8vo. 7s.6d.

KINGSLEY (Charles).—Out of the Deep: Words for the Sorrowful. From the Writings of Charles Kingsley. Ext. fcp. 8vo. 3s. 6d.
—— Daily Thoughts. Selected from the Writings of Charles Kingsley. By His Wife. Cr. 8vo. 6s.
—— From Death to Life. Fragments of Teaching to a Village Congregation. Edit. by His Wife. Fcp. 8vo. 2s. 6d.

MACLEAR (Rev. Canon).—A Manual of Instruction for Confirmation and First Communion, with Prayers and Devotions. 32mo. 2s.
—— The Hour of Sorrow; or, The Office for the Burial of the Dead. 32mo. 2s.

MAURICE (F. D.).—Lessons of Hope Readings from the Works of F. D. Maurice. Selected by Rev. J. Ll. Davies, M.A. Cr. 8vo. 5s.

RAYS OF SUNLIGHT FOR DARK DAYS. With a Preface by Very Rev. C. J. Vaughan. D.D. New Edition. Pott 8vo. 3s. 6d.

SERVICE (Rev. J.).—Prayers for Public Worship. Cr. 8vo. 4s. 6d.

THE WORSHIP OF GOD, AND FELLOWSHIP AMONG MEN. By Prof. Maurice and others. Fcp. 8vo. 3s. 6d.

WELBY-GREGORY (Hon. Lady).—Links and Clues. 2nd Edit. Cr. 8vo. 6s.

WESTCOTT (Rt. Rev. Bishop).—Thoughts on Revelation and Life. Selections from the Writings of Bishop Westcott. Edited by Rev. S. Phillips. Cr. 8vo. 6s.

THEOLOGY.

WILBRAHAM (Francis M.).—IN THE SERE AND YELLOW LEAF: THOUGHTS AND RECOLLECTIONS FOR OLD AND YOUNG. Globe 8vo. 3s. 6d.

The Fathers.

DONALDSON (Prof. James).—THE APOSTOLIC FATHERS. A Critical Account of their Genuine Writings, and of their Doctrines. 2nd Edit. Cr. 8vo. 7s. 6d.

Works of the Greek and Latin Fathers:
THE APOSTOLIC FATHERS. Revised Texts, with Introductions, Notes, Dissertations, and Translations. By Bishop LIGHTFOOT. —Part I. ST. CLEMENT OF ROME. 2 vols. 8vo. 32s.—Part II. ST. IGNATIUS TO ST. POLYCARP. 3 vols. 2nd Edit. 8vo. 48s.
THE APOSTOLIC FATHERS. Abridged Edit. With Short Introductions, Greek Text, and English Translation. By same. 8vo. 16s.
THE EPISTLE OF ST. BARNABAS. Its Date and Authorship. With Greek Text, Latin Version, Translation and Commentary. By Rev. W. CUNNINGHAM. Cr. 8vo. 7s. 6d.
INDEX OF NOTEWORTHY WORDS AND PHRASES FOUND IN THE CLEMENTINE WRITINGS. 8vo. 5s.

Hymnology.

BROOKE (S. A.).—CHRISTIAN HYMNS. Gl. 8vo. 2s. 6d. net.—CHRISTIAN HYMNS AND SERVICE BOOK OF BEDFORD CHAPEL, BLOOMSBURY. Gl. 8vo. 3s. 6d. net.—SERVICE BOOK. Gl. 8vo. 1s. net.

PALGRAVE (Prof. F. T.).—ORIGINAL HYMNS. 3rd Edit. Pott 8vo. 1s. 6d.

SELBORNE (Roundell, Earl of).—THE BOOK OF PRAISE. Pott 8vo. 2s. 6d. net.
—— A HYMNAL. Chiefly from "The Book of Praise."—A. Royal 32mo, limp. 6d.—B. 18mo, larger type. 1s.—C. Fine paper. 1s. 6d. —With Music, Selected, Harmonised, and Composed by JOHN HULLAH. Pott 8vo. 3s. 6d.

WOODS (Miss M. A.).—HYMNS FOR SCHOOL WORSHIP. Pott 8vo. 1s. 6d.

Sermons, Lectures, Addresses, and Theological Essays.

ABBOT (F. E.).—SCIENTIFIC THEISM. Cr. 8vo. 7s. 6d.
—— THE WAY OUT OF AGNOSTICISM; or, The Philosophy of Free Religion. Cr. 8vo. 4s. 6d.

ABBOTT (Rev. E. A.).—CAMBRIDGE SERMONS. 8vo. 6s.
—— OXFORD SERMONS. 8vo. 7s. 6d.
—— PHILOMYTHUS. A discussion of Cardinal Newman's Essay on Ecclesiastical Miracles. Cr. 8vo. 3s. 6d.
—— NEWMANIANISM. Cr. 8vo. 1s. net.

AINGER (Canon).—SERMONS PREACHED IN THE TEMPLE CHURCH. Ext. fcp. 8vo. 6s.

ALEXANDER (W., Bishop of Derry and Raphoe).—THE LEADING IDEAS OF THE GOSPELS. New Edit. Cr. 8vo. 6s.

BAINES (Rev. Edward).—SERMONS. Preface and Memoir by Bishop BARRY. Cr. 8vo. 6s.

BATHER (Archdeacon).—ON SOME MINISTERIAL DUTIES, CATECHISING, PREACHING, Etc. Edited, with a Preface, by Very Rev. C. J. VAUGHAN, D.D. Fcp. 8vo. 4s. 6d.

BERNARD (Canon).—THE CENTRAL TEACHING OF CHRIST. Cr. 8vo. 7s. 6d.

BETHUNE-BAKER (J. F.).—THE INFLUENCE OF CHRISTIANITY ON WAR. 8vo. 5s.
—— THE STERNNESS OF CHRIST'S TEACHING, AND ITS RELATION TO THE LAW OF FORGIVENESS. Cr. 8vo. 2s. 6d.

BINNIE (Rev. W.).—SERMONS. Cr. 8vo. 6s.

BIRKS (Thomas Rawson).—THE DIFFICULTIES OF BELIEF IN CONNECTION WITH THE CREATION AND THE FALL, REDEMPTION, AND JUDGMENT. 2nd Edit. Cr. 8vo. 5s.
—— JUSTIFICATION AND IMPUTED RIGHTEOUSNESS. A Review. Cr. 8vo. 6s.
—— SUPERNATURAL REVELATION; or, First Principles of Moral Theology. 8vo. 8s.

BROOKE (S. A.).—SHORT SERMONS. Crown 8vo. 6s.

BROOKS (Bishop Phillips).—THE CANDLE OF THE LORD: and other Sermons. Cr. 8vo. 6s.
—— SERMONS PREACHED IN ENGLISH CHURCHES. Cr. 8vo. 6s.
—— TWENTY SERMONS. Cr. 8vo. 6s.
—— TOLERANCE. Cr. 8vo. 2s. 6d.
—— THE LIGHT OF THE WORLD. Cr. 8vo. 3s. 6d.
—— THE MYSTERY OF INIQUITY. Cr. 8vo. 6s.

BRUNTON (T. Lauder).—THE BIBLE AND SCIENCE. Illustrated. Cr. 8vo. 10s. 6d.

BUTLER (Archer).—SERMONS, DOCTRINAL AND PRACTICAL. 11th Edit. 8vo. 8s.
—— SECOND SERIES OF SERMONS. 8vo. 7s.
—— LETTERS ON ROMANISM. 8vo. 10s. 6d.

BUTLER (Rev. Geo.).—SERMONS PREACHED IN CHELTENHAM COLL. CHAPEL. 8vo. 7s. 6d.

CAMPBELL (Dr. John M'Leod).—THE NATURE OF THE ATONEMENT. Cr. 8vo. 6s.
—— REMINISCENCES AND REFLECTIONS. Edited by his Son, DONALD CAMPBELL, M.A. Cr. 8vo. 7s. 6d.
—— THOUGHTS ON REVELATION. Cr. 8vo. 5s.
—— RESPONSIBILITY FOR THE GIFT OF ETERNAL LIFE. Compiled from Sermons preached 1829–31. Cr. 8vo. 5s.

CANTERBURY (Edward White, Archbishop of).—BOY-LIFE: ITS TRIAL, ITS STRENGTH, ITS FULNESS. Sundays in Wellington College, 1859–73. Cr. 8vo. 6s.
—— THE SEVEN GIFTS. Primary Visitation Address. Cr. 8vo. 6s.
—— CHRIST AND HIS TIMES. Second Visitation Address. Cr. 8vo. 6s.
—— A PASTORAL LETTER TO THE DIOCESE OF CANTERBURY, 1890. 8vo, sewed. 1d.

CARPENTER (W. Boyd, Bishop of Ripon).—TRUTH IN TALE. Addresses, chiefly to Children. Cr. 8vo. 4s. 6d.
—— TWILIGHT DREAMS. Cr. 8vo. 4s. 6d.
—— THE PERMANENT ELEMENTS OF RELIGION. 2nd Edit. Cr. 8vo. 6s.

CAZENOVE (J. Gibson).—CONCERNING THE BEING AND ATTRIBUTES OF GOD. 8vo. 5s.

SERMONS, LECTURES, ETC. 37

CHURCH (Dean).—HUMAN LIFE AND ITS CONDITIONS. Cr. 8vo. 6s.
—— THE GIFTS OF CIVILISATION: and other Sermons and Letters. Cr. 8vo. 7s. 6d.
—— DISCIPLINE OF THE CHRISTIAN CHARACTER; and other Sermons. Cr. 8vo. 4s. 6d.
—— ADVENT SERMONS, 1885. Cr. 8vo. 4s. 6d.
—— VILLAGE SERMONS. Cr. 8vo. 6s.
—— CATHEDRAL AND UNIVERSITY SERMONS. Cr. 8vo. 6s.

CLERGYMAN'S SELF-EXAMINATION CONCERNING THE APOSTLES' CREED. Ext. fcp. 8vo. 1s. 6d.

CONGREVE (Rev. John).—HIGH HOPES AND PLEADINGS FOR A REASONABLE FAITH, NOBLER THOUGHTS, AND LARGER CHARITY. Cr. 8vo. 5s.

COOKE (Josiah P., jun.).—RELIGION AND CHEMISTRY. Cr. 8vo. 7s. 6d.
—— THE CREDENTIALS OF SCIENCE, THE WARRANT OF FAITH. 8vo. 8s. 6d. net.

COTTON (Bishop).—SERMONS PREACHED TO ENGLISH CONGREGATIONS IN INDIA. Cr. 8vo. 7s. 6d.

CUNNINGHAM (Rev. W.).—CHRISTIAN CIVILISATION, WITH SPECIAL REFERENCE TO INDIA. Cr. 8vo. 5s.

CURTEIS (Rev. G. H.).—THE SCIENTIFIC OBSTACLES TO CHRISTIAN BELIEF. The Boyle Lectures, 1884. Cr. 8vo. 6s.

DAVIES (Rev. J. Llewelyn).—THE GOSPEL AND MODERN LIFE. Ext. fcp. 8vo. 6s.
—— SOCIAL QUESTIONS FROM THE POINT OF VIEW OF CHRISTIAN THEOLOGY. Cr. 8vo. 6s.
—— WARNINGS AGAINST SUPERSTITION. Ext. fcp. 8vo. 2s. 6d.
—— THE CHRISTIAN CALLING. Ext.fp.8vo. 6s.
—— ORDER AND GROWTH AS INVOLVED IN THE SPIRITUAL CONSTITUTION OF HUMAN SOCIETY. Cr. 8vo. 3s. 6d.
—— BAPTISM, CONFIRMATION, AND THE LORD'S SUPPER. Addresses. Pott 8vo. 1s.

DIGGLE (Rev. J. W.).—GODLINESS AND MANLINESS. Cr. 8vo. 6s.

DRUMMOND (Prof. Jas.).—INTRODUCTION TO THE STUDY OF THEOLOGY. Cr. 8vo. 5s.

DU BOSE (W. P.).—THE SOTERIOLOGY OF THE NEW TESTAMENT. By W. P. DU BOSE. Cr. 8vo. 7s. 6d.

ECCE HOMO: A SURVEY OF THE LIFE AND WORK OF JESUS CHRIST. Globe 8vo. 6s.

ELLERTON (Rev. John).—THE HOLIEST MANHOOD, AND ITS LESSONS FOR BUSY LIVES. Cr. 8vo. 6s.

FAITH AND CONDUCT: AN ESSAY ON VERIFIABLE RELIGION. Cr. 8vo. 7s. 6d.

FARRAR (Ven. Archdeacon).—WORKS. Uniform Edition. Cr. 8vo. 3s. 6d. each
SEEKERS AFTER GOD.
ETERNAL HOPE. Westminster Abbey Sermons.
THE FALL OF MAN: and other Sermons.
THE WITNESS OF HISTORY TO CHRIST Hulsean Lectures, 1870.
THE SILENCE AND VOICES OF GOD. Sermons.
IN THE DAYS OF THY YOUTH. Marlborough College Sermons

FARRAR (Ven. Archd.).—WORKS—contd.
SAINTLY WORKERS. Five Lenten Lectures.
EPHPHATHA; or, The Amelioration of the MERCY AND JUDGMENT. [World.
SERMONS AND ADDRESSES DELIVERED IN AMERICA.
—— THE HISTORY OF INTERPRETATION. Bampton Lectures, 1885. 8vo. 16s.

FISKE (John).—MAN'S DESTINY VIEWED IN THE LIGHT OF HIS ORIGIN. Cr. 8vo. 3s. 6d.

FORBES (Rev. Granville).—THE VOICE OF GOD IN THE PSALMS. Cr. 8vo. 6s. 6d.

FOWLE (Rev. T. W.).—A NEW ANALOGY BETWEEN REVEALED RELIGION AND THE COURSE AND CONSTITUTION OF NATURE. Cr. 8vo. 6s.

FRASER (Bishop).—SERMONS. Edited by JOHN W. DIGGLE. 2 vols. Cr. 8vo. 6s. each

HAMILTON (John).—ON TRUTH AND ERROR. Cr. 8vo. 5s.
—— ARTHUR'S SEAT; or, The Church of the Banned. Cr. 8vo. 6s.
—— ABOVE AND AROUND: Thoughts on God and Man. 12mo. 2s. 6d.

HARDWICK (Archdeacon).—CHRIST AND OTHER MASTERS. 6th Edit. Cr. 8vo. 10s. 6d.

HARE (Julius Charles).—THE MISSION OF THE COMFORTER. New Edition. Edited by Dean PLUMPTRE. Cr. 8vo. 7s. 6d.

HARPER (Father Thomas).—THE METAPHYSICS OF THE SCHOOL. Vols. I. and II. 8vo. 18s. each.—Vol. III. Part I. 12s.

HARRIS (Rev. G. C.).—SERMONS. With a Memoir by C. M. YONGE. Ext. fcp. 8vo. 6s.

HORT (F. J. A.).—THE WAY, THE TRUTH, THE LIFE. Cr. 8vo. 6s.

HUTTON (R. H.). (See p. 22.)

ILLINGWORTH (Rev. J. R.).—SERMONS PREACHED IN A COLLEGE CHAPEL. Cr. 8vo. 5s.
—— UNIVERSITY AND CATHEDRAL SERMONS. Crown 8vo. 5s.

JACOB (Rev. J. A.).—BUILDING IN SILENCE: and other Sermons. Ext. fcp. 8vo. 6s.

JAMES (Rev. Herbert).—THE COUNTRY CLERGYMAN AND HIS WORK. Cr. 8vo. 6s.

JEANS (Rev. G. E.).—HAILEYBURY CHAPEL: and other Sermons. Fcp. 8vo. 3s. 6d.

JELLETT (Rev. Dr.).—THE ELDER SON: and other Sermons. Cr. 8vo. 6s.
—— THE EFFICACY OF PRAYER. Cr. 8vo. 5s.

KELLOGG (Rev. S. H.).—THE LIGHT OF ASIA AND THE LIGHT OF THE WORLD. Cr. 8vo. 7s. 6d.
—— GENESIS AND GROWTH OF RELIGION. Cr. 8vo. 6s.

KINGSLEY (Charles). (See COLLECTED WORKS, p. 23.)

KIRKPATRICK (Prof.).—THE DIVINE LIBRARY OF THE OLD TESTAMENT. Cr. 8vo. 2s. net.
—— DOCTRINE OF THE PROPHETS. Cr. 8vo. 6s.

KYNASTON (Rev. Herbert, D.D.).—CHELTENHAM COLLEGE SERMONS. Cr. 8vo. 6s.

LEGGE (A. O.).—THE GROWTH OF THE TEMPORAL POWER OF THE PAPACY. Cr. 8vo. 8s. 6d.

THEOLOGY.

Sermons, Lectures, Addresses, and Theological Essays—continued.

LIGHTFOOT (Bishop).—LEADERS IN THE NORTHERN CHURCH: Sermons. Cr. 8vo. 6s.
—— ORDINATION ADDRESSES AND COUNSELS TO CLERGY. Cr. 8vo. 6s.
—— CAMBRIDGE SERMONS. Cr. 8vo. 6s.
—— SERMONS PREACHED IN ST. PAUL'S CATHEDRAL. Cr. 8vo. 6s.
—— SERMONS ON SPECIAL OCCASIONS. 8vo. 6s.
—— A CHARGE DELIVERED TO THE CLERGY OF THE DIOCESE OF DURHAM, 1886. 8vo. 2s.
—— ESSAYS ON THE WORK ENTITLED "SUPERNATURAL RELIGION." 2nd Edit. 8vo. 10s. 6d.
—— ON A FRESH REVISION OF THE ENGLISH NEW TESTAMENT. Cr. 8vo. 7s. 6d.
—— DISSERTATIONS ON THE APOSTOLIC AGE. 8vo. 14s.
—— BIBLICAL ESSAYS. 8vo. 12s.

MACLAREN (Rev. A.).—SERMONS PREACHED AT MANCHESTER. 11th Ed. Fcp. 8vo. 4s. 6d.
—— SECOND SERIES. 7th Ed. Fcp. 8vo 4s. 6d.
—— THIRD SERIES. 6th Ed. Fcp. 8vo. 4s. 6d.
—— WEEK-DAY EVENING ADDRESSES. 4th Edit. Fcp. 8vo. 2s. 6d.
—— THE SECRET OF POWER: and other Sermons. 4s. 6d.

MACMILLAN (Rev. Hugh).—BIBLE TEACHINGS IN NATURE. 15th Edit. Globe 8vo. 6s.
—— THE TRUE VINE; or, The Analogies of our Lord's Allegory. 5th Edit. Gl. 8vo. 6s.
—— THE MINISTRY OF NATURE. 8th Edit. Globe 8vo. 6s.
—— THE SABBATH OF THE FIELDS. 6th Edit. Globe 8vo. 6s.
—— THE MARRIAGE IN CANA. Globe 8vo. 6s.
—— TWO WORLDS ARE OURS. Gl. 8vo. 6s.
—— THE OLIVE LEAF. Globe 8vo. 6s.
—— THE GATE BEAUTIFUL: and other Bible Teachings for the Young. Cr. 8vo. 3s. 6d.

MAHAFFY (Prof. J. P.).—THE DECAY OF MODERN PREACHING. Cr. 8vo. 3s. 6d.

MATURIN (Rev. W.).—THE BLESSEDNESS OF THE DEAD IN CHRIST. Cr. 8vo. 7s. 6d.

MAURICE (Frederick Denison).—THE KINGDOM OF CHRIST. 3rd Ed. 2 vols. Cr. 8vo. 12s.
—— EXPOSITORY SERMONS ON THE PRAYER-BOOK, AND THE LORD'S PRAYER. Cr. 8vo. 6s.
—— SERMONS PREACHED IN COUNTRY CHURCHES. 2nd Edit. Cr. 8vo. 6s.
—— THE CONSCIENCE: Lectures on Casuistry. 3rd Edit. Cr. 8vo. 4s. 6d.
—— DIALOGUES ON FAMILY WORSHIP. Cr. 8vo. 4s. 6d.
—— THE DOCTRINE OF SACRIFICE DEDUCED FROM THE SCRIPTURES. 2nd Edit. Cr. 8vo. 6s.
—— THE RELIGIONS OF THE WORLD. 6th Edit. Cr. 8vo. 4s. 6d.
—— ON THE SABBATH DAY; THE CHARACTER OF THE WARRIOR; AND ON THE INTERPRETATION OF HISTORY. Fcp. 8vo. 2s. 6d.
—— LEARNING AND WORKING. Cr. 8vo. 4s. 6d.
—— THE LORD'S PRAYER. THE CREED, AND THE COMMANDMENTS. Pott 8vo. 1s.
—— SERMONS PREACHED IN LINCOLN'S INN CHAPEL. 6 vols. Cr. 8vo. 3s. 6d. each.
—— COLLECTED WORKS. Cr. 8vo. 3s. 6d. each.
CHRISTMAS DAY AND OTHER SERMONS.
THEOLOGICAL ESSAYS.
PROPHETS AND KINGS.

MAURICE (Fredk. Denison).—COLLECTED WORKS—continued.
PATRIARCHS AND LAWGIVERS.
THE GOSPEL OF THE KINGDOM OF HEAVEN.
GOSPEL OF ST. JOHN.
EPISTLE OF ST. JOHN.
LECTURES ON THE APOCALYPSE.
FRIENDSHIP OF BOOKS.
SOCIAL MORALITY.
PRAYER BOOK AND LORD'S PRAYER.
THE DOCTRINE OF SACRIFICE.

MILLIGAN (Rev. Prof. W.).—THE RESURRECTION OF OUR LORD. 2nd Edit. Cr. 8vo. 5s.
—— THE ASCENSION AND HEAVENLY PRIESTHOOD OF OUR LORD. Cr. 8vo. 7s. 6d.

MOORHOUSE (J., Bishop of Manchester).—JACOB: Three Sermons. Ext. fcp. 8vo. 3s. 6d.
—— THE TEACHING OF CHRIST: its Conditions, Secret, and Results. Cr. 8vo. 3s. 6d.

MURPHY (J. J.).—NATURAL SELECTION AND SPIRITUAL FREEDOM. Gl. 8vo. 5s.

MYLNE (L. G., Bishop of Bombay).—SERMONS PREACHED IN ST. THOMAS'S CATHEDRAL, BOMBAY. Cr. 8vo. 6s.

NATURAL RELIGION. By the Author of "Ecce Homo." 3rd Edit. Globe 8vo. 6s.

PATTISON (Mark).—SERMONS. Cr. 8vo. 6s.

PAUL OF TARSUS. 8vo. 10s. 6d.

PHILOCHRISTUS: MEMOIRS OF A DISCIPLE OF THE LORD. 3rd. Edit. 8vo. 12s.

PLUMPTRE (Dean).—MOVEMENTS IN RELIGIOUS THOUGHT. Fcp. 8vo. 3s. 6d.

POTTER (R.).—THE RELATION OF ETHICS TO RELIGION. Cr. 8vo. 2s. 6d.

REASONABLE FAITH: A SHORT ESSAY By "Three Friends." Cr. 8vo. 1s.

REICHEL (C. P., Bishop of Meath).—THE LORD'S PRAYER. Cr. 8vo. 7s. 6d.
—— CATHEDRAL AND UNIVERSITY SERMONS. Cr. 8vo. 6s.

RENDALL (Rev. F.).—THE THEOLOGY OF THE HEBREW CHRISTIANS. Cr. 8vo. 5s.

REYNOLDS (H. R.).—NOTES OF THE CHRISTIAN LIFE. Cr. 8vo. 7s. 6d.

ROBINSON (Prebendary H. G.).—MAN IN THE IMAGE OF GOD: and other Sermons. Cr. 8vo. 7s. 6d.

RUSSELL (Dean).—THE LIGHT THAT LIGHTETH EVERY MAN: Sermons. With an Introduction by Dean PLUMPTRE, D.D. Cr. 8vo. 6s.

RYLE (Rev. Prof. H.).—THE EARLY NARRATIVES OF GENESIS. Cr. 8vo. 3s. net.

SALMON (Rev. George, D.D.).—NON-MIRACULOUS CHRISTIANITY: and other Sermons. 2nd Edit. Cr. 8vo. 6s.
—— GNOSTICISM AND AGNOSTICISM: and other Sermons. Cr. 8vo. 7s. 6d.

SANDFORD (Rt. Rev. C. W., Bishop of Gibraltar).—COUNSEL TO ENGLISH CHURCHMEN ABROAD. Cr. 8vo. 6s.

SCOTCH SERMONS, 1880. By Principal CAIRD and others. 3rd Edit. 8vo. 10s. 6d.

SERVICE (Rev. J.).—SERMONS. Cr. 8vo. 6s.

SHIRLEY (W. N.).—ELIJAH: Four University Sermons. Fcp. 8vo. 2s. 6d.

SMITH (Rev. Travers).—MAN'S KNOWLEDGE OF MAN AND OF GOD. Cr. 8vo. 6s.

THEOLOGY—TRANSLATIONS.

SMITH (W. Saumarez).—THE BLOOD OF THE NEW COVENANT: An Essay. Cr. 8vo. 2s. 6d.

STANLEY (Dean).—THE NATIONAL THANKS-GIVING. Sermons Preached in Westminster Abbey. 2nd Edit. Cr. 8vo. 2s. 6d.
—— ADDRESSES AND SERMONS delivered in America, 1878. Cr. 8vo. 6s.

STEWART (Prof. Balfour) and TAIT (Prof. P. G.).—THE UNSEEN UNIVERSE, OR PHYSICAL SPECULATIONS ON A FUTURE STATE. 15th Edit. Cr. 8vo. 6s.
—— PARADOXICAL PHILOSOPHY: A Sequel to the above. Cr. 8vo. 7s. 6d.

STUBBS (Rev. C. W.).—FOR CHRIST AND CITY. Sermons and Addresses. Cr. 8vo. 6s.

TAIT (Archbp.).—THE PRESENT CONDITION OF THE CHURCH OF ENGLAND. Primary Visitation Charge. 3rd Edit. 8vo. 3s. 6d.
—— DUTIES OF THE CHURCH OF ENGLAND Second Visitation Addresses. 8vo. 4s. 6d.
—— THE CHURCH OF THE FUTURE. Quadrennial Visitation Charges. Cr. 8vo. 3s. 6d.

TAYLOR (Isaac).—THE RESTORATION OF BELIEF. Cr. 8vo. 8s. 6d.

TEMPLE (Frederick, Bishop of London).—SERMONS PREACHED IN THE CHAPEL OF RUGBY SCHOOL. Second Series. Ex. fcp. 8vo. 6s. Third Series 4th Edit. Ext. fcp. 8vo. 6s.
—— THE RELATIONS BETWEEN RELIGION AND SCIENCE. Bampton Lectures, 1884 7th and Cheaper Edition. Cr. 8vo. 6s.

TRENCH (Archbishop). — THE HULSEAN LECTURES FOR 1845—6. 8vo. 7s. 6d.

TULLOCH (Principal).—THE CHRIST OF THE GOSPELS AND THE CHRIST OF MODERN CRITICISM. Ext. fcp. 8vo. 4s. 6d.

VAUGHAN (C. J., Dean of Landaff).—MEMORIALS OF HARROW SUNDAYS. 8vo. 10s. 6d.
—— EPIPHANY, LENT, AND EASTER. 8vo. 10s. 6d.
—— HEROES OF FAITH. 2nd Edit. Cr. 8vo. 6s
—— LIFE'S WORK AND GOD'S DISCIPLINE. Ext. fcp. 8vo. 2s. 6d.
—— THE WHOLESOME WORDS OF JESUS CHRIST. 2nd Edit. Fcp. 8vo. 3s. 6d.
—— FOES OF FAITH. 2nd Edit. Fcp.8vo. 3s.6d.
—— CHRIST SATISFYING THE INSTINCTS OF HUMANITY. 2nd Edit. Ext. fcp. 8vo. 3s. 6d.
—— COUNSELS FOR YOUNG STUDENTS. Fcp. 8vo. 2s. 6d.
—— THE TWO GREAT TEMPTATIONS. 2nd Edit. Fcp. 8vo. 3s. 6d.
—— ADDRESSES FOR YOUNG CLERGYMEN. Ext. fcp. 8vo. 4s. 6d.
—— "MY SON, GIVE ME THINE HEART." Ext. fcp. 8vo. 5s.
—— REST AWHILE. Addresses to Toilers in the Ministry. Ext. fcp. 8vo. 5s.
—— TEMPLE SERMONS. Cr. 8vo. 10s. 6d.
—— AUTHORISED OR REVISED? Sermons. Cr. 8vo. 7s. 6d.
—— LESSONS OF THE CROSS AND PASSION; WORDS FROM THE CROSS; THE REIGN OF SIN; THE LORD'S PRAYER. Four Courses of Lent Lectures. Cr. 8vo. 10s. 6d.
—— UNIVERSITY SERMONS, NEW AND OLD. Cr. 8vo. 10s. 6d.
—— THE PRAYERS OF JESUS CHRIST. Globe 8vo. 3s. 6d.
—— DONCASTER SERMONS; LESSONS OF LIFE AND GODLINESS; WORDS FROM THE GOSPELS. Cr. 8vo. 10s. 6d.

VAUGHAN (C. J., Dean of Llandaff).—NOTES FOR LECTURES ON CONFIRMATION. 14th Edit. Fcp. 8vo. 1s. 6d.
—— RESTFUL THOUGHTS IN RESTLESS TIMES. Crown 8vo. 5s.

VAUGHAN (Rev. D. J.).—THE PRESENT TRIAL OF FAITH. Cr. 8vo. 5s.

VAUGHAN (Rev. E. T.)—SOME REASONS OF OUR CHRISTIAN HOPE. Hulsean Lectures for 1875. Cr. 8vo. 6s. 6d.

VAUGHAN (Rev. Robert).—STONES FROM THE QUARRY. Sermons. Cr. 8vo. 5s.

VENN (Rev. John).—ON SOME CHARACTERISTICS OF BELIEF, SCIENTIFIC, AND RELIGIOUS. Hulsean Lectures, 1869. 8vo. 6s.6d.

WELLDON (Rev. J. E. C.).—THE SPIRITUAL LIFE: and other Sermons. Cr. 8vo. 6s.

WESTCOTT (Rt. Rev. B. F., Bishop of Durham).—ON THE RELIGIOUS OFFICE OF THE UNIVERSITIES. Sermons. Cr. 8vo. 4s. 6d.
—— GIFTS FOR MINISTRY. Addresses to Candidates for Ordination. Cr. 8vo. 1s. 6d.
—— THE VICTORY OF THE CROSS. Sermons Preached in 1888. Cr. 8vo. 3s. 6d.
—— FROM STRENGTH TO STRENGTH. Three Sermons (In Memoriam J. B. D.). Cr. 8vo. 2s.
—— THE REVELATION OF THE RISEN LORD. 4th Edit. Cr. 8vo. 6s.
—— THE HISTORIC FAITH. Cr. 8vo. 6s.
—— THE GOSPEL OF THE RESURRECTION. 6th Edit. Cr. 8vo. 6s.
—— THE REVELATION OF THE FATHER. Cr. 8vo. 6s.
—— CHRISTUS CONSUMMATOR. Cr. 8vo. 6s.
—— SOME THOUGHTS FROM THE ORDINAL. Cr. 8vo. 1s. 6d.
—— SOCIAL ASPECTS OF CHRISTIANITY. Cr. 8vo. 6s.
—— THE GOSPEL OF LIFE. Cr. 8vo. 6s.
—— ESSAYS IN THE HISTORY OF RELIGIOUS THOUGHT IN THE WEST. Globe 8vo. 5s.

WHITTUCK (C. A.).—CHURCH OF ENGLAND AND RECENT RELIGIOUS THOUGHT. Cr. 8vo. 7s. 6d.

WICKHAM (Rev. E. C.).—WELLINGTON COLLEGE SERMONS. Cr. 8vo. 6s.

WILKINS (Prof. A. S.).—THE LIGHT OF THE WORLD: An Essay. 2nd Ed. Cr. 8vo. 3s. 6d.

WILLINK (A.).—THE WORLD OF THE UNSEEN. Cr. 8vo. 3s. 6d.

WILSON (J. M., Archdeacon of Manchester).—SERMONS PREACHED IN CLIFTON COLLEGE CHAPEL. 2nd Series, 1888—90. Cr. 8vo. 6s.
—— ESSAYS AND ADDRESSES. Cr. 8vo. 4s. 6d.
—— SOME CONTRIBUTIONS TO THE RELIGIOUS THOUGHT OF OUR TIME. Cr. 8vo. 6s.

WOOD (C. J.).—SURVIVALS IN CHRISTIANITY. Crown 8vo. 6s.

WOOD (Rev. E. G.).—THE REGAL POWER OF THE CHURCH. 8vo. 4s. 6d.

THERAPEUTICS. (See MEDICINE, p. 24.)

TRANSLATIONS.

From the Greek—From the Italian—From the Latin—Into Latin and Greek Verse.

From the Greek.

AESCHYLUS.—THE SUPPLICES. With Translation, by T. G. TUCKER, Litt. D. 8vo. 10s.6d.

TRANSLATIONS—VOYAGES AND TRAVELS.

TRANSLATIONS—*continued.*

AESCHYLUS.—THE SEVEN AGAINST THEBES. With Translation, by A. W. VERRALL, Litt.D. 8vo. 7s. 6d.
— THE CHOEPHORI. With Translation. By the same. 8vo. 12s.
— EUMENIDES. With Verse Translation, by BERNARD DRAKE, M.A. 8vo. 5s.
ARATUS. (*See* PHYSIOGRAPHY, p. 30.)
ARISTOPHANES.—THE BIRDS. Trans. into English Verse, by B. H. KENNEDY. 8vo. 6s.
ARISTOTLE ON FALLACIES; OR, THE SOPHISTICI ELENCHI. With Translation, by E. POSTE M.A. 8vo. 8s. 6d.
ARISTOTLE.—THE FIRST BOOK OF THE METAPHYSICS OF ARISTOTLE. By a Cambridge Graduate. 8vo. 5s.
— THE POLITICS. By J. E. C. WELLDON, M.A. Cr. 8vo. 10s. 6d.
— THE RHETORIC. By same. Cr.8vo. 7s.6d.
— THE NICOMACHEAN ETHICS. By same. Cr. 8vo. 7s. 6d.
— ON THE CONSTITUTION OF ATHENS. By E. POSTE. 2nd Edit. Cr. 8vo. 3s. 6d.
BION. (*See* THEOCRITUS.)
HERODOTUS.—THE HISTORY. By G. C. MACAULAY, M.A. 2 vols. Cr. 8vo. 18s.
HOMER.—THE ODYSSEY DONE INTO ENGLISH PROSE, by S. H. BUTCHER, M.A., and A. LANG, M.A. Cr. 8vo. 6s.
— THE ODYSSEY. Books I.—XII. Transl into English Verse by EARL OF CARNARVON. Cr. 8vo. 7s. 6d.
— THE ILIAD DONE INTO ENGLISH PROSE, by ANDREW LANG, WALTER LEAF, and ERNEST MYERS. Cr. 8vo. 12s. 6d.
MELEAGER.—FIFTY POEMS. Translated into English Verse by WALTER HEADLAM. Fcp. 4to. 7s. 6d.
MOSCHUS. (*See* THEOCRITUS).
PINDAR.—THE EXTANT ODES. By ERNEST MYERS. Cr. 8vo. 5s.
PLATO.—TIMÆUS. With Translation, by R. D. ARCHER-HIND, M.A. 8vo. 16s. (*See also* GOLDEN TREASURY SERIES, p. 22.)
POLYBIUS.—THE HISTORIES. By E. S. SHUCKBURGH. Cr. 8vo. 24s.
SOPHOCLES.—ŒDIPUS THE KING. Translated into English Verse by E. D. A. MORSHEAD, M.A. Fcp. 8vo. 3s. 6d.
THEOCRITUS, BION, AND MOSCHUS. By A. LANG, M.A. 18mo. 2s. 6d. net.—Large Paper Edition. 8vo. 9s.
XENOPHON.—THE COMPLETE WORKS. By H. G. DAKYNS, M.A. Cr. 8vo.—Vols. I. and II. 10s. 6d. each.

From the Italian.

DANTE.—THE PURGATORY. With Transl. and Notes, by A. J. BUTLER. Cr. 8vo. 12s.6d.
— THE PARADISE. By the same. 2nd Edit. Cr. 8vo. 12s. 6d.
— THE HELL. By the same. Cr. 8vo. 12s.6d.
— DE MONARCHIA. By F. J. CHURCH. 8vo. 4s. 6d.
— THE DIVINE COMEDY. By C. E. NORTON. I. HELL. II. PURGATORY. III. PARADISE. Cr. 8vo. 6s. each.

DANTE.—NEW LIFE OF DANTE. Transl. by C. E. NORTON. 5s.
— THE PURGATORY. Transl. by C. L. SHADWELL. Ext. cr. 8vo. 10s. net.

From the Latin.

CICERO.—THE LIFE AND LETTERS OF MARCUS TULLIUS CICERO. By the Rev. G. E. JEANS, M.A. 2nd Edit. Cr. 8vo. 10s. 6d.
— THE ACADEMICS. By J. S. REID. 8vo. 5s.6d.
HORACE: THE WORKS OF. By L. LONSDALE, M.A., and S. LEE, M.A. Gl. 8vo. 3s. 6d.
— THE ODES IN A METRICAL PARAPHRASE. By R. M. HOVENDEN, B.A. Ext. fcp. 8vo. 4s.6d.
— LIFE AND CHARACTER: AN EPITOME OF HIS SATIRES AND EPISTLES. By R. M. HOVENDEN, B.A. Ext. fcp. 8vo. 4s. 6d.
— WORD FOR WORD FROM HORACE: The Odes Literally Versified. By W. T. THORNTON, C.B. Cr. 8vo. 7s. 6d.
JUVENAL.—THIRTEEN SATIRES. By ALEX. LEEPER, LL.D. New Ed. Cr. 8vo. 2s. 6d.
LIVY.—BOOKS XXI.—XXV. THE SECOND PUNIC WAR. By A. J. CHURCH, M.A., and W. J. BRODRIBB, M.A. Cr. 8vo. 7s. 6d.
MARCUS AURELIUS ANTONINUS.—BOOK IV. OF THE MEDITATIONS. With Translation and Commentary, by H. CROSSLEY, M.A. 8vo. 6s.
SALLUST.—THE CONSPIRACY OF CATILINE AND THE JUGURTHINE WAR. By A. W. POLLARD. Cr. 8vo. 6s.—CATILINE. 3s.
TACITUS, THE WORKS OF. By A. J. CHURCH, M.A., and W. J. BRODRIBB, M.A. THE HISTORY. 4th Edit. Cr. 8vo. 6s.
THE AGRICOLA AND GERMANIA. With the Dialogue on Oratory. Cr. 8vo. 4s. 6d.
THE ANNALS. 5th Edit. Cr. 8vo. 7s. 6d.
VIRGIL: THE WORKS OF. By J. LONSDALE, M.A., and S. LEE, M.A. Globe 8vo. 3s. 6d.
— THE ÆNEID. By J. W. MACKAIL, M.A. Cr. 8vo. 7s. 6d.

Into Latin and Greek Verse.

CHURCH (Rev. A. J.).—LATIN VERSION OF SELECTIONS FROM TENNYSON. By Prof. CONINGTON, Prof. SEELEY, Dr. HESSEY, T. E. KEBBEL, &c. Edited by A. J. CHURCH, M.A. Ext. fcp. 8vo. 6s.
GEDDES (Prof. W. D.).—FLOSCULI GRÆCI BOREALES. Cr. 8vo. 6s.
KYNASTON (Herbert D.D.).—EXEMPLARIA CHELTONIENSIA. Ext. fcp. 8vo. 5s.

VOYAGES AND TRAVELS.

(*See also* HISTORY, p. 10; SPORT, p. 32.)

APPLETON (T. G.).—A NILE JOURNAL. Illustrated by EUGENE BENSON. Cr. 8vo. 6s.
"BACCHANTE." THE CRUISE OF H.M.S. "BACCHANTE," 1879—1882. Compiled from the Private Journals, Letters and Note-books of PRINCE ALBERT VICTOR and PRINCE GEORGE OF WALES. By the Rev. Canon DALTON. 2 vols. Med. 8vo. 52s. 6d.
BAKER (Sir Samuel W.).—ISMAILIA. A Narrative of the Expedition to Central Africa for the Suppression of the Slave Trade, organised by ISMAIL, Khedive of Egypt. Cr. 8vo. 6s.

VOYAGES AND TRAVELS—BOOKS FOR THE YOUNG. 41

BAKER (Sir Samuel W.).—THE NILE TRIBUTARIES OF ABYSSINIA, AND THE SWORD HUNTERS OF THE HAMRAN ARABS. Cr. 8vo. 6s.
—— THE ALBERT N'YANZA GREAT BASIN OF THE NILE AND EXPLORATION OF THE NILE SOURCES. Cr. 8vo. 6s.
—— CYPRUS AS I SAW IT IN 1879. 8vo. 12s. 6d.
BARKER (Lady).—A YEAR'S HOUSEKEEPING IN SOUTH AFRICA. Illustr. Cr. 8vo. 3s. 6d.
—— STATION LIFE IN NEW ZEALAND. Cr. 8vo. 3s. 6d.
—— LETTERS TO GUY. Cr. 8vo. 5s.
BLENNERHASSETT (R.) and SLEEMAN (L.)—ADVENTURES IN MASHONALAND. Ext. cr. 8vo. 8s. 6d. net.
BOUGHTON (G. H.) and ABBEY (E. A.).—SKETCHING RAMBLES IN HOLLAND. With Illustrations. Fcp. 4to. 21s.
BROOKS (P.).—LETTERS OF TRAVEL. Ext. cr. 8vo. 8s. 6d. net.
BRYCE (James, M.P.). — TRANSCAUCASIA AND ARARAT. 3rd Edit. Cr. 8vo. 9s.
CAMERON (V. L.).—OUR FUTURE HIGHWAY TO INDIA. 2 vols. Cr. 8vo. 21s.
CAMPBELL (J. F.).—MY CIRCULAR NOTES. Cr. 8vo. 6s.
CARLES(W.R.).—LIFE IN COREA. 8vo. 12s. 6d.
CAUCASUS: NOTES ON THE. By "WANDERER." 8vo. 9s.
CRAIK (Mrs.).—AN UNKNOWN COUNTRY. Illustr. by F. NOEL PATON. Roy. 8vo. 7s. 6d.
—— AN UNSENTIMENTAL JOURNEY THROUGH CORNWALL. Illustrated. 4to. 12s. 6d.
DILKE (Sir Charles). (See pp. 26, 31.)
DUFF (Right Hon. Sir M. E. Grant).—NOTES OF AN INDIAN JOURNEY. 8vo. 10s. 6d
FORBES (Archibald).—SOUVENIRS OF SOME CONTINENTS. Cr. 8vo. 6s.
—— BARRACKS, BIVOUACS, AND BATTLES. Cr. 8vo. 7s. 6d
FORBES-MITCHELL(W.)-REMINISCENCES OF THE GREAT MUTINY. Cr. 8vo. 8s. 6d. net.
FULLERTON (W. M.).—IN CAIRO. Fcp. 8vo. 3s. 6d.
GONE TO TEXAS: LETTERS FROM OUR BOYS. Ed. by THOS. HUGHES. Cr. 8vo. 4s. 6d.
GORDON (Lady Duff). — LAST LETTERS FROM EGYPT, TO WHICH ARE ADDED LETTERS FROM THE CAPE. 2nd Edit. Cr. 8vo. 9s.
GREEN (W. S.).—AMONG THE SELKIRK GLACIERS. Cr. 8vo. 7s. 6d.
HOOKER (Sir Joseph D.) and BALL (J.).—JOURNAL OF A TOUR IN MAROCCO AND THE GREAT ATLAS. 8vo. 21s.
HÜBNER (Baron von).—A RAMBLE ROUND THE WORLD. Cr. 8vo. 6s.
HUGHES (Thos.).—RUGBY, TENNESSEE. Cr. 8vo. 4s. 6d.
KALM.—ACCOUNT OF HIS VISIT TO ENGLAND. Trans. by J. LUCAS. Illus. 8vo. 12s. net.
KINGSLEY (Charles).—AT LAST: A Christmas in the West Indies. Cr. 8vo. 3s. 6d.
KINGSLEY (Henry). — TALES OF OLD TRAVEL. Cr. 8vo. 3s. 6d.
KIPLING (J. L.).—BEAST AND MAN IN INDIA. Illustrated. Ext. cr. 8vo. 7s. 6d.

MAHAFFY (Prof. J. P.).—RAMBLES AND STUDIES IN GREECE. Illust. Cr. 8vo. 10s. 6d.
MAHAFFY (Prof. J. P.) and ROGERS (J. E.).—SKETCHES FROM A TOUR THROUGH HOLLAND AND GERMANY. Illustrated by J. E. ROGERS. Ext. cr. 8vo. 10s. 6d.
NORDENSKIÖLD. — VOYAGE OF THE "VEGA" ROUND ASIA AND EUROPE. By Baron A. E. VON NORDENSKIÖLD. Trans. by ALEX. LESLIE. 400 Illustrations, Maps, etc. 2 vols. 8vo. 45s.—Popular Edit. Cr. 8vo. 6s.
OLIPHANT (Mrs.). (See HISTORY, p. 11.)
OLIVER (Capt. S. P.).—MADAGASCAR: AN HISTORICAL AND DESCRIPTIVE ACCOUNT OF THE ISLAND. 2 vols. Med. 8vo. 52s. 6d.
PALGRAVE (W. Gifford).—A NARRATIVE OF A YEAR'S JOURNEY THROUGH CENTRAL AND EASTERN ARABIA, 1862-63. Cr. 8vo. 6s.
—— DUTCH GUIANA. 8vo. 9s.
—— ULYSSES; or, Scenes and Studies in many Lands. 8vo. 12s. 6d.
PERSIA, EASTERN. AN ACCOUNT OF THE JOURNEYS OF THE PERSIAN BOUNDARY COMMISSION, 1870-71-72. 2 vols. 8vo. 42s.
PIKE(W.)—THE BARREN GROUND OF NORTHERN CANADA. 8vo. 10s. 6d.
ST. JOHNSTON (A.).—CAMPING AMONG CANNIBALS. Cr. 8vo. 4s. 6d.
SANDYS (J. E.).—AN EASTER VACATION IN GREECE. Cr. 8vo. 3s. 6d.
SMITH (G.)—A TRIP TO ENGLAND. Pott 8vo. 3s.
STRANGFORD (Viscountess). — EGYPTIAN SEPULCHRES AND SYRIAN SHRINES. New Edition. Cr. 8vo. 7s. 6d.
TAVERNIER (Baron): TRAVELS IN INDIA OF JEAN BAPTISTE TAVERNIER. Transl. by V. BALL, LL.D. 2 vols. 8vo. 42s.
TRISTRAM. (See ILLUSTRATED BOOKS.)
TURNER (Rev. G.). (See ANTHROPOLOGY.)
WALLACE (A. R.). (See NATURAL HISTORY.)
WATERTON (Charles).—WANDERINGS IN SOUTH AMERICA, THE NORTH-WEST OF THE UNITED STATES, AND THE ANTILLES. Edited by Rev. J. G. WOOD. Illustr. Cr. 8vo. 6s.—People's Edition. 4to. 6d.
WATSON (R. Spence).—A VISIT TO WAZAN, THE SACRED CITY OF MOROCCO. 8vo. 10s. 6d.

YOUNG, Books for the.
(See also BIBLICAL HISTORY, p. 33.)
ÆSOP—CALDECOTT.—SOME OF ÆSOP'S FABLES, with Modern Instances, shown in Designs by RANDOLPH CALDECOTT. 4to. 5s.
ARIOSTO.—PALADIN AND SARACEN. Stories from Ariosto. By H. C. HOLLWAY-CALTHROP. Illustrated. Cr. 8vo. 6s.
ATKINSON (Rev. J. C.).—THE LAST OF THE GIANT KILLERS. Globe 8vo. 3s. 6d.
—— WALKS, TALKS, TRAVELS, AND EXPLOITS OF TWO SCHOOLBOYS. Cr. 8vo. 3s. 6d.
—— PLAYHOURS AND HALF-HOLIDAYS, OR FURTHER EXPERIENCES OF TWO SCHOOLBOYS. Cr. 8vo. 3s 6d
—— SCENES IN FAIRYLAND. Cr. 8vo. 4s. 6d.
AWDRY (Frances).—THE STORY OF A FELLOW SOLDIER. (A Life of Bishop Patteson for the Young.) Globe 8vo. 2s. 6d.

BOOKS FOR THE YOUNG.

BOOKS FOR THE YOUNG—*continued.*

BAKER (Sir S. W.).—TRUE TALES FOR MY GRANDSONS. Illustrated. Cr. 8vo. 3s. 6d.
—— CAST UP BY THE SEA : OR, THE ADVENTURES OF NED GRAY. Illust Cr. 8vo. 6s.

CARROLL (Lewis).—ALICE'S ADVENTURES IN WONDERLAND. With 42 Illustrations by TENNIEL. Cr. 8vo. 6s. net.
People's Edition. With all the original Illustrations. Cr. 8vo. 2s. 6d. net.
A GERMAN TRANSLATION OF THE SAME. Cr. 8vo. 6s. net. A FRENCH TRANSLATION OF THE SAME. Cr. 8vo. 6s. net. AN ITALIAN TRANSLATION OF THE SAME. Cr. 8vo. 6s. net.
—— ALICE'S ADVENTURES UNDER-GROUND. Being a Fascimile of the Original MS. Book, afterwards developed into "Alice's Adventures in Wonderland." With 27 Illustrations by the Author. Cr. 8vo. 4s net.

CARROLL (Lewis).—THROUGH THE LOOKING-GLASS AND WHAT ALICE FOUND THERE. With 50 Illustrations by TENNIEL. Cr. 8vo. 6s. net
People's Edition. With all the original Illustrations. Cr. 8vo. 2s. 6d. net.
People's Edition of "Alice's Adventures in Wonderland," and "Through the Looking-Glass." 1 vol. Cr. 8vo. 4s. 6d. net.
—— RHYME? AND REASON? With 65 Illustrations by ARTHUR B. FROST, and 9 by HENRY HOLIDAY. Cr. 8vo. 6s. net.
—— A TANGLED TALE. With 6 Illustrations by ARTHUR B. FROST. Cr. 8vo. 4s. 6d. net.
—— SYLVIE AND BRUNO. With 46 Illustrations by HARRY FURNISS. Cr. 8vo. 7s. 6d. net.
—— (Concluded.) With Illustrations by HARRY FURNISS. Cr. 8vo. 7s. 6d. net.
—— THE NURSERY "ALICE." Twenty Coloured Enlargements from TENNIEL'S Illustrations to "Alice's Adventures in Wonderland," with Text adapted to Nursery Readers. 4to. 4s. net.—*People's Edition.* 4to. 2s. net.
—— THE HUNTING OF THE SNARK, AN AGONY IN EIGHT FITS. With 9 Illustrations by HENRY HOLIDAY. Cr. 8vo. 4s. 6d. net.

CLIFFORD (Mrs. W. K.).—ANYHOW STORIES. With Illustrations by DOROTHY TENNANT Cr. 8vo. 1s. 6d. ; paper covers, 1s.

CORBETT (Julian).—FOR GOD AND GOLD. Cr. 8vo. 6s.

CRAIK (Mrs.).—ALICE LEARMONT : A FAIRY TALE. Illustrated. Globe 8vo. 2s. 6d.
—— THE ADVENTURES OF A BROWNIE. Illustrated by Mrs. ALLINGHAM. Gl. 8vo. 2s. 6d.
—— THE LITTLE LAME PRINCE AND HIS TRAVELLING CLOAK. Illustrated by J. McL. RALSTON. Globe 8vo. 2s. 6d.
—— OUR YEAR : A CHILD'S BOOK IN PROSE AND VERSE. Illustrated. Gl. 8vo. 2s. 6d.
—— LITTLE SUNSHINE'S HOLIDAY. Globe 8vo. 2s. 6d.
—— THE FAIRY BOOK : THE BEST POPULAR FAIRY STORIES. Pott 8vo. 2s. 6d. net.
—— CHILDREN S POETRY. Ex. fcp. 8vo. 4s. 6d.
—— SONGS OF OUR YOUTH. Small 4to. 6s.

DE MORGAN (Mary).—THE NECKLACE OF PRINCESS FIORIMONDE, AND OTHER STORIES. Illustrated by WALTER CRANE. Ext. fcp. 8vo. 3s. 6d.—Large Paper Ed., with Illustrations on India Paper. 100 copies printed.

FOWLER (W. W.). (*See* NATURAL HISTORY.)

GREENWOOD (Jessy E.).—THE MOON MAIDEN: AND OTHER STORIES. Cr. 8vo. 2s. 6d.

GRIMM'S FAIRY TALES. Translated by LUCY CRANE, and Illustrated by WALTER CRANE. Cr. 8vo. 6s.

KEARY (A. and E.).—THE HEROES OF ASGARD. Tales from Scandinavian Mythology. Globe 8vo. 2s. 6d

KEARY (E.).—THE MAGIC VALLEY. Illustr. by "E. V. B." Globe 8vo. 4s. 6d.

KINGSLEY (Charles).—THE HEROES; or, Greek Fairy Tales for my Children. Cr. 8vo. 3s. 6d.—*Presentation Ed.*, gilt edges. 7s. 6d.
MADAM HOW AND LADY WHY; or, First Lessons in Earth-Lore. Cr. 8vo. 3s. 6d.
THE WATER-BABIES : A Fairy Tale for a Land Baby. Cr. 8vo. 3s. 6d.—New Edit. Illus. by L. SAMBOURNE. Fcp. 4to. 12s. 6d.

MACLAREN (Arch.).—THE FAIRY FAMILY. A Series of Ballads and Metrical Tales. Cr. 8vo. 5s.

MACMILLAN (Hugh). (*See* p. 38.)

MADAME TABBY'S ESTABLISHMENT. By KARI. Illust. by L. WAIN. Cr. 8vo. 4s. 6d.

MAGUIRE (J. F.).—YOUNG PRINCE MARIGOLD. Illustrated. Globe 8vo. 4s. 6d.

MARTIN (Frances).—THE POET'S HOUR. Poetry selected for Children. Pott 8vo. 2s. 6d.
—— SPRING-TIME WITH THE POETS. Pott 8vo. 3s. 6d.

MAZINI (Linda).—IN THE GOLDEN SHELL. With Illustrations. Globe 8vo. 4s. 6d.

MOLESWORTH (Mrs.).—WORKS. Illustr. Globe 8vo. 2s. 6d. each.
"CARROTS," JUST A LITTLE BOY.
A CHRISTMAS CHILD.
CHRISTMAS-TREE LAND.
THE CUCKOO CLOCK.
FOUR WINDS FARM.
GRANDMOTHER DEAR.
HERR BABY.
LITTLE MISS PEGGY.
THE RECTORY CHILDREN.
ROSY.
THE TAPESTRY ROOM.
TELL ME A STORY.
TWO LITTLE WAIFS.
"US" : An Old-Fashioned Story.
CHILDREN OF THE CASTLE.
A CHRISTMAS POSY.
NURSE HEATHERDALE'S STORY.
THE GIRLS AND I.
—— MARY. Illustrated by L. BROOKE. Cr. 8vo. 4s. 6d.
—— FOUR GHOST STORIES. Cr. 8vo. 6s.

OLIPHANT (Mrs.).—AGNES HOPETOUN'S SCHOOLS AND HOLIDAYS. Illust. Gl. 8vo. 2s. 6d.

PALGRAVE (Francis Turner).—THE FIVE DAYS' ENTERTAINMENTS AT WENTWORTH GRANGE. Small 4to. 6s.
—— THE CHILDREN'S TREASURY OF LYRICAL POETRY. Pott 8vo. 2s. 6d.—Or in 2 parts, 1s. each.

PATMORE (C.).—THE CHILDREN'S GARLAND FROM THE BEST POETS. Pott 8vo. 2s. 6d. net.

BOOKS FOR THE YOUNG—ZOOLOGY. 43

ROSSETTI (Christina).—SPEAKING LIKE NESSES. Illust. by A. HUGHES. Cr. 8vo. 4s. 6d
— SING-SONG: A Nursery Rhyme-Book. Small 4to. 4s. 6d.
RUTH AND HER FRIENDS: A STORY FOR GIRLS. Illustrated. Globe 8vo. 2s. 6d.
ST. JOHNSTON (A.).—CAMPING AMONG CANNIBALS. Cr. 8vo. 4s. 6d.
— CHARLIE ASGARDE: THE STORY OF A FRIENDSHIP. Illustrated by HUGH THOMSON. Cr. 8vo. 5s.
"ST. OLAVE'S" (Author of). Illustrated. Globe 8vo.
WHEN I WAS A LITTLE GIRL. 2s. 6d.
NINE YEARS OLD. 2s. 6d.
WHEN PAPA COMES HOME. 4s. 6d.
PANSIE'S FLOUR BIN. 4s. 6d.
STEWART (Aubrey).—THE TALE OF TROY. Done into English. Globe 8vo. 3s. 6d.
TENNYSON (Lord).—JACK AND THE BEAN-STALK. English Hexameters. Illust. by R. CALDECOTT. Fcp. 4to. 3s. 6d.
"WANDERING WILLIE" (Author of).—CONRAD THE SQUIRREL. Globe 8vo. 2s. 6d.
WARD (Mrs. T. Humphry).—MILLY AND OLLY. With Illustrations by Mrs. ALMA TADEMA. Globe 8vo. 2s. 6d.
WEBSTER (Augusta).—DAFFODIL AND THE CROÄXAXICANS. Cr. 8vo. 6s.
WILLOUGHBY (F.).—FAIRY GUARDIANS. Illustr. by TOWNLEY GREEN. Cr. 8vo. 5s.
WOODS (M. A.). (See COLLECTIONS, p. 18.)
YONGE (Charlotte M.).—THE PRINCE AND THE PAGE. Cr. 8vo. 2s. 6d.
— A BOOK OF GOLDEN DEEDS. Pott 8vo. 2s. 6d net. Globe 8vo. 2s.—Abridged Edition. 1s.
— LANCES OF LYNWOOD. Cr. 8vo. 3s. 6d.
— P's AND Q's; and LITTLE LUCY'S WONDERFUL GLOBE. Illustrated. Cr. 8vo. 3s. 6d.
— A STOREHOUSE OF STORIES. 2 vols. Globe 8vo. 2s. 6d. each.
— THE POPULATION OF AN OLD PEAR-TREE; or, Stories of Insect Life. From E. VAN BRUYSSEL. Illustr. Gl. 8vo. 2s. 6d.

ZOOLOGY.

Comparative Anatomy—Practical Zoology—Entomology—Ornithology.

(*See also* BIOLOGY; NATURAL HISTORY; PHYSIOLOGY.)

Comparative Anatomy.

FLOWER (Sir W. H.).—AN INTRODUCTION TO THE OSTEOLOGY OF THE MAMMALIA. Illustrated. 3rd Edit., revised with the assistance of HANS GADOW, Ph.D. Cr. 8vo. 10s. 6d.
HUMPHRY (Prof. Sir G. M.).—OBSERVATIONS IN MYOLOGY. 8vo. 6s.

LANG (Prof. Arnold).—TEXT-BOOK OF COMPARATIVE ANATOMY. Transl. by H. M. and M. BERNARD. Preface by Prof. E. HAECKEL. Illustr. 2 vols. 8vo. Part I. 17s. net.
PARKER (T. Jeffery).—A COURSE OF INSTRUCTION IN ZOOTOMY (VERTEBRATA). Illustrated. Cr. 8vo. 8s. 6d.
PETTIGREW (J. Bell).—THE PHYSIOLOGY OF THE CIRCULATION IN PLANTS, IN THE LOWER ANIMALS, AND IN MAN. 8vo. 12s.
SHUFELDT (R. W.).—THE MYOLOGY OF THE RAVEN (*Corvus corax Sinuatus*). A Guide to the Study of the Muscular System in Birds. Illustrated. 8vo. 13s. net.
WIEDERSHEIM (Prof. R.).—ELEMENTS OF THE COMPARATIVE ANATOMY OF VERTEBRATES. Adapted by W. NEWTON PARKER. With Additions. Illustrated. 8vo. 12s. 6d.

Practical Zoology.

HOWES (Prof. G. B.).—AN ATLAS OF PRACTICAL ELEMENTARY BIOLOGY. With a Preface by Prof. HUXLEY. 4to. 14s.
HUXLEY (T. H.) and MARTIN (H. N.).—A COURSE OF ELEMENTARY INSTRUCTION IN PRACTICAL BIOLOGY. Revised and extended by Prof. G. B. HOWES and D. H. SCOTT, Ph.D. Cr. 8vo. 10s. 6d.
THOMSON (Sir C. Wyville).—THE VOYAGE OF THE "CHALLENGER": THE ATLANTIC. With Illustrations, Coloured Maps, Charts, etc. 2 vols. 8vo. 45s.
THOMSON (Sir C. Wyville).—THE DEPTHS OF THE SEA. An Account of the Results of the Dredging Cruises of H.M.SS. "Lightning" and "Porcupine," 1868-69-70. With Illustrations, Maps, and Plans. 8vo. 31s. 6d.

Entomology.

BADENOCH (L. N.).—ROMANCE OF THE INSECT WORLD. Cr. 8vo. 6s.
BUCKTON (G. B.).—MONOGRAPH OF THE BRITISH CICADÆ, OR TETTIGIDÆ. 2 vols. 42s. net; or in 8 Parts. 8s. each net.
LUBBOCK (Sir John).—THE ORIGIN AND METAMORPHOSES OF INSECTS. Illustrated. Cr. 8vo. 3s. 6d.
SCUDDER (S. H.).—FOSSIL INSECTS OF NORTH AMERICA. Map and Plates. 2 vols. 4to. 90s. net.

Ornithology.

COUES (Elliott).—KEY TO NORTH AMERICAN BIRDS. Illustrated. 8vo. 2l. 2s.
— HANDBOOK OF FIELD AND GENERAL ORNITHOLOGY. Illustrated. 8vo. 10s. net.
FOWLER (W. W.). (*See* NATURAL HISTORY.)
WHITE (Gilbert). (*See* NATURAL HISTORY.)

INDEX.

	PAGE
ABBEY (E. A.)	13, 41
ABBOT (F. E.)	36
ABBOTT (E. A.)	3, 14,, 33, 36
ACLAND (Sir H. W.)	24
ADAMS (Sir F. O.)	31
ADDISON	4, 20, 22
AGASSIZ (L.)	3
AINGER (Rev. A.)	4, 5, 17, 23, 36
AINSLIE (A. D.)	15
AIRY (Sir G. B.)	2, 29
AITKEN (Mary C.)	22
AITKEN (Sir W.)	26
ALBEMARLE (Earl of)	3
ALDOUS (J. C. P.)	35
ALDRICH (T. B.)	14
ALEXANDER (C. F.)	22
ALEXANDER (T.)	9
ALEXANDER (Bishop)	36
ALLBUTT (T. C.)	24
ALLEN (G.)	6
ALLINGHAM (W.)	21
AMIEL (H. F.)	3
ANDERSON (A.)	15
ANDERSON (Dr. McCall)	24
ANDREWS (C. M.)	10
ANDREWS (Dr. Thomas)	29
APPLETON (T. G.)	40
ARCHER-HIND (R. D.)	40
ARNOLD (M.)	8, 15, 21, 22, 31, 33
ARNOLD (Dr. T.)	10
ARNOLD (W. T.)	10
ASHLEY (W. J.)	3
ATKINSON (J. B.)	2
ATKINSON (Rev. J. C.)	1, 41
ATTWELL (H.)	22
AUSTIN (Alfred)	15
AUTENRIETH (Georg)	8
AWDRY (F.)	41
BACON (Francis)	3, 21, 22
BADENOCH (L. N.)	43
BAINES (Rev. E.)	36
BAKER (Sir S. W.)	31, 32, 40, 41, 42
BALCH (Elizabeth)	12
BALDWIN (Prof. J. M.)	28
BALFOUR (F. M.)	6
BALFOUR (J. B.)	6
BALL (V.)	41
BALL (W. Platt)	6
BALL (W. W. R.)	24
BALLANCE (C. A.)	24
BARKER (G. F.)	29
BARKER (Lady)	2, 8, 41
BARNARD (C.)	29
BARNES (W.)	3
BARNETT (E. A)	8
BARTHOLOMEW (J. G.)	3
BARTLETT (J.)	8
BARWELL (R.)	24
BASTABLE (Prof. C. F.)	30
BASTIAN (H. C.)	6, 25
BATES (K. L.)	21
BATESON (W.)	6
BATH (Marquis of)	31
BATHER (Archdeacon)	36
BAXTER (L.)	3

	PAGE
BEESLY (Mrs.)	4, 10
BENHAM (Rev. W.)	5, 21, 22, 35
BENSON (Archbishop)	36
BENSON (W. A. S.)	32
BERLIOZ (H.)	3
BERNARD (C. E.)	3
BERNARD (J. H.)	27
BERNARD (H. M.)	6
BERNARD (M.)	13
BERNARD (T. D.)	36
BERNERS (J.)	17
BESANT (W.)	4
BETHUNE-BAKER (J. F.)	36
BETTANY (G. T.)	6
BICKERTON (T. H.)	25
BIGELOW (M. M.)	13
BIKÉLAS D.)	18
BINNIE (Rev. W.)	36
BIRKS (T. R.)	6, 27, 33, 36
BJÖRNSON (B.)	18
BLACK (W.)	4
BLACKBURNE (E.)	3
BLACKIE (J. S.)	10, 15, 21
BLAKE (J. F.)	3
BLAKE (W.)	3
BLAKISTON (J. R.)	8
BLANFORD (H. F.)	9, 30
BLANFORD (W. T.)	9, 26
BLENNERHASSETT (R.)	41
BLOMFIELD (R.)	9
BLYTH (A. W.)	12
BÖHM-BAWERK (Prof.)	30
BOISSEVAIN (G. M.)	30
BOLDREWOOD (Rolf)	18
BONAR (J.)	30
BOND (Rev. J.)	34
BOOLE (G.)	28
BOOTH (C.)	32
BOSE (W. P. du)	37
BOUGHTON (G. H.)	41
BOUTMY (E.)	13
BOWEN (H. C.)	27
BOWER (F. O.)	6
BRETT (R. B)	10
BRIDGES (J. A.)	21
BRIGHT (H. A.)	9
BRIGHT (John)	31
BRIMLEY (G.)	21
BRODIE (Sir B. C.)	7
BRODRIBB (W. J.)	14, 40
BROOKE (Sir J.)	3
BROOKE (S. A.)	14, 15, 21, 35, 36
BROOKS (Bishop)	36, 41
BROWN (A. C.)	29
BROWN (J. A.)	1
BROWN (Dr. James)	4
BROWN (T. E.)	15
BROWNE (J. H. B.)	12
BROWNE (Sir T.)	22
BRUNTON (Dr. T. Lauder)	25, 36
BRYCE (James)	10, 31, 41
BUCHHEIM (C. A.)	21
BUCKLAND (A.)	5, 31
BUCKLEY (A. B.)	10, 11
BUCKNILL (Dr. J. C)	25

	PAGE
BUCKTON (G. B.)	43
BUNYAN	4, 21, 22
BURGON (J. W.)	15
BURKE (E.)	31
BURN (R.)	1
BURNETT (F. Hodgson)	18
BURNS	15, 21
BURY (J. B.)	10
BUTCHER (Prof. S. H.)	14, 21, 40
BUTLER (A. J.)	14, 40
BUTLER (Rev. G.)	36
BUTLER (Samuel)	15
BUTLER (W. Archer)	36
BUTLER (Sir W. F.)	4
BUXTON (Mrs. S.)	33
BYRON	22
CAIRNES (J. E.)	30, 31
CALDECOTT (R.)	13, 41
CALDERON	15
CALDERWOOD (Prof. H.)	6, 8, 27, 28
CALVERT (Rev. A.)	34
CAMERON (V. L.)	41
CAMPBELL (G.)	3
CAMPBELL (J. D.)	15
CAMPBELL (J. F.)	41
CAMPBELL (Dr. J. M.)	36
CAMPBELL (Prof. Lewis)	5, 14
CANTILLON	30
CAPES (W. W.)	14
CARLES (W. R.)	41
CARLYLE (T.)	3
CARMARTHEN (Lady)	18
CARNARVON (Earl of)	40
CARNOT (N. L. G.)	29
CARPENTER (Bishop)	36
CARR (J. C.)	2
CARROLL (Lewis)	28, 42
CARTER (R. Brudenell)	25
CASSEL (Dr. D.)	10
CAUTLEY (G. S.)	15
CAZENOVE (J. G.)	36
CHALMERS (J. B.)	9
CHALMERS (M. D.)	31
CHAPMAN (Elizabeth R.)	14
CHAPPELL (W)	26
CHASE (Rev. F. H.)	34
CHASSERESSE (Diana)	32
CHERRY (R. R.)	13
CHEYNE (C. H. H.)	3
CHEYNE (T. K.)	33
CHRISTIE (J.)	25
CHRISTIE (W. D.)	21
CHURCH (Prof. A. H.)	6
CHURCH (Rev. A. J.)	4, 33, 40
CHURCH (F. J.)	22, 40
CHURCH (Dean)	4, 5, 21, 34, 37
CLARE (G.)	30
CLARK (J. W.)	22
CLARK (L.)	3
CLARK (R)	32
CLARK (S.)	4
CLARKE (C. B.)	9, 30
CLEVELAND (Duchess)	4
CLIFFORD (Ed.)	4

INDEX. 45

Name	Page
CLIFFORD (W. K.)	21, 28
CLIFFORD (Mrs. W. K.)	42
CLOUGH (A. H.)	15, 21
COBDEN (R.)	31
COHEN (J. B.)	7
COLENSO (J. W.)	35
COLERIDGE (C. R.)	20
COLERIDGE (S. T.)	15
COLLIER (Hon. John)	2
COLLINS (J. Churton)	21
COLQUHOUN (F. S.)	15
COLVIN (Sidney)	4, 22, 23
COMBE (G.)	8
COMMONS (J. R.)	30
CONGREVE (Rev. J.)	37
CONWAY (Hugh)	18
COOK (E. T.)	2
COOKE (C. Kinloch)	26
COOKE (J. P.)	7, 37
COOPER (E. H.)	18
CORBETT (J.)	4, 18, 42
CORFIELD (W. H.)	12
COSSA (L.)	30
COTTERILL (J. H.)	9
COTTON (Bishop)	37
COTTON (C.)	13
COTTON (J. S.)	31
COUES (E.)	43
COURTHOPE (W. J.)	4
COWELL (G.)	25
COWPER	21, 22
COX (G. V.)	10
CRAIK (Mrs.) 15, 18, 21, 22, 41, 42	
CRAIK (H.)	8, 21, 31
CRANE (Lucy)	42
CRANE (Walter)	42
CRAVEN (Mrs. D.)	8
CRAWFORD (F. M.)	18, 21
CREIGHTON (Bishop M.)	4, 11
CRICHTON-BROWNE (Sir J.)	8
CROSS (J. A.)	33
CROSSLEY (R.)	12
CROSSLEY (E.)	3
CROSSLEY (H.)	40
CUMMING (L.)	29
CUNLIFFE (J. W.)	21
CUNNINGHAM (C.)	31
CUNNINGHAM (Sir H. S.)	18
CUNNINGHAM (Rev. J.)	34
CUNNINGHAM (Rev. W.) 34, 36, 37	
CUNYNGHAME (Sir A. T.)	26
CURTEIS (Rev. G. H.)	35, 37
DAHLSTROM (K. P.)	9
DAHN (F.)	18
DAKYNS (H. G.)	40
DALE (A. W. W.)	34
DALTON (Rev. J. N.)	40
DANIELL (Alfred)	29
DANTE	4, 14, 40
DAVIES (Rev. J. Ll.)	34, 35, 37
DAVIES (W.)	5
DAWKINS (W. B.)	1
DAWSON (G. M.)	9
DAWSON (Sir J. W.)	9
DAWSON (W. J.)	15
DAY (L. B.)	18
DAY (R. E.)	29
DEFOE (D.)	4, 21, 22
DEIGHTON (K.)	5, 16
DELAMOTTE (P. H.)	2
DELL (E. C.)	12
DE MORGAN (M.)	42
DE VARIGNY (H.)	6
DE VERE (A.)	15, 21
DICEY (A. V.)	13, 31
DICKENS (C.)	5, 18, 21
DICKENS (M. A.)	18, 21
DIGGLE (Rev. J. W.)	37
DILKE (Ashton W.)	20
DILKE (Sir Charles W.)	26, 31
DILLWYN (E. A.)	18
DOBBIN (L.)	7
DOBSON (A.)	4
DONALDSON (J.)	36
DONISTHORPE (W.)	31
DOWDEN (E.)	4, 14, 17
DOYLE (Sir F. H.)	15
DOYLE (J. A.)	11
DRAKE (B.)	40
DRUMMOND (Prof. J.)	37
DRYDEN	21
DU CANE (E. F.)	31
DUFF (Sir M. E. G.) 5, 21, 31, 41	
DUNSMUIR (A.)	19
DÜNTZER (H.)	5
DURAND (Sir R.)	19
DYER (L.)	2, 30
EADIE (J.)	4, 33, 34
EASTLAKE (Lady)	35
EBERS (G.)	19
ECCLES (A. S.)	25
EDGEWORTH (Prof. F. Y.)	30
EDMUNDS (Dr. W.)	24
EDWARDS-MOSS (Sir J. E.)	32
EIMER (G. H. T.)	6
ELDERTON (W. A.)	9
ELLERTON (Rev. J.)	37
ELLIOT (Hon. A.)	31
ELLIS (T.)	2
EMERSON (R. W.)	4, 21
EVANS (S.)	15
EVERETT (J. D.)	29
FALCONER (Lanoe)	19
FARRAR (Archdeacon)	6, 33, 37
FARRER (Sir T. H.)	31
FAULKNER (F.)	7
FAWCETT (Prof. H.)	30, 32
FAWCETT (M. G.)	6, 31, 32
FAY (Amy)	26
FEARNLEY (W.)	30
FEARON (D. R.)	8
FERREL (W.)	30
FESSENDEN (C.)	29
FINCK (H. T.)	1
FINLAYSON (T. C.)	21
FISHER (Rev. O.)	29, 30
FISKE (J.)	6, 10, 27, 32, 37
FISON (L.)	1
FITCH (J. G.)	8
FITZ GERALD (Caroline)	15
FITZGERALD (Edward)	15, 21
FITZMAURICE (Lord E.)	5
FLEISCHER (E.)	7
FLEMING (G.)	19
FLOWER (Sir W. H.)	43
FLÜCKIGER (F. A.)	25
FORBES (A.)	4, 41
FORBES (Prof. G.)	3
FORBES (Rev. G. H.)	37
FORBES-MITCHELL (W.)	4
FOSTER (Prof. M.)	6, 30
FOTHERGILL (Dr. J. M.)	8, 25
FOWLE (Rev. T. W.)	31, 37
FOWLER (Rev. T.)	4, 28
FOWLER (W. W.)	2, 26
FOX (Dr. Wilson)	25
FOXWELL (Prof. H. S)	31
FRAMJI (D.)	10
FRANKLAND (P. F.)	1
FRASER (Bishop)	37
FRASER-TYTLER (C. C.)	15
FRAZER (J. G.)	1
FREEMAN (Prof. E. A.) 2, 4, 10, 11, 32, 35	
FRENCH (G. R.)	14
FRIEDMANN (P.)	3
FROST (A. B.)	42
FROUDE (J. A.)	4
FULLERTON (W. M.)	41
FURNISS (Harry)	42
FURNIVALL (F. J.)	15
FYFFE (C. A.)	11
FYFE (H. H.)	10
GAIRDNER (J.)	4
GAISFORD (H.)	9
GALTON (F.)	1
GAMGEE (Arthur)	30
GARDNER (Percy)	2
GARNETT (R.)	15
GARNETT (W.)	5
GASKELL (Mrs.)	12
GASKOIN (Mrs. H.)	33
GEDDES (W. D.)	14, 40
GEE (W. H.)	29
GEIKIE (Sir A.)	9, 10, 30
GENNADIUS (J.)	18
GIBBINS (H. de B.)	10
GIBBON (Charles)	4
GILCHRIST (A.)	3
GILES (P.)	27
GILMAN (N. P.)	31, 32
GILMORE (Rev. J.)	13
GLADSTONE (Dr. J. H.)	7, 8
GLADSTONE (W. E.)	14
GLAISTER (E.)	2, 8
GODFRAY (H.)	3
GODKIN (G. S.)	5
GOETHE	3, 5, 15, 21
GOLDSMITH	4, 12, 15, 21, 22
GOODALE (Prof. G. L.)	6
GOODFELLOW (J.)	12
GORDON (General C. G.)	5
GORDON (Lady Duff)	41
GORDON (H.)	29
GOSCHEN (Rt. Hon. G. J.)	31
GOSSE (Edmund)	4, 14
GOW (J.)	2
GRAHAM (D.)	15
GRAHAM (J. W.)	19
GRAND'HOMME (E.)	8
GRAY (Prof. Andrew)	6, 29
GRAY (Asa)	6, 22
GRAY	4, 15, 22
GRAY (J. L.)	22
GREEN (J. R.)	9, 11, 12, 22
GREEN (Mrs. J. R.)	4, 9, 11
GREEN (W. S.)	41
GREENHILL (W. A.)	22
GREENWOOD (F.)	22
GREENWOOD (J. E.)	42
GRENFELL (Mrs.)	8
GRIFFITHS (W. H.)	25
GRIMM	42
GROVE (Sir G.)	9, 26
GUEST (E.)	11
GUEST (M. J.)	11
GUILLEMIN (A.)	26, 29
GUIZOT (F. P. G.)	6
GUNTON (G.)	31
GWATKIN (H. M.)	34
HALES (J. W.)	15, 18, 21
HALLWARD (R. F.)	12
HAMERTON (P. G.)	2, 12, 22
HAMILTON (Prof. D. J.)	25
HAMILTON (J.)	37

INDEX.

	PAGE		PAGE		PAGE
Hanbury (D.)	7, 25	Irving (H.)	17	Leslie (G. D.)	23
Hannay (David)	4	Irving (J.)	10	Lethaby (W. R.)	32
Hardwick (Archd. C.)	34, 37	Irving (Washington)	13	Lethbridge (Sir Roper)	5, 11
Hardy (A. S.)	19	Jackson (D. C.)	29	Levy (Amy)	20
Hardy (T.)	19	Jackson (Helen)	19	Lewis (R.)	13
Hare (A. W.)	22	Jacob (Rev. J. A.)	37	Lightfoot (Bp.)	23, 33, 34, 36, 38
Hare (J. C.)	37	James (Henry)	4, 19, 23	Lightwood (J. M.)	13
Harper (Father Thos.)	37	James (Rev. H.)	37	Lindsay (Dr. J. A.)	25
Harris (Rev. G. C.)	37	James (Prof. W.)	28	Littledale (H.)	14
Harrison (F.)	4, 6, 12, 22	Jardine (Rev. R.)	28	Lockyer (J. N.)	3, 7, 30
Harrison (Miss J.)	2	Jeans (Rev. G E.)	37, 40	Lodge (Prof. O. J.)	3, 23, 29
Harte (Bret)	19	Jebb (Prof. R. C.)	4, 11, 14, 23	Loewy (B.)	29
Hartig (Dr. R.)	7	Jellett (Rev. J. H.)	37	Loftie (Mrs. W. J.)	v
Hartley (Prof. W. N.)	7	Jenks (Prof. Ed.)	32	Longfellow (H. W.)	22
Harwood (G.)	22, 32, 35	Jennings (A. C.)	11, 33	Lonsdale (J.)	21, 40
Hauser (K.)	5	Jephson (H.)	32	Lowe (W. H.)	32, 33
Hayes (A.)	15	Jevons (W. S.)	5, 28, 31, 32	Lowell (J. R.)	13, 16, 23
Headlam (A. C.)	2	Jex-Blake (Sophia)	8	Lubbock (Sir J.)	6, 7, 9, 23, 43
Headlam (W.)	40	Johnson (Amy)	29	Lucas (F.)	16
Heaviside (O.)	29	Johnson (Samuel)	5, 14	Lucas (Joseph)	40
Helps (Sir A.)	22	Jolley (A. J.)	33	Lupton (S.)	7
Hempel (Dr. W.)	7	Jones (H. Arthur)	15	Lyall (Sir Alfred)	4
Herodotus	40	Jones (Prof. D. E.)	29	Lysaght (S. R.)	20
Herrick	22	Jones (F.)	7	Lyte (H. C. M.)	11
Herrmann (G.)	9	Kalm	41	Lyttelton (E.)	23
Hertel (Dr.)	9	Kant	28	Lytton (Earl of)	20
Hickie (W. J.)	33	Kari	42	MacAlister (D.)	26
Hill (D. J.)	28	Kavanagh (Rt. Hn. A. M.)	5	MacArthur (M.)	11
Hill (F. Davenport)	32	Kay (Rev. W.)	34	Macaulay (G. C.)	17, 40
Hill (O.)	32	Keary (Annie)	11, 19, 33, 42	Macaulay (Lord)	23
Hiorns (A. H.)	26	Keary (Eliza)	42	MacColl (Norman)	15
Hobart (Lord)	22	Keats	4, 22, 23	M'Cosh (Dr. J.)	28
Hobday (E.)	9	Kellner (Dr. L.)	37	Macdonald (G.)	18
Hodgson (Rev. J. T.)	5	Kellogg (Rev. S. H.)	37	Mackail (J. W.)	40
Hoffding (Prof. H.)	28	Kelvin (Lord)	27, 29	Maclagan (Dr. T.)	25
Hofmann (A. W.)	7	Kempe (A. B.)	29	Maclaren (Rev. Alex.)	38
Hole (Rev. C.)	8, 11	Kennedy (Prof. A. B. W.)	9	Maclaren (Archibald)	42
Holiday (Henry)	4	Kennedy (B. H.)	40	Maclean (W. C.)	25
Holland (T. E.)	13, 32	Kennedy (P.)	19	Maclear (Rev. Dr.)	32, 33, 35
Hollway-Calthrop (H.)	41	Keynes (J. N.)	28, 31	M'Lennan (J. F.)	1
Holmes (O. W., junr.)	13	Kiepert (H.)	9	M'Lennan (Malcolm)	20
Homer	14, 40	Killen (W. D.)	35	Macmillan (Rev. H.)	23, 38
Hood (T.)	12	Kingsley (Charles)	5, 9, 11, 12, 13, 14, 16, 19, 23, 26, 35, 41, 42	Macmillan (Michael)	5, 16
Hooker (Sir J. D.)	7, 41			Macnamara (C.)	25
Hoole (C. H.)	33	Kingsley (Henry)	21, 41	Macquoid (K. S.)	20
Hooper (G.)	4	Kipling (J. L.)	41	Madoc (F.)	20
Hooper (W. H.)	2	Kipling (Rudyard)	19	Maguire (J. F.)	42
Hope (F. J.)	9	Kirkpatrick (Prof.)	37	Mahaffy (Prof. J. P.)	2, 11, 14, 23, 28, 38, 41
Hopkins (E.)	15	Klein (Dr. E.)	6, 25, 26		
Hoppus (M. A. M.)	19	Knight (W.)	14, 28	Maitland (F. W.)	13, 31
Horace	14, 21, 40	Kuenen (Prof. A.)	33	Malet (L.)	20
Hort (F. J. A.)	33, 35, 37	Kynaston (Rev. H.)	37, 40	Malory (Sir T.)	21
Horton (Hon. S. D.)	31	Labberton (R. H.)	3	Mansfield (C. B.)	7
Hosken (J. D.)	15	Lafargue (P.)	19	Markham (C. R.)	4
Hovenden (R. M.)	40	Lamb	5, 22, 23	Marriott (J. A. R.)	6
Howell (George)	31	Lanciani (Prof. R.)	2	Marshall (Prof. A.)	31
Howes (G. B.)	43	Landauer (J.)	7	Martel (C.)	26
Howitt (A. W.)	1	Landor	4, 22	Martin (Frances)	3, 42
Howson (Very Rev. J. S.)	35	Lane-Poole (S.)	22	Martin (Frederick)	31
Hozier (Col. H. M.)	26	Lanfrey (P.)	5	Martin (H. N.)	43
Hübner (Baron)	41	Lang (Andrew)	13, 22, 40	Martineau (H.)	6
Hughes (T.)	3, 4, 5, 15, 19, 22, 41	Lang (Prof. Arnold)	43	Masson (D.)	4, 5, 16, 21, 28
Hull (E.)	2, 10	Langley (J. N.)	30	Masson (G.)	8, 21
Hullah (J.)	2, 23, 26	Langmaid (T.)	9	Masson (R. O.)	18
Hume (D.)	4	Lankester (Prof. Ray)	6, 23	Maturin (Rev. W.)	38
Humphry (Prof. Sir G. M.)	30, 43	Laslett (T.)	7	Maudsley (Dr. H.)	28
Hunt (W.)	11	Laurie (A. P.)	1	Maurice (F.)	9, 23, 28, 32—35, 38
Hunt (W. M.)	2	Lea (A. S.)	29	Maurice (Col. F.)	4, 5, 26, 31
Hutchinson (G. W. C.)	2	Leaf (W.)	14, 40	Max Müller (F.)	28
Hutton (R. H.)	4, 22	Leahy (Sergeant)	32	Mayer (A. M.)	29
Huxley (T.)	4, 23, 28, 30, 32, 43	Lee (M.)	20	Mayor (J. B.)	34
		Lee (S.)	21, 40	Mayor (Prof. J. E. B.)	3, 5
Illingworth (Rev. J. R.)	37	Leeper (A.)	40	Mazini (L.)	42
Ingram (T. D.)	11	Legge (A. O.)	11, 37	M'Cormick (W. S.)	14
Ireland (A.)	23	Lemon (Mark)	22	Meldola (Prof. R.)	7, 28, 30

INDEX. 47

	PAGE		PAGE		PAGE
MENDENHALL (T. C.)	29	PARKINSON (S.)	29	ROGERS (J. E. T.)	12, 32
MERCIER (Dr. C.)	25	PARKMAN (F.)	11	ROMANES (G. J.)	6
MERCUR (Prof. J.)	26	PARRY (G.)	20	ROSCOE (Sir H. E.)	7, 8
MEREDITH (G.)	16	PARSONS (Alfred)	13	ROSCOE (W. C.)	16
MEREDITH (L. A.)	13	PASTEUR (L.)	7	ROSEBERY (Earl of)	4
MEYER (E. von)	7	PATER (W. H.)	2, 20, 24	ROSEVEAR (E.)	8
MICHELET (M.)	11	PATERSON (J.)	13	ROSS (P.)	20
MIERS (H. A.)	12	PATMORE (Coventry)	22, 42	ROSSETTI (C. G.)	16, 43
MILL (H. R.)	9	PATTESON (J. C.)	5	ROUTLEDGE (J.)	32
MILLER (R. K.)	3	PATTISON (Mark)	4, 5, 38	ROWE (F. J.)	17
MILLIGAN (Rev. W.)	34, 38	PAYNE (E. J.)	11, 31	RÜCKER (Prof. A. W.)	8
MILTON	5, 14, 16, 21	PEABODY (C. H.)	9, 29	RUMFORD (Count)	24
MINTO (Prof. W.)	4, 20	PEARSON (C. H.)	32	RUSHBROOKE (W. G.)	33
MITFORD (A. B.)	20	PEEL (E.)	16	RUSSELL (Dean)	38
MITFORD (M. R.)	13	PEILE (J.)	27	RUSSELL (Sir Charles)	32
MIVART (St. George)	30	PELLISSIER (E.)	27	RUSSELL (W. Clark)	4, 20
MIXTER (W. G.)	7	PENNINGTON (R.)	10	RYLAND (F.)	14
MOHAMMAD	22	PENROSE (F. C.)	1	RYLE (Prof. H. E.)	33, 38
MOLESWORTH (Mrs.)	42	PERCIVAL (H. M.)	16	ST. JOHNSTON (A.)	20, 41, 43
MOLLOY (G.)	29	PERKINS (J. B.)	11	SADLER (H.)	3
MONAHAN (J. H.)	13	PERRY (Prof. J.)	29	SAINTSBURY (G.)	4, 14
MONTELIUS (O.)	1	PETTIGREW (J. B.)	7, 30, 43	SALMON (Rev. G.)	38
MOORE (C. H.)	2	PHILLIMORE (J. G.)	13	SANDFORD (Bishop)	38
MOORHOUSE (Bishop)	38	PHILLIPS (J. A.)	26	SANDFORD (M. E.)	5
MORISON (J. C.)	3, 4	PHILLIPS (W. C.)	2	SANDYS (J. E.)	41
MORLEY (John)	3, 4, 17, 23	PICTON (J. A.)	24	SAYCE (A. H.)	12
MORRIS (Mowbray)	4, 21	PIFFARD (H. G.)	25	SCAIFE (W. B.)	24
MORRIS (R.)	21, 27	PIKE (W.)	41	SCARTAZZINI (G. A.)	14
MORSHEAD (E. D. A.)	40	PLATO	22, 40	SCHLIEMANN (Dr.)	2
MOULTON (L. C.)	16	PLUMPTRE (Dean)	38	SCHORLEMMER (C.)	7
MUDIE (C. E.)	16	POLLARD (A. W.)	14, 40	SCOTT (Sir W.)	16, 21
MUIR (M. M. P.)	7	POLLOCK (Sir Fk., and Bart.)	5	SCRATCHLEY (Sir Peter)	26
MÜLLER (H.)	7	POLLOCK (Sir F., Bt.)	13, 24, 31, 32	SCUDDER (S. H.)	43
MULLINGER (J. B.)	11	POLLOCK (Lady)	2	SEATON (Dr. E. C.)	25
MUNRO (J. E. C.)	9	POLLOCK (W. H.)	2	SEELEY (J. R.)	12
MURPHY (J. J.)	6, 28, 38	POOLE (M. E.)	24	SEILER (Dr. Carl)	25, 30
MURRAY (D. Christie)	20	POOLE (R. L.)	12	SELBORNE (Earl of)	22, 35, 36
MYERS (E.)	16, 40	POPE	4, 21	SELLERS (E.)	2
MYERS (F. W. H.)	4, 16, 23	POSTE (E.)	30, 40	SERVICE (J.)	35, 38
MYLNE (Bishop)	38	POTTER (L.)	24	SEWELL (E. M.)	12
NADAL (E. S.)	23	POTTER (R.)	38	SHADWELL (C. L.)	40
NETTLESHIP (H.)	14	PRESTON (T.)	29	SHAIRP (J. C.)	4, 16
NEWCASTLE (Duke and Duchess)	22	PRICE (L. L. F. R.)	31	SHAKESPEARE	14, 16, 21, 22
NEWCOMB (S.)	3	PRICKARD (A. O.)	24	SHANN (G.)	9, 29
NEWTON (Sir C. T.)	2	PRINCE ALBERT VICTOR	40	SHARP (W.)	5
NICHOL (J.)	4, 14	PRINCE GEORGE	40	SHELLEY	17, 22
NICHOLLS (H. A. A.)	1	PROCTER (F.)	35	SHIRLEY (W. N.)	38
NISBET (J)	7	PROPERT (J. L.)	2	SHORTHOUSE (J. H.)	20
NOEL (Lady A.)	20	RADCLIFFE (C. B.)	3	SHORTLAND (Admiral)	27
NORDENSKIÖLD (A. E.)	41	RAMSAY (W.)	7	SHUCHHARDT (Carl)	2
NORGATE (Kate)	11	RANSOME (C.)	14	SHUCKBURGH (E. S.)	12, 40
NORRIS (W. E.)	20	RATHBONE (W.)	8	SHUFELDT (R. W.)	43
NORTON (Charles Eliot)	3, 40	RAWLINSON (W. G.)	13	SIBSON (Dr. F.)	25
NORTON (Hon. Mrs.)	16, 20	RAWNSLEY (H. D.)	16	SIDGWICK (Prof. H.)	28, 31, 32
OLIPHANT (T. L. K.)	24, 27	RAY (P. K.)	28	SIME (J.)	9, 11
OLIPHANT (Mrs. M. O. W.)	4, 11, 14, 20, 22, 42	RAYLEIGH (Lord)	29	SIMPSON (Rev. W.)	35
		REICHEL (Bishop)	38	SKEAT (W. W.)	14
OLIVER (Prof. D.)	7	REID (J. S.)	40	SKRINE (J. H.)	5
OLIVER (Capt. S. P.)	41	REMSEN (I.)	7	SLADE (J. H.)	9
OMAN (C. W.)	4	RENAN (E.)	5	SLEEMAN (L.)	41
ORR (H. B.)	1	RENDALL (Rev. F.)	34, 38	SLOMAN (Rev. A.)	34
OSTWALD (Prof.)	7	RENDU (M. le C.)	10	SMART (W.)	31
OTTÉ (E. C.)	11	REYNOLDS (H. R.)	38	SMALLEY (G. W.)	24
PAGE (T. E.)	34	REYNOLDS (J. R.)	25	SMETHAM (J. and S.)	5
PALGRAVE (Sir F.)	11	REYNOLDS (O.)	12	SMITH (A.)	21
PALGRAVE (F. T.)	2, 16, 18, 21, 22, 36, 42	RHOADES (J.)	20	SMITH (C. B.)	17
		RHODES (J. F.)	12	SMITH (Goldw.)	4, 6, 18, 24, 32, 41
PALGRAVE (R. H. Inglis)	38	RICHARDSON (B. W.)	12, 25	SMITH (H.)	17
PALGRAVE (W. G.)	16, 32, 41	RICHEY (A. G.)	13	SMITH (J.)	7
PALMER (Lady S.)	20	RITCHIE (A.)	5	SMITH (Rev. T.)	38
PARKER (T. J.)	5, 6, 43	ROBINSON (Preb. H. G.)	38	SMITH (W. G.)	7
PARKER (W. K.)	5	ROBINSON (J. L.)	27	SMITH (W. S.)	39
PARKER (W. N.)	43	ROBINSON (Matthew)	5	SOMERVILLE (Prof. W.)	7
PARKIN (G. R.)	32	ROCHESTER (Bishop of)	5	SOUTHEY	5
		ROCKSTRO (W. S.)	2	SPENDER (J. K.)	25

INDEX.

	PAGE		PAGE		PAGE
Spenser	17, 21	Thring (E.)	9, 24	West (M.)	20
Spottiswoode (W.)	29	Thrupp (J. F.)	33	Westcott (Bp.)	33, 34, 35, 39
Stanley (Dean)	39	Thursfield (J. R.)	4	Westermarck (E.)	1
Stanley (Hon. Maude)	32	Todhunter (I.)	5	Wetherell (J.)	27
Statham (R.)	32	Torrens (W. M.)	5	Wheeler (J. T.)	12
Stebbing (W.)	4	Tourgénief (I. S.)	20	Whewell (W.)	5
Steel (F. A.)	20	Tout (T. F.)	4, 12	White (Gilbert)	26
Stephen (C. E.)	8	Tozer (H. F.)	9	White (Dr. W. Hale)	25
Stephen (H.)	13	Traill (H. D.)	4, 31	White (W.)	30
Stephen (Sir J. F.)	12, 13, 24	Trench (Capt. F.)	32	Whitney (W. D.)	8
Stephen (J. K.)	13	Trench (Archbishop)	39	Whittier (J. G.)	17, 24
Stephen (L.)	4	Trevelyan (Sir G. O.)	12	Whittuck (C. A.)	39
Stephens (J. B.)	17	Tribe (A.)	7	Wickham (Rev. E. C.)	39
Stevenson (F. S.)	6	Tristram (W. O.)	13	Wicksteed (P. H.)	31, 33
Stevenson (J. J.)	2	Trollope (A.)	4	Wiedersheim (R.)	43
Stewart (A.)	43	Truman (J.)	17	Wieser (F. von)	31
Stewart (Balfour)	29, 30, 39	Tucker (T. G.)	39	Wilbraham (F. M.)	36
Stokes (Sir G. G.)	30	Tuckwell (W.)	5	Wilkins (Prof. A. S.)	2, 14, 39
Story (R. H.)	4	Tufts (J. H.)	28	Wilkinson (S.)	26
Stone (W. H.)	30	Tulloch (Principal)	39	Williams (C. M.)	28
Strachey (Sir E.)	21	Turner (C. Tennyson)	17	Williams (G. H.)	10
Strachey (Gen. R.)	9	Turner (G.)	1	Williams (Montagu)	5
Strangford (Viscountess)	41	Turner (H. H.)	29	Williams (S. E.)	13
Strettell (A.)	17	Turner (J. M. W.)	13	Willink (A.)	39
Stubbs (Rev. C. W.)	39	Tylor (E. B.)	1	Willoughby (E. F.)	12
Stubbs (Bishop)	34	Tyrwhitt (R. St. J.)	2, 17	Willoughby (F.)	43
Sutherland (A.)	9	Vaughan (C. J.)	34, 35, 39	Wills (W. G.)	17
Swete (Prof. H. B.)	34	Vaughan (Rev. D. J.)	22, 33	Wilson (A. J.)	31
Symonds (J. A.)	4	Vaughan (Rev. E. T.)	39	Wilson (Sir C.)	4
Symonds (Mrs. J. A.)	5	Vaughan (Rev. R.)	39	Wilson (Sir D.)	1, 4, 14
Symons (A.)	17	Veley (M.)	20	Wilson (Dr. G.)	4, 6, 24
Tainsh (E. C.)	14	Venn (Rev. J.)	28, 39	Wilson (Archdeacon)	39
Tait (Archbishop)	39	Vernon (Hon. W. W.)	14	Wilson (Mary)	14
Tait (C. W. A.)	12	Verrall (A. W.)	14, 40	Windelband (W.)	28
Tait (Prof. P. G.)	29, 30, 39	Verrall (Mrs.)	2	Wingate (Major F. R.)	26
Tanner (H.)	1	Victor (H.)	20	Winkworth (C.)	6
Tavernier (J. B.)	41	Vines (S. H.)	6	Winkworth (S.)	22
Taylor (E. R.)	2	Wain (Louis)	42	Winter (W.)	13
Taylor (Franklin)	26	Waldstein (C.)	2	Wolseley (Gen. Viscount)	26
Taylor (Isaac)	27, 39	Walker (Prof. F. A.)	31	Wood (A. G.)	17
Taylor (Sedley)	26, 30	Walker (Jas.)	7	Wood (C. J.)	39
Tegetmeier (W. B.)	8	Wallace (A. R.)	6, 26, 31	Wood (Rev. E. G.)	39
Temple (Bishop)	39	Wallace (Sir D. M.)	32	Woods (Rev. F. H.)	1
Temple (Sir R.)	4	Walpole (S.)	31	Woods (Miss M. A.)	18, 36
Tennant (Dorothy)	42	Walton (I.)	13	Woodward (C. M.)	9
Tenniel	42	Ward (A. W.)	4, 14, 21	Woolner (T.)	17
Tennyson	14, 17, 22	Ward (H. M.)	6, 7	Wordsworth	6, 14, 17, 22
Tennyson (Frederick)	17	Ward (S.)	17	Worthey (Mrs.)	20
Tennyson (Hallam)	13, 43	Ward (T. H.)	18	Wright (Rev. A.)	33
Theodoli (Marchesa)	20	Ward (Mrs. T. H.)	20, 43	Wright (C. E. G.)	8
Thompson (D'A. W.)	7	Ward (W.)	5, 24, 35	Wright (J.)	9
Thompson (E.)	11	Waters (C. A.)	30	Wright (J.)	22
Thompson (H. M.)	31	Waterton (Charles)	26, 41	Wright (L.)	30
Thompson (S. P.)	29	Watson (E.)	5	Wright (W. A.)	8, 16, 21, 27, 34
Thomson (A. W.)	9	Watson (R. S.)	41	Wurtz (Ad.)	8
Thomson (Sir C. W.)	43	Watson (W.)	17, 21	Wyatt (Sir M. D.)	2
Thomson (Hugh)	12	Webb (W. T.)	17	Yonge (C. M.)	5, 6, 7, 8, 11, 12, 20, 22, 24, 27, 33, 43
Thorne (Dr. Thorne)	25	Webster (Mrs. A.)	17, 43	Young (E. W.)	9
Thornton (J.)	6	Weisbach (J.)	9	Ziegler (Dr. E.)	26
Thornton (W. T.)	28, 32, 40	Welby-Gregory (Lady)	35		
Thorpe (T. E.)	8	Welldon (Rev. J. E. C.)	39, 40		

MACMILLAN AND CO., LONDON.

J. PALMER, PRINTER, ALEXANDRA STREET, CAMBRIDGE.

11/50/1/94

www.ingramcontent.com/pod-product-compliance
Lightning Source LLC
Chambersburg PA
CBHW022059230426
43672CB00008B/1217